D0216541

The Critical Response
to Robert Lowell

Recent Titles in
Critical Responses in Arts and Letters

The Critical Response
to Robert Lowell

Edited by
Steven Gould Axelrod

Critical Responses in Arts and Letters, Number 33
Cameron Northouse, *Series Adviser*

GREENWOOD PRESS
Westport, Connecticut • London

THE PENNSYLVANIA STATE UNIVERSITY
COMMONWEALTH CAMPUS LIBRARIES
DELAWARE COUNTY

Library of Congress Cataloging-in-Publication Data

The critical response to Robert Lowell / edited by Steven Gould
 Axelrod.
    p. cm.—(Critical responses in arts and letters, ISSN
 1057–0993 ; no. 33)
   Includes bibliographical references (p.) and index.
   ISBN 0–313–29037–7 (alk. paper)
   1. Lowell, Robert, 1917–1977—Criticism and interpretation.
 I. Axelrod, Steven Gould, 1944–   . II. Series.
 PS3523.089Z646 1999
 811′.52—dc21   99–11307

British Library Cataloguing in Publication Data is available.

Copyright © 1999 by Steven Gould Axelrod

All rights reserved. No portion of this book may be
reproduced, by any process or technique, without the
express written consent of the publisher.

Library of Congress Catalog Card Number: 99–11307
ISBN: 0–313–29037–7
ISSN: 1057–0993

First published in 1999

Greenwood Press, 88 Post Road West, Westport, CT 06881
An imprint of Greenwood Publishing Group, Inc.
www.greenwood.com

Printed in the United States of America

The paper used in this book complies with the
Permanent Paper Standard issued by the National
Information Standards Organization (Z39.48–1984).

10 9 8 7 6 5 4 3 2 1

Copyright Acknowledgments

The editor and publisher gratefully acknowledge permission for use of the following material:

Excerpts from "The Drunken Fisherman," "The Quaker Graveyard in Nantucket," "Between the Porch and the Altar," "In Memory of Arthur Winslow," "The Death of the Sheriff," and "Rebellion" in *Lord Weary's Castle*, copyright 1946 and renewed 1974 by Robert Lowell, reprinted by permission of Harcourt Brace & Company.

Reprinted by permission of Farrar, Straus & Giroux, Inc.: Excerpts from *Day by Day* by Robert Lowell. Copyright 1977 by Robert Lowell. Excerpt from *The Dolphin* by Robert Lowell. Copyright 1973 by Robert Lowell. Excerpt from *For Lizzie and Harriet*. Copyright 1973 by Robert Lowell. Excerpts from *For the Union Dead* by Robert Lowell. Copyright 1959 by Robert Lowell. Copyright renewed 1987 by Harriet Lowell, Caroline Lowell, and Sheridan Lowell. Excerpts from *History* by Robert Lowell. Copyright 1973 by Robert Lowell. Excerpts from *Imitations* by Robert Lowell. Copyright 1959 by Robert Lowell. Copyright renewed 1987 by Harriet Lowell, Sheridan Lowell, and Caroline Lowell. Excerpts from *Life Studies* by Robert Lowell. Copyright 1959 by Robert Lowell. Copyright renewed 1987 by Harriet Lowell, Sheridan Lowell, and Caroline Lowell. Excerpts from *Near the Ocean* by Robert Lowell. Copyright 1967 by Robert Lowell. Excerpts from *Notebook 1967-68*. Copyright 1967, 1968, 1969 by Robert Lowell. Copyright renewed 1998 by Harriet Lowell. Excerpts from *The Old Glory* by Robert Lowell. Copyright 1965 by Robert Lowell. Copyright renewed 1993 by Harriet Lowell, Sheridan Lowell, and Caroline Lowell. Excerpts from *The Oresteia of Aeschylus* by Robert Lowell. Copyright 1979 by Robert Silvers and State Street Bank and Trust Company.

Reprinted by permission of Faber and Faber, Ltd.: Excerpts from *Day by Day* by Robert Lowell. Copyright 1977 by Robert Lowell. Excerpt from *The Dolphin* by Robert Lowell. Copyright 1973 by Robert Lowell. Excerpt from *For Lizzie and Harriet.* Copyright 1973 by Robert Lowell. Excerpts from *For the Union Dead* by Robert Lowell. Copyright 1959 by Robert Lowell. Copyright renewed 1987 by Harriet Lowell, Caroline Lowell, and Sheridan Lowell. Excerpts from *History* by Robert Lowell. Copyright 1973 by Robert Lowell. Excerpts from *Imitations* by Robert Lowell. Copyright 1959 by Robert Lowell. Copyright renewed 1987 by Harriet Lowell, Sheridan Lowell, and Caroline Lowell. Excerpts from *Life Studies* by Robert Lowell. Copyright 1959 by Robert Lowell. Copyright renewed 1987 by Harriet Lowell, Sheridan Lowell, and Caroline Lowell. Excerpts from *Near the Ocean* by Robert Lowell. Copyright 1967 by Robert Lowell. Excerpts from *Notebook 1967-68.* Copyright 1967, 1968, 1969 by Robert Lowell. Copyright renewed 1998 by Harriet Lowell. Excerpts from *The Old Glory* by Robert Lowell. Copyright 1965 by Robert Lowell. Copyright renewed 1993 by Harriet Lowell, Sheridan Lowell, and Caroline Lowell. Excerpts from *The Oresteia of Aeschylus* by Robert Lowell. Copyright 1979 by Robert Silver and State Street Bank and Trust Company.

Excerpts from Robert Lowell's manuscripts "At Payne-Whitney" (bMS Am 1905 2227-28), "Ante-Bellum Boston" (bMS Am 1905 2209-10), and "The balanced aquarium" (bMS Am 1905 2226) reprinted by permission of the Houghton Library, Harvard University.

Excerpt from "Little Gidding" in *Four Quartets, Collected Poems 1909-62,* copyright 1943 by T. S. Eliot and renewed 1971 by Esme Valerie Eliot, reprinted by permission of Harcourt Brace & Company and Faber and Faber, Ltd.

Excerpt from *The Maximus Poems* by Charles Olson, edited/translated by George Butterick (Berkeley: University of California Press, 1983). Copyright © 1983 The Regents of the University of California. Used by permission.

Excerpt from *The Oresteia* by Aeschylus and Robert Fagles, translator. Translation copyright 1966, 1967, 1975 by Robert Fagles. Used by permission of Viking Penguin, a division of Penguin Putnam, Inc., and Georges Borchart, Inc.

"Agamemnon by Aeschylus," from *Three Greek Plays: Prometheus Bound, Agamemnon, and The Trojan Women* by Edith Hamilton, translator. Copyright 1937 by W. W. Norton & Company, Inc., renewed © 1965 by Doris Fielding Reid. Reprinted by permission of W. W. Norton & Company, Inc.

Excerpts from Richmond Lattimore, translator, *Aeschylus I: Oresteia* (Chicago: University of Chicago Press, 1953). © 1953 by The University of Chicago. *Agamemnon:* © 1947 by Richmond Lattimore. All rights reserved. Permission granted by The University of Chicago Press.

Excerpt from R. P. Blackmur, "Notes on Eleven Poets," *Kenyon Review* 7 (1945): 339-52; rpt. Blackmur, *Language as Gesture: Essays in Poetry,* copyright 1952 by Richard P. Blackmur and renewed 1980 by Elizabeth Blackmur. Reprinted by permission of Harcourt Brace & Company.

Excerpt from Louise Bogan, "Verse" [*Lord Weary's Castle*], *New Yorker* 22 (Nov. 30, 1946): 129-32; rpt. Bogan, *A Poet's Alphabet* (New York: McGraw Hill, 1970). Reprinted by permission of Ruth Limmer, literary executor.

Randall Jarrell, "From the Kingdom of Necessity," *The Nation* 164 (Jan. 11, 1947): 75-77; rpt. Jarrell, *Poetry and the Age* (New York: Knopf, 1953). Permission granted by Rhoda Weyr Agency, New York.

Excerpt from William Van O'Connor, "The Influence of the Metaphysicals on Modern Poetry," *College English,* published by the National Council of Teachers of English (Jan. 1948): 180-87.

Excerpt from Josephine Miles, *The Continuity of Poetic Language* (Berkeley: University of California Press, 1951), 436-39. Copyright 1951 by the Regents of the University of California. Reprinted by permission.

Excerpt from Jerome Mazzaro, *The Poetic Themes of Robert Lowell* (Ann Arbor: University of Michigan Press, 1965), 48-55. Reprinted by permission of the author.

Excerpt from Heather Dubrow, "The Marine in the Garden: Pastoral Elements in Lowell's 'Quaker Graveyard,'" *Philological Quarterly* 62.2 (Spring 1983): 127-45. Reprinted by permission of the author.

Excerpt from Louise Bogan, "Verse" [*The Mills of the Kavanaughs*], *New Yorker* 27 (June 9, 1951): 94. Reprinted by permission of Ruth Limmer, literary executor.

Excerpt from Paul Mariani, *Lost Puritan: A Life of Robert Lowell* (New York: W. W. Norton, 1994), 159-61. Copyright 1994 by Paul Mariani. Reprinted by permission of W. W. Norton & Company, Inc.

M. L. Rosenthal, "Poetry as Confession," *The Nation* 189 (Sept. 19, 1959): 154-55. Reprinted by permission of *The Nation*.

Amiri Baraka [LeRoi Jones], "'Putdown of the Whore of Babylon,'" *Yugen* 7 (1961): 4-5. Copyright 1961 by Amiri Baraka. Reprinted by permission of Sterling Lord Literistic, Inc. for the author.

Marjorie Perloff, "Realism and the Confessional Mode of Robert Lowell," *Contemporary Literature* 11:4 (Autumn 1970): 470-87. Reprinted by permission of The University of Wisconsin Press.

Excerpt from Charles Altieri, *Enlarging the Temple: New Directions in American Poetry During the 1960s* (Lewisburg, Pa.: Bucknell University Press, 1979), 60-68. Permission granted by Associated University Presses.

Excerpt from James E. B. Breslin, *From Modern to Contemporary: American Poetry, 1945-1965* (Chicago: University of Chicago Press, 1984), 118-24. © 1983, 1984 by The University of Chicago. All rights reserved. Permission granted by The University of Chicago Press.

Excerpt from Terri Witek, "Robert Lowell's Tokens of the Self," *American Literature* 63:4 (Dec. 1991): 713-26. Copyright 1991 Duke University Press. Reprinted by permission.

Excerpt from Jahan Ramazani, *Poetry of Mourning* (Chicago: University of Chicago Press, 1994), 232-41. © 1994 by The University of Chicago Press. All rights reserved. Permission granted by The University of Chicago Press.

Excerpt from Stephen Yenser, *Circle to Circle: The Poetry of Robert Lowell* (Berkeley: University of California Press, 1975), 165-74. Copyright 1975 by the Regents of the University of California. Reprinted by permission.

Christopher Ricks, "The Three Lives of Robert Lowell," *New Statesman* 69 (Mar. 26, 1965): 496-97. Copyright 1965 *New Statesman*. Reprinted by permission.

Excerpt from Steven Gould Axelrod, *Robert Lowell: Life and Art* (Princeton: Princeton University Press, 1978), 162-72. Permission granted by Princeton University Press.

Excerpt from Katharine Wallingford, *Robert Lowell's Language of the Self* (Chapel Hill: University of North Carolina Press, 1988), 106-112. Copyright 1988 by the University of North Carolina Press. Used by permission of the publisher.

Albert Gelpi, "He Holds America to Its Ideals" [*The Old Glory*], *The Christian Science Monitor* (Dec. 16, 1965): 11. Copyright 1965 The Christian Science Publishing Society. Reprinted by permission from *The Christian Science Monitor*. All rights reserved.

Albert E. Stone, "A New Version of American Innocence: Robert Lowell's *Benito Cereno*," *The New England Quarterly* 45 (1972): 467-83. Copyright held by *The New England Quarterly*. Reproduced by permission of *The New England Quarterly* and the author.

Hilda Raz [Hilda Link], "A Tempered Triumph," *Prairie Schooner* 41 (Winter 1967): 439-42. Reprinted by permission of the University of Nebraska Press.

Copyright 1967 by University of Nebraska Press, renewed 1995 by University of Nebraska Press.

Excerpt from Alan Williamson, *Pity the Monsters: The Political Vision of Robert Lowell* (New Haven: Yale University Press, 1974), 112-15, 150-55. Copyright Yale University Press. Reprinted by permission.

Mary Kinzie, "The Prophet Is a Fool: On 'Waking Early Sunday Morning,'" *Salmagundi* 37 (Spring 1977): 88-101. Reprinted by permission of the author.

Hilene Flanzbaum, "Surviving the Marketplace: Robert Lowell and the Sixties," *The New England Quarterly* 68 (March 1995), 44-57. Copyright held by *The New England Quarterly*. Reproduced by permission of *The New England Quarterly* and the author.

Richard Gilman, "Still Bound," *Newsweek* 69 (May 22 1967): 109. Copyright 1967 Newsweek, Inc. All rights reserved. Reprinted by permission.

Calvin Bedient, "Visions and Revisions: Three New Volumes by America's Foremost Poet, *New York Times Book Review* (July 29, 1973): 15-16. Copyright 1973 by The New York Times Co. Reprinted by permission.

Excerpt from Adrienne Rich, "Carydid: A Column," *American Poetry Review* 2 (Sept.-Oct. 1973): 42-43. Reprinted by permission of Frances Goldin Literary Agency for the author.

Excerpt from Diane Wakoski, "The Craft of Carpenters, Plumbers & Mechanics: A Column," *American Poetry Review* 3 (Jan.-Feb. 1974): 46; rpt. Wakoski, *Toward a New Poetry* (Ann Arbor: University of Michigan Press, 1979). Copyright 1979 University of Michigan Press. Reprinted by permission.

Excerpt from Robert Pinsky, *The Situation of Poetry* (Princeton: Princeton University Press, 1976), 18-23. Copyright 1976 by Princeton University Press. Reprinted by permission of Princeton University Press.

Excerpt from Steven Gould Axelrod, *Robert Lowell: Life and Art* (Princeton: Princeton University Press, 1978), 225-32. Permission granted by Princeton University Press.

Excerpt from Lawrence Lipking, *The Life of the Poet: Beginning and Ending Poetic Careers* (Chicago: University of Chicago Press, 1981), 184-88. © The University of Chicago. All rights reserved. Permission granted by The University of Chicago Press.

Excerpt from Vereen M. Bell, *Robert Lowell: Nihilist as Hero* (Cambridge, Mass.: Harvard University Press, 1983): 188-94. Copyright 1983 by the

President and Fellows of Harvard College. Reprinted by permission of the publisher.

Excerpt from Robert von Hallberg, *American Poetry and Culture 1945-1980* (Cambridge, Mass.: Harvard University Press, 1985), 158-65. Copyright 1985 by the President and Fellows of Harvard College. Reprinted by permission of the publisher.

Marjorie Perloff, "Robert Lowell: 'Fearlessly Holding Back Nothing,'" *Washington Post Book World* (Sept. 25, 1977), H1. Copyright © Marjorie Perloff. Reprinted by permission.

Excerpt from Harold Bloom, "Harold Bloom on Poetry," *New Republic* 177:22 (Nov. 26, 1977): 24. Permission granted by *New Republic*.

Excerpt from Norma Procopiow, "*Day by Day*: Lowell's Poetics of Imitation," *Ariel: A Review of International English Literature* 14 (1983): 4-14. Reprinted by permission of *Ariel*.

Excerpt from Randall Jarrell, "Fifty Years of American Poetry," *The Third Book of Criticism* (New York: Farrar, Straus & Giroux, 1969), 332-34. Permission granted by Rhoda Weyr Agency, New York.

Frank Bidart, "On Robert Lowell," *Salmagundi* 37 (Spring 1977), 54-55. Permission granted by the author.

Excerpt from Maria Damon, *The Dark End of the Street: Margins in American Vanguard Poetry* (Minneapolis: University of Minnesota Press, 1993), 123-41. Copyright 1993 by The Regents of the University of Minnesota. Reprinted by permission.

Excerpt from Henry Hart, *Robert Lowell and the Sublime* (Syracuse: Syracuse University Press, 1995), 136-42. Permission granted by the publisher.

Richard Tillinghast, "Damaged Grandeur: The Life of Robert Lowell," first published in *Sewanee Review* 102:1 (Winter 1994), 121-31; rpt. Tillinghast, *Robert Lowell's Life and Work: Damaged Grandeur* (Ann Arbor: University of Michigan Press, 1995). Copyright 1994 by Richard Tillinghast. Reprinted with the permission of the editor of *The Sewanee Review* and the author.

Excerpt from Jed Rasula, *The American Poetry Wax Museum: Reality Effects, 1940-1990* (Urbana: NCTE, 1996), 247-56. Copyright 1996 by the National Council of Teachers of English. Reprinted with permission.

Robert Lowell, "After Enjoying Six or Seven Essays On Me," *Salmagundi* 37 (Spring 1977), 112-15. Permission granted by Frank Bidart, literary executor.

Contents

2 MIDDLE PERIOD

3 LATE PERIOD

4 OVERVIEWS

Series Foreword

Critical Responses in Arts and Letters is designed to present a documentary history of highlights in the critical reception to the body of work of writers and artists and to individual works that are generally considered to be of major importance. The focus of each volume in this series is basically historical. The introductions to each volume are themselves brief histories of the critical response an author, artist, or individual work has received. This response is then further illustrated by reprinting a strong representation of the major critical reviews and articles that collectively have produced the author's, artist's or work's critical reputation.

The scope of *Critical Responses in Arts and Letters* knows no chronological or geographical boundaries. Volumes under preparation include studies of individuals from around the world and in both contemporary and historical periods.

Each volume is the work of an individual editor, who surveys the entire body of criticism on a single author, artist, or work. The editor then selects the best material to depict the critical response received by an author or artist over his/her entire career. Documents produced by the author or artist may also be included when the editor finds that they are necessary to a full understanding of the materials at hand. In circumstances where previous, isolated volumes of criticism on a particular individual or work exist, the editor carefully selects material that better reflects the nature and directions of the critical response over time.

In addition to the introduction and the documentary section, the editor of each volume is free to solicit new essays on areas that may not have been adequately dealt with in previous criticism. For volumes on living writers and artists, new interviews may be included, again at the discretion of the volume's editor. The volumes also provide a supplementary bibliography and are fully indexed.

While each volume in *Critical Responses in Arts and Letters* is unique, it is also hoped that in combination they will form a useful, documentary history of the critical response to the arts, and one that can be easily and profitably employed by students and scholars.

Cameron Northouse

Preface

This volume provides a representative sample of the critical discourse concerning Robert Lowell's poetry, drama, and prose. It attempts to display that discourse at its most vital and varied. Lowell's reputation, as this volume makes clear, has had its ups and downs; and in the decades since his death no critical consensus has emerged about any aspect of his work. This degree of liveliness and contention in the reception of Lowell's texts echoes the character of the texts themselves. Surprising, complicated, witty, and at times outrageous, Lowell's writing continues to fascinate us and to inspire what Jean Starobinski once called "words upon words."

The first three sections of this book track Lowell's volumes chronologically. Most of Lowell's volumes receive one or two reviews followed by several scholarly essays, arranged in the order of their publication. *Life Studies* (1959) merits the most ample commentary because it still remains his most interpreted text. But several other volumes—from Lowell's first big success, *Lord Weary's Castle* (1946), to the book published the month he died, *Day by Day* (1977)—have received provocative critiques as well, as the sample included here indicates. Along with the reprinted articles are two essays written especially for this volume by Helen Deese and Jeffrey Gray. The overviews that conclude the book all take a broader perspective, though the chosen perspectives do not necessarily coincide. I have left the last word to Lowell himself, as insightful and eloquent about his own work as he was on other topics.

I have greatly benefited from the advice and help of fellow scholars, whom I would like to thank here: Rise B. Axelrod, John M. Ganim, Paul Mariani, and Marjorie Perloff. The mistakes of fact and judgment that remain are intractably my own. I thank Cameron Northouse and George Butler for their patience. I thank Frank Bidart for favors large and small. Deckard Hodge helped me in the final stages of this project. Jeremiah Axelrod and Max Borenstein pulled me out of computer hell more than once, for which I am incredibly grateful. My wonderful and indefatigable research assistant, Melissa Fabros, accompanied me on all the early steps of this journey. I wish her well on her own journeys to come.

Finally, and again, I dedicate my portion of this book to Rise and Jeremiah with love.

Introduction

Robert Lowell: From Classic to Outlaw

Steven Gould Axelrod

Gertrude Stein, in "Composition as Explanation," wrote that "the creator of the new composition in the arts is an outlaw until he is a classic," but sometimes it works the other way. From the publication of Lowell's first major volume in 1946 to a few years before his death in 1977, he held sway as the premier English-language poet of his time. As Richard Poirier put it, "Robert Lowell is, by something like a critical consensus, the greatest American poet of the mid-century, probably the greatest poet now writing in English." Marjorie Perloff agreed that "Lowell is held by many to be the outstanding poet writing in English in the period since World War II" (*Poetic Art*). M. L. Rosenthal called him "*the* American poet of this age" ("Poets"). And Irvin Ehrenpreis famously termed mid-century "the Age of Lowell" (68).[1]

In 1946, Lowell's *Lord Weary's Castle* seemed to push poetic language and cultural critique in exciting new directions, yet they were directions sanctioned by the ethos of its time. More conspicuously than any other poetic volume of the 1940's, *Lord Weary's Castle* was able to advance the aesthetic and political projects of the New Criticism while maintaining a high level of vitality and idiosyncrasy. In 1959, Lowell's *Life Studies* dramatically junked the very traditions he had previously revitalized, opening poetry to ironic narratives of family malfunction, initiating a sort of subversive and postmodern *poesie verité* that was both disconcerting and immensely influential. Breaking the vessel of the formal poetic object, *Life Studies* became a convenient marker of the death of the New Criticism, the very movement that had facilitated Lowell's early reputation. In the 1960's, *For the Union Dead, The Old Glory, Near the*

---

[1] Unless otherwise noted, all books, articles, and reviews referred to in this essay may be found in "Selected Bibliography" at the end of the book.

Ocean, and *Notebook 1967-68* elaborated Lowell's new poetic mode, engaging personal, political, and historical issues with breathtaking erudition and a radical edge. Like T. S. Eliot a generation before him, Lowell seemed to explain an era to itself. And like Eliot before him, he would not remain unchallenged forever.

The remarkable critical consensus concerning Lowell's classic stature stretched from 1946 through the early 1970's unimpaired by his startling alterations of style and perspective. The consensus cracked, however, with the publication in 1973 of his poetic trilogy, *History*, *For Lizzie and Harriet*, and *The Dolphin*. As Lowell noted with dismay, dissenters outnumbered advocates of these volumes by two to one. Many critics asserted that Lowell had finally lost his formal and moral assurance. The first two volumes of the trilogy contained versions of poems published at least twice before, and some reviewers, especially in Great Britain, thought he had not yet got the poems right. Peter Dale, for example, remarked that "English poets make the odd buck or two by selling their manuscripts to American universities. It has taken Robert Lowell to devise a method of selling his direct to the public." The painfully personal third volume, *The Dolphin*, was attacked by formerly friendly critics like Adrienne Rich and Marjorie Perloff as "mean-spirited" and "sheer soap opera." Lowell's final book of poetry, the autobiographical *Day by Day*, published days before his death in 1977, was favorably received and indeed introduced "heartbreaking" into the critical vocabulary for at least the next decade. Nevertheless, it was already evident that the *zeitgeist* that had carried Lowell aloft for so many years was about to dash him to earth.

In the decade following Lowell's death, his reputation suffered blow after blow. Long-held resentments came to the fore, and new ones emerged. A once-obsessional interest in Lowell's work yielded to hostility and indifference. The river of interpretive books began to peter out, replaced by a stream of negative biographies. George McFadden noted in 1986 that Lowell's reputation was now "under a cloud" ("Prose"), and Harold Bloom—always a canny judge, not to mention precipitator, of standing—concurred in 1987 that time "seems to have darkened Lowell's aura in the decade since his death" ("Introduction"). Jeffrey Meyers replied to McFadden that "no postwar poet now has a greater reputation" than Lowell ("Wild-Genteel"), demonstrating that biographers are sometimes the last to know. Epithets of praise increasingly gave way to laments and ridicule, as the following titles indicate: "Mistah Lowell—He Dead" (Joseph Epstein); "Lowell in the Shadows" (William Logan); and, most resonantly, "The Age of Lowell" (Jed Rasula).

Challenges to Lowell's poetic eminence came from several directions. One was biographical. In 1982, Ian Hamilton published *Robert Lowell: A Biography*, a factually inclusive but devastatingly antagonistic account, which I have compared to an article in the *National Enquirer* ("Lowell's Living Name" 6). Like the attack of a stealth bomber, its destructiveness did not at first appear on the radar screen. Its status as the first full-scale biography, not quite authorized but certainly not *un*authorized, seemed to delude many reviewers, including some of Lowell's best friends, into thinking it a friendly and fair representation, despite its unrelenting negativity and instinct for scandal. This biography all but buried the once-prevailing conception of Lowell as a formal innovator and a moral witness, installing in its place the figure of a man who did little besides bring misery to others. Hamilton's biography— ballasted by other, smaller-scale but still unfriendly biographies— markedly reduced the quantity and the enthusiasm of Lowell commentary. A subsequent biography, Paul Mariani's *Lost Puritan* (1994), provides a much more balanced portrait of the poet, as do several other biographical works of the 1990's. The effect of these more recent biographies has yet to be fully seen.

Another challenge to Lowell's stature came from the direction(s) of linguistic and political postmodernism. Despite their continuing interest in his work, Perloff and Rasula portrayed Lowell as an old-garde exponent of essentialized subjectivity and emotional overstatement, an opponent of irony and linguistic play, a poet too comfortable with retrograde conceptions of language and culture. Maria Damon critiqued Lowell for appropriating perspectives properly belonging to women, minorities, and the poor. Bob Perelman, almost reversing Damon's critique, wrote that in the work of Lowell and his followers one did not find "the poet as engaged, oppositional intellectual, and poetic form and syntax as sites of experiment for political and social purposes."[2] This last was an especially ironic judgment on a poet who in his own day was known as a poetic rebel, and whose principled opposition to war brought him, on one occasion, the wrath of a president and, on another, jail time.

A third challenge came from the direction of the New Formalism (also called Expansive Poetry). Theorists of this movement lambasted Lowell and his circle for their abandonment or derangement of traditional meter and device, their emphasis on individual feeling, and their association with "iconoclasms of the sixties."[3] Publishing in newly

---

[2] Perelman, *Marginalization of Poetry* (Princeton: Princeton UP, 1996), 12.

[3] Timothy Steele, *Missing Measures* (Fayetteville, 1990), 106-108, 281. See also essays by Frederick Feirstein, Richard Moore, and Robert McPhillips that

established or re-established journals like *Kenyon Review*, *The New Criterion*, and *Chronicles*, the poets and ideologues of Expansive Poetry reflected the ideas and energy of Conservatism Militant in the 1980's. They found Lowell and other representatives of the poetic establishment to be inaccessible and self-indulgent—a late emanation of a moribund and harmful liberal tradition. Thus, Lowell found himself under attack from the cultural and linguistic right, the cultural and linguistic avant garde, and a biographism that let its judgment of the poetry be colored by its condemnation of the admittedly flawed man. A scapegoat in René Girard's sense, Lowell was sacrificed so that various intellectual/ aesthetic communities could thrive.

As the culture wars concerning Lowell's status continue to play themselves out, Lowell's readers will surely want to focus on the texts themselves, and on the issues they raise in relation to literary and social history. Some of those issues are apparent now, and others will emerge as the conversation continues. One set of issues concerns Lowell's poetic language and his representation of subjectivity. The assumption that Lowell's language and subject, beginning with *Life Studies*, are clear and straightforward requires critical examination. Indeed, it is this notion itself, rather than Lowell's language and subject, that increasingly appears simplistic and outdated. The verbal and formal play and the subjective decentering that occur in Lowell's texts have yet to be adequately recognized. Another set of issues concerns Lowell's position as public witness and cultural representative. Lowell's discourse of nation, class, race, ethnicity, gender, and sexuality is complex, sophisticated—and "expansive." His engagement with social, political, and cultural history is sustained and challenging. As an oppositional poet, Lowell does not supplant the diversely-cultured poets of his time; he joins them in a communal enterprise and, in surprisingly many cases, participates with them in chains of influence.

Lowell's words are finally not reducible. A poet of contradictions and reversals, he belongs to no camp, though he does bear some relation to Lionel Trilling's aged but still formidable "liberal imagination." Lowell once satirized writing in the United States as a "sequence of demolitions,

---

were published between 1981 and 1988 and later collected in *Expansive Poetry*, ed. Frederick Feirstein (Santa Cruz, 1989), 9-54, 195-208; and Robert Richman's introduction to *The Direction of Poetry* (Boston, 1988), xv-xvi (which, with an imprecision that characterizes many of these polemics, mistakenly asserts that Lowell's *Day by Day* includes free-verse sonnets). An informative critique of the New Formalist/Expansivist movement appears in Thomas B. Byers' "The Closing of the American Line," *Contemporary Literature* 33 (1992): 396-413.

the bravado of perpetual revolution,"[4] a rather apt description of his own career. Readers have been trying to come to terms with him for the last half-century—explaining, celebrating, castigating, problematizing, troping upon and wrestling with his words. The struggle has probably just begun.

Robert Lowell initially experienced life as a contrast between an idealized past and a degraded present. He was related to an array of notables: on his mother's side to Colonial patriarchs Edward, John, and Josiah Winslow; and on his father's side to poets James Russell Lowell and Amy Lowell, astronomer Percival Lowell, and Harvard president A. Lawrence Lowell. Yet he grew up as a single child in a dysfunctional, downwardly mobile nuclear family, caught between his father's dullness and failure and his mother's egotism and frustration. At his prep school, St. Mark's, young Lowell was sullen, rebellious, and unpopular. He earned the nickname of "Cal," referring both to Shakespeare's brutish Caliban and the Roman tyrant Caligula. The behavior problems endured throughout his life, and the nickname stuck.

In two years at Harvard, Lowell received mediocre grades and wrote poems that were disliked by visiting poet Robert Frost and the literary board of the *Harvard Advocate*. Lowell's sense of rejection and his increasingly chaotic emotional life culminated in a physical brawl with his father. In desperation, Lowell drove to Tennessee to meet poet and New Critic Allen Tate, a friend of his mother's psychiatrist. The meeting changed his life. That summer, he dropped out of Harvard, enrolled at Kenyon College, where Tate's friend John Crowe Ransom had taken a position, and slowly discovered his vocation as a poet. For the next years, he experimented with verse that was emotionally and intellectually charged. It resembled Tate's own cryptographic poetry, but with a New England rather than a Southern accent and without Tate's powers of specificity and coherence. Lowell graduated from Kenyon College summa cum laude in Classics. He then married the brilliant young fiction writer Jean Stafford; converted from his parents' passive Episcopalianism to an intensely active Roman Catholicism (as Tate himself was eventually to do); studied for a year with Cleanth Brooks and Robert Penn Warren at LSU; and continued to write.

The religious conversion inspired his poetry. In 1944 he published his first volume, the privately printed *Land of Unlikeness*. The book's poems, heavily rhetorical and symbolic, castigated a materialistic and violent contemporary culture from religious and historical perspectives.

---

[4] "Digressions from Larkin's 20th-Century Verse," *Encounter* 40 (May 1973): 66.

The book received a handful of respectful notices from important critics, including R. P. Blackmur, Elizabeth Drew, and Lowell's friends Randall Jarrell and Allen Tate. Lowell's conversion to Catholicism also inspired a rebellious pacifism that deepened his skepticism about World War II. Although he had previously attempted to enlist in the armed forces, in 1943 he refused induction and was sentenced to a year and a day in prison, of which he served five months. According to Mariani, when the crime boss Louis Lepke said to Lowell, "I'm in for killing, what are you in for?," Lowell replied, "Oh, I'm in for refusing to kill" (109).

Upon release, Lowell revised ten of the *Land of Unlikeness* poems, wrote thirty-two new ones, and published the sequence in 1946 in a volume entitled *Lord Weary's Castle*. This book established Lowell at the age of twenty-nine as a major poet. It received a Pulitzer Prize and critical raves from such critics and poets as John Berryman, Louise Bogan, Babette Deutsch, Richard Eberhart, Leslie Fiedler, and Randall Jarrell. Berryman called Lowell "the most powerful poet to appear in England or America in some years." Bogan compared him to John Donne and Herman Melville. Jarrell wrote: "When I reviewed Mr. Lowell's first book I finished by saying, 'Some of the best poems of the next years ought to be written by him.' The appearance of *Lord Weary's Castle* makes me feel less like Adams or Leverrier than like a rain-maker who predicts rain and gets a flood which drowns everyone in the country."

Composed in a style marked by erudite allusions, emotional extravagance, and intellectual and linguistic complexity, *Lord Weary's Castle* brings the language of Modernism to one kind of conclusion. Formally experimental yet traditional in its fundamental allegiances, the volume represents a culmination of the New Critical aesthetics of tension, ambiguity, and self-enclosed discourse. Yet there is also something in the book's passions and confusions, its grandiloquence and horror, its flamboyant aversions and wild enthusiasms, that will not stay confined within New Critical, Roman Catholic, or politically conservative frames, and that could not have been predicted by a close study of any aesthetic or cultural program. That is to say, although the poetic audience had been prepared to value such a book by the experience of reading the poetry of the high Modernists and the essays of the New Critics, there was also something in poems like "The Quaker Graveyard in Nantucket," "Children of Light," "At the Indian Killer's Grave," "After the Surprising Conversions," and "Where the Rainbow Ends" that eluded the readers' grasp and exceeded their expectations. Such poems afforded both the shock of recognition and the shock of the new. The volume turned out to be a pivot upon which poetic history in the United States could turn: an impressive late manifestation of a certain set of Modernist conventions and an early step in the search for what would succeed them.

In 1951 Lowell published *The Mills of the Kavanaughs*, a volume of obscure and desolate poetic monologues and narratives. In several of these poems, especially "Falling Asleep Over the Aeneid" and "Mother Marie Therese," Lowell succeeded in his attempt to restore character and plot to a prominent position in contemporary poetry. In other texts, however, Lowell's poetic project resembled a car whose motor continued to run even after the engine had been turned off. The book received mixed reviews by such critics as Louise Bogan, Paul Engle, Randall Jarrell, and William Carlos Williams. It struck many readers as transitional—a "dark mid-point" through which the poet must pass, as Bogan put it. In the midst of a review straining to be as positive as possible, Lowell's friend and protector Randall Jarrell cuttingly wrote: "Mr. Lowell too often is either having a nightmare or else is wide awake gritting his teeth and working away at All The Things He Does Best." Always Jarrell's best student, Lowell got the message. As he was later to say, "What you really feel has not got the form, it's not what you can put down in a poem. And the poem you're equipped to write concerns nothing that you care very much about" (*Collected Prose* 266). So Lowell virtually stopped writing for six years, spending his time teaching at several Midwestern universities and then at Boston University and struggling to discover a new poetic direction.

Apart from Lowell's creative dilemma, much else was happening in his personal life during the late 1940's and early 1950's. He divorced his first wife, Jean Stafford, in 1948 and married his second, the novelist and essayist Elizabeth Hardwick, in 1949. He abandoned the conservative political convictions he had inherited from his parents and the Roman Catholic faith he had adopted to defy them. Then he lost his parents themselves: His father died in 1950 and his mother in 1954. And increasingly he suffered from manic-depressive illness. This illness manifested itself in episodes of elation and bizarre behavior followed by paralyzing destitution, a period of institutionalization, recovery, and release—a cycle that would repeat itself at regular intervals until his death.

By the mid-1950's Lowell was taking his cue not from the iconic texts of Modernism but from a new set of contemporary examples: William Carlos Williams' late attempt to render personal topics in the American idiom in such poems as "The Desert Music" and "Asphodel, That Greeny Flower"; Elizabeth Bishop's combination of informality and precise description in such poems as "The Armadillo"; Allen Ginsberg's free-associational epic of himself in "Howl"; and W. D. Snodgrass' elegant and touching manuscript poems about his divorce and his separation from his child, eventually to appear as "Heart's Needle." Lowell, unable to complete a projected prose autobiography, returned to poetry in the fall of 1957, and he began to use his autobiographical material in a new way, as a series of poetic portraits or "life studies" of his family members and himself. Although influenced by the work of Williams, Bishop, Ginsberg, and Snodgrass, this poetry was also distinct from anything that had come before. Mobilizing an amazing dynamic of irony and revelation, coherence and waywardness, it possessed (depending on how one looked at it) the transparency of documents, the narrative drive of fiction, the spontaneity of conversation, or the thick and resonant verbal texture of enduring poetry. A montage of scenes, images, implications, anecdotes, puns, quotations, times, and genres, the new poems provided glimpses of several tragicomic stories at once: of an individual who, as he grows from child to adult, remains remote, mysterious, and marginal even to himself; of his richly dysfunctional family; and of a cultural stew of economic conflict, Cold War politics, and increasingly destabilized categories of gender, race, nation, and class. The volume was entitled *Life Studies*. Published in 1959, it changed the course not only of Lowell's career but of poetry in the United States and, to some degree, the world.

Although labelled "confessional" by M. L. Rosenthal, *Life Studies* is better considered under a variety of different terms. I have proposed "domestic," to emphasize its familial and social aspect (*Sylvia Plath* 59-70), whereas Alan Williamson has proposed "personal" (*Introspection* 7-25) and Thomas Travisano "self-exploratory" (*Mid-century Quartet* passim). Whatever term one prefers, *Life Studies* is obviously not an artless confession but, as Rosenthal himself made clear, an artistic making with social as well as personal implications. The volume traces the disillusion and dissolution of a character named "Robert Lowell" and of his family, but it also constructs a narrative of a nation whose myths about itself are threatened at every point by economic, political, social, military, and cultural changes and by its own difficulty in adjusting the stories it tells about itself to the stories it keeps *to* itself and even *from* itself. Moreover, *Life Studies* reflects on the way the many-told stories and the hidden stories compete with each other on the same field of discourse. Voyeurism, overhearing, secrets, and fantasy appear as recurrent motifs. In "91 Revere Street" the young Lowell overhears what he should not: his parents' bedroom quarrels. In "My Last Afternoon with Uncle Devereux Winslow," he looks out on the world, "unseen and all-seeing," while fantasizing himself as alternatively Huck Finn, Pegasus, or Agrippina the Elder. In "Skunk Hour," he spies on lovers in their cars and, simultaneously, on his own estrangement. This activity of listening, watching, transgressing, inventing fantasies, telling lies, and revealing secrets is at the heart of *Life Studies*. Not only does "Lowell" as a character see and think what he should not; so do Lowell as an author and we as readers. *Life Studies*, rather than a "confession," is an intricate meditation on the complicated roles that observing, imagining, and constructing narratives play for a human being struggling to maintain a space of freedom and agency in a place of surveillance, control, and silence.

Life Studies had an immediate impact on the scene of poetry. It received the National Book Award, shared the Guinness Poetry Award, and received excited and laudatory reviews by such leading poets and critics as A. Alvarez, Louise Bogan, Donald Davie, F. W. Dupee, Richard Eberhart, John Hollander, Alfred Kazin, Stanley Kunitz, M. L. Rosenthal, and Stephen Spender. True, Frank Kermode hinted that the book contained "superior doggerel," Joseph Bennett called it a collection of "snobbish memories," and DeSales Standerwick thought it just "too personal." But the consensus held that, as Hugh Staples put it in an essay reviewing Lowell's career, *Life Studies* proved Lowell to be "the most significant poet of his generation." Elizabeth Bishop wrote on the book's dust jacket: "Somehow or other . . . in the middle of our worst century so far, we have produced a magnificent poet."

Life Studies has had an even more significant long-range impact on poetry and criticism. Its influence may be detected on many of the landmark poetic texts of the 1960's such as Ginsberg's *Kaddish* (1960), Sexton's *To Bedlam and Part Way Back* (1960), Jarrell's *The Lost World* (1965), Plath's *Ariel* (1966), Merrill's *Nights and Days* (1966), and Berryman's *The Dream Songs* (1969)—and (directly or obliquely) on more recent gay, ethnic, and postmodernist texts such as Olga Broumas' *Beginning with O* (1977), Lorna Dee Cervantes' *Emplumada*,(1981), Cathy Song's *Picture Bride* (1982), Lucille Clifton's *Good Woman* (1987), Rita Dove's *Thomas and Beulah* (1987), Lyn Hejinian's *My Life* (1987), Frank Bidart's *In the Western Night* (1990), and Theresa Cha's *Dictée* (1995). The kind of poetry Lowell initiated in *Life Studies* has been interpreted, explained, defended, attacked, and rewritten from a wide variety of perspectives ever since 1959.

In the 1960's Lowell consolidated his achievement and reputation with a series of well-reviewed and important books. These included two volumes of original poetry, *For the Union Dead* (1964) and *Near the Ocean* (1967); a volume of poetic translations called *Imitations* (1961); and a dramatic trilogy based on stories by Nathaniel Hawthorne and Herman Melville entitled *The Old Glory* (1965). Although Lowell disparaged *For the Union Dead* as a way of marking time while uninspired, the volume received enthusiastic reviews by Louise Bogan, G. S Fraser, Geoffrey Hartman, Richard Howard, Josephine Jacobsen, Richard Poirier, Christopher Ricks, William Stafford, and others. Reviewers were especially impressed with the title poem. Indeed, "For the Union Dead"—an elegy for the Massachusetts 54th regiment of African-American soldiers in the Civil War—has proven to be one of Lowell's most anthologized and commented-on texts. On the basis of this poem, Poirier termed Lowell "our truest historian," Jacobsen called him one of the few poets "whose natural idiom is history," and Fraser wrote that Lowell was "not merely a poetic consciousness, but a poetic conscience." Just as *Life Studies* had established Lowell's reputation for personal or domestic poetry, so *For the Union Dead* confirmed his historical sense and his moral awareness.

Lowell's other publications of the 1960's reinforced his reputation as "the official poet of his generation," as Bogan called him. When two of the plays of *The Old Glory* were produced at the American Place Theater in New York in 1964, they received mixed reviews from the daily and weekly press but enthusiastic praise from Robert Brustein, Randall Jarrell, and W. D. Snodgrass. When the complete trilogy was published in book form the following year, the critic John Simon sought to eviscerate it, but Albert Gelpi, Thomas McDonnell, and others rose to the defense. Lowell's dramatic trilogy—and especially the concluding play "Benito Cereno," which Brustein termed a "cultural-poetic masterpiece"—powerfully represented the history and character of the United States as an ironic interplay of violence and idealism, of self-obscured motives and racist, imperialist outcomes. *The Old Glory* clearly raised a momentous topic as civil rights battles continued and the Vietnam War loomed.

Near the Ocean, published in 1967, translated Lowell's strong opposition to the Vietnam War directly into poetry. The volume originated in an audacious political act. In 1965, Lowell protested President Lyndon Johnson's Vietnam policies—just then escalating from a limited conflict to an all-out war—by publicly declining to attend a White House Festival of the Arts. That political intervention, and the controversy it caused, precipitated the composition of the "Near the Ocean" sequence. In typically Lowellian fashion, the poems mix matter from the personal, public, and literary spheres. "Waking Early Sunday Morning" questions the ideology of war and darkly prophesies an endless future of military conflict. "Central Park" laments class division and the suffering of the urban poor. Whereas Louise Bogan and Louis Martz dismissed *Near the Ocean* as interim work, Daniel Hoffman argued that it brilliantly elaborated on Lowell's theme of the "greatness and horror" of the American empire, and such critics as Jean Garrigue, Richard Howard, David Kalstone, and Hilda Raz defended it on similar grounds. By fiercely analyzing American history, Lowell seemed to have become the country's "reigning poet," as William Stafford put it. Several other events indicated Lowell's continued engagement in the political as well as the literary culture of his time: the production of his anti-patriarchal version of Aeschylus's *Prometheus Bound* at Yale in 1967; his participation with Allen Ginsberg, Denise Levertov, Norman Mailer, and others in the anti-Vietnam War march on the Pentagon in that same year; and his participation in Senator Eugene McCarthy's campaign for the presidency in 1968.

In the 1960's, critical books and articles about Lowell began to appear. The first two books—both of them serious and influential—were Hugh Staples' *Robert Lowell: The First Twenty Years* (1962) and Jerome Mazzaro's *The Poetic Themes of Robert Lowell* (1965). These two studies, between them, set the terms in which Lowell's poetry would be discussed for the next two decades.

Staples' study, written with the advice and encouragement of Lowell himself, analyzes Lowell's first four volumes and is especially informative on *Lord Weary's Castle*. Conceived as a work of the New Criticism, this book treats Lowell's poetry as a contained verbal world contextualized only by the traditional canon. It discusses the poems in terms of their formal qualities and their relation to texts by Dante, Villon, Milton, Shelley, Hawthorne, Melville, Pound, and Eliot. It also briefly suggests a thematic development in Lowell's career from "dissatisfaction" through "rebellion" to "partial acceptance." In this study, Staples initiated an enduring tradition of considering Lowell's poems as autotelic literary artifacts; as compendia of rhetorical strategies, techniques, allusions, and influences; as radically isolated from psychological pattern and the social and material world.

Mazzaro's study, while also attending to Lowell's poems as linguistic constructions, pays more attention to such extrinsic contexts as Roman Catholic belief, classical myth, comparative cultures, and the history of ideas. Mazzaro's major thesis is that Lowell's early volumes— *Land of Unlikeness*, *Lord Weary's Castle*, and *The Mills of the Kavanaughs*—try to merge methods from Roman Catholic meditation with those from literary tradition, relying on a range of religious and literary thinkers such as Dante, Joyce, Eliot, St. Ignatius, and St. Bernard of Clairvaux. Conversely, Lowell's subsequent volumes—*Life Studies* and *For the Union Dead*—forgo such supports as they attempt to deal with disordered secular experience. Like Staples' study, Mazzaro's is most illuminating about the early volumes, especially *Lord Weary's Castle*. In counterpoint to Staples, Mazzaro initiated a tradition of considering Lowell's poems in relation to their author's creative drive and the larger contexts of religion, history, art, politics, and culture.

The 1960's also witnessed the appearance of important critical studies in quarterlies, journals, and collections. Among the more general essays, Irvin Ehrenpreis's "The Age of Lowell" helped to confirm Lowell as the leading poet of his time. M. L. Rosenthal's "Robert Lowell and 'Confessional' Poetry" suggested an aesthetics of "confessional poetry." Herbert Leibowitz's "Robert Lowell: Ancestral Voices" represented the poet's sense of history as a dialogue with the past. And Gabriel Pearson's "Robert Lowell," a proto-deconstruction, presciently suggested that Lowell's later poems tend to be frayed, to have holes eaten out, to struggle with their own dissolution. Among the more specialized studies, John Berryman's "Despondency and Madness" provided an early close reading of "Skunk Hour"; Thomas Parkinson's "*For the Union Dead*" provocatively critiqued Lowell's poetic language; and Patricia Meyer Spacks' "From Satire to Description" compared Lowell's use of Juvenal in *Near the Ocean* with Samuel Johnson's. Important studies of Lowell's dramas included Robert Ilson's "*Benito Cereno* from Melville to Lowell," a comparison of Melville's text to Lowell's adaptation; Baruch Hochman's "Robert Lowell's *The Old Glory*," which analyzes antitheses within and between the trilogy's characters; and Jonathan Price's "Fire Against Fire," which similarly analyzes conflicts in *Prometheus Bound*. Three stimulating studies of Lowell's mode of poetic translation also appeared: Donald S. Carne-Ross's "The Two Voices of Translation" and Ben Belitt's "*Imitations*: Translation as Personal Mode," which argued in Lowell's defense; and John Simon's "Abuse of Privilege: Lowell as Translator," which made the case for the prosecution.

Finally, during this period Lowell himself published numerous self-revealing interviews and essays. (Most of these are now reprinted in Lowell's *Collected Prose* and Jeffrey Meyers' *Robert Lowell: Interviews and Memoirs*.) The interviews, which had the cumulative effect of reinforcing Lowell's cultural primacy, were conducted by such notable literary figures as A. Alvarez, Stanley Kunitz, V. S. Naipaul, Frederick Seidel, and Cleanth Brooks and Robert Penn Warren. The essays, which often resembled prose-poems in their eloquent turns of phrase, included memorials to T. S. Eliot, Ford Madox Ford, Robert Frost, Randall Jarrell, Sylvia Plath, and William Carlos Williams.

In 1969 Lowell published *Notebook 1967-68*, a long poem of unrhymed sonnets that, as Lowell said in an interview, "mixes the day-to-day with the history" (*Collected Prose* 270-71). The poem creates a jagged discourse of political and personal events, flashbacks, memories of public violence, textual echoes, and tributes to writers and historical figures—all swirling together in a plot that "rolls with the seasons" (*Notebook 1967-68* 159). A list of dates at the end emphasizes the poem's historical content. The text refers to the assassinations of Martin Luther King and Robert Kennedy, political demonstrations, the Presidential campaign of 1968, the Arab-Israeli Six Day War, the Soviet occupation of Czechoslovakia—and it begins and ends with the Vietnam War. This volume marks the commencement of a slow decline in Lowell's reputation—what seemed for a time like the gradual effacement of his name from the slopes of Mount Parnassus. The book received the weakest reviews Lowell had yet received. Although *Time* magazine called him "an honest madman and an eloquent one," praise echoed by Jerome Mazzaro and Kathleen Spivack, Peter Cooley criticized *Notebook 1967-68* for lapses of form and language, and Burton Feldman witheringly called its politics as "simplistic" as a New Left poster.

What was worse for Lowell's reputation was that he could not seem to finish his poem. Like other long poems of the twentieth century—Pound's *Cantos*, Williams' *Paterson*, and Berryman's *Dream Songs*—Lowell's epic of his consciousness demanded to continue. But instead of simply going on with the story—as Pound, Williams, and Berryman had done—Lowell began a process of revising and back-filling. A second edition of the poem appeared within months of the first. An expanded version of the poem, minus the seasonal plot and now called simply *Notebook*, appeared the following year. And by 1973, the poem had grown (or metastasized) into three. No longer so intent to mix "the day-to-day with the history," Lowell published the sonnets dealing with his love affairs and the eventual break-up of his marriage to Elizabeth Hardwick as a separate sequence, rather bizarrely entitled *For Lizzie and Harriet*. He placed the sonnets about historical, political, and literary matters in a chronological order based on subject matter and published them as *History*. And, to complete the triptych, he composed a new sonnet sequence called *The Dolphin*, which recounted his love affair with Caroline Blackwood and the birth of their child.

Critics decried all this fiddle. They disliked the indeterminacy of Lowell's obsessive revisions and additions, and they hated his revelation of intimate details about his messy emotional life—particularly his inclusion, without permission, of sentences from Hardwick's private letters to him. Calvin Bedient, Christopher Ricks, Diane Wakoski, and a few others tried to be kind. But James Finn Cotter termed the volumes "literary overkill"; Peter Dale thought they showed "delusions of grandeur"; Donald Davie, once an admirer, wrote that Lowell's overheated verse-machine was "throwing up more sludge and waste"; Donald Hall denounced the poems as "self-serving" and "self-exploiting"; and Marjorie Perloff called Lowell's sonnets pseudo, his revisions fruitless, and his personal revelations boring. Adrienne Rich asserted that Lowell's use of Hardwick's letters was one of the "most vindictive" acts in the history of poetry. Robert Bertholf wrote that Lowell's line of poetry was now "dead."

Lowell spent the ensuing years in emotional crisis and declining health. In and out of hospitals, and removed from most public involvements, he lived in relative seclusion, first in England (with his third wife, Caroline Blackwood, their son Sheridan, and her three daughters) and then in the United States (with his second wife, Elizabeth Hardwick, and their daughter Harriet). He was suspended between countries, families, and identities. Yet despite his creative struggles and the querulous reviews his recent volumes had received, the scholarly books and articles kept coming. Indeed, the Lowell cottage industry of the 1960's went multinational in the 1970's. The years between 1970 and 1975 saw the publication of no fewer than thirteen books about the poet published in the United States, Great Britain, and Australia. Five of these are of special interest.

Richard J. Fein's *Robert Lowell* (1970; revised 1979) includes some of the most detailed and illuminating readings of Lowell's poetry and plays available. Mediating between Staples' intrinsic approach and Mazzaro's extrinsic approach, Fein argues that Lowell's texts elucidate "both a private and a common world." He convincingly shows how the poems combine autobiographical, political, and literary elements. Although the first edition of this book discusses Lowell's work only through *Near the Ocean*, the revised edition encompasses Lowell's whole career, though it unfortunately omits the chapter on *Near the Ocean* and gives short shrift to the poems of the 1970's. In Fein's account of Lowell's career, it is the early and middle texts that count most: *Lord Weary's Castle*, *The Mills of the Kavanaughs*, the poem "For the Union Dead," the play "Benito Cereno," and above all *Life Studies*.

Phillip Cooper's *The Autobiographical Myth of Robert Lowell* (1970) finds "ambivalence" or "irony" to be at the core of Lowell's poetic project. Although this thesis is helpful and appropriate, Cooper attempts to present disunity as a unifying principle, in a sense subverting his point or what should have been his point. Like several other books and essays produced during this period, this book may be understood as occupying a space between two worlds—a dying New Criticism and a Poststructuralism struggling to be born. Modest but willing to take interpretive risks, *The Autobiographical Myth of Robert Lowell* focuses on the five volumes it regards as the poet's great achievements: *Lord Weary's Castle, Life Studies, For the Union Dead, Near the Ocean,* and *Notebook 1967-68.* Lowell himself thought this book "sensitive."[5]

Two other books follow in Staples' footsteps by focusing on "purely literary" matters—the formal and the stylistic. Both works, however, replace Staples' New Critical aesthetic of the discrete verbal object with a Structuralist interest in verbal and generic patterns that permeate textual borders. Both books had the effect of modernizing Lowell criticism.

Marjorie Perloff's *The Poetic Art of Robert Lowell* (1970) contains some of the most illuminating and innovative analyses of Lowell's writing ever committed to print: fine studies of his imagery and syntax; a germinal account of his elegiac practice in such poems as "In Memory of Arthur Winslow" and "My Last Afternoon With Uncle Devereux Winslow"; and a ground-breaking study of metonymic language in *Life Studies.* This latter chapter, in particular, remains a crucial text— arguably *the* crucial text—in the history of Lowell criticism. The first scholarly book to avoid a volume-by-volume approach, Perloff's study moves back and forth among Lowell's early and middle texts, investigating their repeating gestures and highlighting what Perloff takes to be their accomplishments and limitations.

Stephen Yenser's *Circle to Circle: The Poetry of Robert Lowell* (1975), less flamboyant and exciting than Perloff's book, gives Lowell's poems perhaps the steadiest and subtlest aesthetic scrutiny they have yet received. Yenser shows that Lowell's early poems characteristically employ contradiction and dialectical symbolism. In the middle and later periods, structural principles extend beyond the boundaries of individual poems. *Life Studies* is a coherent whole in which each poem lends context to the others, cumulatively revealing the condition of "contemporary civilization." *Imitations* takes the shape of an inverted cone, whereas *For the Union Dead, Near the Ocean,* and *Notebook 1967-68* manifest circular designs. Yenser's book serves as an excellent guide to Lowell's microaesthetics of the word and macroaesthetics of the volume.

Alan Williamson's *Pity the Monsters: The Political Vision of Robert Lowell* (1974) is less interested in formal design than in political issues, and less interested in political issues *per se* than in the psychoanalysis of culture. Secularizing Mazzaro's approach, Williamson relates Lowell's poetry to works of cultural theory: Freud's *Civilization and its Discontents,* Herbert Marcuse's *Eros and Civilization,* Norman O. Brown's *Life Against Death,* and others. This resourceful and often

---

[5] Lowell to Axelrod, Feb. 10, 1974 (University of California, Riverside).

brilliant book, which reflects the late 1960's and prefigures the 1990's, might be termed the first cultural critique of Lowell's poetry. Williamson portrays Lowell's work as a dark questioning of civilization. Although he devotes chapters to *Lord Weary's Castle* and *Life Studies*, he finds the subsequent volumes more resonant. *For the Union Dead* begins Lowell's quest to forge a public pacifistic conscience; *Near the Ocean* achieves notable prophetic power based on "tenderness toward humanity"; and *Notebook* discovers a poetic language that balances skepticism with mystical feeling, conservative pessimism with revolutionary identifications. All three of these later Lowell volumes express a desire for political change based on a psychoanalytical model of self and history.

Beyond these books, numerous articles and book chapters in the 1970's contributed to the lively critical conversation swirling around Lowell's texts. Karl Malkoff's *Escape from the Self* argued that Lowell's poems exemplify an abandonment of the ego, whereas Charles Altieri's *Enlarging the Temple* argued conversely that the poems exemplify solipsism. In other general studies, Monroe Spears related alterations in Lowell's career to the break between modernism and postmodernism; Dwight Eddins reviewed Lowell's changing political attitudes; and Robert Pinsky discussed Lowell's use of voices. In more specialized studies, Mazzaro elucidated the conservative politics of *Land of Unlikeness*; Robert Hass provided a trenchant reading of "The Quaker Graveyard in Nantucket"; Joan Bobbitt, Steven K. Hoffman, and George McFadden provided illuminating genre studies of *Life Studies*; John McWilliams and Albert Stone placed *The Old Glory* in historical perspective; and Mary Kinzie and Elizabeth Lunz explicated "Waking Early Sunday Morning."

Lowell's last years were spent in pain. His marriage to Caroline Blackwood disintegrating, he found himself in and out of hospitals as a result of coronary disease as well as his continuing cycles of manic-depression. Nevertheless, he continued to teach and to write. In August of 1977, he published his final book of poetry, the heart-wrenchingly autobiographical *Day by Day*. The following month, he died of a heart attack in a New York City taxicab, returning from a visit with Blackwood and his son in Ireland to the home he shared with Hardwick and his daughter in Manhattan. Following an Episcopalian funeral service in Boston, he was buried in the family plot at Dunbarton, New Hampshire. In obituaries, *Time* magazine called Lowell a poet of "ceaseless self-scrutiny," the *Boston Globe* called him "the Hub's pacifist poet," and the *London Times* wrote that at his death he was generally considered "the most distinguished poet writing in the English language."

Reviews of *Day by Day* were mixed, and the positive notices often assumed the qualities of memorials. Lowell's antagonist Donald

Hall found the book narcissistic and corrupt, and even Denis Donoghue and Alfred Kazin found it disappointing. Harold Bloom gently wondered if the book's readers were "not being moved by a record of human suffering, rather than a making of any kind." Conversely, A. Alvarez called Lowell's last book "as aroused and poignant as anything he has written before." John Bayley pronounced the poems a dazzling hybrid of Hardy and Yeats. Calvin Bedient called them fearless in their "almost posthumous" freedom from and about the self. Marjorie Perloff, often Lowell's severest critic, wrote that *Day by Day*, which resembles Chekhovian fiction, "succeeds brilliantly."

The first critical book on Lowell to appear after his death was my own *Robert Lowell: Life and Art* (1978), a portrait of Lowell as a working artist, from the beginning of his career to the end. It was intended as a preliminary biography of his imagination and textual production, as they interacted with the politics, literature, and culture of his time and place. Based on archival research, the book uncovers Lowell's apprenticeship first to Allen Tate in *Lord Weary's Castle* and then to William Carlos Williams in *Life Studies*; it reveals the complex genealogy, political positioning, and artistry of the poem "For the Union Dead"; it describes the poet's political involvements in the 1960's; it analyzes *The Dolphin* as a self-referential meditation on art and love; and it attempts to place Lowell, despite Harold Bloom's arguments to the contrary, in the tradition of Ralph Waldo Emerson. Providing sustained readings of the major poems within a framework of the developing career, *Robert Lowell: Life and Art* strives to evoke the Lowellian spirit.

My book seemed to conclude a long and active period of generally positive commentary about Lowell. In the 1980's, books and articles appeared with less frequency, and they moved ever further from the celebratory tone that had generally marked criticism through the 1960's. Lowell's chief defender in the intellectual quarterlies and weeklies was now Helen Vendler, who did his cause some good but perhaps also some harm. Vendler was one of the last exponents of the New Criticism, which she stripped of its scientism and redubbed "aesthetic criticism." She gloried in the words and rhythms of Lowell's poems, which she interpreted with brilliance. But she was essentially a critic of the local effect. Her insights were idiosyncratic, and her sympathies aligned with a traditional canon increasingly viewed by others as restrictive. Moreover, she seemed to privilege her own subjectivity over any sort of systematic method and certainly over the judgment of most other Lowell readers. Finally, she regarded poetic language as inherently non-referential, as severed from the author's social and intellectual milieux—except on the rare occasions when she herself wished to make such a connection. Attempting to denude Lowell's discourse of its relations to the world, she produced not only an aesthetic criticism but an anesthetic one. Her work may have had the unintended and ironic effect of making Lowell seem irrelevant to the cultural issues of the late twentieth century.

Even apart from Vendler's perhaps unfortunate advocacy, cultural tides were moving against Lowell in the years following his death. Harold Bloom, the most prominent poetic theorist of the 1970's and 1980's, was at work developing an American poetic tradition that derived from English Romanticism by way of Emerson, Whitman, and Dickinson. In Bloom's literary history, this tradition leads through Wallace Stevens and Hart Crane to Elizabeth Bishop, James Merrill, John Ashbery, A. R. Ammons, and John Hollander—though Ashbery, for one, dissented vigorously from Bloom's notion of his work. Bloom's tradition definitely did not include Lowell. Bloom wrote, devastatingly, that whereas Lowell was initially our William Mason, in later years he wrote mere period pieces. One read a poem by Lowell "and concluded that both poet and reader knew less about poet and reader than they did before the poem was written and read. . . . Time therefore seems to have darkened Lowell's aura in the decade since his death. Elizabeth Bishop is now firmly established as the enduring artist of Lowell's generation" ("Introduction").

Moreover, as I have noted, the projects of multiculturalism, feminism, queer theory, postcoloniality, and language poetry—each of them increasingly important in the decades after Lowell's death—propelled criticism in directions that left Lowell at least temporarily behind. Lowell, after all, despite his difficulties, oppositional stances, self-marginalizations, and aesthetic revolutions might be considered a mainstream and even a privileged poet. And he unfortunately had been portrayed in just that way by some of his well-intentioned supporters. During his lifetime, they had canonized Lowell—and the very canon into which they inserted him now appeared to be dated, patriarchal, ethnocentric, and in desperate need of enlarging or dismantling. The practitioners and advocates of postmodernism deplored Lowell's language use, which they misread as traditional, transparent, and expressionist, and they deplored the impact he had and was continuing to have on poetry. (They seemed not to care that Lowell's impact was probably strongest and most positive among women and minority poets.) On the aesthetic right, exponents of New Formalist or Expansive Poetry also deplored the influence Lowell's poems had exerted—though for the opposite reason that they were insufficiently traditional in form and values. Perhaps even the Reagan administration's dumping of mental patients onto the city streets played a role in the general loss of sympathy for Lowell's representations of mental illness. These various movements were hardly synonymous—some were progressive, some were conservative, and some were at war with each other. But they all shared a feeling that Lowell's hegemony had been outlived.

Into these critical currents, already running against Lowell, an explosive device was dropped: Lowell's biography. At the time of his death in 1977, Lowell was the subject of numerous affectionate memoirs (later collected in volumes edited by Rolando Anzilotti and Jeffrey Meyers). But in the 1980's, Lowell's image dramatically changed from that of poetic exemplar and historical witness to that of a scandal. He threatened to become the John Wayne Bobbitt of American letters, if not the Jeffrey Dahmer. That his greatest poem was called "Skunk Hour" now seemed only too appropriately self-descriptive.

The 1980's saw the appearance of no fewer than four hostile biographies. All focused on Lowell's frequent and regular periods of mania, during which he drank too much, talked obsessively, and injured those he loved with behavior that later filled him with remorse. Lowell's mood disorder was certainly a part of his life story, but the early biographers treated it—and not his creative struggles and political engagements—as the life's most significant feature. First came the group biography *American Aristocracy: The Lives and Times of James Russell, Amy, and Robert Lowell* (1980) by David Heymann, who later found his true calling as the author of celebrity biographies of Barbara Hutton, Jackie Onassis, and Elizabeth Taylor. *American Aristocracy*, largely uninformed about the facts of Lowell's life, made a negligible impact apart from the tone of contempt it initiated. A second group biography, Bruce Bawer's *The Middle Generation: The Lives and Poetry of Delmore Schwartz, Randall Jarrell, John Berryman, and Robert Lowell* (1986) combined rather standard critical commentary with by now familiar representations of Lowell's alienated misbehaviors. It was read by few and cited by none. A third group biography, Jeffrey Meyers' *Manic Power: Robert Lowell and his Circle* (1987), also had a relatively minor impact. Although Meyers is a respected biographer of Katherine Mansfield and Ernest Hemingway, among others, and the editor of a fine book of Lowell interviews and memoirs, he composed *Manic Power* with apparent haste and, like Heymann, seemed to assume that his audience would be more interested in Lowell's personal misadventures than in his texts. All of the group biographies contain a paucity of information, make facile judgments, and rely on popularistic notions of mental illness.

Unlike the group biographies, however, Ian Hamilton's *Robert Lowell* (1982) had an enormous impact on the reception of Lowell. It transformed him overnight from an exemplar of imaginative and political courage to everybody's nightmare of a husband—the kind of person for whom restraining orders were invented. Hamilton—an English reviewer, editor, and journalist—was temperamentally and intellectually unequipped to deal with Lowell's production of poems and plays in the context of American literature and culture. Nevertheless, his book was greatly influential because it was the first to have full access to Lowell's papers. It revealed aspects of the poet's life previously unknown and even unsuspected by readers: his manic drinking, womanizing, and brushes with the law. Inquiring minds could find out everything they wanted to know about Lowell, and in the process they were subjected to a genteel yet devastating wash of hostile comments about the poet's every action and almost every text.

Taken in by the author's clubby air of cultural superiority, early reviewers even termed the biography "sympathetic," but the sympathy was feigned. The book is, in fact, subtly slanted against Lowell from its opening portrait of a little boy who "elected to sulk his way" through childhood to its later representations of an adult Lowell careening from disaster to disaster. Moreover, Hamilton clearly learned to dislike not only Lowell's person but his poems. He portrays the early poetry as a "welter of grabbed myths and pseudo symbols," the middle poetry as "pedestrian" and "complacent," and the later poetry as "sprawling" and "almost meandering." He approves of only "Waking in the Blue" and "Soft Wood"—two poems out of an oeuvre of hundreds. Finally, Hamilton's book is relentlessly superficial, manifesting no interest at all in Lowell's inner life or his creative desire. He labels the poet's mood disorder "almost certainly incurable," making no attempt to fathom its causes or its pressures on Lowell's existence. Nor does he examine the crucial role poetry played in the life of a poet who wrote, "if I stop writing, I stop breathing" (*History* 169). Packed with factual details but skeptical about Lowell's life, work, and conception of art, this biography came not to praise but to bury Lowell, and for a time it succeeded.

As Lowell moved down the food chain, the production of books and essays about his work began to drop. Whereas the 1970's had seen the publication of fifteen English-language books and essay collections, the 1980's saw only nine such works. Of these, three were introductory studies, two were bibliographies, two were essay collections, and only two were significant scholarly analyses. Philip Hobsbaum's *A Reader's Guide to Robert Lowell* (1988) is probably the canniest of the introductory studies. It can be recommended to novice Lowell readers (along with Fein's earlier *Robert Lowell*) as a useful and reader-friendly guide. The other introductions—Burton Raffel's *Robert Lowell* (1981) and Mark

Rudman's *Robert Lowell: An Introduction to the Poetry* (1983)—also contain explications worth reading and pondering. A Japanese-language introduction published during this period is Shozo Tokunaga's *Robert Lowell: Horo to Hangyaku no Bostonian* (1981). *Robert Lowell: A Reference Guide* (1982), which I wrote with Helen Deese, is a complete bibliography of almost forty years of commentary on Lowell. Norma Procopiow's *Robert Lowell: The Poet and the Critics* (1984) attempts to make sense of that commentary. Mixing penetrating insights with more elementary comments, Procopiow's book focuses on themes in Lowell's poetry rather than on trends or strategies in the critical discourse. Although the book is therefore limited as a reception study, it does illuminate the way Lowell and his readers mutually contributed to the construction of textual meaning.

The first major critical study of the 1980's was Vereen Bell's *Robert Lowell: Nihilist as Hero* (1983). Eloquent and informed, this book argues that Lowell's poetry is marked by a chronic pessimism that ultimately becomes an absolute nihilism. The thesis allows Bell to articulate the darkness of Lowell's vision, but it prevents him from noting the redemptive values that are also inscribed into Lowell's texts. For instance, the book elides the moment of freedom at the end of "Skunk Hour," the courage of Colonel Shaw and his African American troops in "For the Union Dead," and the salvatory role of art in *History*, *The Dolphin*, and "Epilogue." Bell's book remains important for the integrity of its position and the quality of its explications, but its portrayal of Lowell's poetry as a black hole may have inadvertently contributed to the poet's growing disesteem in the 1980's.

The other major study of the 1980's was Katharine Wallingford's *Robert Lowell's Language of the Self* (1988). Following in the wake of Alan Williamson, Wallingford shows how Lowell incorporated psychoanalytical techniques of self-examination into his poetry. The book freely crosses the boundaries of Lowell's texts as it focuses in turn on four recurrent motifs: free association, repetition (as both psychic compulsion and therapeutic "working-through"), relations with others, and memory. Some reviewers, seeking a conventional series of close readings, found this book incomprehensible or insignificant. Yet it is the most thorough study to date of the formal congruities between psychoanalysis and Lowell's poetry.

Both collections of essays published during this period reflected and affected the story of Lowell's reputation, though in almost obverse fashion. *Robert Lowell: Essays on the Poetry* (1986), which I edited with Helen Deese, included new (or heavily revised) essays by such scholars as Calvin Bedient, Albert Gelpi, Sandra M. Gilbert, Jay Martin, Lawrence

Kramer, and Marjorie Perloff. The volume was overtly intended to "reassess Robert Lowell's poetry and to restimulate critical thinking about it" (ix). Marked by diversity and controversy, the book seems to have succeeded, at least partly, in restoring focus on Lowell's texts rather than his life. The book has remained in print, and the essays continue to be cited. Harold Bloom's *Robert Lowell* (1987), also still in print, included reprinted essays by such critics as Dwight Eddins, David Kalstone, Helen Vendler, and Stephen Yenser. The essays, which located successes and failures in Lowell's canon, were preceded by Bloom's withering introductory judgment that Lowell terminated the already inconsequential mandarin-modernist line of Eliot, Pound, and Tate. Whereas the Axelrod-Deese volume foresaw a Lowell revival, Bloom (though certainly not all of his contributors) pronounced the last rites.

Apart from the essays included in the two collections, a handful of articles and book chapters about Lowell continued to appear each year. Three deserve special mention. James Breslin's *From Modern to Contemporary: American Poetry, 1945-1965* (1984) includes a thought-provoking chapter on Lowell's poetic renovation in *Life Studies*. Alan Williamson's *Introspection and Contemporary Poetry* (1984) represents Lowell as the key figure in the rise of personal poetry in the 1960's and 1970's. And Robert von Hallberg's *American Poetry and Culture 1945-1980* (1985) contains a superb reading of Lowell's *History*. Among the other essays in this period were my analysis of Lowell's relationship to Gerard Manley Hopkins (1985); Neil Corcoran's essay on *The Dolphin* (1980); Heather Dubrow's study of "The Quaker Graveyard in Nantucket" (1983); Lynda D. McNeil's comparison of Lowell and Rimbaud (1984); Anthony Manousos' study of "Falling Asleep over the Aeneid" (1984); Michael North's consideration of Lowell's poems about statues (1985); Thomas Parkinson's essay on Lowell's final phase in *Poets, Poems, Movements* (1987); Norma Procopiow's interpretation of *Day by Day* (1983); Cushing Strout's essay on *The Old Glory* (1989); and Derek Walcott's overview and memoir.

In the 1990's, fortune's needle shifted direction again. Three new Lowell biographies appeared, each with a tone markedly different from that of the Reagan-era biographies. Paul Mariani's *Lost Puritan: A Life of Robert Lowell* (1994) is the most important of these works and in some ways the central book in the history of Lowell commentary. There will probably never be a "definitive" biography of anybody, least of all a figure as large and protean as Lowell. Nevertheless, *Lost Puritan*, with its blessedly unimperial subtitle, is the book readers will be consulting, arguing with, and relying on for many years to come. Bringing the previous era of flippant, hostile, moralistic, frenetic, and sensationalized biography to an end, this book changes the course of Lowell studies. It enables biographical criticism to rise to a more sophisticated plane, and it frees other approaches from the shadow of biographical obsession.

Unlike Hamilton's biography, which relentlessly stigmatizes mental illness, Mariani's biography takes an even-handed, reportorial approach. Mariani makes little attempt to proffer medical or psychoanalytical insight into Lowell's behavior, a lack which is both a limitation and a strength. He simply tells what happened, maintaining a tone of understated yet dependable empathy for both Lowell and those around him. Lowell regularly hurt those who knew and loved him. As a boy he bullied classmates, and in his twenties he abused his first wife, Jean Stafford. Later on, his misbehaviors were confined to periods of mania preceding hospitalization. His friends and his second wife, Elizabeth Hardwick, understood and tolerated these episodes as a manifestation of illness; but new acquaintances and his young children, toward whom he was nurturing when present but from whom he was periodically absent, could not fully understand. By the end, these episodes seem more painful and sad than reprehensible or exciting—the product of a mood disorder (and probably other disorders as well). Like others, Lowell lived a life of considerable loneliness and unhappiness and some fellowship and joy. When stabilized, he was kind to acquaintances and a source of pleasure and stimulation to friends and loved ones. When ill, he was none of those things. Hidden under the sign of aristocrat and miscreant is a flawed, complex, brilliant, and productive human being, fully engaged with the currents of his time. Faithful to the ethos of Lowell's last poem, "Epilogue," Mariani gives the poet back his "living name."

More than any previous biographer, Mariani focuses on Lowell's continuing creative struggle, his ever-present need "to write in a new way" (318). Mariani does a fine job suggesting the motives and the character of Lowell's many stylistic changes over the years. He is sensitive and thoughtful in his readings of Lowell's texts, particularly such early landmarks as "Colloquy in Black Rock," "The Quaker Graveyard in Nantucket," and "Falling Asleep over the Aeneid." Moreover, he reveals Lowell as a contradictory yet principled spokesperson of conscience, positioning his body and his words against war, racial inequality, and tyranny. *Lost Puritan* provides a well-written narrative of Lowell's life and career. It is especially strong in its first half, recounting Lowell's turbulent efforts to crash into literary history not once but twice: first, in his late twenties with *Lord Weary's Castle*, and again, in his early forties with *Life Studies*. The story comes alive again in the final harrowing chapters, when Lowell derails—certainly in his private life and possibly, as some readers think, in his poetry as well. Overall, Mariani is simply more informed and informative than any previous writer about Lowell's day-by-day existence—the mad scramble and the slow introspection of his life. Scrupulously fair-minded, *Lost Puritan* opens doors into Lowell's world through which readers may walk, their own agendas in hand.

The 1990's witnessed the publication of two additional biographical works, each written in a generous spirit. William Doreski's *The Years of Our Friendship: Robert Lowell and Allen Tate* (1990) provides an extended account of Lowell's beneficial yet conflicted friendship with Tate, a relationship also described in Mariani's *Lost Puritan* and my own *Robert Lowell: Life and Art*. Richard Tillinghast's *Robert Lowell's Life and Work: Damaged Grandeur* (1995) combines a moving memoir—the author was Lowell's student and friend—with perceptive commentary on volumes from Lowell's middle and late periods: *For the Union Dead*, *The Dolphin*, *Day by Day*, and the little-discussed *For Lizzie and Harriet*. At the outset, Tillinghast warns theorists away from his book. This defensive gesture is the work's only unfortunate aspect, because it widens gaps separating theory, criticism, and biography that have bedeviled Lowell discourse for a decade and more. Just as Tillinghast would undoubtedly find ideas worth engaging in contemporary theory, so theorists of many stripes would find much of value in Tillinghast's book if they read it.

Along with the newly sympathetic biographical works, two important critical books appeared in the early and mid-1990's. Terri Witek's *Robert Lowell and "Life Studies": Revising the Self* (1993) provides a thorough manuscript study of *Life Studies*, augmented by a sophisticated theorization of Lowell's practice of revision. Well-grounded in semiotics, psychoanalysis, and autobiography theory, Witek suggests that writing and subjectivity both share a discursive basis. She demonstrates how Lowell's textual revolutions and revisions amount to an endless series of self-recreations. She also shows how the poet typically sets up and then dismantles the voice of the other, leaving him, ambivalently, alone with himself. Witek's chapters focus on Lowell's multiple versions of "Beyond the Alps"; his creation of textual figures of his parents and his childhood self in the initial "Life Studies" poems; his transformation of autobiographical prose into poetry; and his effort to compose figures of his wife, daughter, and his adult self in the later "Life Studies" poems. This book, which everyone fascinated by Lowell will want to read, moves discussion of *Life Studies* to a new level of insight.

Similarly sophisticated in contemporary theory, Henry Hart's *Robert Lowell and the Sublime* (1995) studies Lowell's oeuvre in terms of the sublime. Referring to commentators ranging from Longinus to

Lyotard, Hart argues that Lowell's poetry repeatedly evokes a struggle for visionary power—for an exalted understanding beyond the capacity of ordinary language and ordinary human beings. At the same time, Lowell relates that struggle to megalomaniacal impulses evident in Western history, and he highlights the dangers of such a struggle. Lowell's conflicted allegories of the sublime oscillate among the conceptual systems that most strongly influenced his thought: Transcendentalist and Christian, Freudian and Marxist, New Critical and Postmodern. If his quest for sublimity was both Oedipal and national, his critique of sublime desire—his exposure of its illusions and destructiveness—reveals his ability to regard his own wishes with irony. Hart portrays Lowell's confrontation with the sublime in such poems as "The Quaker Graveyard in Nantucket," "Skunk Hour," and "Waking Early Sunday Morning" as the central narrative of his texts, one that bears meaningfully on our own drives and dilemmas.

Beyond the biographies and critical books, the 1990's witnessed an upsurge in the quantity and quality of book chapters and articles about Lowell as well. Maria Damon, in *The Dark End of the Street* (1993), and Jed Rasula, in *The American Poetry Wax Museum* (1996), provided challenging but compelling accounts of Lowell's ambiguous position at both the center and the margins of official American culture. Jahan Ramazani, in *Poetry of Mourning* (1994), sensitively placed Lowell within the developing traditions of English-language elegy. Alan Williamson returned once more to Lowell as a dominating poetic figure in *Eloquence and Mere Life* (1994), as did Helen Vendler in *The Given and the Made* (1995). Whereas Diane Wood Middlebrook portrayed Lowell as the key exponent of "Confessional Poetry" in the *Columbia History of American Poetry* (1993), Thomas Travisano constructed Lowell not as a "confessionalist" at all but as a "postmodernist" in *Midcentury Quartet* (1999).

In the scholarly journals, Christopher Beach clarified Lowell's debt to Ezra Pound (1991); William Doreski offered an important new reading of *Life Studies* as an exploration of "the crisis in information and representation" in 1950's America (1996); Barbara Estrin provided a provocative new interpretation of the way Lowell problematizes gender and genre in *Day by Day* (1996); Hilene Flanzbaum supplied a shrewd cultural critique of Lowell's literary production in the 1960's (1995); David Gewanter brilliantly juxtaposed the published version of *The Dolphin* with its more radical manuscript version (1995); Allan Johnston shed new light on Lowell's poetry of memory (1990); Ross Labrie powerfully represented Lowell's early poetry as hybridizing his Protestant cultural inheritance with his Roman Catholic beliefs at the time (1995);

Geoffrey Lindsay, following the theoretical leads of Mikhail Bakhtin and Leonard Diepeveen, focused on the agency of quoted voices in *The Dolphin* (1996); James Sullivan described Lowell's publishing practices from a Marxist perspective (1992); and Jonathan Veitch explicated the intertwined literary and psychological projects of *History* (1992). Clearly, Joseph Epstein's report in 1996, "Mistah Lowell—He Dead," was exaggerated. Epstein was recycling yesterday's news. Lowell, outlawed and comatose in the 1980's, jumped to life in the 1990's.

We no longer live in anything so comfortable, hierarchical, and contained as "the Age of Lowell." We never really did. Yet two decades after Lowell's passing, he haunts our awareness, tests our theories, and evokes intense and contradictory feelings. Apparently, he will not leave us alone, nor we him. Lowell once remarked, with characteristic irony, that James Russell Lowell was a poet "pedestaled for oblivion" and Amy Lowell was "big and a scandal, as if Mae West were a cousin" (*Prose* 276). For a while it looked as though he himself might share those fates. But being off the pedestal actually seems to agree with him. Excluded from anthologies, nobody's idea of a well-balanced individual, he speaks now as an outsider, in a voice that confounds our paradigms and generates its own distinctive registers of dissent, wit, and eloquence. Writing under the ambiguous sign of the Hale-Bopp comet, I do not know what the future holds. But the preternatural Randall Jarrell once predicted that people would be reading Lowell as long as English is read—and I would never bet against Jarrell in such matters.

1

Early Period

Land of Unlikeness

R. P. Blackmur

Robert Lowell's *Land of Unlikeness* . . . shows, not examples of high formal organization achieved, but poems that are deliberately moving in that direction and that have things put in to give the appearance of the movement of form when the movement itself was not secured. In fact, Lowell's verse is a beautiful case of citation in any argument in support of the belief in the formal inextricability of the various elements of poetry: meter is not meter by itself, any more than attitude or anecdote or perception, though any one of them can be practiced by itself at the expense of the others, when the tensions become mere fanaticism of spirit and of form: conditions, one would suppose, mutually mutilating. Something of that sort seems to be happening in Lowell's verse. It is as if he demanded to *know* (to judge, to master) both the substance apart from the form with which he handles it and the form apart from the substance handled in order to set them fighting. . . . Lowell is distraught about religion; he does not seem to have decided whether his Roman Catholic belief is the form of a force or the sentiment of a form. The result seems to be that in dealing with men his faith compels him to be fractiously vindictive, and in dealing with faith his experience of men compels him to be nearly blasphemous. By contrast, Dante loved his living Florence and the Florence to come and loved much that he was compelled to envisage in hell, and he wrote throughout in loving meters. In Lowell's *Land of Unlikeness* there is nothing loved unless it be its repellence; and there is not a loving meter in the book. What is thought of as Boston in him fights with what is thought of as Catholic; and the fight produces not a tension but a gritting. It is not the violence, the rage, the denial of this world that grits, but the failure of these to find *in verse* a tension of necessity; necessity has, when recognized, the quality of conflict accepted, not hated. To put a thing, or a quality, or an intimation, *in verse* is for the poet the same job as for the man not a poet the job of putting or holding a thing in mind. Mind and verse are mediums of response. If Lowell, like St. Bernard whom he quotes on his title page, conceives the world only as a place of banishment, and poetry (or theology) only as a means of calling up memories of life before banishment, he has the special problem of maturing a medium, both of mind and verse, in which vision and logic combine; and it is no wonder he has gone no further. *Inde anima dissimilis deo inde dissimilis est et sibi*. His title and his motto suggest that the problem is actual to him; the poems themselves suggest, at least to an alien mind, that he has so far been able to express only the violence of its difficulty. As it is now, logic lacerates the vision and vision turns logic to zealotry. I quote the last section of "The Drunken Fisherman" which seems to me the best-managed poem in the book.

> Is there no way to cast my hook
> Out of this dynamited brook?
> The Fisher's sons must cast about
> When shallow waters peter out.
> I will catch Christ with a greased worm,
> And when the Prince of Darkness stalks
> My bloodstream to its Stygian term . . .
> On water the Man-Fisher walks.

Kenyon Review 7 (1945): 339-52.

Lord Weary's Castle

Louise Bogan

Religious conversion, in the case of two modern poets writing in English—T.S. Eliot and W. H. Auden—brought an atmosphere of peace and relief from tension into their work. But Robert Lowell, a young American who has forsaken his New England Calvinist tradition for the tenets of the Roman Catholic Church, exhibits no great joy and radiance in the forty-odd poems now published under the title *Lord Weary's Castle*. A tremendous struggle is still going on in Lowell's difficult and harsh writings, and nothing is resolved. These poems bring to mind the crucial seventeenth-century battle between two kinds of religious faith, or, in fact, the battle between the human will and any sort of faith at all. They are often at what might be called a high pitch of baroque intensity. They do not have the sweetness of the later English "metaphysical" writers; Lowell faces the facts of modern materialism more with the uncompromising tone and temper of the Jacobean dramatists, Webster and Tourneur, or of Donne, who (to quote Professor Grierson), "concluding that the world, physical and moral, was dissolving in corruptions which human reason could not cure, took refuge in the ark of the Church." (Lowell, it is clear, has not taken refuge anywhere.) He also bears some relationship to Herman Melville, the American with Puritan hellfire in his bones. The more timid reader would do well to remember these forerunners, and the conditions that fostered them, when confronted with young Lowell's fierce indignation.

Lowell's technical competence is remarkable, and this book shows a definite advance over the rather stiff and crusty style of his first volume, *Land of Unlikeness*, published in 1944. This competence shows most clearly in his "imitations" and arrangements of the work of others, which he hesitates to call direct translations. "The Ghost" (after Sextus Propertius), "The Fens" (after Cobbett), and the poems derived from Valéry, Rimbaud, and Rilke reveal a new flexibility and directness. These poems might well be read first, since they show the poet's control of both matter and manner. The impact of the other poems in the book is often so shocking and overwhelming, because of the violent, tightly packed, and allusive style and the frequent effects of nightmare horror, that his control may seem dubious. The extraordinary evocation of the sea's relentlessness and the terror of death at sea, in "The Quaker Graveyard in Nantucket" (an elegy to a drowned merchant seaman), is equaled in dreadfulness by the grisly emblems of "At the Indian Killer's Grave," a poem wherein successive layers of spiritual and social decomposition in the Massachusetts Bay Colony come to light through a descent into the King's' Chapel Burying Ground in Boston. Lowell, again in the seventeenth-century way, continually dwells upon scenes of death and burial. He is at his best when he mingles factual detail with imaginative symbols; his facts are always closely observed down to every last glass-tiered factory and every dingy suburban tree. To Lowell, man is clearly evil and a descendant of Cain, and Abel is the eternal forgotten victim, hustled away from sight and consciousness. And the modern world cannot reward its servants; no worthy pay is received by the good mason who built "Lord Wearie's castle." (The old ballad from which the book's title is taken runs: "It's Lambkin was a mason good As ever built wi' stane: He built Lord Wearie's castle But payment gat he nane.") These are the themes that run through this grim collection. Lowell does not state them so much as present himself in the act of experiencing their weight. It is impossible to read his poems without sharing his desperation. Lowell may be the first of that postwar generation which will write in dead earnest, not content with providing merely a slick superficiality but attempting to find a basis for a working faith, in spite of secretive Nature and in defiance of the frivolous concepts of a gross and complacent society. Or he may simply remain a solitary figure. Certainly his gifts are of a special kind.

New Yorker 22 (Nov. 30, 1946): 129-32.

From the Kingdom of Necessity

Randall Jarrell

Many of the people who reviewed *Lord Weary's Castle* felt that it was as much of an event as Auden's first book; no one younger than Auden has written better poetry than the best of Robert Lowell's, it seems to me. Anyone who reads contemporary poetry will read it; perhaps people will understand the poetry more easily, and find it more congenial, if they see what the poems have developed out of, how they are related to each other, and why they say what they say.

Underneath all these poems "there is one story and one story only"; when this essential theme or subject is understood, the unity of attitudes and judgments underlying the variety of the poems becomes startlingly explicit. The poems understand the world as a sort of conflict of opposites. In this struggle one opposite is that cake of custom in which all of us lie like lungfish—the stasis or inertia of the stubborn self, the obstinate persistence in evil that is damnation. Into this realm of necessity the poems push everything that is closed, turned inward, incestuous, that blinds or blinds: the Old Law, imperialism, militarism, capitalism, Calvinism, Authority, the Father, the "proper Bostonians," the rich who will "do everything for the poor except get off their backs." But struggling within this like leaven, falling to it like light, is everything that is free or open, that grows or is willing to change: here is the generosity or openness or willingness that is itself salvation; here is "accessibility to experience";

this is the realm of freedom, of the Grace that has replaced the Law, of the perfect liberator whom the poet calls Christ.

Consequently the poems can have two possible movements or organizations: they can move from what is closed to what is open, or from what is open to what is closed. The second of these organizations—which corresponds to an "unhappy ending"—is less common, though there are many good examples of it: "The Exile's Return," with its menacing Voi ch'entrate that transforms the exile's old home into a place where even hope must be abandoned; the harsh and extraordinary "Between the Porch and the Altar," with its four parts each ending in constriction and frustration, and its hero who cannot get free of his mother, her punishments, and her world even by dying, but who sees both life and death in terms of her, and thinks at the end that, sword in hand, the Lord "watches me for Mother, and will turn / The bier and baby-carriage where I burn."

But normally the poems move into liberation. Even death is seen as liberation, a widening into darkness: that old closed system Grandfather Arthur Winslow, dying of cancer in his adjusted bed, at the last is the child Arthur whom the swanboats once rode through the Public Garden, whom now "the ghost of risen Jesus walks the waves to run / Upon a trumpeting black swan / Beyond Charles River and the Acheron / Where the wide waters and their voyager are one." (Compare the endings of "The Drunken Fisherman" and "Dea Roma.") "The Death of the Sheriff" moves from closure—the "ordered darkness" of the homicidal sheriff, the "loved sightless smother" of the incestuous lovers, the "unsearchable quicksilver heart / Where spiders stare their eyes out at their own / Spitting and knotted likeness"—up into the open sky, to those "light wanderers" the planets, to the "thirsty Dipper on the arc of night." Just so the cold, blundering, iron confusion of "Christmas Eve Under Hooker's Statue" ends in flowers, the wild fields, a Christ "once again turned wanderer and child." In "Rebellion" the son seals "an everlasting pact / With Dives to contract / The world that spreads in pain"; but at last he rebels against his father and his father's New England commercial theocracy, and "the world spread / When the clubbed flintlock broke my father's brain." The italicized words ought to demonstrate how explicitly, at times, these poems formulate the world in the terms that I have used.

"Where the Rainbow Ends" describes in apocalyptic terms the wintry, Calvinist, capitalist—Mr. Lowell has Weber's unconvincing belief in the necessary connection between capitalism and Calvinism—dead end of God's covenant with man, a frozen Boston where even the cold-blooded serpents "whistle at the cold." (The poems often use cold as a plain and physically correct symbol for what is constricted or static.) There "the scythers, Time and Death, / Helmed locusts, move upon the tree of breath," of the spirit of man; a bridge curves over Charles River like an ironic parody of the rainbow's covenant; both "the wild ingrafted olive and its root / Are withered" [these are Paul's terms for the Judaism of the old Law and the Gentile Christianity grafted upon it]; "every dove [the Holy Ghost, the bringer of the olive leaf to the Ark] is sold" for a commercialized, legalized sacrifice. The whole system seems an abstract, rationalized "graph of Revelations," of the last accusation and judgment brought against man now that "the Chapel's sharp-shinned eagle shifts its hold / on serpent-Time, the rainbow's epitaph." This last line means what the last line in "The Quaker Graveyard"—"The Lord survives the rainbow of His will"—means; both are inexpressibly menacing, since they show the covenant as something that binds only us, as something abrogated merely by the passage of time, as a closed system opening not into liberation but into infinite and overwhelming possibility; they have something of the terror, but none of the pity, of Blake's "Time is the mercy of Eternity."

Then the worshipper, like a victim, climbs to the altar of the terrible I AM, to breathe there the rarefied and intolerable ether of his union with the divinity of the Apocalypse; he despairs even of the wings that beat against his cheek: "What can the dove of Jesus give / You now but wisdom, exile?" When the poem has reached this point of the most extreme closure, when the infinite grace that atones and liberates is seen as no more than the acid and useless wisdom of the exile, it opens with a rush of acceptant joy into: "Stand and live, / The dove has brought an olive branch to eat." The dove of Jesus brings to the worshipper the olive branch that shows him that the flood has receded, opening the whole earth for him; it is the olive branch of peace and reconciliation, the olive branch that he is "to eat" as a symbol of the eaten flesh of Christ, of atonement, identification, and liberation. Both the old covenant and the new still hold, nothing has changed: here as they were and will be-says the poem—are life and salvation.

Mr. Lowell's Christianity has very little to do with the familiar literary Christianity of as if, the belief in the necessity of belief; and it is a kind of photographic negative of the faith of the usual Catholic convert, who distrusts freedom as much as he needs bondage, and who sees the world as a liberal chaos which can be ordered and redeemed only by that rigid and final Authority to Whom men submit without question. Lowell reminds one of those heretical enthusiasts, often disciplined and occasionally sanctified or excommunicated, who are more at home in the Church Triumphant than in the church of this world, which is one more state. A phrase like Mr. Lowell's "St. Peter, the distorted key" is likely to be appreciated outside the church and overlooked inside it, ad maiorem gloriam of Catholic poetry. All Mr. Lowell's earliest poems would seem to suggest that he was, congenitally, the ideal follower of Barth or Calvin: one imagines him a few years ago, supporting neither Franco nor the loyalists, but yearning to send a couple of clippers full of converted minute-men to wipe out the whole bunch —human, hence deserving. (I wish that he could cast a colder eye on minute-men; his treatment of the American Revolution is in the great tradition of Marx, Engels, and Parson Weems.) Freedom is something that he has wished to escape into, by a very strange route. In his poems the Son is pure liberation from the incestuous, complacent, inveterate evil of established society, of which the Law is a part—although the Father, Jehovah, has retained both the violence necessary to break up this inertia and a good deal of the menacing sternness of Authority as such, just as the poems themselves have. It is interesting to compare the figure of the Uncle in early Auden, who sanctifies rebellion by his authority; the authority of Mr. Lowell's Christ is sanctified by his rebellion or liberation.

Anyone who compares Mr. Lowell's earlier and later poems will see this movement from constriction to liberation as his work's ruling principle of growth. The grim, violent, sordid constriction of his earliest poems—most of them omitted from *Lord Weary's Castle*—seems to be temperamental, the old Adam which the poet grew from and only partially transcends; and a good deal of what is excessive in the extraordinary rhetorical machine of a poem like "The Quaker Graveyard at Nantucket," which first traps and then wrings to pieces the helpless reader—who rather enjoys it—is gone from some of his later poems, or else dramatically justified and no longer excessive. "The Quaker Graveyard" is a baroque work, like *Paradise Lost*, but all the extase of baroque has disappeared—the coiling violence of its rhetoric, the harsh and stubborn intensity that accompanies all its verbs and verbals, the clustering stresses learned from accentual verse, come from a man contracting every muscle, grinding his teeth together till his shut eyes ache. Some of Mr. Lowell's later work moved, for a while, in the direction of the poem's quiet contrast-section, "Walsingham"; the denunciatory prophetic tone disappeared, along with the savagely satiric effects that were one of the poet's weaknesses. Some of the later poems depend less on rhetorical description and more on dramatic speech; their wholes have escaped from the hypnotic bondage of the details. Often the elaborate stanzas have changed into a novel sort of dramatic or narrative couplet, run-on but with heavily stressed rhymes. A girl's nightmare, in the late "Katherine's Dream," is clear, open, and speech-like, compared to the poet's own descriptive meditation in an earlier work like "Christmas at Black Rock."

Mr. Lowell has a completely unscientific but thoroughly historical mind. It is literary and traditional as well; he can use the past so effectively because he thinks so much as it did. He seems to be condemned both to read history and to repeat it. His present contains the past—especially Rome, the late Middle Ages, and a couple of centuries of New England—as an operative skeleton just under the skin. (This is rare among contemporary poets, who look at the past more as Blücher is supposed to have looked at London: "What a city to sack!") War, Trade, and Jehovah march side by side through all Mr. Lowell's ages: it is the fundamental likeness of the past and present, and not their disparity, which is insisted upon. "Cold / Snaps the bronze toes and fingers of the Christ / My father fetched from Florence, and the dead / Chatters to nothing in the thankless ground / His father screwed from Charlie Stark and sold / To the selectmen." Here is a good deal of the history of New England's nineteenth century in a sentence.

Of New England Mr. Lowell has the ambivalent knowledge one has of one's damned kin. The poems are crowded with the "fearful Witnesses" who "fenced their gardens with the Redman's bones"; the clippers and the slavers, their iron owners, and their old seamen knitting at the asylum; the Public Garden "where / The bread-stuffed ducks are brooding, where with tub / And strainer the mid-Sunday Irish scare / The sun-struck shallows for the dusky chub"; the faith "that made the Pilgrim Makers take a lathe / To point their wooden steeples lest the Word be dumb." Here his harshest propositions flower out of facts. But some of his earlier satires of present-day politics and its continuation have a severe crudity that suggest Michael Wigglesworth rewriting the "Horatian Ode"; airplanes he treats as Allen Tate does, only more so—he gives the impression of having encountered them in Mother Shipton. But these excesses were temporary; what is permanently excessive is a sort of obstinate violence or violent obstinacy of temperament and perception—in a day when poets long to be irresistible forces, he is an immovable object.

Mr. Lowell's period pieces are notable partly for their details—which are sometimes magically and professionally illusionary—and partly for the empathy, the historical identification, that underlie the details. These period pieces are intimately related to his adaptations of poems from other languages; both are valuable as ways of getting a varied, extensive, and alien experience into his work. Dismissing these adaptations as misguided "translations" is like dismissing "To Celia" or Cathay, and betrays an odd dislike or ignorance of an important and traditional procedure of poets.

Mr. Lowell is a thoroughly professional poet, and the degree of intensity of his poems is equaled by their degree of organization. Inside its elaborate stanzas the poem is put together like a mosaic: the shifts of movement, the varied pauses, the alternation in the length of sentences, and the counterpoint between lines and sentences are the outer form of a subject matter that has been given a dramatic, dialectical internal organization; and it is hard to exaggerate the strength and life, the constant richness and surprise of metaphor and sound and motion, of the language itself. The organization of the poems resembles that of a great deal of traditional English poetry—especially when compared to that type of semi-imagist modern organization in which the things of a poem seem to marshal themselves like Dryden's atoms—but often this is complicated by stream-of-consciousness, dream, or dramatic-monologue types of structure. This makes the poems more difficult, but it is worth the price— many of the most valuable dramatic effects can hardly be attained inside a more logical or abstract organization. Mr. Lowell's poetry is a unique fusion of modernist and traditional poetry, and there exist side by side in it certain effects that one would have thought mutually exclusive; but it is essentially a post- or anti-modernist poetry, and as such is certain to be influential.

This poet is wonderfully good at discovering powerful, homely, grotesque, but exactly appropriate particulars for his poems. "Actuality is something brute," said Peirce. "There is no reason in it. I instance putting your shoulder against a door and trying to force it open against an unseen, silent, and unknown resistance." The things in Mr. Lowell's poems have, necessarily, been wrenched into formal shape, organized under terrific pressure, but they keep to an extraordinary degree their stubborn, unmoved toughness, their senseless originality and contingency: no poet is more notable for what, I have read, Duns Scotus calls haeccitas—the contrary, persisting, and singular thingness of every being in the world; but this detailed factuality is particularly effective because it sets off, or is set off by, the elevation and rhetorical sweep characteristic of much earlier English poetry. Mr. Lowell is obviously a haptic rather than a visual type: a poem like "Colloquy in Black Rock" has some of the most successful kinaesthetic effects in English. It is impossible not to notice the weight and power of his lines, a strength that is sometimes mechanical or exaggerated, and sometimes overwhelming. But because of this strength the smooth, calm, and flowing ease of a few passages, the flat and colloquial ease of others, have even more effectiveness than they ordinarily would have: the dead mistress of Propertius, a black nail dangling from a finger, Lethe oozing from her nether lip, in the end can murmur to the "apple-sweetened Anio": ". . . *Anio, you will please / Me if you whisper upon sliding knees: / 'Propertius, Cynthia is here: / She shakes her blossoms when my waters clear.'"*

Mr. Lowell, at his best and latest, is a dramatic poet: the poet's generalizations are usually implied, and the poem's explicit generalizations are there primarily because they are dramatically necessary—it is not simply the poet who means them. He does not present themes or generalizations but a world; the differences and similarities between it and ours bring home to us themes, generalizations. and the poet himself. It is partly because of this that atheists are vexed by his Catholic views (and Catholics by his heretical ones) considerably less than they normally would be.

But there are other reasons. The poet's rather odd and imaginative Catholicism is thoroughly suitable to his mind, which is so traditional, theocentric, and anthropomorphic that no images from the sciences, next to none from philosophy, occur in his poems. Such a Catholicism is thoroughly suited to literature, since it is essentially literary, anthropomorphic, emotional. It is an advantage to a poet to have a frame of reference, terms of generalization, which are themselves human, affective, and effective as literature. *Bodily Changes in Fear, Rage, Pain, and Hunger* may let the poet know more about the anger of Achilles, but it is hard for him to have to talk about adrenaline and the thalamus; and when the arrows of Apollo are transformed into a "lack of adequate sanitary facilities," everything is lost but understanding. (This helps to explain the dependence of contemporary poetry on particulars, emotions, things—its generalizations, where they are most effective, are fantastic, though often traditionally so.) Naturally the terms of scientific explanation cannot have these poetic and emotional effects, since it is precisely by the exclusion of such effects that science has developed. (Many of the conclusions of the sciences are as poetic as anything in the world, but they have been of little use to poets—how can you use something you are delighted never to have heard of?) Mr. Lowell's Catholicism represents effective realities of human behavior and desire, regardless of whether it is true, false, or absurd; and, as everyone must realize, it is possible to tell part of the truth about the world in terms that are false, limited, and fantastic—else how should we have told it? There is admittedly no "correct" or "scientific" view of a great many things that a poet writes about, and he has to deal with them in dramatic and particular terms, if he has foregone the advantage of pre-scientific ideologies like Christianity or Marxism. Of course it seems to me an advantage that he can well forego; I remember writing about contemporary religious poems, "It is hard to enjoy the ambergris for thinking of all those suffering whales," and most people will feel this when they encounter a passage in Mr. Lowell's poetry telling them how Bernadette's miraculous vision of our Lady "puts out reason's eyes." It does indeed.

It is unusually difficult to say which are the best poems in *Lord Weary's Castle:* several are realized past changing, successes that vary only in scope and intensity—others are poems that almost any living poet would be pleased to have written. But certainly some of the best things in the book are "Colloquy in Black Rock," "Between the Porch and the Altar," the first of the two poem that compose "The Death of the Sheriff," and "Where the Rainbow Ends"; "The Quaker Graveyard at Nantucket" and "At the Indian-Killer's Grave" have extremely good parts; some other moving, powerful, and unusual poems are "Death from Cancer," "The Exile's Return," "Mr. Edwards and the Spider," and "Mary Winslow"— and I hate to leave entirely unmentioned poems like "After the Surprising Conversions," "The Blind Leading the Blind," "The Drunken Fisherman," and "New Year's Day."

When I reviewed Mr. Lowell's first book I finished by saying, "Some of the best poems of the next years ought to be written by him." The appearance of *Lord Weary's Castle* makes me feel less like Adams or Leverrier than like a rainmaker who predicts rain and gets a flood which drowns everyone in the country. One or two of these poems, I think, will be read as long as men remember English.

Nation 164 (Jan. 11, 1947): 75-77.

The Influence of the Metaphysicals on Lowell

William Van O'Connor

That the influence of the Metaphysicals is now a part of the growing and developing body of modern poetry is illustrated by its presence in the work of a poet as young as Robert Lowell. In his *Lord Weary's Castle* one finds the elements that characterize the metaphysical moderns—the ease in incorporating the antipoetic into the poetic structure, the unexpected but appropriate adjective, the ironic and analytical mind, the varied but strong metrical pattern, and the constant awareness of the bones beneath the flesh. The mood and manner is in these lines from "The Drunken Fisherman": "Is there no way to cast my hook / Out of this dynamited brook? / The Fisher's sons must cast about / When shallow waters peter out." The tension between the traditional ideals and the modern sense of formlessness and heterogeneity is especially strong in Lowell's work because of his sense of his age and his own religious orthodoxy.

College English (Jan. 1948):180-87.

Lowell's Language

Josephine Miles

A younger poet who has been critically hailed in the past years, and descriptively related to Auden, makes much the same sort of combination:

> There mounts in squalls a sort of rusty mire,
> Not ice, not snow, to leaguer the Hotel
> De Ville, where braced pig-iron dragons grip
> The blizzard to their rigor mortis. A bell
> Grumbles when the reverberations strip
> The thatching from its spire,
> The search-guns click and spit and split up timber
> And nick the slate roofs on the Holstenwall
> Where torn-up tilestones crown the victor. . . .
>
> ("Exile's Return")

So begins Robert Lowell's *Lord Weary's Castle*. Since there is less variety in his work from poem to poem, these lines are the more representative of them all, and they indicate how action can be turned to quality. *Mounts, leaguer, grip, grumbles, strip, click, spit, split up, nick, crown,* all ten in nine lines, couldn't be more variously and vigorously active. The adjectives are meager and subordinated to verbs: *rusty, braced, slate, torn-up.* The twenty nouns are a tremendous load, mixed and specific. The whole is devoted to precision of context, not scene merely, but situation; the poem ends, "your life is in your hands," and it has devoted itself to telling you the particularities of event in that life. Event becomes quality.

  Lowell's main verbs are, as here, besides standard actions the verbs of shattering: *break, cry, die, fall.* His adjectives, besides *old* and *dead* and *great,* are colored: *black, red, blue.* His nouns are multitudinous: besides most of the major ones, his own and his decade's *water, father, child, snow, ice, king, Christ, Lord*, the anatomy of *bones, blood, body, face*, the nature of *tree, stone, wind, sea, house, glass*; over these the major *time, head, light, death* preside. Nouns so outweigh adjectives for him because they take on the function of adjectives, as, in the lines above, the materials of pig iron and slate are used to modify. The proportion of 7A-2IN-10V in its subordination of epithet links him with Frost and Auden and the seventeenth century, but its excess of nouns links him with the most substantial poets like his contemporary Thomas. Any twenty nouns in any average ten lines are apt to make a strong substantial burden, and in Lowell it is their quality that is their burden.

We may see a good example of resulting structure in such a relatively short poem as "To Peter Taylor on the Feast of the Epiphany." The title suggests the address and the occasion of seventeenth-century verse; the eighteen verbs in twenty-two lines come close to fitting a metaphysical predication; the minor *thin, allegoric, sacred, fabulous, sharp, old*, and others, paint no scene and are subordinate to concept; the couplets are regular, the thought complex. But the more than fifty nouns control. . . .

The poem sets power and wealth against fear. The first sentence explains, addressing Peter, why the poet thinks only Armageddon will suffice against the shapes of fear. The second defines: Fear is where we hunger, . . . where the Magi went in sacred terror, . . . and where the airplane industry builds to government contract; . . . there the bugs of Armageddon. The third sentence wears the time away to twilight and continues the battle which by its persistence and money power catches fear suspended, mid-air. The total effect of all three sentences is this mid-air poise. The long middle one describes a number of scenes of activity of fear; in all there is much bustling and going about, but all are framed and set off as examples. The shorter first and last statements parallel each other, making the balance of opposition, keeping the hero skating on thin ice, the grandsires battling, the stop-watch fingered, the fabulous gold offered in terror. Where is Peter? Unlike the lady or the lord of seventeenth-century address, he does not even seem to reply. The active, personal, "Peter, the war has taught me to revere," turns quickly to solid Whore and Beast and Dragon and "Fear with its fingered stop-watch in mid-air," and relationship of persons is less poetic than relationship of mass.

If such development from active to qualitative context is characteristic of Lowell, as I think it is, then his structures follow the turn of his vocabulary. They make substantives of verbs and qualities. They arrive at a generalized particularity. The sound pattern aids by subordination. The common rough five-accent couplet gives a sense of workmanship and effort; not much agility or delight in sound, but a sense of achievement in bringing a sort of serial order from a great many rough syllables and objects. "And the sharp barker rigs his pre-war planes" is hard to say, but important to think and feel; in its ugliness it has a kind of onomatopoeia which is characteristic throughout. All efforts turn toward getting the significant particularity of situation built up before us; and the situation is not a pleasant one. The spirit is caught in it and must deal with it.

As Lowell's concern for difficult context turns ostensible nouns and verbs to defining qualities and makes him less a reasoning or active poet than one would surmise from his proportioning, so too the most extremely predicative poets in the decade are not as extreme as they look, though for a different reason. They do not alter the standard parts of speech so much as they alter line length. William Carlos Williams, E. E. Cummings, and H. D. belong at the extreme of the list, in other words, not because, like Googe and Barclay in the sixteenth century, or like Harvey, Suckling, Jonson in the seventeenth, they used so few adjectives and nouns in proportion to verbs, whatever the line length, but rather because the use of short and broken lines itself cuts down amounts. In proportioning, Williams and H. D. belong with Eliot, Pound, Spender, Stevens, the middle group of balance or slight adjectival emphasis. Cummings, maintaining predicative emphasis, fits closer to Frost.

Nevertheless, it is significant to consider the poets at an extreme, for the reasons that put them there. With Auden and Lowell they represent a breaking down, a revision, of traditional language structures. To the juggling of parts of speech they add the juggling of linear units. Where through four centuries we have seen a constant correlation between proportioning, linear quantity, and vocabulary, now in the twentieth we find experimentation in cross-cutting which disturbs such correlation though preserving much of it.

Continuity of Poetic Language (Berkeley, 1951), 436-39.

Lord Weary's Castle

Jerome Mazzaro

Lord Weary's Castle (1946), in which Lowell first makes extensive use of his contemplative predilections, lets the reader know at the outset that it is in part a continuation of the ideas and techniques present in *Land of Unlikeness*. The sketch on the title page depicts the murder of Abel, and the title for the volume derives from a Scottish ballad in which injustice leads to blood and eventually to more blood for retribution. Much of the book continues the meditational tradition: The experiences continue to be objectified by relating them to epic events of the past or of literature, and the vision remains that of an Old Testament prophet in ungodly times. The major figures of St. Bernard, Christian Pilgrim, Faust, and Cain recur, and the major themes of mysticism, war, materialism, man's unlikeness to God, and man's salvation are repeated. New impetuses are suggested in such poems as "Charles the Fifth and the Peasant," "The Fens," "Buttercups," and "The First Sunday in Lent," but generally, the tone remains expository, didactic and critical.

The opening poem, "The Exile's Return," indicates that the volume's main concern is the world recovering from the war. It pictures the occupation of Germany as a parallel of Dante's famous descent into Hell. Yet, as in the poems of *Land of Unlikeness, this* Hell contains symbols of the country's return to Christianity—"already lily-stands / Burgeon the risen Rhineland, and a rough / Cathedral lifts its eye." It is the "Exile's" return, the epical echo of the return of the faithful from their Babylonian captivity. Told in imagery borrowed from Kröger's dream return to Lubeck in Thomas Mann's "Tonio Kröger," both this and the second poem of the volume, aptly called "The Holy Innocents," manifest the sublime faith of the earlier "Leviathan" that God will provide a new means for the remission of sins.

But soon the reader is back in the bleak war world of Cain and *Land of Unlikeness.* "Christmas Eve Under Hooker's Statue," "In Memory of Arthur Winslow," "Salem," "Concord," "Children of Light," "The Drunken Fisherman," "Napoleon Crosses the Berezina," "The Crucifix," "Dea Roma," and "The Slough of Despond" are reprinted from the earlier volume. A new sonnet, "France," portrays a view of the world war from the Crucifix, with Christ again the image of brotherhood. The opening line is a translation of the opening line of François Villon's "Epitaph," and the setting as well as other words and phrases owe much to Villon's poem. In such a world where Christ and Abel together hang forgotten on the gibbet, Lowell can only call in vain for love and understanding. It seems that with such an initial vision, the purgatorial trek up St. Peter's hill he describes in "The Holy Innocents" is doomed to failure.

Nevertheless, whereas frequently the poems in *Land of Unlikeness* did not altogether succeed in merging meditation and poetry, many of the later poems do. "At the Indian Killer's Grave," for example, despite its bleak outlook, becomes the newest, most ambitious, and most successful treatment of Lowell's Cain-Abel theme. Composed in part of segments from "The Park Street Cemetery" and "Cistercians in Germany" [in *Land of Unlikeness*], it returns the reader to the accusations of "Children of Light" and the indictments of John Easton. Added now is a description of King Philip's death at Mount Hope Neck, based on a letter by Richard Hutchinson: "This seasonable Prey was soon divided, they cut off his Head and Hands, and conveyed them to Rhode-Island, and quartered his Body, and hung it upon four Trees." A quotation from Nathaniel Hawthorne's story, "The Grey Champion," forms its inscription: "Here, also, are the veterans of King Philip's War, who burned villages and slaughtered young and old, with pious fierceness, while the godly souls throughout the land were helping them with prayer."

Like Hawthorne, Lowell is considering his Cain-Abel analogy in light of the end of an era during which the godly souls of our land were helping win World War II with prayer while young and old were being slaughtered. Coined especially for the new poem, the opening lines form an indictment against the "godly souls" of the Hawthorne story (and by analogy of our own day), whom history held in honor but subsequently forgot. Lowell wonders if at the Last Judgment they, too, will be so honored, or if their crimes, personified by King Philip's noose, will eventually hang them. In this speculation Jehoshaphat serves a dual purpose, being both the name of the valley of God's Last Judgment and of a ruler of Judah whose son Jocam murdered his brothers to gain control of the kingdom. As a reference to the book of Joel it stresses the moral nature of Lowell's vision; as an Adam figure it suggests the archetypal patterning of history.

Lapsing into the underworld descent of "The Park Street Cemetery," the poem continues with a description of modern Boston and the changes that have occurred since the deaths of the "stern Colonial magistrates and wards / Of Charles the Second." The Irish "hold the golden Statehouse / For good and always," and those colonists among the "dusty leaves and the frizzled lilac" lie decayed amid the whir and whirl of life. Returning to its initial theme of justice, the poem repeats its original Cain accusation more concretely.

King Philip speaks to these dead, taunting them with the results of their efforts to found a new Canaan. His taunts parody the peace pictured in "On the Eve of the Feast of the Immaculate Conception, 1942," where "mankind's Mother" like another Nimrod "danced on Satan's head": ". . . *But, Sirs, the trollop dances on your skulls. . . .*" The trollop, too, recalls Pearl, Hawthorne's symbol of God's mercy in *The Scarlet Letter,* and her dance over these same graves: "She now skipped irreverently from one grave to another; until, coming to the broad, flat, armorial tombstone of a departed worthy,—perhaps of Isaac Johnson himself,—she began to dance upon it." "The Judgment is at hand," King Philip warns, and it is unremitting.

The remainder of the poem shifts to Lowell's engulfing contemplative interests. Repeating the Deucalion-Jason image of "Cistercians in Germany," it goes on to entreat John, Matthew, Luke, and Mark to "gospel" the poet to the contemplative garden. There Mary rather than Bernard will become the "ecstatic womb, / As through the trellis peers the sudden Bridegroom." In the end, the poem remains one step farther away from contemplative vision, for in the earlier poem, the monks went beyond the Gospel into the "bedchamber."

In stressing the need for contemplative Truth, the poem conveys the energy and single-mindedness with which Lowell pursues his new vision. Its use of previous writings suggests the maelstrom of his imagination and engenders the belief that despite his ranging far and wide into issues derived from readings or conversations, Lowell's work will continue within quite narrow limits. Ironically, except for a possible pun on Major Thomas Savage, the Indian killer of the title does not figure at all in the main directions of the poem, let alone in its quest for Truth. Resting in the same underworld of "The Park Street Cemetery," his soul like the souls of "Adams, Otis, Hancock, Mather, Revere, and Franklin's mother" is beyond reviving

With this poem Lowell's references to Indians and King Philip's War cease, and he ends his Cain-Abel analogy, leaving to God and time the ultimate judgment of the extent of the State's crimes. Why, one might ask, the abandonment? Perhaps with the immediacy of world war gone, the immediacy of this theme also disappears. With the "Ship of State" no longer asking "Christ to walk on blood," no need exists to press Cain-Abel analogies since there are neither Cains nor Abels. Still his position calls for blood to beget blood, war to beget war, injustice to beget injustice, and the concept of man as a descendant of Cain remains a shadowy, uneasy force.

The other new, successful, time-possessed poems of the volume seek also by brimstone to restore a balance of contemplation and meditation. "To Peter Taylor on the Feast of the Epiphany," "The Dead in Europe," "As a Plane Tree by the Water," and "Where the Rainbow Ends" move beyond the themes of war, Cain, and mysticism to the themes of world destruction. Abandoning his belief that man can reform, Lowell maintains in these poems that only the world-ending Last Judgment described in St. John's Apocalypse may suffice to turn man from his present evil course. Therefore, he resumes the admonishing voice of *Land of Unlikeness*, selecting his images from Ezekiel, Joel, and John. . . .

In each of these poems the nature of man is contemporary, passive, and ambiguous. In "To Peter Taylor on the Feast of the Epiphany," man is the "hero skating on thin ice." In "The Dead in Europe," he is merely an unidentified "we." In both cases, he is universal and much different from the active Cain and Faust archetypes of *Land of Unlikeness*, for here man has lost his definitely assigned role. He can be anyone.

"As a Plane Tree by the Water" describes his society. Its title derives from Ecclesiasticus (24:19): "As a plane tree by the water in the streets, I was exalted." There the exaltation is of the contemplative after his mystical experience. Here "Darkness has called to darkness," suggesting an opposite view. The darkness seems in part taken from Psalms (43:18-21), where David describes man's state in God's covenant: "All this has come upon us, though we have not forgotten you, nor have we been disloyal to your covenant . . . though you thrust us down into a place of misery and covered us over with darkness." It also seems to derive from the ninth plague of Exodus (10:21-22): "And the Lord said . . . : Stretch out thy hand towards heaven: and may there be darkness upon the land of Egypt . . . and Moses stretched forth his hand towards heaven: and there came a horrible darkness in all the land of Egypt for three days." Likewise the poem's refrain seems to derive from the fourth plague of Exodus (8:20-21): "Thus said the Lord: Let my people go to sacrifice to me. But if thou wilt not let them go, behold I will send in upon thee, and upon thy servants, and upon thy houses all kinds of flies." These echoes and the poem's picture of "Babel-Boston" thus reverse the title, for darkness bespeaks a knowledge of evil, and in a land like ancient Babel wicked pride brings God's curse. The confusion of tongues is rampant.

Money is again the besetting evil as the Egyptian and Babylonian exiles are combined with man's current self-imposed exile from God. The poem indicates that the new world is a modern Babylon, a land of preparation for God, filled with the images of the Blessed Mother of God. As Walsingham had its Lady's shrine, so, too, Babylonian Boston has its Mary, "our Lady of Babylon." Once the city was the apple of her eye. Now it is crusted with flies. As in Exodus, these flies symbolize God's intent that the people be released to worship Him. Thus, the signs of destruction are in full force. The sea walls of the poem become the cursed walls of Jericho, whose building caused Hiel, another Adam figure, to lose his sons (3 Kings 16:34), and the streets sing for the exodus, the world-ending flood of "A Prayer for My Grandfather to our Lady" to set the people free to enter the contemplative life of the new covenant with God, where "all the world shall come to Walsingham."

Similarly, "Where the Rainbow Ends" suggests by its title that it is an extension of the contemplative direction begun in "In Memory of Arthur Winslow." The title, too, is ironic. The rainbow image of "The Quaker Graveyard in Nantucket" suggests a willful renewal of God's hopeful covenant with man now that World War II has ended. Here, in a vision, the poet sees Boston as the end of the rainbow: "I saw the sky descending, black and white, / Not blue, on Boston." The vision parallels St. John's in Apocalypse 21:2: "And I saw the holy city, New Jerusalem, coming down out of heaven from God, made ready as a bride adorned for her husband." But, as the reader soon learns, Boston exists outside the rainbow of God's will.

The deadwood at the foot of Ararat, where God made His covenant with Noah by sending him a rainbow, is being eaten by worms. Time and Death move upon the "thorn tree" of breath, symbolic of Christ. Time, as the second stanza makes explicit, is again damnation; it is the "serpent-Time, the rainbow's epitaph." The "serpent" is the Uroboros, the life-time serpent of medieval magic, as well as Satan. Caught up in time, the modern hero becomes an echo of his "damned" archetypal predecessor. Lowell, the prophet, describes himself as "a red arrow on this graph / of Revelations, pointing the direction of mankind. As "Boston serpents whistle at the cold," he is at the high altar kneeling, asking for the wisdom implied, but not gained in "As a Plane Tree by the Water." The war has ended. "The dove has brought an olive branch to eat." Paralleling the action of Noah's dove in bringing the news of the new world, it is the Holy Ghost indicating to man that the olive branch of eternal peace is the direction of his salvation

The poem's epithets for cold symbolize constriction and narrowness, greed and selfishness, Satan and evil. There is little hope for salvation except for the mystic who can achieve the mystical marriage of man and God and so escape: *"The victim climbs the altar steps and sings: / 'Hosannah to see the lion, lamb, and beast / Who fans the furnace-face of IS with wings: / I breathe the ether of my marriage feast.'"* Thus, in spite of the "olive branch," the world has grown narrower by the two years of war separating the publication of the two volumes, and, in Lowell's mind, mankind's salvation has been made more

difficult. This poem, the last one in the volume, ends the panoramic view
begun in *Land of Unlikeness* on a pessimistic note. Not all men can be
saved. Only those capable of achieving anagogic Truth can escape their
Cain archetypes into salvation. These, as St. Bernard notes, are few
compared to those who can live actively as Marthas and Lazaruses. They
have been made even fewer, according to Lowell, by the materialism
about them which minimizes their ability to contemplate. This
materialism, in all of its aspects, gnaws most deeply at man's soul and
prevents him from achieving the mystical experience he needs for
salvation. The modern world, as a result, has become a Babel or a Vanity
Fair avoiding God's worship in folly, and only destruction can save its
inhabitants. Unless one accepts the implications of Walsingham that
everyone is potentially a mystic, one wonders where the hope expressed in
"Leviathan" has gone, the hope that God would send His saving Grace to
man.

The Poetic Themes of Robert Lowell (Ann Arbor, 1965), 48-55.

The Marine in the Garden:
Pastoral Elements in Lowell's "Quaker Graveyard"

Heather Dubrow

. . . Inherent in the geographical milieu and chronological period in which
Lowell sets "The Quaker Graveyard in Nantucket" are the complex
responses to pastoral traditions that we will repeatedly encounter in the
text itself: Lowell's setting at once announces an overt and radical
disjunction between his vision and that in many other pastorals, while at
the same time asserting more subterranean parallels between his poem and
others in its genre.[1] To begin with, his landscape is not a generalized and

---

[1] [Several critics have briefly noted similarities between Lowell's poem and
Milton's "Lycidas."] See, e. g., the enumeration of the parallels in Hugh B.
Staples, *Robert Lowell: The First Twenty Years* (London, 1962), 45-46. Alan
Williamson suggests that the conventions of the pastoral elegy were present in
Lowell's mind but that he gradually lost interest in them as he composed the
poem (*Pity the Monsters*, New Haven, 1974, 35); this essay argues instead that
those conventions inform the whole elegy.

idealized Arcadia, but rather a carefully particularized section of the American coast—"A brackish reach of shoal off Madaket" (1).[2] Other pastoral poets do, of course, refer to specific places, often in a mythologized form, as Milton does when he transforms the river Cam into the river god Camus, but Lowell studs his poem with far more place-names than most of his predecessors: he crams no fewer than twenty-six into "The Quaker Graveyard in Nantucket," of which seven are references to the Atlantic itself. Like the geographical allusions in the passages from *Paradise Lost* that Lowell had been copying [into his notebooks], these proper nouns bring to the poem a sense of grandeur. Another function they serve, however, is to hint at one important explanation for the many distinctions between Lowell's poem and other pastorals: the place-names with which we are virtually bombarded from the opening of the elegy lead us to speculate on whether some of the less conventional qualities of this pastoral vision are influenced by, or even determined by, the fact that the poem focuses on New England.

One of those qualities is the marine setting of the elegy: the writer who was to compose such volumes as *Near the Ocean* and *The Dolphin* selects for his locale here not the rural or sylvan milieu of most pastoral elegies but rather the sea. If meadows normally connote peace and induce tranquillity, a stormy sea, in contrast, symbolizes destruction and generates suffering. Shepherds customarily enjoy a symbiotic relationship with their flocks and, indeed, with the natural landscape in which they figure; whalers threaten and are threatened by the natural world. Shepherds are rooted in one dear, perpetual place. (When a poet deviates from that assumption, as Virgil so effectively does in Eclogue I, we are all the more startled because a homeless shepherd represents a striking violation of our generic expectations.) In contrast, a sailor is a wanderer—in a sense, like the character who figures in the first and last poems in *Lord Weary's Castle,* an Exile.

As early as his third line ("Had steamed into our North Atlantic fleet") Lowell reminds us that for the peace of the garden he is substituting the turbulence of World War II, that his landscape is populated not by shepherds but by servicemen. This is not to imply that militaristic violence is wholly absent from more traditional pastorals, as Marvell's Nymph, say, learns to her cost, but usually such violence represents an intrusion, a contrast to the pastoral norms. In Lowell's

---

[2] [Parenthetical citations indicate line number.] All citations from "The Quaker Graveyard in Nantucket" and other poems are to *Lord Weary's Castle,* 3rd ed. (New York, 1947). Lowell published a truncated version of the elegy subsequently but later rejected those revisions.

poem, the military violence and the earlier materialism that it echoes are themselves the norms. He is exploring pastoral conventions while evoking a series of confrontations more reminiscent of epic—and the pastoral and epic repeatedly call each other's values into question.[3]

Though the setting of Lowell's poem differs so strikingly from that of conventional elegies like Theocritus I or Spenser's "Astrophel," his genre offers a number of precedents both for the natural landscape he chooses and for the attitudes to nature implied by that choice. The Renaissance piscatory eclogue, pioneered by the Italian poet Jacopo Sannazaro and imitated by Phineas Fletcher, transposes the topoi of pastoral from the shepherd's meadows to the fisherman's streams; Sannazaro's own eclogues do in fact include a funeral elegy. But in most piscatory eclogues the change in setting is not accompanied by a significant change in mood or values; the lives of the fishermen exemplify the otium that customarily characterizes the lives of shepherds, and their streams are no more threatening than the dales inhabited by their counterparts in other poems. Perhaps the primary inspiration behind Lowell's transformation of the pastoral milieu is instead to be found in the metaphysical poets who interested him so much early in his career.[4] By converting the shepherd into a Mower, by focusing on the destructive side of a harvest, Marvell draws attention to the violence latent in seemingly innocent pastoral activities and the tensions inherent in the relationship between man and nature. Similarly, in "The Baite" Donne transposes Marlowe's "The Passionate Shepherd to his Love" from the meadows to "golden sands, and cristall brookes." He then proceeds to describe love in terms of the most exploitative aspects of fishing, the "strangling snare, or windowie net." In so doing he criticizes the idealized vision with which Marlowe's shepherd tempts his beloved—and the idealizing literary form

---

[3] Lowell's battle imagery and many characteristics of his diction recall epic poetry. The juxtaposition of pastoral and epic has been analyzed by many critics; see, e. g., Claudio Guillén, *Literature as System* (Princeton, 1971), 159-217. On epic elements in Lowell's poetry, see Peter R. Remaley "Epic Machinery in Robert Lowell's *Lord Weary's Castle*," *Ball State U. Forum* 18 (1977): 9-64; Thomas A. Vogler, "Robert Lowell and the Classical Tradition," *Pacific Coast Philology* 4 (1969), 59-64.

[4] On the influence of the metaphysical poets on Lowell, see, e. g., his own comments in an interview with Frederick Seidel published in the *Paris Review* 25 (1961): esp. 64-65. If the ways those poets transform pastoral conventions did indeed influence Lowell, then "The Quaker Graveyard in Nantucket" exemplifies the curious fact that some of the major influences behind a poem may not be manifest in its text (cf. Guillén, esp. Chs. I and II).

in which he does so. And American literature of course includes many works that, like Lowell's elegy, play a more optimistic interpretation of the pastoral world against the violence of a sea or river—among the most suggestive of these precedents is the contrast between the idyllic descriptions in *Moby-Dick* and the "Try-Works" chapter.

As such analogues imply, "The Quaker Graveyard in Nantucket" has many affinities with works generally classified as "hard" rather than "soft" pastoral, works that stress the harshness of the natural world rather than its pleasures and focus on how that world teaches us the uses of adversity, not how it delights or comforts us.[5] The violent milieu in which Lowell sets his elegy also prepares us for the fact that the poem will invert many pastoral topoi and in so doing recall works that are often labelled anti-pastoral, notably *King Lear* itself. But terms like "anti-pastoral" and "hard" pastoral can at best illuminate—not encapsulate—Lowell's approach to pastoral topoi. For the two labels in question too often encourage reductionistic readings: does not even a "straight" pastoral like Marlowe's "The Passionate Shepherd to his Love" in fact hint at the critique of its genre that we normally associate with anti-pastoral? in which category should we place "Lycidas" itself? and so on. Like "Lycidas" and so many other works sometimes defined as "hard" or as anti-pastoral, "The Quaker Graveyard in Nantucket" in fact moves back and forth between the cynicism of those modes and a vision not unlike that found in the most conventional pastoral elegies.

Most elegies allude to the burial of their subject near the end of the poem; in Lowell's elegy we witness a funeral of sorts, though a very odd one, as early as the first stanza. A body appears and is cast back into the sea: "We weight the body, close / Its eyes and heave it seaward whence it came" (12-13). Neither the historical facts behind this stanza nor its literary source provides an adequate explanation: the body of Lowell's cousin Warren Winslow was never recovered,[6] and the passage from Thoreau on which Lowell is modeling his description depicts a shipwreck, rather than the discovery of a body at sea. By reshaping that model as he does, Lowell introduces an idea that will prove to be among the central

---

[5] One of the most illuminating commentaries on the distinction is in Rosalie Colie's *Shakespeare's Living Art* (Princeton, 1974), 302-16.

[6] Warren Winslow died in the "home waters" (30) of the Atlantic: not enemy action but rather a series of explosions on board destroyed his ship, the *Turner*. For the details of this accident and a suggestive interpretation of what they symbolized to Lowell, see Stephen Fender, "What Really Happened to Warren Winslow?," *Journal of American Studies* 7 (1973), 187-90.

motifs of his poem, the interconnectedness of birth (or rebirth) and death. In so doing he foreshadows one of the most significant ways his elegy will differ from those composed by most Christian poets and many pagan ones as well: their works customarily culminate on the celebration of some sort of rebirth, while the somber and temporary rebirth of Lowell's protagonist as early as stanza one anticipates the fact that he will not enjoy other and more lasting forms of resurrection.

This deviation from the normal chronological pattern of a pastoral elegy signals Lowell's deviation from the underlying attitudes towards time shared by many other writers in that genre. Those poets offer us an essentially optimistic, even amelioristic, view of experience: the speaker can in time assuage his grief and move to "pastures new" ("Lycidas"), the dead man can enjoy some form of rebirth, and the natural world itself can be reborn from diurnal darkness or seasonal aridity. This faith that experience proceeds progressively is mirrored in the narrative pattern of the poems themselves: while the stanzas in many other lyric poems are interchangeable, or else simply move in accordance with gradual shifts in the speaker's emotions, those in the pastoral elegy describe a series of sequentially ordered events in the external world. In Lowell's elegy, in contrast, the opposition between the "blue-lung'd combers" (142) and the men they attack is established at the moment of creation and continued without essential variation whether the adversary in question be Ahab or Winslow. Hence it is wholly appropriate that the topoi of the elegy are wrested from their normal sequence: the poem itself will not culminate in a resurrection any more than life itself changes for the better or, indeed, changes significantly at all.

If Lowell's description of the drowned sailor deviates from Thoreau's *Cape Cod* in some respects, in many other ways it is insistently close to its model, borrowing as it does a long string of phrases and images. By alluding to Thoreau's work in this stanza and to Melville's throughout the poem, Lowell is reinforcing the implication behind his place names: he is recasting the melodies of classical and British elegies in an American key. The writers whom Lowell is imitating function as symbols of their respective cultures and in so doing illuminate the broader meaning of those imitations: just as the poem reinterprets topoi developed by such figures as Theocritus and Milton to explore events like those described by Thoreau and Melville, so it plays the attitudes expressed in or exemplified by more conventional elegies against life in the New World.

As stanza one continues Lowell deviates even more sharply from most other works in the same literary form: "When you are powerless / To sand-bag this Atlantic bulwark, faced / By the earth-shaker, green, unwearied, chaste / In his steel scales. . ." (20-23). While pastoral elegies occasionally allude to conflicts between the man they are mourning and some of the gods, the main role assumed by mythological deities is to lament the death and in so doing to suggest that the man who has died is worthy of even a god's homage. In contrast, Lowell's allusions to Poseidon imply that the sea-god is not an ally who will mourn Winslow with us but rather an enemy we must fight, and fight in vain.

Despite the violence with which he is connected, the adjectives describing Poseidon—"green, unwearied, chaste"—establish a momentary but memorable parallel between this figure and the denizens of the pastoral world in more traditional elegies: he is associated with the kind of vitality and innocence enjoyed by, say, Milton's speaker and the young Lycidas as they lead their flocks "under the opening eye-lids of the morn." But as so often happens when we read Lowell's poem, our awareness of similarities between his work and that of other elegists quickly yields to an acute consciousness of the differences. The joy that Milton's persona experiences at that moment of innocence may perhaps never be recovered in quite the same form, but he may still in some senses participate in a world that is "green, unwearied, chaste"; at the end of the poem he plans to set out for those new pastures. But the one figure in "The Quaker Graveyard in Nantucket" who is associated with the joys that pastoral customarily offers is inhuman, not a model we can readily emulate. In fact, the main effect of the subsequent allusion to his "steel scales" is to suggest his affinity to the "dark and downward vegetating kingdom" of marine life ("For the Union Dead").[7] In other words, Lowell is anticipating here a pattern that is to find fuller realization in his more mature poems: he is connecting pastoral values and virtues not with men or even with anthropomorphic forces with which men can identify, but rather with a realm of creation from which we are cut off.

While pastoral elegies customarily celebrate the power of poesy to bring immortality to the dead and joy to the living, "Lycidas" of course questions that optimistic vision of art. In his attitudes to poesy, as in so many other respects, Lowell repeats and intensifies the troubling questions posed by Milton—and rejects even the hard won answers that his predecessor proffers.[8] For at the end of the opening stanza, as at the conclusion of a subsequent one (86-88), Lowell declares that it is pointless

---

[7] The citation is to *For the Union Dead* (New York, 1964).

[8] Lowell's allusion to rejecting the orphean lute is also discussed in Paul J. Dolan, "Lowell's *Quaker Graveyard:* Poem and Tradition," *Renascence* 21 (1969), 173 and Steven Gould Axelrod, *Robert Lowell: Life and Art* (Princeton, 1978), 57.

for art to attempt the kinds of immortalization that other writers in his genre claim to have achieved: ". . . ask for no Orphean lute / To pluck life back. The guns of the steeled fleet / Recoil and then repeat / The hoarse salute" (23-26). Instead of musical harmony between man and the natural world, Lowell offers us the dissonant sounds of the guns. (He intensified the contrast between those two types of music by changing the adjective "last," which appeared in an earlier version, to "hoarse" [26]).[9] The speaker rejects the claims of art for a less comforting but more honest acceptance of the inevitability of death.

One of the most common topoi of pastoral elegies is a description of the natural world mourning the death in question: "Nulla neque amnem / libauit quadripes nec graminis attigit herbam" (Virgil, Eclogue V). Behind this convention lies an assumption normally central to pastoral—nature mirrors the moods of the human beings within it. In his second stanza Lowell moves closer to traditional pastoral in that he is incorporating both the topos in question and the assumption behind it—"The terns and sea-gulls tremble at your death" (29). At the same time, however, Lowell's version of the pathetic fallacy deviates sharply from that in many other pastorals: "And questioned every gust of rugged wings / That blows from off each beaked promontory. . ." ("Lycidas"); ". . . The winds' wings beat upon the stones / Cousin, and scream for you . . ." ("Graveyard" 39-40).Though Lowell echoes the image of winged winds closely enough to suggest that "Lycidas" was very much on his mind, that figure functions quite differently in his poem. Milton asserts that the winds were not to blame for the death of King; in contrast, even when describing the way nature mourns for Winslow, Lowell also underlines the antagonism between man and the natural world. Though the winds seem to be bemoaning Winslow, their responses are at best ambiguous: is the world of nature screaming in the sense of lamenting Winslow's death or in the sense of threatening him with yet more violence?

Shortly after his evocation of Lycidas' idyllic childhood, Milton turns to one of the most common conventions of the pastoral elegy: his speaker demands to know where those who might have saved the young swain from drowning were when the dread event took place. Lowell does not overtly incorporate this convention into his poem. Nor does he wholly omit it, as readers have assumed: in a sense "The Quaker Graveyard in Nantucket" as a whole represents a version of that question. For, as we will see, one of the underlying dilemmas that charges the poem with

---

[9] See the first published version of the poem in the *Partisan Review* 12 (1945), 170). Professor Dolan also draws attention to the change but interprets it differently (173).

tension is whether God Himself has, despite his promises, not merely allowed Winslow to drown but also abandoned all the world.

Stanzas three and four contain dirge-like laments reminiscent of similar passages in other elegies: "This is the end of the whaleroad and the whale / Who spewed Nantucket bones on the thrashed swell" (69-70). Lowell's satirical commentary in these stanzas suggests yet another parallel between his pastoral elegy and other works in the same tradition: influenced by the models composed by Mantuan, Boccaccio, and Petrarch, English poets writing in the genre weave long passages of satire into their elegies, a practice that culminates in Milton's attack on the church.

But within these same stanzas we also find yet more examples of the radical ways Lowell has been transforming his literary heritage throughout the poem. The whalers, we are informed, died, "When time was open-eyed / Wooden and childish" (58-59). The adjectives "open-eyed" and "childish," like the attributes attached to Poseidon, recall the freshness and innocence normally associated with the pastoral world, and the very act of looking backward historically is reminiscent of the way so many pastoral poets locate those ideal qualities in the Golden Age preceding their own. Just as he does in his first allusion to Poseidon, however, Lowell is here recalling certain pastoral values only to remind us of their absence in the brave New World that he is describing. The childishness of the Quakers issues, ironically enough, not in shepherds like Milton's who gambol "under the opening eye-lids of the morn," but rather in whalers who destroy their prey while naively hoping that God will prevent their own destruction.

Many other pastoral elegies include at around this point a vision of destruction, destruction at once symbolized and generated by the death that is being mourned. Lowell's elegy devotes less attention to Warren Winslow than many other works in his genre bestow on their subjects (this is yet another regard in which the poem resembles "Lycidas"), and stanza five is no exception. The apocalyptic vision bodied forth in that stanza, an evident continuation of the violence that has characterized New England all along, is only tangentially related to Winslow.[10]

---

[10] The coexistence of apocalyptic imagery and pastoral conventions is no more surprising than Lowell's juxtaposition of epic and pastoral elements. On the relationship between imagery of the apocalypse and the garden, see Northrop Frye, *Anatomy of Criticism* (Princeton, 1957), 141-46. The apocalyptic imagery of the poem has been most fully explicated in Philip Furia, "'IS, the whited monster': Lowell's Quaker Graveyard Revisited," *TSLL* 17 (1976), 837-54, and Jerome Mazzaro, "Robert Lowell's Early Politics of Apocalypse," *Modern American Poetry*, ed. Jerome Mazzaro (New York, 1970), 321-50. Though otherwise useful, these and other studies neglect the possible literary sources of

Other poets in the genre follow their dirges and their lamentations with the soothing promises of the *consolatio*. Milton's adaptation of the *consolatio* describes the same patterns as his adaptations of other pastoral topoi; though troubled with grave doubts about the easy solutions that other pastoral elegies have proffered, he achieves and offers to his readers an acceptance of King's death that is rooted at once in pagan myth, in art, and in Christianity itself. Many critics have found in the final line of stanza five and in the next two stanzas as a whole an analogue to Milton's *consolatio*. But if we read those passages without preconceptions based on our knowledge that their author was "a fire breathing Catholic c.o." ("Memories of West Street and Lepke")[11] at the time he composed "The Quaker Graveyard in Nantucket," we do not in fact find in them the promise that Catholicism can save us from spiritual or military destruction.

Certainly the prayer on which the fifth stanza ends, "Hide, / our steel, Jonas Messias, in thy side" (l05-06) is at the very least ambiguous.[12] This appeal to Christ is followed immediately by the description of our Lady of Walsingham shrine:

> And the small trees, a stream and hedgerows file
> Slowly along the munching English lane,
> Like cows to the old shrine, . . .
> Our Lady, too small for her canopy,
> Sits near the altar. There's no comeliness
> At all or charm in that expressionless
> Face with its heavy eyelids . . . (109-11, 117-20)

The critical reaction to this section of the poem has hardly been marked by the beatific calm that the statue itself supposedly embodies.[13] Some

---

Lowell's millenarianism, concentrating exclusively on religious ones. But it is suggestive that several of the poets who interested Lowell during the period when he was composing *Lord Weary's Castle* themselves wrote apocalyptic poetry; among the examples one could cite are Donne's *Anniversaries* and Yeats's "The Second Coming" (which Lowell himself copied out in his notebooks) and Blake's "The Tyger," which he echoes in the elegy.

[11] The citation is to *Life Studies*, 2nd ed. (London, 1959).

[12] On the ambiguities of this line, cf. Williamson, 42-43.

[13] Among the critics who find peaceful affirmation of Catholicism in this stanza is Sr. Mary Theresa Rink ("The Sea in Lowell's 'Quaker Graveyard in Nantucket,' "*Renascence* 20 (1967): 39-43). Marjorie Perloff sees the inaccessibility of the Virgin as an artistic failure (*Poetic Art of Robert Lowell*, Ithaca, 1973, 144). Revising his earlier position on the poem, Richard J. Fein,

readers assert that to Lowell this English shrine indeed represents a satisfying alternative to the Sturm und Drang of contemporary society, as it indubitably does to the Catholic mystic whose descriptions Lowell is copying, E. I. Watkin. Others, however, noting that the description of the Virgin is unappealing in many ways, have traced that fact either to the aesthetic limitations that they also find elsewhere in the poem or to the psychological turmoil of a poet who, despite his Catholic conversion, was certainly Protestant by birth and training and probably Calvinist by inclination. While Lowell's description of Walsingham is indeed primarily negative, one need not attribute this to artistic or emotional failings. Acknowledging the role of pastoral in the poem enables us to recognize that Lowell's criticisms of the shrine figure prominently in the debate about that genre that is articulated and developed throughout the elegy.

In stanza six Lowell repeatedly stresses the difficulty of entering into the world of Walsingham. "Expressionless" (119, 123) and "too small for her canopy" (117), Mary seems distant from, cut off from, both her environment and those who come to worship her. The geographical distance between this world and New England is in turn underscored by a linguistic shift. Lowell has repeatedly used the proximals "this" and "these" and "here" until now (e. g., the demonstrative adjective reinforces the point made by the noun in the phrase "these home-waters" [30]). In stanza six, however, he writes "There once" (107) and "that stream" (116), as if to remind us through these distals that for the speaker, as for the Sailor and reader, Walsingham is far away.

The shrine is ultimately as unattractive as it is inaccessible. Admittedly, in certain ways Walsingham does seem appealing; for example, the fact that she "knows what God knows" (124) evidently testifies to Mary's wisdom. Yet the notion of an uncommunicative, Buddha-like Virgin is ipso facto very troubling. Nor are our negative reactions to the Virgin lessened by the "open-eyed, / Wooden and childish" (58-59) setting in which she figures. "Gurgle" (114) suggests not comfort and solace but rather something coy and distastefully childish. "Munching" (110), with its evident connotations of bovine simplicity, conveys a similar mood. Lowell's view of England's green and pleasant lands is no more pleasing than that in a suggestively analogous poem that also appears in *Lord Weary's Castle*, the imitation of William Cobbett's

---

like several other readers, suggests that the figure of Mary reflects Lowell's discomfort with some of the Catholic doctrines that he was attempting to espouse ("*Lord Weary's Castle* Revisited," *PMLA* 89, 1974, 36-37). One of the most acute commentaries is the observation Lowell's friend and fellow poet Randall Jarrell wrote on a copy of the poem: "This is as frightening as anything could be, after the beautiful beginning" (Harvard collection).

Rural Rides entitled "The Fens."

Many other poems in *Lord Weary's Castle* suggest that the answers of Catholicism, while in practice unavailable to the corrupted community that "out-Herods Herod" ("The Holy Innocents"), still in theory remain viable. In his description of our Lady of Walsingham, however, Lowell implicitly questions whether those answers are in fact practicable or desirable for Americans or even for the English. Like the pastoral landscape with which they are associated, they may represent an overly neat and smug response to complexities that cannot be so readily resolved. Because the poet has so repeatedly invited us to compare his vision with Milton's, we may even suspect that he is again in a sense rebutting "Lycidas": Milton's speaker eventually comes to accept and rejoice in the very antidotes to grief—the peace of religion and the pleasures of nature—that Lowell is here renouncing.

"The Quaker Graveyard in Nantucket" mirrors the movement it is advocating: just as we must abandon the deceptive peace of Walsingham for the harsh truths of Nantucket, so Lowell's elegy moves form the English countryside described in stanza six to the New England landscape of stanza seven. Near the conclusion of many elegies, the poet describes the way the tomb is strewn with flowers. In stanza seven, however, Lowell writes, "the oak / Splatters and splatters on the cenotaph (127-28). The implicit contrast with more conventional funeral rites reminds us yet again that the kinds of consolation that flowers symbolize in other poems are absent from this one.

Towards the end of the same stanza the poet suggests that creation and destruction are indissolubly linked. He almost seems to be implying a Manichean opposition between the God who creates man and the natural forces that attempt to destroy him, and in so doing recalls the attitudes to the natural world in many anti-pastorals: ". . . the Lord God formed man from the sea's slime / And breathed into his face the breath of life, / And blue lung'd combers lumbered to the kill" (140-42).The word "blue" here not only echoes Lowell's other references to that color but also encourages us to remember and contrast Milton's concluding promise of diurnal and personal rebirth, a promise whose optimism is intensified by the fact that blue normally signifies hope: "At last he rose, and twitched his mantle blue: / Tomorrow to fresh woods, and pastures new."

Like so many other poems in its intensely self-conscious genre, then, "The Quaker Graveyard in Nantucket" is a pastoral among whose chief preoccupations is the pastoral mode itself. Throughout the poem Lowell effects a series of contrasts between the peace and stability promised by more conventional pastorals and his speaker's very different assumptions;

he variously plays off "Lycidas" against his own modern version of pastoral, "soft" against "hard" pastoral, pastoral against anti-pastoral, the English landscape against the American, and so forth. In the process of comparing those versions of pastoral, he examines many of the most traditional pastoral themes—how nature mirrors man's psyche, whether humankind is indeed kind rather than cruel, and whether civilization is indeed more civilized than barbaric. Perhaps the main suggestion behind Lowell's exploration of pastoral, however, is that a conventional pastoral elegy would be inappropriate to the harshness of New England: like so many American writers before him, he is implying that the New World may demand new genres.

One reason Lowell's approach to pastoral is so central to the poem is that it is but one example of the pattern that shapes his elegy at so many different levels, the contrast between forms of peace on the one hand and forms of turmoil on the other. Most obviously, this pattern is established through certain recurrent themes and ideas. In stanza six, as we have seen, the serenity of traditional religion and that of traditional pastoral are linked together and both found wanting. Another possible source of security is God's promise about man's domination over the beasts, quoted in Lowell's epigraph, but as the poem progresses both the substance of that promise and the contractual relationship with God that it represents come to be questioned.

The argumentative structure of the poem mirrors this thematic pattern: again and again what seems to be a clear-cut concluding statement proves in more senses than one to be far from conclusive. Stanza six at first seems to be a conclusion and resolution—but it is quickly succeeded by stanza seven. On another level, observations like the ones on which stanzas five, six, and seven end may appear on first reading to represent an unambiguous resolution of problems—"the world shall come to Walsingham" (126), for example, sounds like a straightforward and eminently reliable pronouncement—but when we read these comments more closely, or when we reexamine them in light of subsequent lines, we discover that they are no more trustworthy than the promise of peace that Walsingham itself ostensibly offers.[14] And in those concluding lines of stanzas six and seven Lowell heightens the contrast between confusion and seeming serenity by shaping his highly ambiguous pronouncements into a crystalline syntactical unit, subject plus verb (and its object, in the case of stanza seven) plus short prepositional phrase.

---

[14] Vivian Smith notes that several poems in *Lord Weary's Castle* end ambiguously but explains the phenomenon differently *(Poetry of Robert Lowell,* Sydney, 1979, 16-17).

Within one of the central images of the poem is embedded the same duality of peace and conflict, resolution and doubt. It is no accident that a poem so concerned with havens from chaos—whether they be religious, pastoral, or stylistic—and with the violation of those havens should return repeatedly to the image of a castle. A castle may seem to represent impregnable security; but the other side of the coin becomes explicit in Lowell's allusion to "castles in Spain, / Nantucket's westward haven" (48-49) and implicit but no less troubling when he suggests that the Sailor will not reach the "castled Sion" (124) that he seeks. And the ballad from which the title *Lord Weary's Castle* is taken tells the tale of the man who finds that his seemingly secure home, and all his pretty ones, have been destroyed.

The shift between trusting in impregnable castles and recognizing them for castles in the air is not merely discussed in the poem, not merely bodied forth in its language and imagery, but also enacted by both the Sailor and the reader. The Sailor approaches Walsingham with high hopes, whistling; the phrase "But see" (116) alerts us to the fact that he fails to find the peace he anticipates. The experience of the reader closely parallels that of this deceived pilgrim. We too reach out for the religious security that stanza six seems to offer, or the ideological certainty suggested by the epigraph and by the epigrammatic concluding lines, or the assurances inherent in traditional pastoral assumptions; we try to believe that certain ideas in the poem represent clear-cut promises, not ambiguous observations. Like the Sailor, we learn we must settle not for the peace of the garden but rather for the chaos of the sea, not for an idealized English or Arcadian landscape but rather for the locale so clearly defined by Lowell's place-names. . . .

Philological Quarterly 62.2 (Spring 1983): 127-45.

The Mills of the Kavanaughs

Louise Bogan

Lowell is not without his baffling idiosyncrasies. He is drawn to highly specialized characters and situations, his writing is compressed often to the point of obscurity, and his tendency toward moral rigidity and emotional morbidity is marked. But Lowell's relation to his subjects, peculiar as they may be, is absolutely and dramatically direct, and the smallest details of character and setting make an unforgettable impact upon the attentive reader because they are so clearly a living part of the poet's emotional and imaginative being. The closely woven texture of the writing is not an added effect but an integral part of method. The title poem is particularly impressive. Yet Lowell, for all his gifts, is still incapable of expressing daylight simplicities at any length. His deepest predilections are toward spiritual regions where the season is always one of autumnal desolation and the hour is always hair-raising midnight. This is the dark mid-point of a poet's development which must in some way be transcended. That it can be transcended, even in our own tragic day, has been already demonstrated by Yeats and Eliot.

New Yorker 27 (June 9, 1951): 94.

Lowell, Santayana, and "Falling Asleep over the Aeneid"

Paul Mariani

That December [1947] Santayana wrote Lowell in care of the embassy in Istanbul, asking for some information on his background, noting that his poetry had a power "greater than any recent poetry" he'd read in English, and that he'd discovered there many beautiful passages.

When Cal [Lowell] returned to Washington in January 1948, after spending Christmas and New Year's with the Jarrells and Taylors in North Carolina, he found Santayana's letter waiting for him. In his reply, he sketched out his background, then noted that he was no longer in the Church. " I think that what Catholics believe is true, in a way," he added, because it had "a world of experience behind it." But it was not *the* truth. Actually, he no longer knew what he believed, and was just as glad. He was probably "something of a mild secular quietist—usually in trouble though—and an anarchical conservative." But he blushed "to toss these rude terms to a philosopher" of Santayana's stature. He'd been honored to hear form Santayana, whom he'd been reading for the past ten years—his

Character and Opinion in America, his autobiography, his essays on Christ, as well as those on Browning and Whitman. Except for Plato, Lowell admitted, he'd read too little philosophy, though he'd read Santayana's *Dialogues in Limbo* with the same intensity with which he'd read Shakespeare. He enclosed copies of "Falling Asleep over the Aeneid" and "Mother Marie Therese."[1]

"I can think of you only as friend and not merely as a celebrity," Santayana replied. "In spite of the great differences in our ages—I could be your grandfather—in our backgrounds, and also, no doubt, in our characters, there is a notable parallelism in our minds." In Lowell's stance toward the Church, for instance, "feeling its historic and moral authority, and yet seeing that its doctrine is not true," he had arrived at exactly the place where Santayana himself was. Then he turned to Lowell's imitation of Virgil in "Falling Asleep over the Aeneid." Virgil was probably too mild for Lowell's taste, he could see, which perhaps explained why he'd turned the Roman poet's Trojans and Italian barbarians into American Indians. And surely, Santayana remonstrated, Virgil would never have called Venus a "whore." She had lovers, he explained, "no end of lovers including the young Anchises," but that was "because she was the goddess of fecundity and beauty." But then, perhaps Lowell did not "feel the sacredness of nature in paganism"? And yet it was clear he did feel the sacredness of Catholicism, which, in its fundamental perception, "Jewish as well as Greek," was, at bottom, but another form of paganism.

Lowell was delighted to have someone of Santayana's stature take his work so seriously, especially where his own relatives had only gaped blindly. Then, with all the overreaching vigor of the young, perhaps unaware that he was critiquing his own practice, he explained that he had set out in his own dramatic monologue to correct the deficiencies of the form as Browning had practiced it, since Browning, in spite of "all the right ideas about what the poetry of his time should take in" had "muffed it" with his "ingenious, terrific metrics," which in the long run only shook "the heart out of what he was saying." If only he'd been patient, Lowell added, Browning could have been "one of the great poets of the world." In spite of which, Browning had often enough managed to find himself on the side of the angels.

"Falling Asleep over the Aeneid" is the first of Lowell's Sunday Morning poems, his occasional meditations on the current state of affairs during the time usually given over to Church attendance. Here he turns away from Christianity and the Bible—Lowell's earlier preoccupations— to the classics. The speaker of this dramatic monologue (which employs,

---

[1] Both later published in *The Mills of the Kavanaughs* (New York, 1951).

as Browning had, enjambed heroic couplets) is named Vergil, the name creating an immediate historical palimpsest which links this New World figure in Concord, Massachusetts, to the author of the Aeneid, the two worlds in the speaker's dream state having suddenly become very much like each other. The time is the present—1945 or '46—eighty years after the end of the Civil War, and—in the wake of the destruction by fire of Dresden, Hamburg, and Nagasaki (figured by the terrible funeral pyre which dominates the poem)—one is reminded of the death of the thousand-year reign of the Third Reich, with its heilings and flickering torchlight rallies, the burnt corpse of Hitler in his Berlin bunker and the beginnings of an American Empire. For Lowell, the Republic is dead, as dead as Pallas, killed by Prince Turnus, as dead as Colonel Charles Russell Lowell, killed charging the entrenchments at the Wilderness, as dead too as Colonel Robert Shaw, killed in the assault on Fort Wagner.

Virgil foreshadowed it all—war and war's aftermath—in his bittersweet epic, weeping (lacrimae rerum) as he recalled the solid virtues of the Roman Republic, even as Caesar continued to consolidate his new Roman Empire. Santayana was right, of course: Lowell has whipped the quieter landscapes of Virgil into a frenzy, for much of the anger and despair of "Quaker Graveyard" has spilled over into this poem as well. Here in Lowell—as Robert Fitzgerald, himself a superb translator of the Aeneid, would note—"reanimated, plumed and clopping," one hears again "the barbaric Ausonian cavalry."[2] There is in fact a barbarous dignity about Lowell's language here, a language close to what Pound did in his Englishing of Propertius, and Lowell has been careful to play the Latin idiom ("With snapping twigs and flying" and "armored horses, bronze") against the American idiom ("Boy, it's late and Vergil must keep the Sabbath").

"History," Joyce's Stephen Daedalus says: "a nightmare from which I am trying to awake." And Lowell, in late 1947, from Washington: "When the next atom bombs fall, there won't be any more inhabitable Atlantic coast in our life-time." So too with Vergil, dreaming the deaths of good men and the unleashing of a new savagery upon the world as the infant Empire (Rome then, America now) begins to consolidate its gains.

Lost Puritan: A Life of Robert Lowell (New York, 1994), 159-61.

---

[2] Fitzgerald, "Robert Lowell, 1917-1977," *Harvard Advocate* 113 (1979): 41.

Middle Period

On *Life Studies*

Elizabeth Bishop

As a child, I used to look at my grandfather's Bible under a powerful reading-glass. The letters assembled beneath the lens were suddenly like a Lowell poem, as big as life and as alive, and rainbow-edged. It seemed to illuminate as it magnified; it could also be used as a burning-glass.

This new book begins on Robert Lowell's now-familiar trumpet-notes (see "Inauguration Day"), then with the auto-biographical group the tone changes. In these poems, heartbreaking, shocking, grotesque and gentle, the unhesitant attack, the imagery and construction, are as brilliant as ever, but the mood is nostalgic and the meter is refined. A poem like "My Last Afternoon with Uncle Devereux Winslow," or "Skunk Hour," can tell us much about the state of society as a volume of Henry James at his best.

Whenever I read a poem by Robert Lowell I have a chilling sensation of here-and-now, of exact contemporaneity: more aware of those "ironies of American History," grimmer about them, and yet hopeful. If more people read poetry, if it were more exportable and translatable, surely his poems would go far towards changing, or at least unsettling, minds made up against us. Somehow or other, by fair means or foul, and in the middle of our worst century so far, we have produced a magnificent poet.

Dust jacket, Robert Lowell, *Life Studies* (New York, 1959).

Poetry as Confession

M. L. Rosenthal

Emily Dickinson once called publication "the auction of the mind." Robert Lowell seems to regard it more as soul's therapy. The use of poetry for the most naked kind of confession grows apace in our day. We are now far from the great Romantics who, it is true, spoke directly of their emotions but did not give the game away even to themselves. They found, instead, cosmic equations and symbols, transcendental reconciliations with "this lime-tree bower my prison," titanic melancholia in the course of which, merging his sense of tragic fatality with the evocations of the nightingale's song, the poet lost his personal complaint in the music of universal forlornness. Later, Whitman took American poetry to the very edge of the confessional in his *Calamus* poems and in the quivering avowal of his helplessness before the seductions of "blind loving wrestling touch, sheath'd hooded sharp-tooth'd touch." More recently, under the influence of the Symbolists, Eliot and Pound brought us into the forbidden realm itself, yet even in their work a certain indirection masks the poet's actual face and psyche from greedy eyes.

Lowell removes the mask. His speaker is unequivocally himself, and it is hard not to think of *Life Studies* as a series of personal confidences, rather shameful, that one is honor-bound not to reveal. About half the book, the prose section called "91 Revere Street," is essentially a public discrediting of his father's manliness and character, as well as of the family and social milieu of his childhood. Another section, the concluding the sequence of poems grouped under the heading "Life Studies," reinforces and even repeats these motifs, bringing them to bear on the poet's psychological problems as an adult. The father, naval officer *manqué* and then businessman and speculator *manqué*, becomes a humiliating symbol of the failure of a class and of a kind of personality. Lowell's contempt for him is at last mitigated by adult compassion, though I wonder if a man can allow himself this kind of ghoulish operation on his father without doing his own spirit incalculable damage. But the damage has clearly been in the making a long time, and Lowell knows very well that he is doing violence to himself most of all: "I hear / my ill-spirit sob in each blood cell, / as if my hand were at its throat. . . ."

He does not spare himself in these poems, at least two of which have to do with sojourns in mental hospitals and his return home from them. We have grotesque glimpses into his marital life. "Man and Wife," for instance, begins: "Tamed by *Miltown,* we lie on Mother's bed." It later tells how

> All night I've held your hand,
> as if you had
> a fourth time faced the kingdom of the mad—
> its hackneyed speech, its homicidal eye—
> and dragged me home alive. . . .

"My mind's not right," says the speaker in "Skunk Hour," the poem which ends the book. It is partly Lowell's apology for what he has been saying in these pieces, like Gerontion's mumbling that he is only "an old man, a dull head among windy spaces." And it is partly his assertion that he cannot breathe without these confessions, however rank they may be, and that the things he has been talking about are too stubbornly alive to be ignored:

> I stand on top
> of our back steps and breathe the rich air—
> a mother skunk with her column of kittens swills the
>   garbage pail.
> She jabs her wedge-head in a cup
> of sour cream, drops her ostrich tail,
> and will not scare.

It will be clear that my first impression while reading *Life Studies* was that it is impure art, magnificently stated but unpleasantly egocentric—somehow resembling the triumph of the skunks over the garbage cans. Since its self-therapeutic motive is so obvious and persistent, something of this impression sticks all the way. But as the whole work floods into view the balance shifts decisively. Lowell is still the wonderful poet of "The Quaker Graveyard in Nantucket," the poet of power and passion whose driving aesthetic of anguish belies the "frizzled, stale and small" condition he attributes to himself. He may be wrong in believing that what has happened to New England's elite is necessarily an embodiment of the state of American culture, the whole maggoty character of which he feels he carries about in his own person. But he is not wrong in looking at the culture through the window of psychological breakdown. Too many other American poets, no matter what their social class and family history, have reached the same point in recent years. Lowell is foremost among them in the energy of his uncompromising honesty.

Furthermore, *Life Studies* is not merely a collection of small moment-by-moment victories over hysteria and self-concealment. It is also a beautifully articulated poetic sequence. I say "articulated," but the impact of the sequence is of four intensifying waves of movement that smash at the reader's feelings and break repeatedly over his mind. The poems that make up the opening movement are not personal in the sense of the rest of the book. They are poems of violent contradiction, a historical overture to define the disintegration of a world. In the first a train journeys from Rome to Paris at mid-century. The "querulous hush-hush" of its wheels passes over the Alps and beyond them, but nowhere in the altitudes to which it rises does it touch the sanely brilliant heights of ancient myth and thought. For its riders there are, at one terminal, the hysteria of *bella Roma,* where "the crowds at San Pietro screamed *Papa*" at the pronouncement of the dogma of Mary's assumption and where "the Duce's lynched, bare, booted skull still spoke"; and at the other terminal, the self-destructive freedom of "Paris, our black classic." The next poem reaches far enough back in time to reveal the welter of grossly sensual, mindlessly grasping egotism that attended the birth of the modern age. Marie de Medici "the banker's daughter," soliloquizes about "blood and pastime," the struggle between monarchy and the "pilfering, pillaging democracies," the assassination of her husband. The third poem returns from modern Europe and its bloody beginnings to our own American moment. All that turbulence of recent centuries now seems frozen into intellectual and moral death. . . .

But then the fourth poem hurls at us the monologue of a mad Negro soldier confined at Munich. Here the wit, the audacious intimacy, the acutely bizarre tragic sense of Lowell's language take on jet-speed. In this monologue the breakdown of traditional meanings and cultural distinctions is dramatized in the frenzy of one contemporary figure. Thus Lowell begins to zero in on his main target, himself as the damned speaking-sensibility of his world. The humiliated, homicidal fury of the Negro soldier throws its premonitory shadow over the disturbed "comedy" of "91 Revere Street" which follows. It helps us to see, beneath the "Jamesian" nuances of relationship in a society of ritual pretensions but no center of gravity, how anguished is this prose section's murderous dissection of the poet's parents and its complaint against a childhood gone awry. In this way it prepares us for the personal horrors with which the book closes.

But before that long, devastating final wave of poems, there is a smaller one, corresponding in gathering force with the first group. This third wave is again made up of four poems, each of them about a modern writer with whom Lowell feels kinship as an embattled and alienated spirit. Following hard upon the prose, these poems clearly say: "This is what the predatory centuries, and the soul-devouring world in which I walked the maze of my childhood, have done to man's creativity." Lowell first portrays Ford Madox Ford, the "mammoth mumbler" cheated out of his earned rewards, standing up to Lloyd George and, later, scratching along in America, sick and "gagged for air." Then, dear to Lowell's heart, the self-exiled Santayana looms before us—"free-thinking Catholic infidel." The third poem recreates with sentimental bitterness a winter Lowell and Delmore Schwartz spent at Harvard in 1946. Nothing could be more pathetically open about Lowell's state of mind concerning himself and his art than the parts of their conversation he chooses to record and even to italicize:

> . . . "Let Joyce and Freud,
> the Masters of Joy,
> be our guests here," you said. The room was filled
> with cigarette smoke circling the paranoid,
> inert gaze of Coleridge, back
> from Malta—his eyes lost in flesh, lips baked and black.
> . . . You said:
> *"We poets in our youth begin in sadness;*
> *thereof in the end come despondency and madness;*
> Stalin has had two cerebral hemorrhages!"

The ironic facetiousness that so often marks Schwartz's writing and conversation is here absorbed by Lowell into a vision of unrelieved breakdown centered on the image of Coleridge's "paranoid gaze" in the picture. That image, together with the mocking allusion to Stalin as one of "we poets" who come at last to madness, brings past and present, and all political and psychological realities, into a single focus of defeat. Then in the fourth poem, "Words for Hart Crane," the group comes to a climax paralleling that of "A Mad Negro Soldier" in the first group. Crane's brief, self-destructive career is seen as the demand of the creative spirit, deliberately wearing the most loathsome mask it can find, for unquestioning love from the culture that has rejected it. Here, just before he plunges back into his major theme, the "life studies" of himself and his family, Lowell again—at the most savagely committed pitch he can command—presents the monologue of a dramatically suffering figure whose predicament has crucial bearing on his own.

In large part, the fourteen poems of the final section echo the prose of "91 Revere Street." But they echo it as a storm echoes the foreboding sultriness of a threatening spell of weather before it. Apart from the obvious differences that verse makes, they break out of the cocoon of childhood-mentality that somehow envelops "91 Revere Street" despite its more sophisticated aspects. Lowell, like Yeats and Thomas, casts over his autobiographical prose a certain whimsy (though often morbid) and childlike half-awareness. But the poems are overborne by sadness first and then by the crash of disaster. Side by side Lowell places memories of his confinement in mental hospitals and a denigration of his great act of defiance as a conscientious objector in World War II which led to his imprisonment for a year: "I was a fire-breathing Catholic C. O., / and made my manic statement, / telling off the state and president. . . ." The only poem of this group in which he does not talk in his own person, "'To Speak of Woe That Is in Marriage,'" is a monologue by the wife of a lecherous, "hopped-up" drunkard. It is placed strategically just before the last poem, "Skunk Hour," and after "Man and Wife," in which Lowell makes certain we know he is discussing his own marriage, and it is a deliberate plunge into the depths of the theme of degradation at all but the last moment. Finally, "Skunk Hour," full of indirections and nuances that bring the sickness of our world as a whole back into the scene to restore a more universal vision, reaches a climax of self-contempt and of pure symbol-making. This is Lowell's fantastic, terrifying skunk-image for the secret self's inescapable drive to assure itself of continued life—

> I myself am hell;
> nobody's here—
>
> only skunks, that search
> in the moonlight for a bite to eat.
> They march on their soles up Main Street:
> white stripes, moonstruck eyes' red fire
> under the chalk dry and spar spire
> of the Trinitarian Church.

Life Studies brings to culmination one line of development in our poetry of the utmost importance. Technically, it is an experiment in the form of the poetic sequence comparable to *Mauberley* and *The Bridge*. To build a great poem out of the predicament and horror of the lost Self has been the recurrent effort of the most ambitious poetry of the last century. It is too early to say whether *Life Studies* is great art. Enough, for the moment, to realize that it is inescapably encompassing art.

Nation 189 (Sept. 19, 1959): 154-55.

"Putdown of the Whore of Babylon"
(a Lamantia title)

Amiri Baraka

To give The National Book Award to Robert Lowell is a simple & representative methodology. A fixture. It is not literary: or, to get at it from another way, it is *merely* literary. *Life Studies* is a good book. And *yes*, there were better books of poetry in 1959. But *Life Studies* can be accepted as "what is going on, &c." I. e., Robert Lowell is a more than "competent" poet. A serious and accomplished *younger* (the way we use that) poet. And *yes*, there are better ynger (& not so ynger) poets. I mean, let me propose that Olson, Creeley and Duncan are better. (A loose chronology, tho.) Let me also propose that there is another, even ynger segment, whose work is also Superior (from "On Yr Mark". Intent. I. e., in what it, the work, *intends. And* the actual writing) to Lowell's. I. e., Ginsberg, O'Hara, Dorn, McClure, and some others. And I still mean to say Lowell is the best of a bunch. Another bunch.

But in giving The Pulitzer Prize for poetry to W. D. Snodgrass, it becomes viciously apparent that the methodology, the fixture, the cookie tournament, is one (if we squint in hopeless paranoia at all the phenomena of our lives) of actual *filth.*

To begin with *A.*, Robert Lowell is certainly a better poet than W. D. Snodgrass. A much more *honest* man. *Life Studies* is the champ of that league (the cookie people/ & better'n that). A better book than *Heart's Needle*. It is (*L. S.*) a terribly impressive voice out of all those stacks of dead tomes (that form official USKulchur). & Because of this. This impressiveness. The N.B.A. was easy to accept (& with only a slight, say, grimace of ironic prehension). But if the prize is to be *Only* a gift. I. e., "he got *one* . . . let's give ol' Snod the other" . It, this "fixture", becomes more than just another example of the simplemindedness &/or immaturity of the official literary hierarchy. It is suddenly an ugly dishonesty, horribly obscene, that shd scare the hell out of anyone unfortunate enough not to be in on it. An ugliness that screams at us to injure it. (If we would call *honesty a* substance we *must* have in our lives. If we are *anything.*

But it is virtually impossible to *injure* it. It will abide/as long as there is at least one liar in a high place. ". . . the darkness sur- / rounds us," & nothing has *ever* given us any reason to believe that anything else will ever be the case. "what / can we do against / it," The one aim of his life, Porphyry said, "was to rise to God and become one with Him." Plotinus: "The soul is unlit without that experience. Lit thereby, it possesses that which is sought. This is the true goal set before the soul, to attain that light, to perceive God in His own radiance and not by any other light. . . *Let all else go!"* (That bugged Augustine. The West wall.) A defense? ? ?

There ain't none. ". . . or else, shall we & / by not, buy a goddamn big car,"

I went to see John Coltrane last night and came back trembling.

> drive, he sd, for
> christ's sake, look
> out where yr going.

Yugen 7 (1961): 4-5.

Realism and the Confessional Mode of Robert Lowell

Marjorie Perloff

. . . As long ago as 1925, Boris Tomashevsky, a leading Russian formalist critic, observed that the "autobiographical poem" is one that mythologizes the poet's life in accordance with the conventions of his time. It relates not what has occurred but what should have occurred, presenting an idealized image of the poet as representative of his literary school. James Merrill made the same point with reference to the so-called confessional poems in his *Nights and Days* (1967): "Confessional Poetry . . . is a literary convention like any other, the problem being to make it sound as if it were true." Whether or not the poet is presenting the actual facts of his experience is irrelevant, but he must give the "illusion of a True Confession."[1] "There's a good deal of tinkering with fact," Lowell said of *Life Studies* in the *Paris Review* interview, but of course "the reader was to believe he was getting the *real* Robert Lowell."[2]

---

[1] Donald Sheehan, "Interview with James Merrill," *Contemporary Literature* 9 (1968): 1-2.
[2] Frederick Seidel, "Robert Lowell," *Writers at Work, 2nd Series* (New York, 1963), 349.

These reminders of the role convention plays in even autobiographical poetry are salutary at a time when the confessional poem—surely our predominant lyric genre today—is consistently treated by critics as *confession* rather than as poetry. When M. L. Rosenthal, in his seminal study of post-war poetry, defines the confessional poem as one in which "the private life of the poet himself, especially under stress of psychological crisis, becomes a major theme,"[3] he is telling us something about the typical subject matter of Robert Lowell or Allen Ginsberg or Anne Sexton, but this and similar definitions give us no way of distinguishing between, say, Anne Sexton's frequently maudlin revelations of her reactions to menstruation or masturbation and a poem like Lowell's "Skunk Hour"—generally considered one of the major poems of the last decade.

Again, when critics argue, as Roger Bowen has done,[4] that *Life Studies* functioned mainly as a "personal catharsis" for the poet, and that, once Lowell had been liberated from the "personal neurosis" and the "obsessive involvement with personal history" which characterize these confessional poems, he was psychologically ready to move on to a more "responsible" and more "public" poetry, I suspect that the nature of the confessional poem as a literary genre has been completely misunderstood. The publication of *Notebook 1967-68* must in fact have come as a great surprise to critics of Bowen's persuasion, for here, ten years after *Life Studies*, were poems about Lowell's precise sensations during the Pentagon March of 1967, his idyllic romance during a brief stay at Harvard, his ambivalent feelings toward Allen Tate and Randall Jarrell, and his reactions to too much liquor. Read as a whole, *Notebook 1967-68* is, despite Lowell's disclaimer in the "Afterthought," an autobiographical sequence in which one year in the life of Robert Lowell is recaptured. Although the stanza form—the blank verse sonnet—of *Notebook* is new, the mode of the poems is still that of *Life Studies*.

How does a poet like Lowell "mythologize" his personal life? What are the conventions that govern the structure of his poems, and conversely, what conventions does he reject? These are the questions I shall try to answer in this chapter. My text is one of the best-known poems in the final section of *Life Studies*, "Man and Wife":

> Tamed by Miltown, we lie on Mother's bed;
> the rising sun in war paint dyes us red;
> in broad daylight her gilded bed-posts shine,

---

[3] Rosenthal, *The New Poets* (New York, 1967), 15.
[4] Bowen, "Confession and Equilibrium," *Criticism* 11 (1969): 79.

abandoned, almost Dionysian.
At last the trees are green on Marlborough Street,
blossoms on our magnolia ignite
the morning with their murderous five days' white.
All night I've held your hand,
as if you had
a fourth time faced the kingdom of the mad—
its hackneyed speech, its homicidal eye—
and dragged me home alive.... Oh my *Petite*,
dearest of all God's creatures, still all air and nerve:
you were in your twenties, and I,
once hand on glass
and heart in mouth,
outdrank the Rahvs in the heat
of Greenwich Village, fainting at your feet—
too boiled and shy
and poker-faced to make a pass,
while the shrill verve
of your invective scorched the traditional South.

Now twelve years later, you turn your back.
Sleepless, you hold
your pillow to your hollows like a child;
your old-fashioned tirade—
loving, rapid, merciless—
breaks like the Atlantic Ocean on my head.[5]

I suppose that the most obvious thing to say about this poem is that it marks a return to the romantic mode in which the "I," clearly designated as the poet himself, undergoes a highly personal experience. Whatever else "Man and Wife" is like, it surely represents a reaction against Eliot's dictum that poetry is not the turning loose of emotion but an escape from emotion; it is a reaction against the autonomous, "impersonal" symbolist mode of Eliot, Pound, Stevens, the early Auden, and of the Robert Lowell of *Lord Weary's Castle*—the mode that dominated the first half of our century. Lowell himself has said that when he wrote *Life Studies*, he wanted to get away from the doctrine that poetry is first of all a craft. "Any number of people are guilty of writing a complicated poem that has a certain amount of symbolism in it and really difficult meaning, a wonderful poem to teach. Then you unwind it and you

---

[5] *Life Studies* (New York, 1959), 87.

feel that the intelligence, the experience, whatever goes into it, is skin deep"(Seidel 347). More explicitly, W. D. Snodgrass has said in a panel discussion, "I read *The Waste Land* if somebody tells me to, but I never tell myself to. Similarly with Pound, I am much attracted to his early work but I find that as he goes on he becomes less and less a poet and more and more a kind of flash card machine." As for Stevens, his whole middle period is "a desert of philosophy." Interestingly, the only early twentieth-century poet exempt from these charges is Yeats. He was, Snodgrass believes, "the last and certainly the finest symbolist in English. Yet in some very essential sense he never gave in to it." He could not submit to any "system of ideas" because he was essentially "talking about his own feelings."[6] Yeats is, in other words, a romantic and therefore, unlike Eliot and Pound, he is acceptable to a confessional poet of the mid-sixties.

M. H. Abrams defines the structure of what he calls "the greater Romantic Lyric" as follows:

> [It presents] a determinate speaker in a particularized, and usually a localized, outdoor setting, whom we overhear as he carries on, in a fluent vernacular which rises easily to a more formal speech, a sustained colloquy, sometimes with himself or with the outer scene, but more frequently with a silent human auditor, present or absent. The speaker begins with a description of the landscape; an aspect or change of aspect in the landscape evokes a varied but integral process of memory, thought, anticipation, and feeling which remains closely involved with the outer scene. In the course of this meditation the lyric speaker achieves an insight, faces up to a tragic loss, comes to a moral decision, or resolves an emotional problem. Often the poem rounds upon itself to end where it began, at the outer scene, but with an altered mood and deepened understanding which is the result of the intervening meditation.[7]

This definition is generally applicable to the structure of "Man and Wife," even though the bedroom has replaced the outdoor setting of romantic poetry. Lowell's poem does have a determinate speaker—the poet himself—in a specific setting at a particular moment in time, who carries on a colloquy with a silent human auditor—his wife. Again, the

---

[6] Snodgrass, "Poetry Since Yeats," *TriQuarterly* 4 (1965): 101-102.

[7] Abrams, "Structure and Style in the Greater Romantic Lyric," *Sensibility to Romanticism*, ed. Frederick Hilles and Harold Bloom (New York, 1965), 527-28.

poet does use a "fluent vernacular" ("All night I've held your hand") which "rises easily to a more formal speech" as in "Oh my *Petite*, / clearest of all God's creatures." The poem begins in the present: husband and wife face the beginning of another day not after a happy night of love, but after sleepless hours of argument, hysteria, and anxiety, made bearable only by tranquilizers. As the poet contemplates the scene, he recalls the very different night of their first meeting. The memory of his former enthusiastic and romantic self enables the poet to face the present with some return to equanimity: wryly he capitulates to his wife's "old-fashioned tirade" which "breaks like the Atlantic" on his head. The poem thus "rounds upon itself"; it moves in a circle from present to past and back to the present, imitating the structure of the poet's meditation as he struggles toward self-understanding.

Generically, then, "Man and Wife" can be placed in the romantic tradition, and yet even a cursory reading of the poem suggests that it is, in fact, quite unlike "Resolution and Independence" or "Frost at Midnight" or "Ode to a Nightingale." One notices immediately the factual documentation quite alien to the romantics: the allusions to *Miltown*, to Marlborough Street, to the Rahvs of Greenwich Village, as well as the peculiar insistence on numerical accuracy: "five days' white," "a fourth time," "you were in your twenties," "twelve years later." Conversely, "Man and Wife" does not have the dense web of symbolic implication that characterizes romantic and symbolist poetry. The magnolia tree of line 6, for example, unlike the "great-rooted blossomer" of Yeats's "Among School Children" or the "green laurel" of his "A Prayer for my Daughter," is not a central symbol around which the whole poem is built. It would have no place, for example, in the rich catalogue of tree images discussed by Frank Kermode in *Romantic Image*. One finds it difficult, moreover, to discern what relates one line or one image to the next in "Man and Wife." Why, for example, does the poem begin with the image of the tranquilized couple reclining on "Mother's bed"—an image rich with latent meanings about the failure of this particular marriage—and then suddenly switch to the optical effect created when bright sunlight shines on bed-posts? Although the syntax is perfectly straight-forward—a sequence of simple declarative sentences—the poet's meditation is not sustained. It focuses first on one object and then on another without explicit connection.

How, then, can we characterize the technique of "Man and Wife"? Lowell himself gives us an important hint when, in the *Paris Review* interview, he explains why he rejected the technically sophisticated poetry of his contemporaries, a poetry exhibiting "tremendous skill" but "divorced from culture somehow." "Prose," Lowell argues, "is in many ways better off than poetry. It's quite hard to think of a young poet who has the vitality, say, of Salinger or Saul Bellow. . . . Some of this Alexandrian poetry is very brilliant. . . . But I thought it was getting increasingly stifling. I couldn't get my experience into tight metrical forms." (Seidel 346)

"Almost the whole problem of writing poetry," Lowell insists, "is to bring it back to what you really feel." The "ideal modern form" for capturing "personal vibrance" is the novel. "Maybe Tolstoy would be the perfect example—his work is imagistic, it deals with all experience, and there seems to be no conflict of the form and content. So one thing is to get into poetry that kind of human richness in rather simple descriptive language" (Seidel 368, 343). In a later discussion of *Life Studies* Lowell made this point even more emphatic: "I felt that the best style for poetry was none of the many poetic styles in English, but something like the prose of Chekhov or Flaubert."[8]

In *Life Studies*, one concludes, Lowell is trying to fuse the romantic mode, which projects the poet's "I" in the act of self-discovery, and the Tolstoyan or Chekhovian mode, usually called realism. I would posit that it is his superb manipulation of the realistic convention, rather than the titillating confessional content, that is responsible for the so-called breakthrough of *Life Studies* and that distinguishes Lowell's confessional poetry from the work of his less accomplished disciples.

Realism is one of the most difficult terms to define, as René Wellek's and Harry Levin's comprehensive discussions of the term in literary scholarship make clear. Tolstoyan realism is perhaps best defined in an excellent essay on *Anna Karenina* by Robert Louis Jackson: "The principle of realism guiding Tolstoy . . . is one which Chekhov will develop to the highest point of perfection; the view that our casual everyday appearance, behavior, conversation—in short, our everyday 'character' and confrontations—contain, reflect, anticipate the larger shape of our destiny." Tolstoy's genius is "to maintain a primary focus upon the 'natural' movement of surface action . . . while at the same time revealing in this seemingly routine material the texture of a dynamic reality, rapidly acquiring design and shape."[9]

But how does the realistic writer organize "seemingly routine material" so that it will reveal the "texture of a dynamic reality"? It was Roman Jakobson, I believe, who first associated realism with metonymy as a stylistic device. Any verbal discourse, Jakobson argues, has two

---

[8] Anthony Ostroff, ed., *Contemporary Poet as Artist and Critic* (Boston, 1964), 108.
[9] Jackson, "Chance and Design in *Anna Karenina*," *Disciplines of Criticism*, ed. Peter Demetz et al. (New Haven, 1968), 325-26.

possible poles of semantic connection between words or word groups: relations of similarity or of contiguity. If, for example, the stimulus *hut* produces the response *poor little house*, the relationship is one of semantic similarity, since the second term can obviously be substituted for the first. If, on the other hand, the response to the stimulus *hut* is *poverty*, the link is one of contiguity, the focus shifting from one term to a closely related one.[10]

In literature, Jakobson observes, the figures of semantic similarity are simile and metaphor, whereas contiguity produces the figures traditionally known as metonymy and synecdoche. "The primacy of the metaphoric process in the literary schools of romanticism and symbolism has been repeatedly acknowledged," writes Jakobson, "but it is still insufficiently realized that it is the predominance of metonymy which underlies and actually predetermines the so-called 'realist' trend. Following the path of contiguous relations, the realistic author metonymically digresses from the plot to the atmosphere and from the characters to the setting in space and time" (Jacobson 78). . . .

In *Theory of Literature*, René Wellek and Austin Warren seem to echo Jakobson when they say that "metonymy and metaphor may be the characterizing structures of two poetic types—poetry of association by contiguity, of movement within a single world of discourse, and poetry of association by comparison, joining a plurality of worlds."[11] But most critics have been extremely reluctant to follow this lead, no doubt because their own orientation is toward symbolism and romanticism. Jerome Mazzaro, for example, has complained that "the most serious defect" of Lowell's confessional poetry is "the poet's inability to rise above simplified diction and imagery to a comment on life";[12] he takes for granted that the dense symbolic mode of "The Quaker Graveyard in Nantucket," with its allusions to *Genesis*, *Revelation*, and *Moby Dick*, is somehow superior.

Yet metonymic structure is far from artless. Before examining this technique in Lowell's poetry, it may be helpful to show how metonymy works in a realist novel like *Anna Karenina*. In chapter 30 of Part I, when Anna's train pulls into Petersburg after her fateful interview with Vronsky, she suddenly becomes aware of her husband, waiting on the station platform. "'Oh mercy! Why do his ears look like that?' she thought, looking at his frigid and imposing figure, and especially at the

---

[10] Jacobson, "The Metaphoric and Metonymic Poles," *Fundamentals of Language* (The Hague, 1956), 77.
[11] Wellek and Warren, *Theory of Literature*, 3d ed. (New York, 1956), 195.
[12] Mazzaro, *Poetic Themes of Robert Lowell* (Ann Arbor, 1965), 113.

ears that struck her at the moment as propping up the brim of his round hat." Here the physical attribute—the protruding ears—metonymically stand for the whole man. To Anna, who has never really "seen" her husband before, he instantaneously becomes ridiculous and physically repulsive. . . .

Let us now return to our original text: Lowell's "Man and Wife." In this intensely personal poem, Lowell dramatizes the strains and stresses of his twelve-year-old marriage to Elizabeth Hardwick, a marriage in which, the poem implies, sexual passion has gradually given way to mutual psychological dependency. The poet's self is clearly at the center, but there is little direct expression of the complex feeling—a mixture of devotion and ironic detachment—that the poet has for his wife. Rather, the poem is organized around a metonymic network of images: the speaker is characterized by his environment while his wife is known only by her speech habits ("the shrill verve / of your invective," "your old-fashioned tirade—loving, rapid, merciless") and by certain physical gestures ("you turn your back," "you hold / your pillow to your hollows").

Although the mode of "Man and Wife" is essentially realistic, there are a number of local metaphors. The "rising sun" of line 2 becomes, in the diseased imagination of the poet who fears passion and vitality, an Indian savage in "war paint" who "dyes us red," the pun on "dyes" intensifying the death-in-life existence of the couple. Paradoxically, from the poet's point of view only inert objects receive the sun's life-giving warmth: the "gilded bed-posts" of line 3, which evidently have an antique floral motif, are seen as thyrsi, the phallic staffs carried by the Bacchantes in their rites honoring Dionysus. The magnolia blossoms, further reminders that April is the cruelest month, are murderous creatures who set the morning air on fire. And finally, the tirade of the poet's wife bombards his ear like an ocean wave breaking against a rock.

But the condition which causes the poet to see the sun as a feared savage and the white magnolia blossoms as "murderous" is defined by a larger metonymic sequence of alliterating nouns: "Miltown"—"Mother's bed"—"Marlborough Street"—"our magnolia." The first line of the poem looks casual and matter-of-fact until certain connections become apparent. The reference to Miltown, the first and most famous of the tranquilizers that came on the market in the fifties, rather than to, say, Equanil or Valium, is not coincidental. For one thing, the liquids and nasals ("Tamed by Miltown, we lie on Mother's bed") point up the speaker's torpor and lassitude, but, more important, the name Miltown metonymically suggests such terms as Mill town, mill stone, and small town. The poet's state of anxiety is thus immediately seen as somehow representative of a larger

American dilemma, of a crisis that occurs in Small Town or Any Town, U.S.A. The image of neurotic fracture is intensified in the second half of the line: the nuptial bed has been replaced by "Mother's bed"; her shadow, as it were, lies between husband and wife. In lines 8-12, moreover, it becomes clear that the poet's wife must act the role of mother to him; for the "fourth time" she has had to hold his hand and drag him "home alive."

The reference to Marlborough Street in line 5 introduces a new dimension: the poet's Beacon Hill background. "Hardly passionate Marlborough Street," as Lowell, paraphrasing [William] James, calls it in "Memories of West Street and Lepke," is the prototype of puritan, snobbish Back Bay Boston. In this environment, the poem suggests, the communion of marriage will forever be denied; the trees, even though they can be owned like "our magnolia," turn green too late. The metonymic sequence *Miltown—Mother's bed—Marlborough Street—our magnolia* thus establishes the nature of the poet's milieu: his is a tradition which is deadening. The economy of the seven-line portrait is striking; the word "abandoned," for example, is charged with meaning: it refers both to the "Dionysian" abandon that is denied to the tranquilized couple, and to the ironic fact that, although Mother has indeed "abandoned" her bed because, as we know from the preceding poems, she is dead, her ghost continues to haunt it.

In the second section (lines 8-22), the poet addresses his wife directly. The phrase "Oh my *Petite*, / clearest of all God's creatures, still all air and nerve" sounds mawkish when detached from the poem, but within the context it defines the speaker's wish to let his wife know that he still admires and loves her even if his love is impotent and destructive. Although she must act the role of Mother to him, he wants to think of her as his "*Petite*." And now he recalls the night, so different from this "homicidal" one, when he first met her. Again the focus is on setting rather than on emotion. The scene is diametrically opposed to that of Marlborough Street: it is the noisy, hot, alcoholic, left-wing Greenwich Village of Philip Rahv, the editor of *Partisan Review*. The poet wryly recalls his former self, "hand on glass / and heart in mouth," trying to outdrink the Rahvs and "fainting" at the feet of his future wife, the Southern-born lady intellectual whose "shrill invective" denounced the traditionalism of the Old South.

Past and present are related by an interesting shift in fire imagery. In the opening tableau, the fire is always outside the poet's self: only the bed-posts and the magnolia blossoms are capable of burning. But during their first meeting, the lovers had fire within themselves: in "the *heat* of Greenwich Village," the poet was "too *boiled* and shy / and poker-faced to make a pass," while his beloved's "invective *scorched* the traditional South."

The turn in the final section is quietly ironic: "Now twelve years later, you turn your back." Husband and wife no longer even try to touch. "Sleepless," she holds not him but her pillow to the "hollows" of her unsatisfied body. As in the past, rhetoric is her weapon, but whereas at the Rahvs the attack was good-humored and academic, now on "Mother's bed" life itself is at stake. But this is not to say that the poem is wholly pessimistic. The first water image in the poem—the image of the ocean wave breaking against the speaker's head—marks a turning point. The life-giving water rouses the poet from his *Miltown*-induced lethargy, a lethargy in which he envies the thyrsus-like bed-post, and brings him back to reality.

"Man and Wife" is a highly condensed presentation of a complex personal drama: the movement from a tranquilized present in which life itself is feared and denied, to the memory of a romanticized bohemian past, and back to the present with its open-eyed realization that marriage is torture but also salvation. That the poem has been accused of being too "prosaic" is ironic, for it is intentionally prosaic in a special sense of the word. Unlike, say, Donne's lovers in "The Canonization," Lowell's are not compared to anything; their plight is dramatized in terms of selected, patterned detail. The repeated references to numbers, for example, help to establish the reliability of the speaker as witness: he knows that magnolia blossoms turn brown after five days; he recalls that he has had four bouts with mental illness; he contrasts the image of his wife when she was in her twenties with what she has become "twelve years later." Again, by characterizing the poet's wife chiefly by her rhetoric, Lowell is able to magnify the threat she poses: her deceptively old-fashioned accent belies the mercilessness of her attack, an attack that not even *Miltown* can "tame."

So far I have regarded "Man and Wife" as an isolated text, and of course the poem must first of all exist in its own right. But it becomes immeasurably richer when read against the background of the adjacent poems in *Life Studies* as well as the prose autobiographical sketch "91 Revere Street," which stands at the center of the volume. Names of persons and places, settings, objects, and key incidents in one poem are woven into the total fabric, which becomes something like a novel, but a novel conceived in spatial rather than in temporal terms. In weaving together the "vast number of remembered things" (13), Lowell creates what Yeats called "the tradition of myself."

The prose memoir "91 Revere Street" provides the background for the painful situation described in "Man and Wife." It creates a poignant and ironic image of the tension between the poet's naval officer-father and his refined Beacon Hill mother—a tension that inevitably turns their only child into a hypersensitive, neurotic little boy. The poet places his childhood self in the center of a triangle at whose apex is the romantic figure of his ancestor, Major Mordecai Myers—dark, Mediterranean, part Jewish, "moorish-looking"—and whose base has two points, his father and mother, figures equally lifeless and futile, but strangely unlike each other and constantly at war. The theme of "91 Revere Street" and, by extension, of the whole volume, is the poet's struggle to reach the apex and move away from the Lowell-Winslow base. But he does not succeed. In "Man and Wife," the poet survives only by taking tranquilizers, and the poetic sequence culminates in the terrifying "Skunk Hour," Lowell's self-proclaimed dark night of the soul (Ostroff 107).

The prose autobiography has a narrative framework, but, as in the case of the poems, its theme is conveyed not by a causally related sequence of events, but by the juxtaposition of realistic images describing the Revere Street house, the Brimmer School, the Boston Public Gardens, typical conversations, or visits from relatives. The subject matter seems Jamesian, but Lowell's style is quite unlike [Henry] James's; it is, as the very title "91 Revere Street" suggests, concrete, documentary, factual, realistic.

The reference to "Mother's bed" in "Man and Wife," for example, is metonymically related to the sequence of images in the following passage, which defines Mrs. Lowell's taste in interior decorating:

> Mother's comfort was chic, romantic, impulsive. If her silver service shone, it shone with hectic perfection to rebuke the functional domesticity of naval wives. She had determined to make her ambiance beautiful and luxurious, but wanted neither her beauty nor her luxury unaccompanied. . . . Beauty alone meant the maudlin ignominy of having one's investments managed by interfering relatives. Luxury alone, on the other hand, meant for Mother the "paste and fool's-gold polish" that one met with in the foyer of the new Statler Hotel. She loathed the "undernourishment" of Professor Burckhard's Bauhaus modernism, yet in moments of pique she denounced our pompous Myers mahoganies as "suitable for politicians at the Bellevue Hotel." She kept a middle-of-the-road position, and much admired Italian pottery with its fresh peasant colors and puritanical clean-cut lines. She was fond of saying, "The French do have taste," but spoke with a double-edged irony which implied the French, with

no moral standards to support their finish, were really no better
than naval yahoos. Mother's beautiful house was dignified by a
rich veneer of the useful. (33-34)

In this passage, Mother's neurotic fear of existence is defined
metonymically by the seemingly random inventory of her likes and dislikes
in decor. Almost every possible style represents some sort of threat. Silver
services that do not shine with "hectic perfection" suggest the careless
housekeeping of naval wives, and yet the shiny "fool's-gold polish" of the
Statler Hotel foyer is a sign of *nouveau riche* ostentation." The French *do*
have taste," but they have no morals; Boston Brahmins on the other hand
have morals but no taste: their "pompous" mahoganies are suitable only
for cheap politicians. Worst of all is the "undernourishment" of modern
functionalism, espoused by such middle-European intellectuals as
Professor Burckhard. Having rejected the cult of beauty that leads to
genteel poverty, the luxury of the new rich, the Bauhaus style of central
Europe, the antiques of New England, and the exquisite taste of the
frivolous French, Mother is left with nothing but her predilection for
Italian pottery. The images establish the absurdity of Mother's
"ambiance": she herself emerges as the brittle little Italian urn, whose
"peasant colors" have rapidly faded so that only its "puritanical, clean-cut
lines" remain.
    The motif reappears in the poem "During Fever":

> Mother, your master-bedroom
> looked away from the ocean.
> You had a window-seat,
> an electric blanket,
> a silver hot water bottle
> monogrammed like a hip-flask,
> Italian china fruity
> with bunches and berries
> and proper *putti*.
> Gold, yellow and green,
> the nuptial bed
> was as big as a bathroom. (79-80)

Mother turns her back on the ceaseless life of the ocean; she prefers the
artificial "silver hot water bottle," pointlessly "monogrammed like a hip-
flask," and takes refuge in her "electric blanket" and her Italian pottery,
decorated with artificial fruit and "proper"—note the double meaning—
putti. The "nuptial bed," which is, of course, the bed on which the poet

and his wife recline in "Man and Wife," is "as big as a bathroom"—in other words, clean, antiseptic, and never occupied by two people at the same time.

Lowell's technique in "91 Revere Street" is to resolve the image of his mother into a series of surrounding objects or typical turns of speech. She is, for example, fond of accusing her weak husband of "backsliding" and "living in the fool's paradise of habitual retarding and retarded do-nothing inertia." Or again, she nags him into resigning from the Navy so that he will have the chance to earn more money at Lever Brothers, declaring solemnly, "'A *man* must make up his *own* mind. Oh Bob, if you are going to resign, do it *now* so I can at least plan for your son's *survival* and education on a single continent'" (19-20).

Unaware that it is she who will not let her husband be a *man*, Mrs. Lowell is characterized by these fragments of conversation as a selfish, supercilious and embittered woman, whose air of refinement cannot mask her persistent fear of human experience. Her husband's ineffectuality is just as extreme as hers, but it is more practical, more genial, better intentioned. The following catalogue of the items in Commander Lowell's den should be read in conjunction with the account of his wife's taste in furnishings:

> The walls of Father's minute Revere Street den-parlor were bare and white. His bookshelves were bare and white. The den's one adornment was a ten-tube home-assembled battery radio set, whose loudspeaker had the shape and color of a Mexican sombrero. The radio's specialty was getting programs from Australia and New Zealand in the early hours of the morning.
> My father's favorite piece of den furniture was his oak and "rhinoceros hide" armchair. It was ostentatiously a masculine, or rather a bachelor's, chair. It had a notched, adjustable back; it was black, cracked, hacked, scratched, splintered, gouged, initialed, gunpowder-charred and tumbler-ringed. It looked like pale tobacco leaves laid on dark tobacco leaves. I doubt if Father, a considerate man, was responsible for any of the marring. The chair dated from his plebe days at the Naval Academy, and had been bought from a shady, shadowy, roaring character, mid-ship-man "Beauty" Burford. Father loved each disfigured inch. (17)

Unlike his wife, Father makes no pretense of loving luxury, beauty, or culture. The walls and bookshelves of his den are "bare and white." Rather, Commander Lowell's hobby is gadgetry: his creativity finds an outlet in assembling a ten-tube radio set, whose cute loudspeaker looks like a Mexican sombrero. The function of this radio is even more ridiculous than its appearance: it can broadcast programs from Australia and New Zealand (one wonders what programs would be coming over the air from New Zealand in the early thirties)—programs which can only be heard "in the early hours of the morning," presumably when Father is fast asleep.

The comic futility of Commander Lowell is now intensified as the focus shifts from his homemade radio to his favorite armchair, from the new gadget to the treasured "antique." No veteran of heroic naval combats, this officer comes closest to adventure in the purchase of an ugly "rhinoceros hide armchair" from that glamorous midshipman, "Beauty" Burford. Like the home-assembled radio, this chair is "unique" in a pointless way. Although it has been subject to all sorts of wear and tear, Father, who is a "considerate man," is not responsible for the spots and scratches; he would not dream of disfiguring a chair. Ironically, then, he loves the chair's aura of age and adventure, which has nothing whatever to do with him. The implication is that Father's fondness of tradition is purely surface; it is a tradition from which he himself is completely cut off. What he secretly likes best about the chair, no doubt, is the comfort of its "adjustable back" and its "ostentatiously" masculine air. Emasculated by his wife and reduced to sneaking out at night when he wants to return to the naval yard, Commander Lowell can assert his manhood only in his ridiculous affection for his "sacred 'rhino' chair."

The mode of "91 Revere Street" is essentially realistic in the sense that, as Robert Louis Jackson puts it, "our casual everyday appearance, behavior, conversation . . . contain, reflect, anticipate the larger shape of our destiny." By presenting his parents in terms of a metonymic series of objects, Lowell creates a devastating image of a tradition gone sour. Father's "rhino" chair and Mother's monogrammed hot water bottle stand metonymically for the materialistic debasement of the American dream, the dream of the Mayflower Lowells and Winslows. Given his ancestry and childhood environment, the Robert Lowell of *Life Studies* inevitably fails as a husband: the line "Tamed by *Miltown,* we lie on Mother's bed" becomes increasingly poignant when read in conjunction with its neighboring poems and with "91 Revere Street."

Whether or not the references in *Life Studies* tell "the truth" about Lowell seems beside the point. Because he is writing autobiography, Lowell cannot, of course, tinker with the basic facts of his life: geographical locale, dates, the names and positions of friends and relatives, the schools attended, the three months spent in a mental hospital, and so on. Despite such restrictions, however, Lowell has a great deal of leeway: for all we know, his mother never owned an electric blanket nor his father a "rhino" armchair; for all we know, Lowell never spent a sleepless night arguing with his wife Elizabeth. The accuracy of Lowell's confessional poetry is of interest to the biographer, but for the critic, the exciting thing is to discern how thoroughly Lowell mythologizes his private life. He begins with one established convention—the projection of the romantic lyrical "I"—and fuses the romantic "poetry of experience" with the metonymic mode perfected by the great realist novelists of the late nineteenth century. The style born of this fusion marks a turning point in the history of twentieth-century poetry.

Contemporary Literature 11:4 (Autumn 1970): 470-87; rpt. *Poetic Art of Robert Lowell* (Ithaca, 1973), 80-99.

Robert Lowell and the Difficulties of Escaping Modernism

Charles Altieri

Robert Lowell has never been a very playful man, at least in his poetry. In his earlier work he exemplified the more radical and philosophic New Critical style of his masters Tate and Ransom. Yet it is precisely because he took the incarnation so seriously, as the basis for both his religious and his poetic lives, that he could so thoroughly alter those lives when his faith was no longer adequate to sustain their demands. It is a testament to the seriousness with which he took both religion and poetry that his shift from the dense linguistic structures and typology of his earlier mode to the confessional style constitutes the single most important phenomenon in the movement from a modernist to a postmodernist sensibility in American poetry. But one must not misunderstand the revolution he was instrumental in creating by overlooking the essential transitional quality of the self-criticism in *Life Studies*. Many critics have claimed that the confessional style, with its radical emphasis on subjective, psychological experience, was the central style of postmodernism in the sixties. It is difficult, of course, to imagine objective ways of determining the truth value in any claim for the centrality of a given style, hut from the perspective of recent poetry and poetics it seems clear that, important as it was, confessional poetry is perhaps best seen as the necessary radical break with modernism that allowed other less extreme and self-destructive modes to develop. Confessional poetry broke with symbolism and popularized ideals of presence and immediacy, but, as I shall soon demonstrate, its particular version of these ideals seemed much too solipsistic and extreme to solve the poets' needs for new nonhumanist values.

Lowell's *Life Studies* provides the terms one needs to comprehend the historical genesis of confessional poetry. The volume, taken as a unified set of poems, both interprets Lowell's own break with his past and self-consciously reflects on the implications of the new mode he is creating. The volume's first poem, "Beyond the Alps," introduces the break with the past by returning with a fresh perspective to the oppositions between natural process and an incarnational structure of values. On the one side, the poem indicates, are Rome, altitude, secular and religious authorities, church dogma, traditional symbols, and the heroic classical world; on the other, Paris breaking up, earth, landscape, and "pure prose." The old values have become fictions that no longer meet the test of fact or keep off Stevens's "pressure of reality." Mussolini is not the reincarnation of an Imperial Rome but "one of us / only, pure prose";[1] the pope's devotional candles are offset by his purring electric razor. Even Paris, the city of art, which might restore a Hellas or a viable paganism to replace Rome's authority, cannot do so, for it is breaking up. Man's dream of conquering mountains has not prevailed, and the train must "come to earth" for Lowell to begin the search anew. These oppositions are summarized in the line "Life changed to landscape," which one critic rightly sees could "serve as an epigraph for the volume as a whole."[2] For this line dramatizes Lowell's sense of the only models of meaning left when an essentially vertical symbolic order grounded by the doctrine of incarnation gives way to a primarily horizontal secular one. Landscape is the perfect secular horizontal form of art, for it has no objective center of meaning and depends for its resonance entirely on details and implications created by the painter's stance in relation to his materials. Landscape reveals no hierarchy, nothing valuable in itself. Its horizontality opposes both the typologies of Christianity and the symbolism of Romanticism where specific objects and actions take on sacred or privileged existences.

To appreciate what is at stake in this shift to landscape, one needs to examine a typical early poem based both thematically and stylistically on the incarnation as the reconciliation of secular experience with a timeless vertical order giving events significance. The typological style of

---

[1] *Life Studies* (New York, 1959), 3.
[2] Jerome Mazzaro, *Poetic Themes of Robert Lowell* (Ann Arbor, 1965), 90.

"Colloquy in Black Rock" [in *Lord Weary's Castle*] ends on the poet's ability to find patterns and symbolic schema capable of investing a moment of intense vision with intellectual and ethical significance. And thematically the poem depends literally on the incarnation as the typological moment that transforms suffering into value. . . .

How different it is when one crosses the Alps from Rome to Paris and must imagine landscape as his artistic model. Lowell's insistence on the oppressive reality of the "prose" world indicates the historical and philosophical implications of his journey. For where poetry once defined itself in allegorical and symbolic terms, it now must recognize that it must take what sustenance it can from the affinities it shares with the novel, with the view of literary art developed when men turned from God to the landscape. The novel is the literary form born from the death of the epic.

In all great epics, a vertical force—fate or destiny or the gods— invests the actions with significance and creates the values defining noble conduct. In the novel, on the other hand, action and value tend to be defined horizontally—by the flux of history, by the sociological conditions of the novel world, and by the interactions of the characters. Lowell's task then is to accept the empirical reductions of the old values to mere fictions, but not to stop there. He must suffer the pains of a naturalistic world—hence the volume's pervasive animal images and Lowell's stress on the past as the field of quest; but he must, at the same time, transform the landscape by finding through his suffering a secular basis for value that will make endurance possible. Lowell expresses this manner of quest most succinctly in a review of Robert Penn Warren's *Brother to Dragons,* where he speculates on poetry's need to reabsorb the prose world: "Eternal providence has warned us that our world lies all before us and nowhere else. Only the fissured atoms which destroyed Hiroshima and Nagasaki can build our New Atlantis."[3] Lowell's "New Atlantis" (the image is Plato's) will retain most of the old humanistic values, but now the values will be secularly grounded. Lowell calls these poems in *Life Studies* that seek the New Atlantis "more religious than the early ones,"[4] but religion now is immanent and not transcendental, more informed by the dynamic qualities of natural experience than informing that experience with meaningful patterns.

For value to emerge in the prose world, the poet must develop a style that can convey its glimpses of meaning within contingency without the aid of allegorical or paradigmatic structures. Poems must appear to

---

[3] "Prose Genius in Verse," *Kenyon Review* 15 (1953): 120.
[4] Frederick Seidel, "Robert Lowell," *Writers at Work, 2nd Series* (New York, 1965): 352.

remain faithful to the casual flux of experience even while actions and qualities recur so that some kind of generalization, however problematic, can make its appearance. What the mind seeks to bring together seems to yield a little, but nonetheless remains essentially rooted in a horizontal world, asserting its own inviolable uniqueness. Lowell solves the problem of making his poems seem contingent and moments of direct experience while providing patterns allowing interpretive structures by appropriating techniques from the prose tradition. He makes the primary source of interpretive meaning the volume as a whole. Hence what appears casual and momentary in individual poems becomes resonant and yields general significance when the reader learns to relate the instance, expression, or image to similar ones in other poems and to seek out a dramatic structure for the entire volume. I have worked out these patterns and their structure at some length in an essay on *Life Studies*,[5] so here I shall content myself with summarizing those patterns and showing how they all contribute to the climactic poem "Skunk Hour." As these patterns culminate in that poem, one can see the poem itself as a final interpretation of the confessional process leading up to it.

Thematically, the dramatic movement of the volume develops the quest exemplified in "Beyond the Alps." First the volume explores the tragedy of decaying fictions—in the culture as a whole and then in Lowell's private life. Left without external models of authority and faced with his own breakdown, Lowell must come to some self-definition. Yet his only materials for that definition are the *disjecta membra* of his own past and those of fellow artists in the same situation. The confessional style, then, is inextricable from the cultural and personal breakdowns that make one's self-consciousness at once the only imaginative force and the only locus of materials one can employ to achieve some tentative balance with the prose world. Finally, after articulating that plight, Lowell manages to wrest from the flux some bases for value and a source of dignity.

Complementing the dramatic movement are three patterns of recurrent images and actions that allow the intellect to interpret and grasp the emotional resonance of the contingent events. The first two patterns balance one another. Recurrent animal images (for example, in "The Banker's Daughter," "A Mad Negro Soldier Confined at Munich," and "My Last Afternoon with Uncle Devereux Winslow") evoke the metaphysical and psychological plight of men deprived of transcendence and condemned to an essentially biological frame of reference. Reinforcing this subhuman state are repeated images of failed authority

---

[5] Altieri, "Poetry in a Prose World," *Modern Poetry Studies* 1 (1970): 182-98.

figures—pope, president, father, and ancestors—who should mediate the
child from natural existence into a meaningful social order and provide
him with viable models of human conduct. No wonder that a child "quite
without hero-worship for my father, who actually seemed so inferior to the
photographs in uniform he once mailed to us" (13) should find himself in
an asylum seeking to define his identity amid a society of men all imaged
as animals (81-82). Even the domestic order of life, that simplest and
perhaps most assuring form of culture, is now horribly reversed and offers
only momentary terror and a sense of time as infinite repetition. No
wonder also that Lowell's isolation leaves him only the mirror as means
for self-definition and for reconciling inner and outer realities. Yet this
mirror is no ordinary domestic mirror: to see oneself in a metal mirror is
here not to be given back one's ordinary selfhood but to be reminded, in
the very attempt to grasp the self, how close one is to self-destruction.
Even the ordinary tools of cultural life, like the razor, now are potential
elements for suicide.

The one way beyond the mirror for Lowell is to find some form of
communication or communion. Indeed, the dominant quest in the first
three sections of the volume is for some form of communication, some
external source of consolation. But the closest Lowell comes to a feeling
of communion is his sense of sharing Hart Crane's plight. This
identification, however, only drives him back to the solipsism of
confession: "Who asks for me, the Shelley of my age, / must lay his heart
out for my bed and board" (55). Yet in the midst of these failures, Lowell
establishes a set of recurrent images of eating, which allow him to deepen
the symbolic implications of his final encounter with the skunk. The
volume progresses from the demonic, subhuman "feeding" of the mad
Negro soldier, through the more humane pathos of his drinking with
Delmore Schwartz, to his identification with the skunk's quest for
sustenance, a quest John Berryman sees as culminating in a parody of the
Eucharist.[6] The basic context for Lowell's gradual recovery of ritual
possibilities is provided by "Home After Three Months Away." For in this
poem Lowell nicely returns to his earlier references to shaving in order to
mark a recognition that domestic life need not repeat the farce played out
by his parents. The domestic context can, in fact, provide a secular
approximation of the symbolic order by making shaving a kind of ritual
and creating a sense of shared humanity that redeems animal references.
The reference to himself as a polar bear becomes now a playful epithet
and allows him to play a role that creates a moment of tender love.

---

[6] Anthony Ostroff, ed., *Contemporary Poet as Artist and Critic* (Boston, 1964),
99-104.

The possible redeeming qualities of domestic life enable the starker context of "Skunk Hour" to provide a somewhat satisfactory conclusion to the volume's spiritual journey. In the context of the entire volume, "Skunk Hour" articulates a ground of values that make it possible to endure, if not to overcome, the anxieties of contemporary life and the loss of traditional grounds for value. The poem first of all embodies the ultimate lucidity, the denial of all imaginative evasions, which Lowell has been seeking. This then brings him to a dark night of the soul, a traditional religious image he takes now as "secular, puritan and agnostical" (Ostroff 107). There he encounters the ultimate nothingness or absence of meaning, which is perhaps the result of all pursuits of sheer lucidity (I am thinking of the nineteenth-century novel, particularly of Flaubert). For Lowell the absence is dual—an emptiness he witnesses in the scene of perverted love among the love cars, mirrored by a horrifying sense of his own inner emptiness: "I myself am hell; / nobody's here" (90). Hell here is the ultimate prose—a profound sense of the absence of all sources of meaning and value in the public world represented by the landscape and in the private realm where one defines his personal identity. Yet Lowell has not lost his imaginative sense of redemptive archetypes; having fallen to the depths of despair where the ascent beckons, Lowell turns to the skunk—the figure of whatever possibilities Lowell can find for a secular redemption from his despair. . . .

Thematically the skunk resolves several problems in the volume. By returning to the prereflective natural order symbolized by the many animal images. Lowell makes the skunk embody the determination and self-concern of all living beings and beyond that, as mother, a willingness to face danger in order to accept the responsibility of her role. (Family existence once again has value independent of all fictive or interpretative frames.) Now one sees both a parody of the Eucharist and, on another level, a genuine moment of communion, for, as the skunk swills from the garbage pail, Lowell finds precisely the image of endurance and survival he had sought in vain in the rest of the volume. In fact, Lowell's evening service to some extent reverses one of the final images of his father's impotence. For Commander Lowell's lettering his garbage cans was a pathetic alternative to Sunday church service he saw as beneath the dignity of a naval man. Here the very order his father so stupidly rejected is recovered precisely through those images of modern emptiness.

As the skunk makes her way beneath the "chalk-dry church spire," reminding the reader of the dead vertical world, she embodies whatever possibilities Lowell can find for restoring a context of value within secular and biological necessity. These possibilities are not very encouraging; man may learn to endure, but it must be with a dogged single-minded concentration that omits much of the old humanist possibilities for human development and enjoyment of the world. And the poetic process itself calls one's attention to these reduced possibilities. The skunk here plays the resolving role performed by Christ in much of *Lord Weary's Castle.* Christ as a resolving figure functions "metaphorically"; he pulls into himself all the disparate strands and adds an element that completes them and develops their meaning. Thus Christ's suffering both gives Lowell a personal meaning and adds to it a value not evident within secular experience. Lowell imaginatively participates in the same metaphorical project as poet by having the details he uses [in "Colloquy in Black Rock"] in describing Christ, particularly the name kingfisher and the redeeming fire, both define and give value to Lowell's pulsing blood and his resistance to the mud. (Only because Christ evokes an entire mythic structure, a structure of metaphors, can such specific details do so much work.) The skunk, on the other hand, functions metonymically. The analogy between man and skunk now creates only a partial contiguous resolution, so that the summary remains incomplete and ambiguous in relation to the conditions being explained. The presence of the skunk, in other words, forces on the reader a solution to the poem's despair, but it is a solution that does not incorporate the human and religious terms in which the despair had been framed. The analogical link, then, between Lowell and the skunk's not-quite-human resolve to endure can only be known sympathetically. The relation is too complex and diffuse for analysis, and the identification of man and skunk too foreign to one's sensibilities for there to be a completely affirmative resolution. Finally, Lowell's identification with the skunk provides an emblem for the confessional style in the volume. Lowell learned in "Words for Hart Crane" that self-analysis and debasement were the preconditions for salvation in the American Wasteland. Now the skunk summarizes what it means to search for value and self-definition when all the sustaining fictions have failed. One is left only with the garbage of one's own past, which he must have the determination to explore and the courage to endure: "With Berryman, too, I go on a strange journey! Thank God, we both came out clinging to spars, enough floating matter to save us, though faithless" (Ostroff 110).

Enlarging the Temple (Lewisburg, Penn., 1979), 60-68.

From Modern to Contemporary: *Life Studies*

James E. B. Breslin

Strenuous, compressed, and oracular, the language of *Lord Weary's Castle* seems inspired by such poets as Hopkins, Thomas, and Crane. "Like Thomas, Crane is subjective, mystical, obscure and Elizabethan," an admiring Lowell wrote in 1947,[1] and as late as 1961 Lowell ranked Crane as "the great poet" of the generation before his own, because "all the chaos of his life missed getting sidetracked the way the other poets' did."[2] Yet from the beginning Lowell was equally "preoccupied with technique, fascinated by the past, and tempted by other languages."[3] If he wanted his poems to be "loaded and rich," he also wanted (unlike Crane) to build them on a foundation that was "perfectly logical" (Seidel 69). His characterization of Hopkins in a 1945 essay reveals the young Lowell's personal and literary ideal: an "inebriating exuberance" "balanced" by a "strict fastidiousness."[4] The appeal of such fastidiousness explains Lowell's enthusiasm when he first met Allen Tate: "I became converted to formalism and changed my style from brilliant free verse, all in two months" (Seidel 65). Crane might be the greater poet, but Tate "was somehow more of a model and he had a lot of wildness and a lot of construction" (Seidel 68). Combining wildness and construction, loaded language and formal severity, the young Lowell aimed at becoming the total poet, the culmination of the modern movement.

But in his own more impatient and imperious way Lowell participated in the postwar domestication of modernism. Unlike Wilbur and Rich. Lowell saw that traditional poetic forms could not simply be inherited, that in the modern era such forms require justification *in the work.* "Shelley can just rattle off terza rima by the page, and it's very smooth, doesn't seem an obstruction to him," Lowell observed; but when "someone does that today and in modern style it looks as though he's wrestling with every line and may be pushed into confusion, as though he's having a real struggle with form and content" (Seidel 52-53). Of course, this is just how it should look if such forms are to seem authentic. In other words, Lowell energizes—and validates—his external forms by making the poem record the resistance to such forms posed by

---

[1] "Thomas, Bishop, and Williams," *Sewanee Review* 55 (1947): 493.
[2] Fredrick Seidel, "Robert Lowell," rpt. Jeffrey Meyers, ed., *Robert Lowell* (Ann Arbor, 1988), 68.
[3] Stanley Kunitz, "Talk with Robert Lowell," rpt. Meyers, 85.
[4] "The Hopkins Centennial," *Kenyon Review* 6 (1944): 583.

contemporary chaos and confusion. Yet it remains the case that in both religious and poetic ways *Lord Weary's Castle* contains disruptive energies by submission to a preexisting order—precisely the kind of order modernism had tried to abolish.

Lowell's Puritan severity, his "symbolic armor" and his gnarled Miltonic splendor make a peculiar combination, but all three manifest a desire for what he later called "the attenuate ideal."[5] Reservations about this poetic project began to trouble Lowell in the late forties. As Steven Axelrod points out, "Lowell was clearly at odds with his own style of poetry for at least a decade before *Life Studies.*"[6] In a 1947 review ("Thomas" 495), Lowell continues to admire Thomas but he spends considerable time cataloging the excesses of his old literary hero ("self-imitation," "verbal overloading" that creates a "crowded and muscle-bound impression") in a list that sounds like a critique of Lowell's own manner. "If Thomas kept his eye on the object and depended less on his rhetoric," Lowell admonishes, "his poems would be better organized and have more to say." So would Lowell's, as he was apparently coming to see. Lowell then went on to praise the two poets, Bishop and Williams, who became the leading models for *Life Studies* precisely because they did keep their eye on the object and, as Lowell later put it in a letter to Williams, "give rhetoric a nap."[7] Bishop's poems are "unrhetorical, cool, and beautifully thought out"; hers is a poetry—unlike Thomas's, but like Williams's—"absorbed in its subjects" ("Thomas" 496-97). "For experience and observation," Lowell concludes, "*Paterson I* has, along with a few poems of Frost, a richness that makes almost all other contemporary poetry look a little second-hand" ("Thomas" 503).

Fears that his own writing had become overly rhetorical, narrowly literary, and more than a little secondhand prompted Lowell to explore character and plot in the dramatic monologues of *The Mills of the Kavanaughs* (1951). But Lowell's move toward narrative only made clearer the limits of his "intemperate, apocalyptic" style,[8] as the reviewers were quick to point out. Williams connected the tragic mood of the poems with their acceptance of external constraints and he, predictably, imagined "a poet of broader range of feeling" who might be released by dispensing with the poems' iambic pentameter couplets.[9] William Arrowsmith, too, accused Lowell of a narrowness of feeling and language: "a loss of

---

[5] Ian Hamilton, "A Conversation with Robert Lowell," rpt. Meyers, 162.
[6] Axelrod, *Robert Lowell: Life and Art* (Princeton, 1978), 85-86.
[7] Lowell to Williams, June 19, 1957, Williams collection (Yale).
[8] The phrase is from "Marriage," in *History.*
[9] Williams, "In a Mood of Tragedy," *Selected Essays* (New York, 1954), 325.

delicacy, a forcing of effect, a monotony of violence in both language and subject."[10] Peter Viereck complained of self-imitation: "By now, his style is beginning to freeze in its particular 'fine excesses,' so that its surprises, though ever more skillful, are ever less surprising."[11] And in a review that Lowell said affected him deeply, Jarrell noted that Lowell's style was too cumbersome for the narrative poems he was now writing and that it was therefore merely self-imitative. "Sometimes Mr. Lowell is having great difficulties," Jarrell wrote, "and the rest of the time he is seeking refuge from them in some of the effects that he has produced so well and so often before."[12] Lowell remarked that "a true review sinks into the reviewed's mind causing change and discovery," as these reviews did—in part because they articulated the poet's own doubts (Hamilton 160).

"The anguish of the most original" symbolism, Lowell once remarked, "is its tension and ungainliness in descending to the actual, the riches of days."[13] The interval of eight years between *The Mills of the Kavanaughs* (1951) and *Life Studies* (1959) felt like "a slack of eternity" until his autobiographical poems came as a "windfall" in two "spurts" of writing in 1957 and 1958 (Hamilton 156). The interval was a time of personal anguish and literary frustration for Lowell; but it was also a time of gathering of forces in Lowell's struggle to renounce a tense, ungainly symbolic mode and descend to the actual, the riches of days. Like Pound before him, Lowell sought restoration for a decadent poetry in "the prose tradition"; but unlike Pound, he was not looking for *le mot juste* of Stendhal or Flaubert. Rather, he was after a realistic fullness of representation that he found in writers like Chekhov and Tolstoy. "The ideal modern form seems to be the novel and certain short stories," Lowell said in the *Paris Review* interview: "Maybe Tolstoy would be the perfect example—his work is imagistic, it deals with all experience, and there seems to be no conflict of the form and content. So one thing is to get into poetry that kind of human richness in rather simple descriptive language (Seidel 53). Lowell was moving toward a poetics of reference that would diverge from an overly restrictive notion of literariness. As early as 1953, in a review of Robert Penn Warren's *Brother to Dragons*, Lowell proposed "the prose genius in verse" as counter to the symbolist tradition.[14] Ceding the ephemeral to prose, "our traumatically self-conscious and expert modern poetry" has achieved, according to Lowell,

[10] Arrowsmith, "Five Poets," *Hudson Review* 4 (1952): 624.

[11] Viereck, "Technique and Inspiration," *Atlantic Monthly* (Jan. 1952): 82

[12] Jarrell, "A View of Three Poets," *Partisan Review* 18 (1951): 697.

[13] Review of Stanley Kunitz, *The Testing Tree*, *NYTBR* (Mar. 21, 1971), 1.

[14] "Prose Genius in Verse," *Kenyon Review* 15 (1953): 620-21.

the "scrupulous and electrical" but at the cost of exclusion. "These amazing new poems could," it seems, "absorb everything—everything, that is, except plot and characters, just those things long poems have usually relied upon." But Warren's narrative poem, "though tactless and voluminous," is "alive": "Warren has written his best book, a big book; he has crossed the Alps and, like Napoleon's shoeless army, entered the fat, populated riverbottom of the novel." In the crossing of Warren, "one of the bosses of the New Criticism," Lowell found support for the journey "beyond the Alps" that his own work would take in *Life Studies*.

By 1953 Lowell was a poet alienated from his own achievements but without the new matter that might generate a more vigorous style. No grave Blakean voices appeared to fill the void. Rather, as he later sardonically recalled, "I thought that civilization was going to break down, and instead I did."[15] His mother died in early 1954, and he "began to feel tireless, madly sanguine, menaced, and menacing."[16] By the summer of that year he had been hospitalized at Payne-Whitney in New York City, the first of two serious breakdowns in the fifties. Unlike Roethke who yearned for his psychotic bouts as "breaks with reality," Lowell never romanticized his illnesses, but he was able to make creative use of the collapse of his personal life and of the self-examination encouraged by his treatment. At the suggestion of his psychiatrist Lowell began an autobiography, and we have already seen how this peculiar form which exists at the margin between the creative and the factual, the imaginative and the historical, inspired him to turn from verse to prose. The earliest version of this autobiography, "At Payne-Whitney," alternates episodes from his life at the clinic with remembered episodes from both his recent and early life. Lowell hoped, he wrote, that the autobiography would "supply me with my swaddling clothes, with a sort of immense bandage for my hurt nerves." Even at this early point Lowell's aim was not to bare but restore the self. The fragments that are available in the Harvard collection suggest that Lowell expended considerable time and effort on this project. Eventually, he evolved a full-length, chronologically organized autobiography, with formal characterizations, dramatic scenes, dialogue—the story related by the adult author who is relaxed and playful at times, devastatingly ironic at others. These worksheets also reveal that as Lowell worked and reworked his material he wrapped more and more bandages around his wounds, so that the most finished section, "Ante-Bellum Boston" (the only part professionally typed), has a stiff formality. It begins, "I, too, was born under the shadow

---

[15] A. Alvarez, "Robert Lowell in Conversation," rpt. Meyers, 77.
[16] "At Payne-Whitney," Lowell collection (Harvard).

of the Boston State House, and under Pisces, the Fish, on the first of March, 1917," and on one copy Lowell has written in "like Henry Adams" lest we miss the point.[17] In 1957, however, Lowell abandoned his prose project for the more selective, more condensed, and more discontinuous representation of his life that we get in the "Life Studies" sequence—or, rather than abandoning, he renovated his prose work: he returned to "At Payne-Whitney," the earliest and most urgent version, and made its prose the source for such poems as "My Last Afternoon," "Commander Lowell," "Terminal Days at Beverly Farm," "Father's Bedroom," "For Sale," "Sailing Home from Rapallo," and "During Fever."

In "At Payne-Whitney" Lowell had crossed the Alps and entered the rich, populated riverbottom of autobiographical prose. His problem was to explore and mine this fertile ground without draining the life out of it, as he had in the successive revisions of his prose work. His solution was the "Life Studies" sequence in which a poetry that renounced such crucial markers of literariness as regular rhyme and meter kept close to its invigorating prose origins. In the mid-fifties, reading Williams's *Collected Later Poems* had made Lowell wonder (in a letter to the older poet) "if my characters and plots aren't a bit trifling and cumbersome—a bit in the way of the eye, and what one lives" (Apr. 26, 1957). But the New Englander was still hesitant and concluded that "I'd feel as unhappy out of rime and meter as you would in them." By September 1957, as he was in the first of the two "spurts" that produced "Life Studies," Lowell was crossing to William's side of the river, but still determined to bring along as much baggage as he could. He wrote to Williams: "I've been experimenting with mixing loose and free meters with strict in order to get the accuracy, naturalness, and multiplicity of prose, yet I also want the state and surge of the old verse, the carpentry of definite meter that tells me when to stop rambling" (Sept. 30, 1957). Just a few months later—in December 1957—the journey had been completed. "At forty, I've written my first unmeasured verse. It seems to ask for tremendous fire, if it is to come off at all. I've only tried it in a few of these poems, those that are most personal. It's great to have no hurdle of rhyme and scansion between yourself and what you want to say most forcibly. . ." (Dec. 3, 1957).

In November 1958 Williams read a manuscript of *Life Studies,* praised its "terrible wonderful poems," and acknowledged that "the book must have caused you some difficulty to write," for "there is no lying permitted to a man who writes that way."[18] Lowell wrote back to express

---

[17] "Ante-Bellum Boston," Lowell collection (Harvard).

[18] Williams to Lowell, November 24, 1958, Lowell collection (Harvard).

his gratitude and declared that "dropping rhyme does seem to get rid of a thick soapy cloth of artificiality. The true spoken language beats any scholarly alchemist's pseudo-language" (Nov. 29, 1958). But the correspondence between the two poets, along with Lowell's actual practice, makes clear that Lowell's engagement with Williams did not issue in the kind of self-annihilating conversion experience that it did for many less talented poets. The autobiographical subjects and the psychological acuity with which they are explored in *Life Studies* are both foreign to Williams. Lowell still dissents, in February 1958, from the older poet's dogmatic refusal of meter: "I wouldn't like ever to completely give up meter," he says; "it's wonderful opposition to wrench against and revise with" (Feb. 19, 1958). The "Life Studies" poems do, of course, make irregular use of rhyme, and "the ghost of an iambic pentameter" can often be heard in the background. Skeptical of the professed revolutionary violence of a Ginsberg or Williams, Lowell's preservation of these conventions is integral to his meaning in *Life Studies;* the book strives for a relation to both the personal and the literary past that is neither a mere repetition nor an absolute break.

 Life Studies ultimately renounces tight, external forms and preestablished symbolism; it discards rhetorical sublimity and religious myth in a quest to enter a demystified present. Lowell touches what had hurt him most, the prosaic and everyday, and he finds that his fiery creative self can survive within the quotidian. In literary terms, the achievement of *Life Studies is* twofold. Lowell creates what he calls "the confession given rather directly with hidden artifice" (Alvarez 75); at the same time he makes the book as a whole a self-conscious meditation on the problem of a confessional language. In a letter to Henry James, Henry Adams described *The Education* as "a mere shield of protection in the grave." "I advise you," he went on, "to take your own life in the same way, in order to prevent biographers from taking it in theirs." The difference between biography and autobiography was, for Adams, the difference between murder and suicide, and his remark articulates a fear felt by many autobiographies that by fixing the self in words, they have eternalized the self at the cost of its life. "Is the frame of a portrait a coffin?" Lowell once asked (Hamilton 167). Throughout *Life Studies* Lowell remains aware of the tension between the flux of temporal experience and the stasis of literary form; he constantly calls attention to the dangers of turning "life" experiences into poetic "studies." Lowell's critics, arguing the book's coherence by naming its political, religious, and familial *themes,* have imagined a unity that is static, as if *Life Studies* were suicidal. But the four parts of *Life Studies* are stages in the process of finding a language of process, so my own reading attends to the changes and movements of Lowell's language, his effort to find a way of writing that would preserve, rather than annihilate, his life.

From Modern to Contemporary (Chicago, 1984), 118-24.

Robert Lowell's Tokens of the Self

Terri Witek

. . . Lowell's anxiety about his position in a world without his earliest mentors is fueled by his conviction that the self is deeply, irreparably divided. This division ensures that he is perennially pulled in at least two directions: he is attracted both by the idea that the self should be a possession firmly within one's grasp and the idea that the self is an object which should be elusive, beyond the control of its possessor. In the autobiographical prose, Lowell often images these two possibilities as the figures of his own complex and embattled parents, each of whom offers a problematic alternative role model His depiction of these two conflicting forces, each with its claim on him, is as painful as it is informative; his choices show the powerful dilemma into which the poet is thrust each time he tries to choose between alternative images of his own identity.

The allure of an identity which acquires its power through sheer pervasive immobility is represented in the autobiographical prose by Mother. Secure in the Boston of Lowell's youth, fixed forever by being dead, Charlotte Lowell is the unchanging star around whom the male Lowells group, set into motion by her changeless vigor. The prose which became "91 Revere Street" in the finished *Life Studies* volume includes an account of the Lowells' attempt to find a school for the problematic Bobby which is typical of the family dynamic: "I was promised an improved future and taken on Sunday afternoon drives through the suburbs to inspect boys' schools: Rivers, Dexter, Country Day. These expeditions were stratagems designed to give me a chance to know my father; Mother noisily stayed behind and amazed me by pretending that I had forbidden her to embark on 'men's work.'"[1] Bob Lowell, Senior, does all the driving, but it is clear that from her Boston stronghold Charlotte is

---

[1] *Life Studies* and *For the Union Dead* (New York, 1964), 27.

the family mover and shaker. She criticizes the results of these enforced male outings and goes back to interview the headmasters herself: "she expressed astonishment that a wishy-washy desire to be everything to everybody had robbed a naval man of any reliable concern for his son's welfare" (27). . . .

The effect of this presence on the child and then man who is her son is nearly overwhelming: over and over again in the autobiographical prose, Mother's "furniture," symbols of her central presence, must be reckoned with.[2] During Lowell's stay at Payne Whitney [Clinic] following his mother's death, the poet seems to think of himself literally as an object confined within a more powerful structure. When he writes about Payne Whitney, the hospital architecture itself is perversely threatening. Looking out his window at the other buildings of the complex, he describes them as mysteriously female: "First I saw the hospital's architecture as a wedding-cake; no, not a wedding cake but the tall bride standing with her sacrificial silver knife beside the wedding cake; no, not the bride of flesh and blood, but a narrow, late Gothic bride, all arches, groins and stone lace-work; no bride, but a building. . . ."[3]

Lowell writes himself away from dangerous associations by an effort of will in this passage, but it is well worth identifying the bride who seems to engulf him on all sides. In another version of this episode, the bridal building is linked to the bridal photograph Bob Lowell keeps on his dresser, and in the drafts of "Sailing Home from Rapallo" the dead Mother is also a bride. The powerful Mother thus seems to hold her son at the center of her being, but for him the position is fraught with peril: he is trapped almost as if he had been ingested by the bridal buildings of the New York hospital which remind him of the powerful center of his own family. . . .

Lowell said, much later, that the *Life Studies* poems were grouped around his Father, an assessment which seems skewed when the book is considered as a whole. It seems even more so in a consideration of the manuscripts, in which Mother's character is so pervasive: "Unanswerable Motherhood!" Lowell exclaims at one point, as if throwing up his hands at her character's perfect power.[4] But while *Life Studies* often seems to orbit around the fixed center represented by Mother, the figure of Father acts as a counterstrategy for identification of the self. Lowell tries more than once

---

[2] This point is made again in *Life Studies* when the couple who lie untouching and unhappy in "Man and Wife" are strategically located in "Mother's bed."

[3] "The balanced aquarium," Lowell collection (Harvard). Lowell's *Collected Prose* (New York, 1987), 346 offers a version of this description.

[4] "―――," Lowell collection (Harvard).

to make Father the central object of the autobiographical prose. These efforts demonstrate the psychologically different problem incurred by putting his male parent at the center of power.

In one such story, Lowell describes himself writing a poem during his stay at the Payne Whitney Clinic, a process which is interrupted by "Prince Scharnhorst," a hospital inmate. The poet hides a piece of paper on which he'd written "the first and last lines of a sonnet entitled TO MY FATHER": "You sailed to China, Father, and knew your math . . . / Friendly to all, and loving none, perhaps."[5] The prose then switches into a detailed description of the Prince, and Father disappears from the text except for the presence in his stead of a toy boat, which the Prince offers to lend him because Lowell's father, "a naval man, had admired Count von Luckner, the Sea Devil." This miniature is another token provided in place of the absent Father, who is now dead in the present tense of the story itself. Like the other tokens, this one cannot be Lowell's own: it is to borrow, not to keep. Father himself has disappeared; the Prince takes over the text as the controlling presence of the story, and one which defies reason: "He flamed in my doorway, a sunbeam—a man so various in his moonshines and virtuosity that I half-imagined he was an apparition, an actor."

In this version of the prose which offers an embedded poem, Father has been superseded by the colorful Prince Scharnhorst who now seems to control both the story and the talisman that recalls Father. If this appropriation acts as a sudden end to Father's power in the story, it is one prefigured by the poetry insert, itself a clandestine object. This "hidden" manuscript acts as its own cogent dismissal: the sonnet form has been reduced to a summary couplet, the first descriptive line of which is itself overpowered by the dismissive bite of the conclusion.

The unexpected force of this dismissal depends on the central paradox of Father's character. Unlike Mother, whose "furniture" never changes, the figure of Father—"Friendly to all, and loving none, perhaps"—is essentially mysterious. Appearances aren't useful, in his case, as keys to the inner man: the smile Lowell describes elsewhere as "anxious" and "repetitive" does not necessarily indicate love. If Father loves "none," then he is without tie to them; he is free from their power. But it is a terrible thing for a child, even a grown-up one, to acknowledge that his parent might not love him, and the man who writes the bitterly concise couplet provides only the most minimal of escape routes from the awful possibility in the last "perhaps." Robert Lowell, Senior, despite his seeming powerlessness in those sections of the autobiographical prose in

---

[5] "At Payne-Whitney," Lowell collection (Harvard).

which his ineffectiveness is contrasted with the power of Mother, emerges in this couplet as a figure who wields a mysterious authority of his own. While Mother is consuming and all identification with her is psychologically dangerous, Father is no help either against Mother or as an authoritative role model because he is an enigma, as inaccessible to his son as those mysterious talismans of his youth. At the period of Lowell's life in which he writes of his parents they are already dead, but as he structures the story of his life he situates his persona at every stage as a psychological orphan, one whose Identity must be sequestered from Mother's at the same time that his rightful role model has effectually removed himself from the scene.

Lowell's efforts to put Father at the heart of *Life Studies* are showcased in "91 Revere Street," the prose centerpiece of the finished *Life Studies* volume. Earlier manuscripts help get to the source of his ambivalence about his subject: "91 Revere Street" is a compilation of several manuscript sources, and Lowell combines and shapes them so they are loosely structured around he figure of Robert Lowell, Senior. Ruling all as an opening trope of the opening passages is a piece of Father's own "furniture": the ancestral portrait of a dashing progenitor, identified variously in the manuscripts but called Major Mordecai Myers in the published work. Thus "91 Revere Street" begins surprisingly auspiciously for Father, but the crucial ambivalence Lowell associates with this figure undermines the project from the start. The ambivalence surfaces in the text itself. The admired ancestor is somehow "double-faced"; while he looks quite dashing, Myers' "exotic" eye seems to have "shunned the outrageous" (12). In one version of the story, Father tells young Bobby that Myers was actually a civilian, and the boy abandons the ancestor as a role model, much as Lowell seems to have abandoned his own father as a role model when that parent left the Navy at his wife's insistence. In the *Life Studies* version of "91 Revere Street" this effect has been softened considerably, and Lowell conveys pity with his dismissal of his father's ancestor: "Poor sheepdog in wolf's clothing!" But when he talks of Father's disappointing reality in contrast to pictures of the man in naval uniform, and then brings in Mother "to insist to all new visitors" that Bobby's "real LOVE" is his toy soldiers, the child's willed distancing of the "double-faced" Father is complete. Any hope that Bobby Lowell will be able to take Father as a powerful role model has thus been stifled within the opening movements of "91 Revere Street," and the symbolic replacement of Father by a cartoonish "real" sailor at the end, much like his replacement by Prince Scharnhorst in the Payne Whitney story, is hardly surprising.

The elusiveness of the Father, frustrating as it is to the beleaguered son who describes him in the autobiographical prose, ultimately suggests that Lowell *does* identify with his father, albeit unwillingly, and that this identification is the source of his ambiguous descriptions and his damning dismissals. The figure of the Mother with whom he must be careful not to identify is both whole and forceful: she makes Bobby feel impotent, and in this Bobby is surely the son of the man Lowell identifies as Bob in the manuscripts. The source of identity needs to be unambivalently masculine for the boy to stay psychologically secure, and in this way the identification with his elusive Father is both problematic and absolutely necessary. . . .

Whatever the son does to displace Mother is a blow in favor of his own masculinity, and therefore in favor of his own identity. Bob stands in for Bobby in this regard, and if Father is portrayed as indecisive and fundamentally enigmatic, then the son who is even less of a real soldier shares in the fundamental ambivalence of the male Lowell line. Consequently, the problems of the Father are the problems of the son, an identification made again thematically in *Life Studies* when the persona himself becomes, at book's end, a problematic spouse and a "dim-bulb father" (79). For the poet who tries to create an object that will adequately represent the self in his autobiographical prose, the dilemma remains wearyingly familiar, another version of the question of where to locate the source of one's identity and how to inhabit safely the center of one's work. In the Freudian scenario posed in the autobiographical prose, the unalloyed central power of Mother is both forbidden and dangerous to the identity; but the power of the Father is enigmatic and so highly ambiguous that it is impotent. Siding necessarily with Father despite his own sympathies, Lowell presents himself as caught between nearly impossible alternatives, owner of the chronically dispossessed identity which will become the identifying voice of *Life Studies*. . . .

American Literature 63:4 (Dec. 1991): 713-26.

Lowell as Elegist

Jahan Ramazani

. . . After the death of his parents, Lowell wrote *Life Studies* (1959), a book dominated by ambivalent elegies for other poets, for himself, but especially for his father, mother, and grandfather. In Lowell's turn from a more impersonal to a more personal mode of poetry—the genre of both mask and feeling—both myth and intimacy plays a pivotal role. Having generalized and diffused oedipal violence in "Quaker Graveyard," and having aimed it more narrowly at close relatives in the Winslow elegies, Lowell makes his parents themselves the object of sustained attack in *Life Studies*. What Lowell calls "my adolescent war on my parents"[1] is the subject and impetus not only of the elegies in *Life Studies* but also of "91 Revere Street," a prose memoir that prepares for the satiric family elegies in the "Life Studies" sequence. In both "91 Revere Street" and "Life Studies," the central narrative is the story the father's decline, his "downhill progress as a civilian and Bostonian" (43). Even before resigning from the Navy and commencing his social tumble, his father betrayed a "morbidly hesitant" and "Unmasterful" character, which presaged a dismal future and humiliated both wife and son (16, 18). Lowell, in turn, uses his memoir and elegies to humiliate his father. At the same time, he more subtly prosecutes his "war" at the discursive level, making his style the "masculine" opposite of his father's effeminacy. Much as his father's armchair is described as the antithesis of its owner—"black, cracked, hacked, scratched, splintered, gouged, initialed, gunpowder-charred and tumbler-ringed"—so too this vehement, verb-compacted description distinguishes the poet's muscular rhetoric over against his father's weakness. "I doubt if Father, a considerate man," Lowell facetiously adds, "was responsible for any of the marring" visible on this "'rhinoceros hide'" (17). Though his father was a naval officer, it is Lowell who proves himself the man of combat in this memoir and in the elegies of "Life Studies," contending with the dead man in a rhetoric that, as he says of the battered chair, leaves the father "disfigured." Lowell's unresolved oedipal antagonism bears on even the most famous aspect of his poetic practice in *Life Studies*: he invents a lyric mode often said to be more "personal" than any before to elegize a father "who trusted in statistics and was dubious of personal experience." The only artistic acts of which his father is capable are "lettering his three new galvanized garbage cans: R.T.S. LOWELL—U.S.N." (an image subsequently

---

[1] *Life Studies* (New York, 1959), 12.

repeated) and carving with "formal rightness" the Sunday roast, his brow wet with perspiration from the strain of reproducing "stroke by stroke his last carving lesson" at a carving school (32, 34). Lowell recalls having been "furious" at the time (35), and he responds even in the prosody of the "Life Studies" elegies—elegies that, for the first time in his published poetry, eschew the "formal rightness" of regular rhyme and meter. Although Lowell's dissociation from his father tentatively allies him with his mother, she too endures harsh treatment for, among other things, her "ruthlessly neat" aesthetic of house-cleaning and her preference in pottery for "puritanical, clean-cut lines" (37, 34). In contrast, the lines in which Lowell memorializes his mother are ostentatiously irregular, loose, jagged, unhampered. Knowing that both of his parents disdained the "effrontery" of Amy Lowell's "free verse" and that they relished "Robert Frost's remark that writing free verse was like playing tennis without a net,'" the son elegizes his parents in precisely the style that would have irked them most (38): In his prosodic, modal, and stylistic affronts, Lowell turns inside out the elegiac tradition of imitative homage, as practiced by elegists from Spenser to Swinburne and Auden: the rhetoric he adopts was not preferred but despised by the dead.

While male elegists had long assumed the stance of sons grappling with parental figures, they had typically accomplished the transition from competitor to successor by incorporating the dead into their own language and identity, recapitulating ego-formation in a story of professional inheritance.[2] But Lowell deforms this psychodynamic paradigm in the elegies of *Life Studies*, regressing to the unresolved oedipal position of the child, refusing the complete reincorporation of his parental imagos, and reanimating antagonisms without bringing them to closure. The "Life Studies" sequence begins with a memory of youthful rebellion: Lowell "threw cold water" on his parents' "watery martini pipe dreams" because he wanted to stay with his grandfather at the summer home; but rather than merely relate this act of insubordination, Lowell repeats it by mocking his parents in the jarring conflation of these clichés ("My Last Afternoon with Uncle Devereux Winslow," 59-64). As we have seen, the very style of the sequence is a rebuke to his father's weakness and mother's propriety; it more nearly resembles his grandfather's person and decor—"manly, comfortable, / overbearing, disproportioned." His grandfather, though hammered in the earlier elegy, now functions as a bulwark against the greater vexation of his parents. In the bric-à-brac that filled his grandfather's summer place, Lowell finds an

---

[2] On the elegy and ego-formation, see Peter Sacks, *English Elegy* (Baltimore, 1985), 8-12.

objective correlative for his discontinuous psychology and poetry. The imagery of discrete items and the metonymic language could be seen as part of Lowell's larger refusal to subsume the dead parents and the dead past within himself.[3] He describes objects that, like the poet and his elegies, only half incorporate the dead "other," leaving it in partial suspension: the cuckoo dock is "slung with strangled, wooden game," much as the couch legs are "shellacked saplings." The summer home abounds in other elegiac simulacra of extinct worlds, including "snapshots" that recall vanished instants and tiles "crummy with ant-stale," Aunt Sarah's "dummy piano" and Uncle Devereux's student posters of prewar "belles" and "bushwhacked" soldiers. Throughout the sequence, Lowell's ambivalence toward his father and mother prevents him from reinstating the parental "objects," as Klein terms them, within his own identity—an identity that therefore finds itself strangely externalized, fractured, even in peril.

At the same time that Lowell elegizes dead relatives without assimilating them completely, he also recalls his dead youth without absorbing it, holding it instead at an ironic distance. In describing moments of youthful self-reflection, Lowell brings to mind the Lacanian "mirror stage" that Sacks finds recapitulated in the traditional elegy; but whereas this moment in the elegy and in psychoanalysis normally affords growth and self-creation, Lowell emphasizes self-division and paralysis (Sacks 9-10, 16). In "My Last Afternoon," he remembers having seen his image mirrored in the water, where it seemed a "stuffed toucan," and in the next elegy he recalls, "I saw myself as a young newt, / neurasthenic" and "numb" (65-67). These moments in which the young Lowell saw his dead reflection anticipate these very elegies, in which the mature Lowell peers at the dead selves of his youth, not lovingly embraced but ironized, not incorporated but objectified. The sequence's tendency toward reflective self-division manifests Lowell's pervasive ambivalence toward his paternal imagos, the poet separating himself into reflector and reflected, subjective mourner and object of mourning. Instead of re-creating his identity out of a normative process of inheriting parental imagos and the past, Lowell keeps his dead parents and his dead selves abjected, discrete, suspended outside himself. Instead of dissolving his youth with a soft focus, he fixes with precision the date (1922), his age (five and a half), and how long he had worn his shorts (three minutes), much as his grandfather penciled the heights of the doomed Uncle Devereux on a "white measuring-door." Presented as a collection of discontinuous pictures, poetic memory is epitaphic in the sequence.

---

[3] Perloff discusses the importance of metonymy in Lowell (*Poetic Art*, 87-93).

Elegizing his dead uncle, Lowell also elegizes moment-to-moment perceptions, each dead at the instant in which it was lived. The last visual image of Uncle Devereux "grew sharper and straighter" as the poet distills it to a one-dimensional picture, "like a ginger snap man in a clothespress." Painterly but also photographic, these poems approximate some of the harsh instantaneity of the "snapshots" they allude to, "every poem an epitaph" or photograph, a vertical slice of time that mummifies the moment and declares the loss of contiguous duration.

In the ensuing elegy, "Dunbarton," Lowell continues implicitly to link his elegiac craft to his grandfather while maintaining a distance from his parents: each autumn his grandfather drove him to the family graveyard, where together they "raked leaves from our dead forebears" (65-67). Indeed, this strategic alliance with his grandfather helps him to keep his parents at bay: Lowell calls himself his grandfather's "son" and "paramour," and his martially tinged lament in "Grandparents" (68-69) shows up his different attitude toward his parents: "Grandpa! Have me, hold me, cherish me!" While sorry that his grandfather can "Never again" rejoin him, Lowell begins to betray impatience even with his grandfather, associating him with figures of overbearing but impotent authority. "Back in my throw-away and shaggy span / of adolescence," Lowell remarks with amusement, "Grandpa still waves his stick / like a policeman." Lowell freezes his grandfather in a ridiculous pose, granting him only the apotheosis of adolescent caricature. For all Lowell's concessions to his grandfather, the poet represents his overriding elegiac impulse not as idealization but disfiguration: "I hold an *Illustrated London News*—; / disloyal still, / I doodle handlebar / mustaches on the last Russian Czar." Lowell self-mockingly associates his rebellion with Bolshevism, but he nevertheless subjects his grandfather to a dual defacement, refiguring him as anachronistic royalty and then disfiguring his refigured face. At the moment when transcendence might be expected, Lowell eternizes his grandfather as hapless autocrat and shows him to be forever trapped beneath his pen—faced, defaced, refaced according to the elegist's ambivalent impulses. Once again, self-representation, though long traditional in the elegy, evokes not a stabilizing authorial ground but the play of mirror on mirror, poetic identity floating among contradictory impulses toward abjected imagos and selves.

Meanwhile, Lowell's father has fared far worse than his grandfather: the son has not only thrown "cold water" on his parent's dreams but conspired to supplant him as "Father" with his grandfather. He recalls having persistently "dug" and "picked with a clean finger nail at the blue anchor / on my sailor blouse," an image that may seem innocent enough, except that repetition clearly associates it with a specific naval officer (64, 62). When the anchor reappears in "Commander Lowell" (70-72), it has dropped from the boy's shirt and into the ex-officer's ridiculous bath-time chant: "'Anchors aweigh,' Daddy boomed in his bathtub, / 'Anchors aweigh'". . . . Whereas the son picked at the anchor that figured his immovable paternal burden, the father imagines anchoring himself as he drifts aimlessly from jobs in the navy to soap-sales to investments. As with the trope of the anchor, Lowell wages his unresolved "war" on his father in ironic contrasts, both overt and subtle. He had borrowed from his grandfather a thyrsus-like cane, "more a weapon than a crutch," but this phallic inheritance dwindles into the father's mere "dress sword with gold braid" and "ivory Annapolis slide rule"—phony, ineffectual instruments that signify the father's impotence and self-delusion (66, 71, 72). Much as Lowell implicitly defines his poetry of self-scrutiny and force over against his father, so too the noncompensatory logic of his elegiac sequence eschews redemption, while his father compensates himself for failure by singing songs about anchors and buying fancy cars—tokens of the stability, power, and success that have eluded him.

Lowell allows that his father "once" had a heroic moment at the age of nineteen, but he satirizes his father's more recent existence as a sham in "Terminal Days at Beverly Farms" (73-74). Landlocked for many years, ex-commander Lowell "swayed as if on deck duty." About to die, he seems "vitally trim," while his head, useless as ever, looks "efficient." Still squandering money, he convinces himself he has pulled off a great victory in the form of a car deal. As if risking high dangers, he "stole off" to "loaf in the Maritime Museum," the second verb ironically deflating the first. At the hour of death, he is still trying to fake appearances. . . . Although "unprotesting" and "smiling," he does not die the "happy death" of the traditional hero. At the moment when tragic and elegiac convention might lead us to expect heightened utterance, the father's last words are hardly revelatory. And at the moment when penetrating spiritual insight might be expected, only his physical "vision" is keen. While the poet recurs once more in the ensuing elegy to his father's single heroic hour—his gunboat voyage on the Yangtze—the double inscription in the book diminishes this achievement by placing it under the wing of maternal guidance ("Father's Bedroom," 75). Near death as throughout life, the father seems tempted by "anxious, repetitive" fraud and self-deception, while the son represents his own art as the exact opposite—an elegiac sequence of authentic memory and self-revelation. But even though this ironic contrast enhances the poet's definition of his craft and himself, it does not issue in the elegy's typical reconstituted and integral identity, since the son, perpetuating rather than resolving oedipal strife, remains haunted by the very discontinuity that he impugns in his father.

Last to die, his mother is also last among the people elegized in the "Life Studies" sequence, unless we count Lowell's tense glance at his own death in "Skunk Hour." Although the poet portrays himself as weeping at his mother's death, the biographical Lowell also experienced manic elation at the time. Even without this hint, we might detect a troubled joy in the violent, even exuberant descriptions of the shoreline "breaking into fiery flower" and the gaily colored "sea-sleds / blasting like jack-hammers across / the *spumante*-bubbling wake of our liner" ("Sailing Home from Rapallo," 77-78). Vivid flowers, wild colors, and a sea bubbling like champagne—the scene seems more like a celebration than a mourning procession. Having selected her casket, Lowell relishes his little joke on her character and social pretensions: "Mother traveled first-class in the hold; / her *Risorgimento* black and gold casket / was like Napoleon's at the *Invalides*. . . ." Even in death she seems to demand her prerogatives. The Italian undertaker has unwittingly contributed a further joke on Lowell's mother, who used to insist on having her name spelled accurately: "In the grandiloquent lettering on Mother's coffin, / *Lowell* had been misspelled *LOVEL*. / The corpse / was wrapped like *panetone* in Italian tinfoil." Yet on the real coffin, her name was actually misspelled *LOWEL*,[4] so it is once again the poet who disfigures the dead person, much as he doodled mustaches on the displaced picture of his grandfather and attached ironic tags like "vitally trim" to his dying father. Disfiguring her name, he strangely reveals the reason behind his poetic vandalism, for it was his mother's insufficient *LOVE* that he blamed for turning his love to anger.[5] In disfiguring her name, he also, of course, disfigures his own name, much as throughout the entire sequence his abuse of dead family members has also been self-abuse—battering the imperfectly internalized imagos that constitute his own psyche. This incomplete internalization is briefly hinted at in the poem's final comparison of the dead mother with bread to be consumed. After a number of elegies that aggressively ironize and mock the poet's parents, the sequence logically proceeds with poems that explore the precarious structure of the poet's own ego. As Rosenthal wrote in an early review of *Life Studies*, "I wonder if a man can allow himself this kind of ghoulish operation on his father [and mother] without doing his own spirit incalculable damage. But the damage has clearly been in the making a long time, and Lowell knows very well that he is doing

---

[4] Ian Hamilton, *Robert Lowell: A Biography* (New York, 1982), 203.
[5] See Lowell's "Unwanted" in *Day by Day* (New York, 1977), 121-24.

violence to himself most of all. . . ."[6] Rather than strengthen the ego, as the elegiac quest for origins had traditionally done, Lowell's troubled quest reveals the origins of his ego's instability—an instability only exacerbated by the sustained aggression of his work. The poet's rebellion against his family ends not in the triumph of the strong post-oedipal self but in a mind "not right," fractured by its impulses to disinherit and expel the dead, to reappropriate and disinherit the past, to elevate and demolish the ego.

In later years, Lowell went on to write more affectionate elegies for his parents, grandparents, and other relatives. His elegies for Harriet Winslow, from "Soft Wood" (1964) and "Fourth of July in Maine" (1967) to the final "Endings" (1974) are tender, free of the rancor that runs through most of his domestic elegies. In his last volume, *Day by Day* (1977), Lowell rewrites some of his earlier elegies, producing poems that recant his youthful combativeness. In "Phillips House Revisited," for example, Lowell revisits not only the house but also his earliest, harshest elegy for his grandfather. After forty years he recalls the imagery of the House, the crab, and the gold mine, but now he is eager to grant his grandfather's brilliance, magnetic attractiveness, and inexhaustible energy. In "To Mother," he still seems to feel reproved by the militaristic neatness of his mother's housecleaning, but he has now been able "to discover you are as human as I am," her humor no longer his "opposite" but "mine now," her white-pebbled, white-potted lilies now "seductive" in memory. And in "Robert T. S. Lowell" he even grants his father his own voice, the "Son" reproaching himself for not having reached out to his father, the "Father" compounding this self-reproach with a meditation on "loneliness." These retractions are moving, indicating a son's heightened awareness that he shares many of his parents' unfortunate qualities. But they defer more to the traditional codes of elegy than do Lowell's earlier poems of harassed intensity. Much praised, these final poems had a lesser literary impact than Lowell's elegies from "Quaker Graveyard" to *Life Studies*, which were decisive in helping Sexton, Plath, Berryman, Bidart, and others articulate an aggression toward the dead that had never before been uttered in the genre of elegy, especially in its parental form.

Poetry of Mourning (Chicago, 1994), 232-41.

---

[6] M. L. Rosenthal, "Poetry as Confession," rpt. *Our Life in Poetry* (New York, 1991), 109.

Many Personalities, One Voice: *Imitations*

Stephen Yenser

The opening paragraph of the introduction to *Imitations* includes these pointed statements:

> This book is partly self-sufficient and separate from its sources, and should be first read as a sequence, one voice running through many personalities, contrasts and repetitions. I have hoped somehow for a whole. . . . The dark and against the grain stand out, but there are other modifying strands.

If one were not acquainted with Lowell's habit of constructing whole books of poems as distinct from collecting poems and placing them between two covers, these claims might seem enigmatic or pretentious. It is certain that in spite of these remarks, many reviewers and critics have regarded *Imitations* as a collection of more or less free translations that bear little relationship to one another. Ben Belitt, himself a translator and poet and one of Lowell's most competent critics, is typical in this respect. After declaring that the first sentence quoted above is a "startling expectation" for a poet-translator to have, Belitt simply disregards it and proceeds to discuss (quite perceptively) several individual imitations.[1] Frequently, even the claim about the independence of individual poems is not taken quite seriously, and perhaps partly for this reason *Imitations* has not had the undivided critical attention that most of Lowell's other volumes have received. . . .

Lowell's *Imitations* have been brilliantly chosen and scrupulously arranged. The organization of this book resembles that of *Lord Weary's Castle* in that emphases are placed upon the beginning, middle, and concluding poems; in both cases, by repeating key words and images at these points, Lowell calls attention to the generally symmetrical structure of the books. But if in the placing of emphases by means of motif *Imitations* recalls *Lord Weary's Castle*, the extent of the use of motif reminds us of *Life Studies*. The title of this volume itself indicates its relationship to its predecessor, for in addition to its literary meaning, imitation has a pertinent musical denotation. According to the *Harvard Brief Dictionary of Music*, imitation is "the restatement in close succession of a musical idea (theme, subject, motive, or figure) in

---

[1] "*Imitations*: Translation as Personal Mode," *Salmagundi* 1 (1966-67): 44-56.

different voice parts of a contrapuntal texture," and it "may involve certain modifications of the musical idea, e. g., inversion, augmentation, diminution, etc." From the concept of modified "restatement" of materials to that of "different voice parts," this definition is parallel to Lowell's talk of "modifying strands" and of "one voice running through many personalities, contrasts and repetitions."

The organization of *Imitations* is thus more closely related to that of *Life Studies* than to that of *Lord Weary's Castle*, but it is probably most closely related to that of the book that succeeds this one in Lowell's canon. As the brief comparison with *Lord Weary's Castle* has suggested, *Imitations* has a basically symmetrical structure in which the central section is the crux, and . . . the profile of *For the Union Dead* is remarkably similar. Moreover, within the symmetrical framework of each book, there is a series of interrelated groups of poems which function in the manner of a narrative.

One can distinguish two principles upon which the narrative of *Imitations* rests, the most important of which corresponds to the development of character in a more conventional narrative and the other of which corresponds to the development of action or plot. The first of these principles, which is the one upon which Lowell's introduction focuses, provides for the changes in the outlook of a persona who, depending upon one's immediate point of view, either undergoes or emerges from the experiences reported in these poems; for if it is true that there are "many personalities" in this volume, it is also true that there is but this "one voice." Lowell's two phrases, which seem contradictory at first glance, can be reconciled easily enough by means of a simple but unorthodox distinction. This distinction is between the two terms, often considered synonymous, *poet-speaker* and *persona*. For present purposes, the former term refers to the speaking figure in any single poem, while the latter designates the figure who is capable of speaking in all of these voices. The poet-speaker in a given poem, then, although not identical with the persona, is one facet of the latter, or one of the instances from which we infer his development. The other instances include all of the other poet-speakers and a few of the more properly dramatic figures, such as Achilles in the imitation of Homer, who seem to be projections of the persona. If the persona is not identical with any of the poet-speakers or dramatic figures, neither is it identical with the poet, since the poet is the creator of this collective mask just as he is the imitator of the individual masks. Lowell's "many personalities" are the points that comprise the curve of his "one voice."

Perhaps the mixture in that last metaphor indicates the advisability of positing a second principle upon which this poetic narrative operates. The course of the persona's experience is frequently best described in terms of spatial metaphors, and one reason for this is that there is something like a plot in *Imitations*. This principle is harder to analyze than the first because it is both less consistently and more variously invoked. Since thought and feeling rather than deed and event are the concerns of the lyric, action is as necessarily intermittent as character is unavoidably present in this volume; and since lyric themes are fewer than the settings that they involve, action at this most rudimentary level is bound to be more diverse than the "personalities" in *Imitations*. Nevertheless, there are enough references to similar events to constitute a sketchy plot, and this plot is demonstrably of the epic variety. These poems were selected and arranged with an eye to the events and the settings which they involve, and their events and settings are often those one would expect to encounter in a heroic poem—battles, shipwrecks, descents to hell, and the like. *Imitations* opens with Achilles at Troy, and its next to last stanza concerns Leonidas at Thermopylae. But the clearest instance of the use of such a plot is in the central section, which is the nadir of the persona's development, the dark night of the soul, and in which most important poems describe voyages and shipwrecks. If Ovid, whose *Metamorphoses* is the source of the drawing on the title page, provides the model for the changing personalities in this book, then Homer, whose *Iliad* is the source of the first poem, is the guiding spirit for its ghost of a plot.

　　To catch these two principles at their point of intersection, one might say that *Imitations* presents the metamorphosis of Achilles, the type of the warrior, into Odysseus, the type of the voyager. Such a description, however, would still be limited, not only because many of the poems are not concerned with wars or voyages, but also because even the combination of the two heroic figures would only be symbolic of the fundamental subject of the book. Another type that might be singled out as representative of this subject, and which would be more comprehensive than either of the heroic figures because it would conceivably include them, is that of the poet. Almost as many of these imitations are concerned with poets and writing as are concerned with wars and voyages; moreover, as E. R. Curtius has pointed out, there is a seemingly inherent connection between composing poetry and voyaging, and the "boat of the mind" was a commonplace in antiquity.[2] Indeed, just to mention the metaphor is to call to mind a host of poems in English much older than Pound's *Cantos*, Crane's "Voyages," and Stevens's "Prologues to What Is Possible," as well as several of those imitated in this volume, including Baudelaire's

---

[2] *European Literature and the Latin Middle Ages* (New York, 1953), 128-29.

"Voyage" and Rimbaud's "Bateau ivre." Lowell's volume is another of these symbolic voyages, but it is to be distinguished from most other such symbols in that what it signifies (the life of the poet) is virtually identical with what it is (a series of closely related, many-voiced poems). *Imitations* is a particularly apt synecdoche for the poet's life because the poet, be he Homer or Ovid or Lowell, undergoes in the course of his work those changes of personality which Lowell insists are at the heart of this book.

Because it is an intricately organized whole with the requisite beginning, middle, and end, it seems that the volume must remain a symbol for the poet's life rather than a reflection of any particular life. The persona, it will be remembered, is not necessarily Robert Lowell. At the same time, as we shall see, the structure of *Imitations* is not such as to preclude its being a reflection of Lowell's own life as well as a symbol of the life of the poet.

With these general observations in the background, it is possible to examine the structure of *Imitations* in more detail. Although any such analysis must ignore some of the more subtle transitions between poems and the quite natural deviations from the overriding scheme, *Imitations* can be divided into seven sections. The ordering of these sections constitutes both a symmetrical arrangement, in which poems and short sequences approximately equidistant from the center counterbalance one another, and a progressive structure, in which a spiritual descent turns into an ascent and an affirmative conclusion grows out of a nihilistic beginning. On several occasions, Lowell goes out of his way to indicate some of the more salient points of this scheme, and it is mildly surprising that almost no one has yet taken his hints. The earliest of these indications, and the one which has been admirably glossed,[3] appears in the first line of the first poem, "The Killing of Lykaon," which is based on two separate passages from the *Iliad*. In Lowell's translation, Homer's line becomes "Sing for me, Muse, the mania of Achilles." The remarkable aspect of this line is that the Greek word which corresponds to Lowell's "mania" is "ménin," which means "enduring anger" or "divine wrath" and is invariably rendered as such by Homer's translators. While the Greek word is cognate with "mania" and Lowell is therefore more "literal" in a peculiar sense than other translators, the denotations of the two words in their respective languages are significantly different. Lowell's choice, then, enables him to declare in the opening line of the volume his imitative license. That it has an even more important function might be suggested by quotation of another line, this time from one of the poems at the center of the book. In Rimbaud's "Les poètes de sept ans" there is the line

---

[3] Irvin Ehrenpreis, "Age of Lowell," *American Poetry* (New York, 1965), 89.

"Vertige, écroulements, déroutes et pitié," which in Lowell's version becomes "dizziness, mania, revulsions, pity." Since neither "écroulements" ("ruins" or "failings") nor "déroutes" ("routs" or "confusions") would ordinarily be rendered with "mania," one might suspect a connection of some sort between this line and the one in "The Killing of Lykaon." Nonetheless, it is likely that the suspicion would be dismissed if one were not to notice that Lowell makes a similar alteration in translating the last line of Rilke's "Die Tauben" in the poem that ends the book. In the course of transfiguring Rilke's entire last stanza, Lowell turns the last line into "miraculously multiplied by its mania to return." Especially since this imitation has been conspicuously displaced from the chronological order that obtains almost everywhere else, it is clear that Lowell intends "to return" us to the volume's initial line; and once this connection of end and beginning has been noticed, it is likely that we will pay more attention to the line in the Rimbaud poem in the middle of the book.

Simply by placing the word "mania" in these critical positions, Lowell outlines the general curve of *Imitations*, or designates three of the seven sections noted above: the introductory poem, the central sequence, and the concluding poem. Comparable devices are used to designate other groups of poems and the relationships among them. Just after the imitation of Homer and just before the imitation of Rilke, there are short sequences (selections from Sappho and Der Wilde Alexander, on the one end, and from Annensky and Pasternak, on the other) which serve as transitions between these poems and the core of the volume; and Lowell points up the parallelism of these sequences (our second and sixth sections) by making them reflect one another. The concluding lines of the third poem based on Sappho and some lines near the end of "Hamlet in Russia, A Soliloquy," based on several poems by Pasternak, stand in such a relationship. Lowell's version of Sappho runs: "The moon slides west, / it is midnight, / the time is gone— / I lie alone!" The poem derived from Pasternak recalls the preceding lines with this image: "The sequence of scenes was well thought out; / the last bow is in the cards, or the stars— / but I am alone, and there is none. . . ." Both passages deal with the solitariness of the speaker, both address themselves to a darkness not only of the night, and both stress the passing of time. The chief difference between them is that "The sequence of scenes," which is to say the majority of these imitations, has passed. The significance of this distinction, which involves a discussion of the progressive or incremental structure of the volume, is the subject of a later inquiry. At this point, it is necessary to touch upon some of the other indications of our tentative division of this "sequence of scenes."

The transitional sections under consideration reflect one another
by means of several other anticipations and echoes, the most important of
which concern a symbolic forest. In "Children," the forest is a
mysteriously dangerous place, "'alive with snakes,'" which must be
avoided if one is not to be lost. As the herdsman admonished the children:

> "Well then, get out of the woods!
> If you don't hurry away quickly,
> I'll tell you what will happen—
> if you don't leave the forest
> behind you by daylight,
> you'll lose yourselves;
> your pleasure will end in bawling."

The children, however, did not leave the woods, and the poem intimates
that they did indeed lose themselves: "Where we picked up violets / on
lucky days, / you can now see cattle gadding about." In a note in *The
Penguin Book of German Verse*, whose prose translation Lowell seems to
have consulted, the editor remarks that "this poem is probably an
allegory." Like the lyric itself, this note is probably disingenuous, since
the former is certainly allegorical; but the specific subject is sufficiently
ambiguous to justify editorial reticence, and it is this ambiguity which
Lowell exploits later by means of oblique allusions. When we find, near
the end of the book, one poem in which the speaker enters the woods and
is advised by them, and several poems set in the forest, and one poem
entitled "In the Woods," we must suspect that the persona was one of the
children who never got "out of the woods" and that Lowell is bending the
allegory to his own purposes. The suspicion is enforced and more
specifically directed by the reference to the woods as a place where one
must suffer strange transformations, where "'you'll lose yourselves,'" a
reference that is recalled by the last stanza of "The Landlord," another
imitation of Pasternak: "as if life were only an instant, of course, / the
dissolution of ourselves into others, / like a wedding party approaching the
window." This loss of the self repeats but radically revises the notion as it
is allegorized in "Children." More will be said of the nature of this
revision in connection with the progressive structure of the book; what is
important to notice here is that "The Landlord" and "Children" parallel
one another by virtue of both position and subject and thus help to
establish the ordonnance of the *Imitations*.

The titles of several key poems exemplify most simply this
structural use of parallelism. The beginning of what might be called the
third section of *Imitations*, for example, is marked by an imitation of

Villon's "Le grand testament," a title that is translated by Lowell's "The Great Testament." Lowell's title, apparently unremarkable, assumes some importance when it is realized, first, that the adjective "grand," while often interpolated, was not originally in Villon's title and, second, that its inclusion and translation as "Great" suggests more immediately a relationship between this poem and an imitation of Montale called "Little Testament." Since it occurs late in this volume, at the end of the Montale poems, and since it and the poems just preceding provide a thematic response to "The Great Testament" and the poems succeeding it, "Little Testament" concludes our fifth section.

Similarly, if more dramatically, Lowell translates Hugo's "A Théophile Gautier" as "At Gautier's Grave" and then alters the title of Mallarmé's "Toast funèbre" to "At Gautier's Grave" too. The clear implication is that these poems are to be paired, and this implication is strengthened by the positions of the two poems: on either side of the long selections of poems from Baudelaire and Rimbaud. Just as the two "testaments" seem to begin a third section and conclude a fifth, so the two poems on Gautier seem to conclude the third and begin the fifth.

Between the two poems on Gautier, there are twenty-six poems based on Baudelaire and Rimbaud. Since the number of imitations of Baudelaire (fourteen) is the largest of any author, while the number of imitations of Rimbaud (twelve) is second, and since these two are the ninth and tenth of eighteen authors, there is no doubt that what we will call the fourth section is the heart of this volume. Throughout this section there are so many repetitions of phrase and image that it is difficult not to regard them as allusions intended to lace these two sets of imitations together. Of course it might be coincidental that the first Baudelaire poem opens with the indictment that "we spoonfeed our adorable remorse, / like whores and beggars nourishing their lice," while the last Rimbaud poem is "The Lice-Hunters"; and that in the one poem the devil sat by the sickbeds and "hissed," while in the other "the royal sisters" sat there and "hissed"; and that the tone of the first poem, which occurs before the spiritual crisis discussed below, is summarized in the phrase "yawning for the guillotine," while that of the second, which follows this book's dark night, is epitomized by the phrase "begged the fairies for his life"; and so on through the other poems. But even if these echoes are considered accidental, the whole question of whether they are so could not have suggested itself without a recognition of such definite structural indicators as have been noted. From one point of view, *Imitations* is a dense reticulation of internal allusions; and once this self-allusive quality has been noticed, the problem is not so much in showing how the allusions create a structure as in keeping that structure from seeming to fade into the texture of allusions. . . .

Circle to Circle: The Poetry of Robert Lowell (Berkeley, 1975), 165-74.

The Three Lives of Robert Lowell

Christopher Ricks

The singular strength of Robert Lowell's poetry has always been a matter of his power to enforce a sense of context. He has been determined as few poets have been, to face the implications of the dramatic monologue, the only new poetic kind of any importance for centuries and the one which has established itself as peculiarly apt for the modern poet. A sense context becomes a point of urgency, because otherwise a dramatic monologue will be merely a speech from a missing play. Lowell's gift has been to bring a sense of context to bear upon his poems, not just in local effects but as a whole. And the best poems in *For the Union Dead* go beyond their predecessors precisely their ability to enforce simultaneously the three contexts which in Lowell's earlier work had tended to get hived off into separate poems.[1]

First, his personal experience, an "I" who really does live here and now and who comes across as individual and yet not idiosyncratic. Second, the way we live now, a social and political we in which "the Republic summons Ike," and underground parking is gouged out beneath Boston Common, and bombs may and indeed do go off. Third, the outer context, historical, literary and religious, dealing with the old unhappy things which are not far off, the diverse deaths of Jesus, Caligula and Mussolini.

The achievement of this new volume is manifest in a fact which could be misread as a lack of focus: the fact that the book is not predominantly identified with any one of the three contexts that have always both liberated and channelled Lowell's imagination. *Imitations*, by its nature as free-standing translation, was committed only to enforcing a

---

[1] *For the Union Dead* (London, 1965).

historical and literary context. "Only," not because that is a trivial thing, but because the decision entailed leaving out quite a lot of Lowell. That Lowell's French was corrected by T. S. Eliot was no substitute. *Imitations* may be in one sense a more sharply focused book than *For the Union Dead*—but in a lesser sense. Similarly with *Life Studies*, a collection which included poems of various modes (historical monologues and "Inauguration Day: January 1953") but which was predominantly devoted to poems of a personal context: those piercing and affectionate poems about Lowell's own pains and those of his family. *Life Studies* was, after all, Lowell's title for both the volume and for this, the main section. Faber managed to disguise this emphasis (as well as to deprive Englishmen of an important work by Lowell) by omitting from the English edition "91 Revere St.," 36 pages of reminiscential prose which confirmed the emphasis as central to *Life Studies* (poems which are mainly studies in death).

For the Union Dead does not represent any dramatic break. All along, Lowell has written poems which embody the three contexts. But hitherto each collection had tended to manifest an emphasis which was also something of an exclusion. (In the earliest poems, Roman Catholicism was inclined to upstage the others.) And hitherto he had not managed to write many poems in which justice was done to all three, each worthy of the others in their convergence. The sheer distinction of the present title-poem (like that of "Fall 1961," "Florence", and the reprinted "Beyond the Alps") comes from its marrying the three sources of Lowell's imagination—and of our own. "For the Union Dead" outdoes the previous poems, and by multiplying them, not adding. Its setting is "the old South Boston Aquarium" together with the statues of Colonel Shaw and his infantry. The personal context is established at once, with a childhood memory of the Aquarium, a memory later to be hideously distorted or parodied: "Once my nose crawled like a snail on the glass; / my hand tingled / to burst the bubbles / drifting from the noses of the cowed, compliant fish."

The social, civic and political context defines itself by contrast both with this memory (the Aquarium is now derelict) and with the historical memory of what Shaw and his soldiers represented.

> There are no statues for the last war here;
> on Boyleston Street, a commercial photograph
> shows Hiroshima boiling
> over a Mosler Safe, the "Rock of Ages"
> that survived the blast.

The audacity of "Boyleston . . . boiling" is an attempt to match the effrontery of the photograph itself, with trade-name accomplishing, gratuitously, all that Lowell could ask *sub specie aeternitatis*. The poem is superbly organised and yet wonderfully free, so that to point to its bubble-imagery, say, is to schemtise rawly, It finally circles back to its memory of childhood, at which there dawns, unvoiced, the fear that the Aquarium's tanks are now dry because the sea-world has broken loose: "The Aquarium is gone. Everywhere, / giant finned cars nose forward like fish; / a savage servility / slides by on grease." The accurate and the suggestive here combine, permitting Lowell to intimate without pretentiousness that humanity is preying on itself like monsters of the deep. How right to eschew a hyphen in "giant finned." And there is an equivocation (itself sliding) in "slides by on grease," where "on," used here as it is of cars, suggests ("runs on oil") that grease is the fuel as well as what you slide on, both the internal motive-power and the external slippery slope.

In its relating of the internal and the external, as of the personal, the political and the historic, "For the Union Dead" is one of the finest poems Lowell has written. And if it is about sea-monsters we remember the urgent cry in one of the other poems: "Pity the monsters!" Lowell—and it is the crown—does persuade us of his pity. If, like many other people, he sees in present-day America some desolating illness, his tone is very different from that in which Allen Tate spoke when introducing Lowell's first book poems. For Tate in 1944, Lowell was to be warmly contrasted with "the democratic poets who enthusiastically greet the advent of the slave society." Lowell's recent work holds no brief for the right of Southern gentlemen to impugn only one kind of "slave-society." Nor are Lowell's poems so sure that what America is suffering from is an excess of democracy.

"Caligula" shows another meeting of the three. Its starting point, as with all poems, is arbitrary: the fact that as a child Lowell gained (chose?) the nickname Caligula: "My namesake, Little Boots, Caligula, / you disappoint me. Tell me what I saw / to make me like you when we met at school?" The whole poem unfolds that altogether convincing hesitation in "like you"—a verb or not? Does Lowell like Caligula or is he like him? The latter possibility is cunningly held open, with an unobtrusiveness which shows Lowell's mature confidence. The success of the poem comes from the fusion of the personal anecdote with the historical and political.

Historical, because of the passionate skill with which we are shown Caligula's appalling life and death. (Lowell has always found in Rome a combination of the marmoreal and the frenzied which permits him to use a true hyperbole.) Political, because even if Caligula was in one sense "the last Caligula" (its closing words), these have been other such men. The political, historical and personal meet in the psychopathology of Caligula, and Lowell has seized a setting which demands a violence which elsewhere could be suspect:

> You hear you household panting on all fours,
> and itemize your features—sleep's old aide!
> *Item*: your body hairy and badly made,
> head hairless, smoother than your marble head;
> *Item*: eyes hollow, hollow temples, red
> cheeks rough with rouge, legs spindly, hands that leave
> a clammy snail's trail on your soggy sleeve . . .
> a hand no hand will hold . . . nose thin, thin neck—
> you wish the Romans had a single neck!

The shrieking inarticulacy of that last famous wish (embodied in the mad rhyme of "neck" with "neck") springs out in murderous contrast to the itemising of features, and Lowell manages to make us remember, because the poem is both then and now, that nuclear war has indeed given us all one neck. One might add that Lowell's quotation makes use of the very strong anti-democratic feelings which lunge impatiently through American life today, and yet doesn't yield to those feelings.

It is not important that the lines by Lowell so much resemble the great poetry of Jonson's *Sejanus*, the opening speech of which itemises the human features in a way which similarly suggests a disintegration in Rome that is at once spiritual, physical and social: "We have no shift of faces, no cleft tongues, / No soft and glutinous bodies that can stick / Like snails on painted walls." The comparison with Jonson's tragedies, here and elsewhere (cp. Lowell's translation of *Phèdre*), deserves to be demonstrated at length. Both can write with a physical force about he body politic. (*For the Union Dead* is a grimly punning title.) Both are masters of the glacial, the heated and the poisonous, and both create a poetry of dignity and yet profoundly of its time in its sense of turbulence. Jonson would not have despised the couplet: "You stare down hallways, mile on stoney mile, / where statues of the gods return your smile." The assurance manifest in the unsignalled pun on "stare down" (as the couplet unrolls, the suggestion becomes Gorgonian); the way the couplet congeals around "stoney"; the chilling force here given to the cliché "return your smile" (not the reciprocity of love, in the circumstances); and the explicit feeling of vista'd repetition which is enforced by the near-identity of the rhyme "mile" / "smile"—all these show a technical mastery that is inseparable from imaginative mastery.

With the straight historical poems Lowell now seems rather less happy. There was a fine monologue in *Life Studies*, "The Banker's Daughter", in which Marie de Medici speaks "shortly after the assassination of her husband, Henri IV." One of the new poems, "Lady Ralegh's Lament, 1618," invites comparison but then finds itself snubbed—Lady Ralegh is inferior, and not just socially. There is a real problem about historical allusiveness: how much can Lowell legitimately expect us to know? And if he expects us to know quite a lot, what happens when there swims in mind a famous historical anecdote which Lowell apparently would prefer excluded? Lady Ralegh begins "Sir Walter, oh, oh, my own Sir Walter." If it is the case that those are her very words they nevertheless remain uncomfortable close to Aubrey's notorious anecdote about Ralegh:

> He loved a wench well: and one time getting up one of the Mayds of Honour up against a tree in a Wood ('twas his first Lady) who seemed at first boarding the be something fearfull of her Honour, and modest, she cryed, sweet Sir Walter, what doe you me ask? Will you undoe me? Nay, sweet Sir Walter! Sweet Sir Walter! At last, as the danger and the pleasure at the same time grew higher, she cryed in the extasey, Swisser Swatter Swisser Swatter.

Allusiveness creates problems for Lowell. Is a line like "I dabble in the dapple of the day" in any way making use of our awareness that it is Spelt from Hopkins' Leaves? Nor is the problem less when the allusions are to quotations previously quoted in Lowell's own work. "Jonathan Edwards in Western Massachusetts" has a few touching moments—though it does occasionally sound like a kind of Jonathan Edwards Revisited. But what about this?: "you saw the spiders fly, / basking at their ease, / swimming from tree to tree." Lowell-lovers will already have leaped to their feet to intone the unforgettable opening of "Mr Edwards and the Spider": "I saw the spiders marching through the air, / Swimming from tree to tree that / mildewed day. . . ." The simply historical poems seem to have suffered an attenuation, most apparent in the sentimentality of "Hawthorne." Written for a centenary edition, the poem "draws heavily on prose sentences" by Hawthorne, which does not justify the fungoid phrasing.

New Statesman (Mar. 26, 1965): 496-97.

"For the Union Dead"

Steven Gould Axelrod

In contemplating the doomed, heroic charge of Colonel Robert Gould Shaw and his regiment on a Southern fortress, Lowell consciously placed himself within a remarkably rich, century-long artistic tradition that includes poems by Phoebe Cary, Ralph Waldo Emerson, James Russell Lowell, Paul Laurence Dunbar, William Vaughn Moody, John Berryman, and many others; orations by Frederick Douglass, Booker T. Washington, William James, and Oliver Wendell Holmes Jr.; a program by Charles Ives; and the bas-relief in Boston Common by Augustus Saint-Gaudens. [See also the subsequent film *Glory*.] "I knew," Lowell said, "that Colonel Shaw was a heroic, an overworked subject." In composing "For the Union Dead" he entered deliberately into literary history—into dialogue with his respected predecessors and with his comrade in art, John Berryman. His poem demonstrates the survival of literary tradition by breathing life into one of its branches. By its very existence the poem reinforces those values of civilization which are its essential concern. In retrospect it seems almost a matter of destiny that Lowell should have contributed to this tradition of artworks about Shaw. Colonel Shaw, whose sister married Lowell's favorite ancestor, Charles Russell Lowell Jr., is an altogether suitable subject for a poem in his most characteristic mode, the family elegy. But far more important, Robert Lowell, with his sense of history and his moral sensitivity, was perfectly suited by temperament to engage the themes suggested by Shaw's story.

In spring of 1863 Robert Gould Shaw, a twenty-five-year-old Boston Brahmin and family friend of the Lowells, was given command of the Negro 54th Massachusetts Volunteers. The 54th Massachusetts was the first Union Army regiment to be composed below officer rank entirely of free northern blacks. On July 18, 1863, after being in combat for just a few weeks, Colonel Shaw and his regiment were ordered to lead the advance on Fort Wagner, the outermost defense of the Charleston harbor. The assault proved suicidal. Almost half of the members of the 54th were killed, including Shaw who was shot with a dozen of his men after having scaled the parapet wall of the fort. By all accounts Shaw and the black soldiers had fought gallantly, proceeding with their charge even after realizing that they were caught in an ambush. Because the enlisted men were black, the Confederate commander of Fort Wagner refused Shaw the honorable burial to which his rank entitled him, and instead had him buried with his men in a common grave. Later, when efforts were initiated in the North to rebury him more ceremonially, Shaw's father quietly forbade this to be done, holding that "a soldier's most appropriate burial place is on the field where he has fallen."

Colonel Shaw's "picturesque and gallant death" made an immense impact on a northern public confused about the war and eager for heroes. Shaw came to represent for the North, and especially for New England, its own capacity for idealism and courage. His life and death were taken as justification for the Union cause and, more importantly, as justification for the essential Yankee character. Because of the symbolic quality his story assumed and indeed invited, it became a subject for poems, all of which serve as a matrix for "For the Union Dead." Characteristic of the works composed in the months immediately following the assault on Fort Wagner is Phoebe Cary's "The Hero of Fort Wagner," in which a fallen black soldier selflessly exhorts a white officer, "I'm done gone, Massa; step on me; / And you can scale the wall!" In a similar bathetic spirit, Anna Cabot Lowell Quincy Waterston, a friend of both the Lowell and Shaw families, wrote an ode to Shaw entitled "Together," four lines of which were later inscribed on the Saint-Gaudens memorial: "O fair-haired Northern hero, / With thy guard of dusky hue, / Up from the field of battle / Rise to the last review." Less pretentious were many anonymous and widely circulated pieces of doggerel, one of which purported to describe Fort Wagner's commanding officer ordering his troops to bury Shaw "with his niggers," a phrase Lowell alludes to in stanza thirteen of "For the Union Dead."

Two of the earliest poems took the form of generalized tributes. Ralph Waldo Emerson had young Shaw in mind when he composed these famous lines for his Civil War dirge "Voluntaries":

> In an age of fops and toys,
> Wanting wisdom, void of right,
> Who shall nerve heroic boys
> To hazard all in Freedom's fight? . . .
> So nigh is grandeur to our dust,
> So near is God to man,
> When Duty whispers low, *Thou must,*
> The youth replies, *I can.*

In an early version of "For the Union Dead," Robert Lowell wrote that Shaw "replied" to his general "I will," a possible echo of Emerson's "I can." Although the published version contains no verbal echoing of Emerson, its portrayal of Shaw accords with Emerson's depiction of him as an exemplar of duty in an age of "sloth and ease." The second generalized tribute was James Russell Lowell's "Ode Recited at the Harvard Commemoration," which he contributed to a volume of *Harvard Memorial Biographies* containing a life of Shaw written by his mother. Although the "Ode" names no soldier specifically, its fervid rhetoric was doubtless inspired by the death of Shaw as well as the deaths of two of Lowell's nephews. This poem, however, is just the kind of "set-piece and official ode" that Robert Lowell sought to avoid in "For the Union Dead," just the kind of poem that caused him to call his great-granduncle a poet "pedestalled for oblivion."

Perhaps the most impressive of all the Shaw poems written during this period was another poem by James Russell Lowell called "Memoriae Positum R.G.S." This poem, begun in the weeks following Shaw's death and published in the following year, shows its author for once descended from his pedestal. A result of intense "brooding in [the] heart," it possesses a quiet dignity and pained self-questioning very different from the inflated tone of the "Commemoration Ode." In "Memoriae Positum" the poet attempts, with very little self-assurance, to justify both Shaw's death and his own survival, and to renew his shaken faith in his country at a time when the country's future was still in doubt. Complex, ambiguous, and ultimately quite personal, "Memoriae Positum" is perhaps James Russell Lowell's most "modern" poem. Foreshadowing "For the Union Dead," the poem contrasts Colonel Shaw's ideal of moral purity with society's reality of moral bankruptcy. It pictures Shaw as a "saintly shape of fame" whose memory now will goad survivors into goodness. But it also expresses a deep fear that the masses will prove "heedless" of Shaw, and heedless of poetry celebrating him. The poem thus takes the form of a dialectic between James Russell Lowell's constitutional need to affirm and his underlying philosophical fears and doubts. Predictably, the lines chosen to be inscribed on the Saint-Gaudens memorial are the most yea-saying of the poem, ending "death for noble ends makes dying sweet." Yet two stanzas later, Shaw and his band are pessimistically termed "Hope's *forlorn-hopes* that plant the *desperate* good." (Robert Lowell similarly referred to Shaw's "forlorn hope" in one draft of "For the Union Dead," but ultimately abandoned the image.) By allowing his compassion for Shaw to radiate outward to include all of life's innocents, James Russell Lowell is able to end his poem with renewed faith in America and the future. He thus makes an affirmation that Robert Lowell cannot. His earnest hopes for a union reborn are answered a century later by his descendant's lamentations for a union dead.

Three decades later, the dedication of Augustus Saint-Gaudens' bronze bas-relief memorial to Shaw and his regiment in Boston Common inspired a second spate of poems and recitations on the topic. The memorial itself, completed in 1897, was obviously intended in part as a compliment by the Boston cultural elite to itself. The monument is scrupulously inscribed with the names of every one of the killed white officers but none of the killed black soldiers. Its epigraph, "Omnia Relinquit Servare Rempublicam," is the motto of the Society of the Cincinnati, the exclusive military club to which Shaw belonged by right of descent. Yet both the overall conception of Saint-Gaudens' design, giving prominence as it does to the individuality of each of the black soldiers, and the passionately egalitarian speeches given at the unveiling ceremonies, attest to Boston's real moral fervor. The Shaw family itself refused initial plans for an equestrian statue of Shaw alone, insisting that the memorial give equal importance to the black soldiers. William James, in the major address of the unveiling, called the black soldiers "champions of a better day for man" and said that they and Shaw "represent with such typical purity the profounder meaning of the Union cause." Thomas Bailey Aldrich recited a grandiloquent dedicatory poem entitled "Shaw Memorial Ode," and speeches suitable to the occasion were given by Booker T. Washington and several government officials. The next several years saw the publication of poems about Shaw by Richard Watson Gilder, Benjamin Brawley, Percy MacKaye, Paul Laurence Dunbar, and William Vaughn Moody. Of these, the most enduring are Dunbar's eloquent sonnet "Robert Gould Shaw," which laments the lack of racial progress since Shaw's time, and Moody's idealistic, angry "Ode in Time of Hesitation." Like Emerson and James Russell Lowell before him, Moody presents Shaw as a moral example whose heroism contrasts tellingly with endemic civic corruption (specifically, American imperialism). To this basic contrast, however, he adds a new historical dimension. He associates Shaw's heroic ideal with the past, and unheroic reality with the present, thus suggesting a pattern of moral degeneration similar to that suggested by "For the Union Dead."

   Apart from "For the Union Dead" itself, the only later addition to the tradition of Shaw poems is "Boston Common" by John Berryman, Lowell's friend and an acknowledged influence on his work. Writing during World War II, Berryman portrays Colonel Shaw in even a darker aspect than Moody does. His Shaw can no longer even speak to us: "Fiery night consumes a summoned ghost." For Berryman, the mass slaughter of modern war has rendered Shaw and his regiment obsolete, even as symbols. Whereas James Russell Lowell once looked hopefully to a nobler future, Paul Laurence Dunbar, William Vaughn Moody, John Berryman, and finally Robert Lowell himself all lament, with increasing bitterness, the passing of a nobler past. This alteration signals a dimming of hopes, a process of disillusionment, the darkening glass of the twentieth century.

"For the Union Dead" clearly responds to the themes and motifs present in the previous poems on Colonel Shaw and his troops. It even more openly echoes two eloquent speeches on the subject: William James's oration dedicating the Shaw memorial and a short address by Justice Oliver Wendell Holmes called "Harvard College in the War." In a sense, Lowell's poem may be viewed as an ironic commentary on both these speeches, which were several notches more optimistic in their idealism than any of the major poems about Shaw dared to be. James, for example, had consecrated "Shaw's beautiful image to stand here for all time, an inciter to similarly unselfish public deeds." Holmes had thought Shaw's example "necessary" to future generations. Instead, Lowell sees Shaw as being "out of bounds now" (st. 10), both literally and spiritually. His beautiful image incites only civic hostility. He "sticks" in the city's throat" (st. 8).

Both of Lowell's descriptions of statuary in "For the Union Dead" echo phrases from William James's speech. He remarks of the Saint-Gaudens bas-relief that "William James could almost hear the bronze Negroes breathe" (st. 7), an allusion to James's description of them as "so true to nature that one can almost hear them breathing." And he goes on to describe the "stone statues of the abstract Union Soldier" which are found "on a thousand small town New England greens" (st. 11-12), a paraphrase of James's statement that "the abstract soldiers'-monuments have been reared on every village green." In both of these borrowings Lowell deliberately turns James's words of hope and praise into lament. He comments that the Union Soldier statues "grow slimmer and younger each year" in contrast to the increasingly fat and venal general populace (st. 12). And now, far from almost hearing Saint-Gaudens' blacks breathing, the general populace roundly ignores them; values them less than parking places; seeks half-consciously to rid itself of their symbolic reproach. James had written that nothing "can save us from degeneration if the inner mystery is lost," defining this inner mystery as "trained and disciplined good temper" and "fierce and merciless resentment toward every man or set of men who break the public peace." Lowell, however, everywhere sees savagery rather than good temper and servility rather than righteous resentment. The degeneration James feared has become Lowell's theme.

"For the Union Dead" stands in a similarly ironic relation to Justice Holmes's speech. In its initial drafts, the poem included explicit quotations from this speech, but by the time the poem assumed its final form Holmes had become merely another of the figures standing dimly behind it, his own possibly facile optimism corrected by Lowell's revision. Holmes had professed to believe that succeeding generations would continue to heed Shaw as a symbol of "man's destiny and power for duty," and of the willingness "to toss life and hope like a flower" before the feet of one's country. Lowell, of course, tells us that Shaw goes generally unheeded by succeeding generations. Further, Lowell intends his statement that Shaw "rejoices" in man's "peculiar power to choose life and die" (st. 10) as a faint parodic echo of several of Holmes's characteristic remarks. Holmes once said of the casualties of the Civil War that "our dead brothers still live for us, and bid us think of life, not death," and on another occasion proclaimed that "life is action, the use of one's powers. . . . To use them to their height is our joy and duty." Yet Lowell believes that this justification of the heroically strenuous life masks an unconscious urge toward its opposite: "How we mean the opposite of what we first say or habitually say." "For the Union Dead" makes manifest the note of suicidalism implicit but unacknowledged in Holmes's assertions. Lowell's Shaw finds his joy and duty in his power not merely to think of life or "choose life" but also to "die," and even to lead others "to death." Thus, Lowell converts Holmes's attractive but simplistic affirmations into a vision more richly ambiguous. His poem praises the military valor of Shaw, but also suggests dark, mixed motives beneath that valor.

"For the Union Dead," then, is first of all a poem about American history. It pays a complex but sincere tribute to Colonel Shaw and the Massachusetts 54th, and it responds to and subtly alters a distinguished tradition of works of art about that regiment, through a process Emerson would term "creative reading." Lowell's purpose in harkening to the past is to expose and dramatize the moral squalor of the historical present. The heroic idealism of Colonel Shaw and his troops—and the preservation of their honored memory in various works of art—contrasts devastatingly with the only memento Boston cares to keep of World War II: a commercial photograph of the Hiroshima mushroom cloud with a caption advertising the Mosler Safe as "the 'Rock of Ages' that survived the blast" (st. 15). (Paul C. Doherty has reported that the Mosler Safe Company entitled this advertising display "The Hiroshima Story Comes to Life with a Bang.") In contrast to nineteenth-century Boston, which cheered Shaw and his men off to war in 1863 and celebrated their valor in memorials, orations, and poems after their death, the "New Boston" can only pride itself blasphemously upon a receptacle for lucre sturdy enough to "survive" atomic explosion—unlike 80,000 human beings. Colonel Shaw's "civic courage (in James's phrase) has given way to a complacent merchandising of nuclear annihilation.

Yet in Lowell's complex vision, the past explains as well as rebukes the present. The circumstances of Shaw's brutal death and burial, in what Lowell called "the first modern war," suggests that Fort Wagner and Hiroshima are both part of the same historical curve of increasing technological barbarity. Equally disturbing, the hidden homicidal or suicidal strain that Lowell detects in Shaw himself (and in some of his nineteenth-century celebrators) corresponds to the Ahab-like spirit he finds deep in the American character, a spirit of "violence and idealism" capable in our day of producing nuclear holocaust.

Nevertheless, there is another, more hopeful historical comparison in "For the Union Dead": that between Shaw's black regiment and the black students of the desegregation battles of the 1950s. These young students, nonviolent counterparts of the Massachusetts 54th, are the only unambiguous heroes in the poem. Lowell has said of the political aspect of "For the Union Dead": "In 1959 I had a message here; since then the blacks have found their 'break,' but the landscape remains." This landscape is one of continuing injustice and increasing political terror. The flawed but very real idealism of Shaw and his celebrators has given way to a "commercial optimism" (in a phrase from one of the poem's drafts) which serves as a cover for mass murder, for servility, for savagery. Yet however dark the prospects, the black schoolchildren, lonely but determined disciples of Gandhi and King, provide reason for hope.

In "For the Union Dead," Lowell has substituted a prophetic historicism for the prophetic mythology of his earliest public poems. The poem is literally born of time, focusing on various historical moments: Colonel Shaw and the 54th marching through Boston in 1863 and then defeated at Fort Wagner two months later; William James dedicating their monument in 1897; Hiroshima "boiling" in 1945; the Boston Common being torn open "one morning last March"; the teeming city thoroughfares of time present. Even within the poem itself, the process of time, Philip Rahv's "powerhouse of change," can be observed: in the first stanza the aquarium still "stands" but by the last it "is gone." By his act of historical memory, Lowell seeks to counter the prevailing mood of his age, which is fiercely antagonistic to traces of the past—aquarium, St. Gaudens memorial, and all else. By obliterating its own past, modern society has become a stranger to itself, without identity or inherited moral values (such as those promulgated by James and other writers about the 54th). As a result we ignorantly repeat the worst sins of our ancestors: the brutal death and burial of Shaw and his soldiers become, immensely magnified, the bombing of Hiroshima. But by applying his historical consciousness to a land actively hostile to history, Lowell hopes to redeem time by restoring its significance. He identifies Colonel Shaw and the Massachusetts 54th, William James, and (above all) the black school-children as models of a humane and liberal tradition; one which, however flawed and beleaguered, is still alive and worthy of allegiance. As G. S. Fraser has said, Lowell's national elegy ultimately becomes a "song of praise"—praise for the enduring forms and values of human civilization.

Robert Lowell: Life and Art (Princeton, 1978), 162-72.

A Poetry of Memory: *For the Union Dead*

Katharine Wallingford

"Children, the raging memory drools / Over the glory of past pools," Robert Lowell declaimed in his first volume of poetry.[1] Throughout his career he would acknowledge again and again the power of memory in his poetry and in his life. By the time he wrote *Life Studies*, Lowell was using memory deliberately as a therapeutic instrument; many of the poems in that volume had their beginnings in prose reminiscences he wrote on the advice of his doctors. As we know, the use of memory to probe the past to remember and to come to terms with conflicts that arise out of past experience is one of the standard techniques of psychoanalysis and other forms of psychotherapy. According to Freud, "If a pathological idea . . . can be traced back to its elements in the patient's mental life from which it originated, it simultaneously crumbles away and the patient is freed from it."[2] Philip Rieff paraphrases Freud's definition of psychological illness as "the failure to become emancipated from one's past," and Rieff pinpoints the "peculiar and central place" of memory in psychoanalysis: "It is constraining, since by remembering our bondages to the past we appreciate their enormity; but it is also, Freud believed, liberating, since by remembering we understand the terrors and pleasures of the past and move toward mastering them."[3]

Jacques Lacan and others have stressed one particular aspect of this technique of using memory to investigate one's personal history. Concentrating on what Lacan calls the "intersubjective continuity of the discourse in which the subject's history is constituted," these

---

[1] "The Drunken Fisherman," *Lord Weary's Castle* (New York, 1946), 37.
[2] Freud, "Interpretation of Dreams," *Standard Edition* 4: 100.
[3] Rieff, *Freud*, 3d ed. (Chicago, 1979), 49, 334.

psychoanalysts call for the subject to construct from his or her memories a personal narrative that will make sense of the past and its relation to the present.[4] But this approach too . . . has its detractors—critics who decry the emphasis on the continuity of the personal narrative. Here psychoanalysis confronts the problem of the nature of the self in the twentieth century. In his fine book *Being in the Text*, Paul Jay points to Henry Adams as the great enunciator not only of this problem but of a possible, if limited, solution. Both the problem and the solution are considered (and I use this next pun deliberately) in terms of language: "[Adams's] frank admission of the inadequacy of narrative as a form for modern self-representation and his conviction that the modern ego was a chaos of 'multiplicities' looks forward to a self-reflexive practice that articulates, and sometimes embraces, such a chaos."[5] This characterization of the self as a chaos of multiplicities to be embraced rather than as a tidy entity to be pinned down in a coherent narrative has its counterpart in contemporary theories of history. Given Lowell's lifelong habit of seeing himself as a reflection of history and history as a reflection of himself, we will need to consider at least briefly the application of these theories in Lowell's poetry.

We may appear to have wandered far from the subject of memory, but in fact memory, like association, like repetition, like relation, is inextricably bound up in our discussion of self-examination in Robert Lowell's poetry. His history was crucial in determining what he was to make of his self, both in his life and in his poetry, and he was well aware of the significance of memory in that process. Particularly in *For the Union Dead* and *Day by Day*, he addressed himself specifically to the question of the nature of that puzzling phenomenon. "Both fascinated and imprisoned by memories," John Crick says of the poet in *For the Union Dead*, "he seeks freedom through deliberate appropriations of them, and throughout the book weaves patterns of recollection."[6] The first four poems in the volume treat memory explicitly. In the first poem, "Water," the poet addresses a woman with whom he has shared an experience in the past. "Remember?" he asks. "We sat on a slab of rock. / From this distance in time, / it seems the color / of iris, rotting and turning purpler." But the poet's memory errs: "it was only / the usual gray rock / turning the usual green / when drenched by the sea."[7]

---

[4] Lacan, "Function and Field," *Ecrits* (New York, 1977), 49.
[5] Jay, *Being in the Text* (Ithaca, 1984), 37.
[6] Crick, *Robert Lowell* (New York, 1974), 37.
[7] *For the Union Dead* (New York, 1964), 3.

This knowledge of the distorting properties of memory hovers in the background throughout the rest of the volume, even when, as in the next poem, the poet expresses no doubts as to the accuracy of his recollections. The remembered past in "The Old Flame" (5) is unpleasant: the poet and his wife were "quivering and fierce"; they lay "awake all night. / In one bed and apart," and listened to the snow-plow "groaning up hill." But now "Everything's changed for the best"—visiting the house in which the two had lived, the poet finds a "new landlord, / a new wife, a new broom." The house has been "swept bare, / furnished, garnished and aired," and the resulting sense of total discontinuity between past and present hints at what will become, for Lowell, one of the disturbing aspects of memory. Another of its alarming features takes concrete form in the next poem, "Middle Age" (7). Lowell sets the scene, describing the "midwinter grind" of New York which "drills through [his] nerves" as he walks "the chewed-up streets." The dental imagery is unobtrusive enough to be effective and chilling, and thus to prepare the reader for the ominous next lines. "At forty-five, / what next, what next?" the poet asks. "At every comer, / I meet my Father, / my age, still alive." To come face to face with the father is terrifying, the more so since the poet at this stage of life has no answer to his own question. He has only the excruciating memory of the father in whose "dinosaur / death steps" he must walk.

As is so often the case for Lowell, memory brings with it pain; he eschews autobiography in the next poem, "The Scream" (8), which explores the way in which an uncomfortable memory acts upon a child. He bases the poem on "In the Village," a short story by Elizabeth Bishop about a young girl whose life is colored by the memory of her deranged mother's scream. Bishop begins her story with these words:

> A scream, the echo of a scream, hangs over that Nova Scotian village. No one hears it; it hangs there forever, a slight stain in those pure blue skies . . . too dark, too blue, so that they seem to keep on darkening. . . over the woods and waters as well as the sky. The scream hangs like that, unheard, in memory in the past, in the present, and those years between.

The echo of a scream, hanging in memory, a slight stain in the sky, darkening over the woods and waters—this thinning echo becomes for Lowell a metaphor for memory itself.

In "The Scream," Lowell imagines memory as an echo thinning away, finally, to nothing, but much more often in *For the Union Dead* he insists upon its persistence. He plays with the notion of the instability of memory, the way remembered objects seem to change shape with the passage of time, as when, in "For the Union Dead" (70), "The stone statues of the abstract Union Soldier / grow slimmer and younger each year." In that poem, as in "The Public Garden" (26) and "Returning" (34), the remembered past is superior to the present. Usually, however, the memories themselves are disappointing at best, and, at their worst, crippling. Lowell was taught that he must use his memory to explore the past in order better to understand the present, and in *For the Union Dead* he accepts the unpleasant truth that the darkening stain of memory colors the past with pain and grief. Later he will admit, "I return then, but not to what I wanted."[8]

Sometimes the memories cause pain because they reveal qualities in the young child that the remembering adult finds abhorrent. In "Florence" (13), the poet remembers "How vulnerable the horseshoe crabs," which were "made for a child to grab / and throw strangling ashore!" Similarly, in "The Neo-Classical Urn" (47), Lowell rubs his head and feels "a turtle shell," which he associates with memories of an early cruelty: he remembers "the plop and splash / of turtle on turtle" as he dropped the helpless creatures into a garden urn. In "Dunbarton," in *Life Studies*, the poet had recalled a similar incident from his childhood: catching and imprisoning newts in a tobacco tin, he saw himself "as a young newt, / neurasthenic, scarlet / and wild in the wild coffee-colored water"; in "The Neo-Classical Urn" he identifies himself not only with the turtles confined in the urn but also with their unfeeling captor: Lowell himself as a child. The garden urn is transmuted, in "Night Sweat" (68), into the urn of the body, a container for memories: "always inside me is the child who died."

Lowell's most extensive and thorough treatment of the subject of memory in *For the Union Dead* is "Eye and Tooth" (18), in which he dramatizes the complicated nature of that shadowy filter through which the poet sees the past. Irvin Ehrenpreis describes the poem in these words: "The poem depends on a brilliant use of the *eye*—I pun. Treating vision as memory or id, Lowell presents the voyeur poet's eye as an unwreckable showcase of displeasing memories that both shape and torment the person. The dominating metaphor is, so to speak, 'I've got something in my I and can't get it out.'"[9] This poem was not the first occasion on which Lowell had associated his eye and his I. Writing to Cousin Harriet in December of 1955, he describes "our first movie in two months, The eye of a Camera." But the typed words "The eye of" are crossed out, and written above them in Elizabeth Hardwick's handwriting are the words "I am"; at the end of

---

[8] "Searchings 1," *Notebook* (New York, 1970), 35.
[9] Ehrenpreis, "Age of Lowell," *American Poetry* (New York, 1965), 94.

the letter she has added a note saying that "You will see the marks of my editing here."[10] And in "Near the Unbalanced Aquarium," one of the prose reminiscences that Lowell wrote as part of his therapy, and which would serve as the basis for some of the poems in *Life Studies*, he made this association explicit. "Nearly blind with myopia" as a result of having dropped his eyeglasses from a third-story window, "I was reborn each time I saw my blurred, now unspectacled, now unprofessorial face in the mirror."[11] Here the fuzzy vision has the potential to banish bad memories, to give him a fresh start; but as the rest of the story makes dear, no such beginning is forthcoming.

"Eye and Tooth," too, begins with a juxtaposition of the eye and the I: "My whole eye was sunset red, / the old cut cornea throbbed, / I saw things darkly, / as through an unwashed goldfish globe." As the rest of the poem will make clear, the "old cut cornea" represents among other things, in Stephen Yenser's words, "the flaw in man's nature, original sin, which 'Nothing can dislodge.'"[12] "My eyes throb," the poet complains in the fourth stanza. "Nothing can dislodge / the house with my first tooth / noosed in a knot to the doorknob." Apparently remembering an incident from his childhood, Lowell here represents this memory of an unpleasant experience as a tangible, physical object in his eye (I).

The association of memory with sin begins in the next stanzas, which, as several critics have noticed, are closely related to a prose passage in Lowell's essay on William Carlos Williams:

> An image held my mind . . .Can old-fashioned New England cottage freshly painted white. I saw a shaggy, triangular shade on the house, trees, a hedge, or their shadows, the blotch of decay. The house . . . came from the time when I was a child, still unable to read, and living in the small town of Bamstable on Cape Cod. Inside the house was a bird book with an old stiff and steely engraving of a sharp-shinned hawk. The hawk's legs had a reddish-brown buffalo fuzz on them; behind was the blue sky, bare and abstracted from the world (*Collected Prose* 37-38).[13]

In his description of the triangular shade on the house, the shadows, "the blotch of decay," we may perhaps sense a similarity to the darkening stain

---

[10] Lowell to Winslow, Dec. 27, 1955, Lowell collection (Harvard).

[11] *Collected Prose* (New York, 1987), 354.

[12] Yenser, *Circle to Circle* (Berkeley, 1975), 216.

[13] See Steven Axelrod, *Robert Lowell: Life and Art* (Princeton 1978), 155; Phillip Cooper, *Autobiographical Myth* (Chapel Hill, 1970), 114; Crick, 97-98.

of memory Lowell adapted from Elizabeth Bishop in "The Scream." In any event, the poet in "Eye and Tooth" juxtaposes the memory of the triangular blotch with the remembered image of the hawk, whose cold eye seemed to pronounce judgment on the small boy:

> Nothing can dislodge
> the triangular blotch
> of rot on the red roof,
> a cedar hedge, or the shade of a hedge.
>
> No ease from the eye
> of the sharp-shinned hawk in the birdbook there,
> with reddish brown buffalo hair
> on its shanks, one ascetic talon
>
> clasping the abstract imperial sky.
> It says:
> *an eye for an eye,*
> *a tooth for a tooth.*

The eye is both judge and instrument of punishment, the super-ego made concrete. And the eye is the instrument of the crime as well: "No ease for the boy at the keyhole, / his telescope, / when the women's white bodies flashed / in the bathroom. Young, my eyes began to fail." As Alan Holder has pointed out, we learn in "Art of the Possible" [in *Day by Day*] that "for a winter or so, / when eleven or twelve," the poet "nightly enjoyed [his] mother bathing" in the bathroom;[14] and there is no ease for the boy, no ease from the eye, no ease, now, for the man whose eyes are full of memories: "Nothing! No oil / for the eye, nothing to pour / on those waters or flames. / I am tired. Everyone's tired of my turmoil."

Robert Lowell's Language of the Self (Chapel Hill, 1988), 106-112.

---

[14] Holder, "Going Back," *Robert Lowell*, ed. Steven Axelrod and Helen Deese (New York, 1986), 162.

He Holds America to Its Ideals: *The Old Glory*

Albert Gelpi

The Old Glory is, for many reasons, an event in American literature. Robert Lowell, by wide recognition the most distinguished poet of mid-century America, has written a trilogy of plays adapted from stories by two of our most renowned nineteenth-century writers, Nathaniel Hawthorne and Herman Melville.

In Lowell's own development *The Old Glory* extends his involvement in the condition of life around him. The auto-biographical poet of *Life Studies* has come more and more to feel his tragic conviction confirmed in the world in which he lives; his last volume of poems was called, with a sense of tragedy, *For the Union Dead*. These three one-act plays turn on incidents from seventeenth, eighteenth, and early nineteenth-century American history to become, for the twentieth century, a profoundly disturbing dramatic reading of the development of the American character. Looking back, Lowell writes for the troubled present with a dread of impending doom.

The stories are not so much models as points of reference and departure. In place of Hawthorne's elaborate cadences and Melville's rich rhetoric, Lowell has made a lean and flexible line—spare yet responsive to the varied needs of the dramatic situation. The result is verse clean of all obtrusive ornament and tinglingly clear to the ear—yet capable of the full range of effects from introspection to atmospheric description to passionate declamation, from broad jokes to subtle ironies to heightened recognitions.

The finely controlled lines are tuned and timed to a fully orchestrated production which would coordinate speech, action, costume, and scenery; they were not written to be read, though they read superbly, but to be heard in vital expression on the stage. Lowell's masterful achievement initiates serious poetic drama in America.

The flag of identify and identification—or rather a series of flags—is the developing symbol as the plays move, each in its own tempo and style, to the same violent conclusion: in the name of or under the guise of freedom, a bloody outbreak as ruthless as the force it vanquishes.

The first play, "Endecott and the Red Cross," delineates the intellectual and moral ambiguities which lie at the heart of Lowell's vision. The dramatist has brought together two Hawthorne stories about Endecott: "The Maypole of Merry Mount" and the story of the title. In the first story the Puritan soldier-governor of Salem overruns an enclave of riotous, pleasure-seeking Anglicans headed by Thomas Morton; in the second he leads the resistance to the Rev. Blackstone, the emissary of the new Royal Governor. Lowell yokes these two acts of defiance in a single dramatic action.

Blackstone speaks for the established authority of Church and Crown, while Morton represents a new American type, willing to use church and state for a façade as he greedily pursues his selfish goals, money and pleasure. When the fierce Puritan Elder Palfry, speaking for an opposing theocracy, tries to pressure Endecott into a more rigorous exercise of power, Endecott emerges as the pivotal figure and fullest consciousness in the play.

This man of conscience temporizes until faced by a power alliance of the Church and Crown of England with Morton the amoral American tradesman. The "calamitous moment" of choice has been forced on him. Much against his will and painfully aware of the implication, Endecott rallies his troops with a martial call to strike against the king and bishops of England in the name of their freedom and religion. Morton and Blackstone are clamped into irons; Merry Mount is razed.

The last image of the play is Endecott, alone and brooding over the trampled flag of England. He knows, if no one else does, that the first declaration of American independence was vitiated in its inception. His patriotic speech was a practical expediency: "a hollow, dishonest harangue, / half truth, half bombast," declaimed to rouse the ignorant to violence. He had already foreseen the inevitable course of empire: "Only God goes on existing. We'll be over quickly. . . ."

"My Kinsman, Major Molyneux," the simplest of the three plays, follows Hawthorne more closely, but Lowell makes the action more explicitly political. During the outbreak of the Revolution in Boston, two country boys arrive to look for their wealthy and influential relative, who had promised them an easy life and profitable career. A Charon-like ferryman deposits the boy in an infernal "city of the dead"; the citizens of Boston are no democrats intent upon the rights of man but bizarre figures in a ghastly nightmare. Oblivious to the rebellious ferment and to the fact that their kinsman is a hated Tory tea-trader, the boys wander through the streets only to be rebuffed and reviled.

Finally the rabble drag Major Molyneux forward and in orgiastic fury execute their victim, stripping him of his possessions as they proclaim hypocritically: "All tyrants must die as this man died." And, caught up in this bloodletting, the boys have been initiated into manhood, into city life, into urban America.

"Benito Cereno" is the most fully developed drama of the three. It takes place in 1800 in the Caribbean on the orderly, shipshape President

Adams flying the stars and stripes in the China trade, and on a decaying Spanish slave vessel named the San Domingo (Columbus's landing place). Lowell has changed Melville's tale of illusion and reality, American innocence and European corruption, into a weird fable that defines an authoritarian and imperialist disposition toward the Negro and toward other nations in terms that suggest recurring problems of American history down to the present difficulties with civil rights and foreign policy.

Captain Delano of the President Adams is "a true American" who intones: "when a man's in office, Sir, we all pull behind him!" When he meets the diseased and demented Captain Cereno, he spots him as an example of the Old World in his practical "inexperience, sickness, impotence, and aristocracy."

As for slavery itself, shortly after declaring "each man will have his share" of the provision he has brought because "that's how we do things in the States," he confesses blandly: "Sometimes I think we overdo our talk of freedom. / If you looked into our hearts, we all want slaves." His naive invulnerability keeps him from guessing the menacing eruption of the blacks until the very last.

As the rioting slaves are slaughtered by the American sailors, Cereno's servant Babu becomes the spokesman of the awakening new peoples: "Yankee Master understand me. The future is with us." The insensible Delano cries "This is your future" and thinks he is extinguishing the threat by pumping six bullets into Babu.

The Old Glory is a heroic act of dissenting patriotism. The title is bitterly ironic: the glory is more than past and gone, it never existed. And yet Robert Lowell's unflinching honesty displays a peculiarly American insistence on demanding the most of ourselves and on probing all the ambiguities of our motives and intentions.

Many of our artists have found themselves saying NO in thunder to the main thrust of the nation's course, but their dissent has proceeded from the conscience of a peculiarly American idealism: we are not what we say, what we ought to be. Not just Hawthorne and Melville, but even so serene a spirit as Emerson could turn angrily on his country because of its materialism, its use of slaves, its imperialism against Mexico: "Virtue falters; Right is hence; / Freedom praised, but hid; / Funeral eloquence / Rattles the coffin-lid."

Robert Lowell has become a presence in the nation, not as a smiling sage like Emerson and Whitman and the public Frost, but as a blackly blazing New England prophet of the Apocalypse whose funeral eloquence rattles the coffin lid without expecting to avert the doom and whose jeremiads spell out in flaming letters these words—half warning, half prayer—from the final play of the trilogy: "God save America from Americans."

Taken together, *The Old Glory* is an immense and impressive feat of imaginative assimilation and imaginative projection. No one concerned with American letters—and America—can overlook these plays; they are the first successful American poetic drama, and a tragic reading of our destiny pronounced with the measured ferocity of a moral concern as deep as it is dark.

Christian Science Monitor (Dec. 16, 1965), 11.

A New Version of American Innocence: Robert Lowell's *Benito Cereno*

Albert E. Stone

An important cultural event occurred on November 1, 1964, when Robert Lowell's *The Old Glory* had its premiere at the American Place Theatre in New York. Audience and critics alike responded enthusiastically to the adaptation in verse of two classic American stories—Hawthorne's "My Kinsman, Major Molineux" and Melville's *Benito Cereno*. In spite of staging difficulties, Lowell's play was hailed as a major achievement. A highlight of the 1964-1965 season, it won five prizes. To many it appeared that the American stage, divorced since the death of T. S. Eliot from contact with poets of the first rank, had now found an impressive ally, a poet with theatrical flair to go with gifts of language and imagination. "The American drama has finally developed an important subject and an eloquent voice," declared Robert Brustein. "*The Old Glory* may well mark the beginning of a dramatic renaissance in America. . . ."[1]

Whether Brustein's prophecy has been fulfilled is unclear, but there seems little doubt that Lowell's achievement has given fresh impetus to a movement, the revival of interest in historical literature, much underrated by some critics of contemporary American culture. Such a revival has been dismissed by historians like Warren I. Susman, who in 1964 declared that "the last two decades in America have been marked by

---

[1] Introduction, *The Old Glory*, rev. ed (New York, 1968), 217.

a singularly anti-historical spirit among the leading figures of our intellectual life."[2] Such pronouncements, drawing support from "end-to-ideology" social scientists like Daniel Bell, seem inappropriate to the literary situation, however, when one recalls careers like Faulkner's, Warren's and Conrad Richter's, the distinguished group of works issued during these decades, including *The Crucible* (1953), *The Sot-Weed Factor* (1960), *Little Big Man* (1964), and *The Confessions of Nat Turner* (1967), as well as less well-known works on similar themes like Martin Duberman's *In White America* (1964) and Ishmael Reed's recent *Yellow Back Radio Broke-Down* (1969). Robert Lowell's play about the American past by no means stands alone. It is further proof of the fact that the Fifties and Sixties were actually decades in which many of our most imaginative artists were engaged in confronting the national past and finding forms for its configurations and complexities.

Announcing either rebirth or continuity, *The Old Glory* speaks with Lowell's typically emphatic voice. Many readers or playgoers would say: too loud and harsh, and not very subtle as compared to the modulated ironies of Hawthorne and Melville. Such critics lament particularly Lowell's ideological transformation of Melville's original tale of the slave insurrection aboard a Spanish ship at the beginning of the nineteenth century. Long a favorite among ambiguity-relishing critics, Melville's *Benito Cereno* seems to surrender its gray web of subtleties to Lowell's strident black-and-white assertions. We are reminded of Herbert Blau's well-known comment about Arthur Miller's *The Crucible*, another drama ostensibly cast in black-and-white categories. "This absence of doubt," declared Blau, "reduced the import of *The Crucible* for those who thought about it, while increasing the impact for those who didn't."[3] So, too, for many traditionalists in Robert Lowell's audiences who see the tale's complexity sacrificed to melodramatic "relevance."

There is no doubt that *Benito Cereno*, as the climactic part of *The Old Glory*, closes with a brutal directness more reminiscent of LeRoi Jones [Amiri Baraka] than of Melville. How else to characterize Lowell's quite original denouement? Captain Amasa Delano, having rescued Don Benito from his rebellious slaves, advances upon Babu who has surrendered and empties six pistol shots into the defenseless black's body. "This is your future," cries the captain in whose "enduring innocence" we have nearly all believed.[4] The "rockslide force" of this and earlier scenes

---

[2] "History and the American Intellectual," *American Quarterly* 16 (1964): 260.
[3] *The Impossible Theatre* (New York, 1964), 191.
[4] Allen Guttmann, "The Enduring Innocence of Captain Amasa Delano," *Boston University Studies in English* 5 (1961): 35-45.

goes as far in stripping innocence from the American past as Lowell's autobiographical verse goes to remove traditional wraps from the poet's private life.[5] The two effects are related, for Lowell's play—like *Life Studies* and *For the Union Dead*—brings into history and art some of the bitter clarifying insights of psychotherapy. But its affective power derives less from psychology than from the playwright's uncompromising gaze into the past—into the faces of American corruption and innocence, of violence and aggression, as common bonds between past and present, between history and autobiography. *The Old Glory* will endure as an important work of art and cultural document precisely because it compresses history and personal experience into a form of "literary power," which as Leo Marx has recently reasserted is far more important than "representative value" for determining a book's permanent worth.[6] This essay will consider three components of that literary power. The first two—achieved dramatic form and appropriate poetic language—help make possible the third, that characteristic historical imagination of Lowell's which expresses the complexities of the historical record in the stark simplicities of image and scene. Each of these aspects of *Benito Cereno* is heightened and sharpened by the spirit of Herman Melville, the angel or father with whom the modern poet wrestled. For it was Melville who first opened the pages of Captain Amasa Delano's *Narrative of Voyages and Travels* (1817) and translated its Chapter XVIII into fictional art.

One might begin by asking why Lowell's choice of this particular story involved him also in choosing drama, and especially poetic drama, as the necessary form of his re-creation. The glib biographical answer would be to say that, shortly before commencing on *The Old Glory*, Lowell held a fellowship as poet-librettist with the Metropolitan and New York City Operas. A more fundamental explanation in the same vein would be to note how much of Lowell's verse is "imitation" wherein the reader is invited, in Lowell's own words, to hear "one voice running through many personalities, contrasts and repetitions."[7] *Benito Cereno* is one such imitation, with his own voice as undertone to Melville's, as his own form of poetic drama is the translation of essential qualities of the original.

---

[5] The phrase is W. D. Snodgrass's; see "In Praise of Robert Lowell," *New York Review of Books* (Dec. 3, 1964): 8.
[6] Marx, "American Studies—A Defense of an Unscientific Method," *New Literary History* 1 (1969): 80.
[7] *Imitations* (New York, 1961), xi.

The *Benito Cereno* of 1855 is a leisurely-paced narrative of some seventy or eighty pages, but it possesses also a dramatic form and spirit, in spite of Melville's preoccupation with point of view. This dual nature is suggested early. When Delano first boards the *San Dominick*, he reflects that the scene "seems unreal; these strange costumes, gestures, and faces, but a shadowy tableau just emerged from the deep, which directly must receive back what it gave." The sense of life here as "a shadowy tableau" increases all day. To the Yankee's perplexed mind, the Spaniard's decks resemble a stagebox and a pit. At the shaving ceremony Don Benito wears a "theatrical aspect . . . in his harlequin ensign." This effect of theatrical enchantment or charade is crucial, describing as it does not only atmosphere but the shape of the action, the revelation of character (or, rather, its masking), and ultimately the very meaning of experience itself. Everything in Melville's sea-world is prolonged mystification, "dreamy inquietude" suddenly dispelled by violence. Lowell was inspired, I suspect, to adapt *Benito Cereno* not only by its theme but also because he saw that this tone and atmosphere could be handled dramatically and poetically through modern versions of Melville's own devices, tableau and imagery.

The chief means Lowell has used to dramatize prolonged mystery is poetic language itself, which by its formality, rhythm, and economy creates a speech deliberately measured but subtly heightened in tempo. Melville's topics, tropes, and vocabulary are employed but never apart from Lowell's modern idiom. Sometimes there is more Lowell than Melville, but where this is the case the tone manages to evoke both writers and both epochs. A prime example of this mixing is the revealing pair of "dream" speeches which the two captains exchange just before the shaving scene (*Old Glory* 180-82). . . . Here, in the Kafkaesque insect imagery used earlier in *The Old Glory*, the Spaniard describes symbolically the situation aboard the *San Domingo* while ostensibly commenting upon his own childhood innocence. Each dreamy detail affects the mood and increases dramatic irony. For Captain Delano wholly misses the message of Benito's dream; indeed, its full meaning is hid even from Benito himself. Delano replies: "Ha, ha, Captain. We are like two dreams meeting head-on" (182). Lowell's deceptively simple language, by avoiding extremes of poetic eloquence or flat naturalism, points in two directions at once—*back* at Melville's context if the reader remembers it and at Lowell's present moment in case he doesn't. The slight puzzlement or dislocation this produces becomes a part of the theme and mood of the play. Moreover, many other speeches share the thematic shape of this one of Benito's—which begins in innocence and stasis, modulates through mystery and defilement, and arrives at death. Thus the pattern of the whole is often repeated in the part, the poetic method of synecdoche which tightens rather than distracts from the dramatic form.

If Lowell's *Benito Cereno* is *poetic* drama it is just as clearly poetic *drama*. The poet-playwright has used several devices to translate Melville's metaphysical and character-probing tale into a theatrical expression. The most obvious of these translations, as Robert Ilson has pointed out, is the alteration and addition of characters.[8] But apart from the recasting of Delano's character—signaled most conclusively in those six deliberately anachronistic pistol shots—the most arresting device is the tableau. Picking up Melville's own term, Lowell has created a series of allegorical "entertainments" which Babu, the other slaves, and the captive Spanish sailors present for Delano's bewilderment and enlightenment as he passes the day on the *San Domingo*. Each of these brief plays-within-the-play has its source in Melville, yet each bears a modern meaning as well. The not-so-secret significance of each tableau is slavery, the "yellow fever" which is man's curse and rebellion's justification. Slavery's saffron hue is literally and symbolically presented both in the Spanish flag and in Francesco, the mulatto waiter on Don Benito's table, who is "as yellow as a goldenrod" (194). In living color he manifests the linked sexual and economic exploitation of slavery. (This meaning is extended into history through the images of Benito's yellow hands, Delano's yellow life-giving pumpkins, Atufal's golden ear-wedges, and the rising and setting sun, all of which hint at the corrupting legacy America inherits from the "absentee empire" of Spain.) Slavery is represented in the other tableaux by a white doll-baby. This doll is first dipped in tar, next entered in a chess match, and then cuddled by a black Virgin Mary while a white Saint Joseph looks uncomfortably on. Thus slavery is both a black and a yellow plague.

These grim charades dramatize Melville's vignettes while at the same time they carry out the de-mythification of these very scenes. For in place of Melville's religious and cultural generalizations Lowell substitutes, or adds, the far more specific realities of American politics, economics, and sex as these factors focus historically upon race. Thus Lowell transforms Melville's largely mythical pattern of details and images into an ideological series of dramatic actions. In the process, a certain loss of dramatic pace and focus may be the price of Lowell's historicism. The force of his *Benito Cereno* flows in large measure from the way in which poetic language and dramatic structure combine to move

---

[8] Ilson, "*Benito Cereno* from Melville to Lowell," *Robert Lowell*, ed. Thomas Parkinson (Englewood Cliffs, 1968), 135-142. I am indebted to Mr. Ilson's analysis, though I disagree with his interpretation of Delano as a "liberal." Imprecise as such tags are, I would apply it rather to John Perkins.

the action from a mythic plane into the historical and ideological without wholly destroying the range of resonances Melville has established. The play's movement, from desultory dialogue to enigmatic tableau to violent, sudden action, results in a compacting of the loose riches of Melville's story into a powerful and dramatic historical parable.

To regard *Benito Cereno* as an ideological parable of our past is to be reminded that Robert Lowell's verse since the beginning of his career has been characterized by stark moral energy and violence. His friendly critic Randall Jarrell (to whom *The Old Glory* is dedicated) once observed with wry honesty that "some of his earlier satires of present-day politics . . . have a severe crudity that suggest Michael Wigglesworth rewriting the Horatian Ode."[9] Yet if *Benito Cereno* is a latter-day jeremiad, it thunders with a range of historical references at least as rich and organized as the literary and theological references of earlier works like *Lord Weary's Castle*. No playgoer can miss the ironic interplay between different aspects and eras of American experiences evoked on the deck of the San Domingo. Lowell's *Benito Cereno* reeks with relevance. The play recalls Melville's pre-Civil War world of 1855, largely by way of making contrasts with Lowell's world of 1964. These contrasts emphasize the related themes of national character, politics, and racial violence. This shift is signaled in small but significant ways. We note, for instance, that although Melville places his story in 1799, Lowell has moved the action to July 4, 1800. Captain Delano's original account in the *Narrative*, however, specifies that the insurrection actually occurred in February, 1805. Similarly, the two ships' names are again changed. Melville had already made one symbolic substitution: the original *Tryal* became the *San Dominick*, while Delano's ship the *Perseverance*, became the *Bachelor's Delight*. Lowell re-christens the vessels the San Domingo and the *President Adams* and moves the locale from the coast of Chile to the Caribbean. The playwright emphasizes the political implications of these shifts by introducing into the dialogue echoes of many other times, persons, and events. The American and French Revolutions, Toussaint L'Ouverture, Gabriel Prosser, the election of 1800, Civil War and Emancipation, Caribbean history and dollar diplomacy, the contemporary civil rights struggle—all these and other connections are suggested. Lowell's cultural perspective reaches even into the future. Though he could not have anticipated them, the American intervention in the Dominican Republic in 1965 and the rhetoric of present-day Black

---

[9] Jarrell, "From the Kingdom of Necessity," *Poetry and the Age* (New York, 1955), 194.

Panthers are developments which the reader of Lowell's play can readily relate to Babu's later speeches on the deck of the *San Domingo*.

This rich pattern of historical allusion becomes part of the overall theme of *The Old Glory*. Beginning with *Endecott and the Red Cross*, the opening play Lowell found too difficult to stage but which forms part of the printed version, and proceeding through *My Kinsman, Major Molineux* and *Benito Cereno*, Lowell's trilogy traces the emergence of an American national identity from seventeenth-century beginnings in New England, through the Revolutionary trauma, to a point of definition with Jefferson's election in 1800. The flag, the Old Glory, is the ironic symbol of this identity. Its various shades of red all announce that power, aggression, violence of all sorts (including specifically sexual) is the inherited keynote of American character. Like Sigmund Freud, Robert Lowell has an essentializing imagination. Yet innocent idealism, too, is part of the pattern of history. In each play, these twin aspects, the major and the minor, are represented dramatically by a young person, placed at or near the center of the action, and an older figure (ultimately sinister) who conducts, as it were, the younger's initiation. In *My Kinsman, Major Molineux*, to be sure, the pattern is slightly different; Robin Molineux, the Deerfield youth, is the innocent, while a number of the townspeople assist the Man with the Mask in educating Robin and his bloodthirsty younger brother. Here, of course, the innocent initiate is John Perkins, the youthful bosun of the *President Adams* and Delano's relative. To see Amasa Delano himself as the sinister older man is to recognize at once the chief difference between Melville's story and Lowell's play. Delano's pistol points the moral as it symbolically demonstrates the later development of American racism between Delano's first incarnation in 1855 and his second in 1964. Between the two dates, Lowell reminds us, has intervened a century of war, reconstruction, lynching, and racial discrimination. Thus Babu suffers his recurring historical fate as he falls under the white man's bullets. John Perkins, as well, enacts his future, and it is indeed an ambiguous one. At the very moment that his kinsman reveals with brutal suddenness his hitherto masked violence and racism, Perkins is crying out: "Let him surrender. Let him surrender. / We want to save someone" (214).

The audience, seeing the juxtaposed acts of the two white Yankees, is both dismayed and reassured. We recognize that, although the promise of American life was once brotherhood, its actual fulfillment in history has too often been racial murder. More cynically, of course, we can view Perkins simply as a decoy. Innocent and well-meaning as he may now appear, this green Yankee liberal can only lose his altruism and flexibility. As he grows up he will inevitably resemble his urbane, racist relative. John Perkins represents Lowell's bow to Melville's original man of obtuse good will, Amasa Delano. His own Captain expresses the grimmer realities of American experience which Melville, despite his political sympathies, could not have anticipated in 1855. Lowell's recognition of American history both as innocent promise and corrupt fullfillment is embodied in the two Yankee characters he has put in the place of Melville's one.

Lowell's historicism displays itself most clearly as it realizes for his audience the pastness of our present, the contemporaneity of our past. However, many readers or playgoers, wedded to the metaphysical subtleties of Melville's version of *Benito Cereno*, resist Lowell's reformulations. Such ideological treatment, they feel, represents both a misunderstanding of Melville's broader intentions and of the historical record of the real Captain Delano on which Melville based his tale. The nub of the issue has been stated in classic form by Yvor Winters:

> When Cereno is finally rescued by Captain Delano, he is broken in spirit, and says that he can return home but to die. When Captain Delano inquires what has cast such a shadow upon him, he answers: "The negro." His reply in Spanish would have signified not only the negro, or the black man, but by metaphorical extension the basic evil in human nature. The morality of slavery is not an issue in this story; the issue is this, . . . the fundamental evil of groups of men, evil which normally should have been kept in abeyance, was freed to act.[10]

Now this interpretation, Lowell would assert emphatically, may be a moral and perhaps a metaphysical reading of Melville's novella, but it is no longer historically valid. Not only is it ahistorical with respect to what we know of the history of the Spanish empire and of American history, it is ahistorical with respect to Captain Delano's *Narrative of Voyages and Travels*, a piece of American history published in 1817.

Anyone who has looked into the book which inspired Melville recognizes several dimensions to the relationship between the three works. First of all, one sees that Chapter XVIII of Delano's *Narrative* is, like all narrative history, itself a *literary* account with a rudimentary plot and theme of its own. Moreover, as Rosalie Feltenstein has demonstrated,[11] one perceives how radically Melville rearranged the facts of Delano's

---

[10] Winters, *Maule's Curse;* rpt. in *In Defense of Reason* (Denver, 1947), 222.
[11] Feltenstein, "Melville's 'Benito Cereno,'" *American Literature* 19 (1947): 245-55.

account to suit his own fictional and philosophical purposes." Furthermore, even casual inspection should convince us that Lowell's melodramatic alterations actually fit the historical source at least as well as Melville's fiction does. This, in spite of the fact that Lowell acknowledges no specific debt to Delano's *Narrative*; it is not one of the sources listed in the prefatory note to *The Old Glory*. For the "fundamental evil" which Melville's story assigns in one way to blacks and whites is distributed quite differently in Delano's book. The brutality, violence, and sordid motives belong there chiefly to the whites—to the Spaniards but also to the Americans. "History," in short, took in this case more closely the shape of Lowell's melodrama than of Melville's metaphysics.

Three or four details from the *Narrative* history of the insurrection may illustrate and substantiate Lowell's intuitive or backward-working historical awareness. First—and least important—is Amasa Delano's innocent, well-intentioned American character. By his own account, the real Delano was a middle-aged, tough-minded disciplinarian as well as a cheerful giver. With a gang of Botany Bay convicts for a crew—hardly the "comfortable family" of the *Bachelor's Delight*—Delano describes himself as a ready flogger and perfectly prepared to lead the boarding party himself. Speaking to the boarders, he said:

> I told them that Don Bonito [*sic*] considered the ship and what was in her as lost; that the value was more than one hundred thousand dollars; that if we would take her, it should be all our own; and that if we should afterwards be disposed to give him up one half, I would be considered as a present. I likewise reminded them of suffering condition of the poor Spaniards remaining on board, whom I then saw with my spy-glass as high aloft as they could get on the top-gallant-masts, and knowing that death must be their fate if they came down. I told them, never to see my face again, if they did not take her; and these were all of them pretty powerful stimulants.[12]

Economic gain, it seems clear, was central to the motives of the Americans in this rescue, and bloody violence was a natural means to that end. Melville plays down or ignores this side of Delano's nature; Lowell binds it, through imagery, into every part of his drama. His Delano shares

---

[12] Amasa Delano, *Narrative of Voyages and Travels in the Northern and Southern Hemispheres* (Boston 1887), 327.

the complexity of the historical captain. Other details show how "unhistorically" Melville draws the other white man in the tale. Don Benito, by Delano's account, was as far from Melville's melancholy monk as could be imagined. Benito—and not Babu—had the secreted dirk with which he tried to stab a defenseless slave who had already surrendered. Rather than retreating to Mount Agonia to die, the actual Don solicited accusations of piracy against Delano from his own crew, so as to avoid paying the Americans for the rescue of his ship and slaves. A final detail concerns Babu, the ringleader who was actually killed by an American sailor in the attack. It was another black's head on that pole in the plaza (Delano 320, 328, 334). Lowell's dramatized version of these events, though it subordinates Cereno and suppresses much of *his* historical identity, preserves the economic and racial realities of Delano's *Narrative*. If Lowell did not consult Delano's *Narrative* directly, he clearly did consult his own sense of American historical realities. The result is drama curiously faithful to its ultimate source.

Thus in radically different ways and to quite different ends Lowell and Melville explore and exploit an isolated, representative episode out of our past. Both approaches enlarge the implications of Delano's Chapter XVIII by incorporating it within an imaginative structure. Melville, toward the close of his fictional narrative, openly embraces history by reprinting long selections from Delano's account of the Peruvian court records. But this recapitulation of the "facts" establishes no certainties; it simply demonstrates anew the inadequacy of what passes for history as a trustworthy source of the truth of human motivation. The historical report then gives way to the captain's enigmatic conversation about "the negro," which in turn is succeeded by the final scene of Babu's Iago-like death. Thus, for Melville, myth absorbs ideology and the reader is left with a triple puzzle to contemplate—the mystery of innocence, of morbidity, and of iniquity.

Lowell's finale, on the contrary, moves in precisely the opposite direction—away from myth towards ideology. After the American seamen have rescued the whites with their muskets and bayonets, an unwounded and defiant Babu shouts:

> I freed my people from their Egyptian bondage.
> The heartless Spaniards slaved for me like slaves.
> [*Babu steps back, and quickly picks up a crown from the litter*]
> This is my crown.
> [*Puts crown on his head. He snatches Benito's rattan cane*]
> This is my rod.
> [*Picks up silver ball*]

This is the earth.
[*Holds the ball out with one hand and raises the cane*]
   This is the arm of the angry God.
[*Smashes the ball*]
Perkins: Let him surrender. Let him surrender.
   We want to save someone.
Benito: My God how little these people understand!
Babu: [*Holding a white handkerchief and raising both hands*]
   Yankee Master understand me. The future is with us.
Delano: [*Raising his pistol.*]
   This is your future.
[*Babu falls and lies still. Delano pauses, then slowly empties the five remaining barrels of his pistol into the body. Lights dim*]
                         CURTAIN   (213-14)

If Babu's Biblical language and symbolic gestures begin to focus this climax within Melville's framework of religious and monarchical images, this reach for universal implication is immediately destroyed by the white men's words and acts. Dream is overwhelmed by actuality as Lowell brings his audience back with chilling speed to the world of 1964—and after.

There is, of course, no single form of the historical imagination appropriate to the poet, playwright, or novelist of this age. Lowell's strategy of historical melodrama is one among many. Superficially, his *Benito Cereno* resembles Arthur Miller's *The Crucible*; both dramatize isolated episodes freighted with violence and passion and bearing a persistently contemporary significance; both fabricate a special theatrical language for the occasion, neither archaic nor modern. Yet if as historical literature, *Benito Cereno* represents the more arresting achievement, this may be due not simply to Lowell's greater respect for the *facts* of history (about which Miller is so cavalier) but to his special aptitude for the imitation. Beginning with his earliest verses, Lowell has been stimulated to his finest work by the dual act of plunging into the American past and imitating or translating older writers. In tones of unmitigated indignation and despair, he has voiced his kinship with nay-sayers like Hawthorne and Melville in opposing what Randall Jarrell has termed the "incestuous, complacent, inveterate evil of established society" (Jarrell 192). As social critic, Lowell has drawn special inspiration not only from the American tradition of dissent but from still older satirists as well, including Greek and Latin authors. "The Roman frankness interests me," Lowell once admitted to an interviewer. "Until recently our literature hasn't been as raw as the Roman, translations had to have stars. And their history has a terrible human frankness that isn't customary with us—corrosive attacks on the establishment, comments on politics and the decay of morals, all felt terribly strongly, by poets as well as historians."[13] This remark goes far toward defining—and limiting perhaps—the achievement of *The Old Glory* as contrasted with Melville's story on which its climax is based. If some readers find the play as devoid of compassion as it is of Melville's special kind of complexity this may be excused as inappropriate both to Lowell's artistic method and to his vision of American history. Unlike the philosophical meditation on history which was its inspiration, Lowell's *Benito Cereno* is as "raw as the Roman." It is a translation without stars, whose unconsoling motto may be found in Captain Delano's ironic remark about his innocent kinsman, John Perkins: "God save America from Americans!"

New England Quarterly 45 (1972):467-83.

A Tempered Triumph: *Near the Ocean*

Hilda Raz

Near the Ocean, Robert Lowell's most recent book, includes a sequence of five poems, two shorter poems, and nine translations. In the preface, Lowell explains that "the theme that connects my translations is Rome, the greatness and horror of her Empire." In his original poems, Rome becomes America. The themes are the same: the degeneration of a civilization that is rich and powerful into one that is sterile and impotent; the fall of man and God; the misuse of power in a failing world. But there is one difference between Rome and America: we have the technological ingenuity to destroy whatever life may rise from our ruin.

In the original poems, Lowell describes the physical reality of twentieth-century civilization: Central Park become a jungle, his Aunt's old house in Maine, skiing at the Mittersill, the death of a friend by water in the swimming pool of his own house. And he describes also the spirit of

---

[13] Frederick Seidel, "Robert Lowell," rpt. Parkinson, 26.

our country. Lowell's reaction to the world he displays is despair, tempered by a fine irony and controlled by symbol and form. Water, the ocean, is everywhere: now destroying, now creating, always witness to the passing of time. "Waking Early Sunday Morning," the first of the five-poem sequence, is set by the sea. It is the morning of a holy day. The constant desire for freedom of soul and self is expressed in the image of the salmon, splendid in his suffering, the suffering that allows him to die to live. The first cry—"O to break loose . . ."—is lyric; the water is white, moving. But there is a sharp discrepancy between lyric cry and actuality: "A field-mouse rolls / a marble, hours on end, then stops." We are on land, and splendid deaths are not easily achieved. The use of water has become tawdry and drab: the "wine-dark hulls of yawl and ketch" now leave a "wake of refuse" outside his window. Inside, the poet watches water that is contained by glass. Through it, he sees "some object made of wood, / background behind it of brown grain, / to darken it but not to stain." The image of small water in a glass is enlarged, and the cry breaks through again: "O that the spirit could remain / tinged but untarnished by its strain!"

Religion, the instrument by which men organize and give form to the spirit, Lowell rejects. He sees himself as "old lumber banished from the Temple, / damned by Paul's precept and example, / cast from the kingdom, banned in Israel." Still he longs for God: "When will we see Him face to face? / Each day, He shines through darker glass." After the cry comes the contrast: steeple and flagpole, God's vanished emblems, are "like old white china doorknobs, sad, / slight, useless things to calm the mad." Throughout, the form is shaped by the struggle between compelling irrationality (the cries) and the frustration that results from a rational consideration of reality. The interior dialogue concludes with a query: if the alternative to irrationality is a "sanity of self-deception / fixed and kicked by reckless caution," which is the better choice? Answering himself by tone and image in the last stanza, he equates the human body with the body politic, and the poem becomes an elegy mourning a sterile world without God or gods. He resigns hope in favor of passionless despair, saved at last only by irony.

The description of a joyless world becomes in the second poem a personal paean of despair. Entitled "Fourth of July in Maine," it is about a secular holiday commemorating a civil past that was as splendid in its way as the original holy day, God's day of rest. The central image is his Aunt's house in Maine, once fine and ordered, now filled with disorder and family dissent. A parallel contrast is implied between the national past and present. He concludes not with an elegy but with a prayer: "Great ash and sun of freedom, give / us this day the warmth to live, / and face the household fire." But the prayer is not answered: "We turn our backs, and feel the whiskey burn."

The third and fourth poems focus on objects made emblems of our society: an abandoned police garage and New York's Central Park. The garage is transformed by terror and death into "Some Spanish *casa*, luminous / with heraldry and murder." The excitement attracts a mob which is controlled only by the police: "Deterrent terror!" The poet comments, "*Viva la muerte!*" And Central Park is the product of a society in which the deterrent terror breeds only an answering violence: "We beg delinquents for our life. / Behind each bush, perhaps a knife; / each landscaped crag, each flowering shrub, / hides a policeman with a club." Lowell here transforms the octosyllabics of nursery rhyme into a brutal indictment of a brutal society.

The last poem in the sequence is the one which gives the book its title. A long poem, it is a kind of internal monologue: the poet in his many guises musing to himself, selecting those myths and memories which most clearly present his experience. The most difficult poem in the book, it is also the most brilliant, and thus inevitably assumes a central importance. Gnarled, superficially obscure, it recreates intense feeling through a rich layering of images. . . .

The first four lines dramatize the Theseus myth, the severing of the Gorgon's head; the double audience is seen as brutal, applauding not the destruction of a monster but the fact of death itself—behaving, in fact, as "a mob." There follows a more personal, less allusive kind of memory: a brother and sister facing their mother. The destructive power of the Medusa is here associated with the mother ("old iron-bruises"), but with an added sexuality ("powder"). Both hero and child know that the destruction of the woman will not destroy her power, so they become one in their search for the Medusa-mother, a woman who is at once alive yet deprived of her power: "And if she's killed . . . shifting over on his back . . . ." The search involves the penalty for a possessive closeness between mother and son: loveless and compulsive coupling.

Another twist comes in line four of the second stanza. Having presented two aspects of a feeling without presenting the events which evoke it, he then merges them through an act of memory. Consciousness and memory are the water through which filters "the severed radiance" of the Gorgon head. What is real is the dead monster, "athirst for nightlife," dredged up by memory from the ocean bed. The poet then removes himself to comment, chorus-like, on the levelling effect of time. "Lost in the Near Eastern dreck, / the tyrant and tyrannicide / lie like the bridegroom and the bride"; "Older seas / and deserts give asylum, peace / to each abortion and mistake." Here, water is time, eroding memory, healing. Peace, says the chorus. But no, the quest is never ended until the suffering begins. The speaker, as one grown, describes a relationship between a man and a woman. Their situation is described in terms of their physical surroundings, and in images which have already been established in the sequence. The first night is spent inland, away from fresh, moving water; there is only swamp and "frogs / chirring from the dark trees." There is no light, either of memory or of peace. The scene then shifts to New York, having progressed south from New England (toward the Aegean?). Some water here, cold from the faucets of the flat. Some light, but neon, manmade; and some alcoholic splendor. The lovers are sterile, surrounded by the dry "steel and coal dust" of the largest metropolis in the world, ironically situated on the ocean. Time passes. They meet, "lying like people out of work, / dead sober, cured, recovered, on / the downslope of some gritty green, / all access barred with broken Glass. . . ." The grass is brown here; there is no splendor, and no water.

In the next stanza, the water imagery returns: lost in the sea, they have found the shore. The narrator says, "Sand built the lost Atlantis." All that richness was built on the rubble of past cities, on eroded stones and rotted civilizations. The implicit question is whether we can build something splendid on our sand, on the rubble of our personal past. The final stanza explicitly unites the powerful and destructive figure of the Medusa with the speaker's companion, his wife: "I'm afraid to touch the crisp hairs on your head." And with the recognition of their unity comes a kind of peace. The ocean, here again, is time, grinding the stones of present experience into sand which is ultimately land: "Monster loved for what you are, / till time, that buries us, lay bare." The poem is an analysis of a personal relationship that offers no hope of salvation, only the temporary suspension of consciousness, the peace which is sleep. There is no ultimate ecstasy, no ultimate meaning. The best that man can do is to recognize the human condition, to suffer it and to wait. There is no grand tragedy in the corruption of our civilization; it too will be eroded by the sea, and will rise again with the same potential for corruption.

Two short poems separate the translations from the opening sequence. The first, "For Theodore Roethke," celebrates Lowell's close contemporary as one who "quickened" the "Waters under the earth" until "the mother" made him "nonexistent, / the ocean's anchor, our high tide." The second, called simply "1958," is a love poem; it recalls once more the salmon image from ["Waking Early Sunday Morning"].

Lowell's translations, which he has issued over a period of some twenty years, have won the respect of poet and scholar alike. It might well be said that if a great poet can show his genius in many ways, he is most generous when he uses it to translate and so enrich the poets of other times and civilizations. But it is also clear that the translations Lowell includes in this volume maintain his theme and expand the ironic vision: the harshly rhythmic but unrhymed verse which he uses for the Juvenal, for example, recreates the moral impact of Juvenal in the idiom of our own day. In like manner, the four translations from Quevedo and Gongora—joined under the title of "The Ruins of Time"—parallel the original poems in mood and structure. Here, too, Lowell reminds us that we live near the ocean, our world wasting around us, our civilization rank with decay and we no more able to renew it than were those civilizations that sank before us.

Robert Lowell is a great poet, and this book reconfirms it. His continued growth, evident to anyone who compares *Near the Ocean* with his earlier work, is good evidence that the human spirit can still achieve at least the salmon's triumph.

Prairie Schooner 41 (Winter 1967): 439-42.

The Achievement of *Near the Ocean*

Alan Williamson

In June, 1965, Robert Lowell refused to attend President Johnson's White House Festival of the Arts, as a protest against the war in Vietnam. It was Lowell's most widely publicized political act since his conscientious objection (later in the anti-war movement, he again risked imprisonment by joining Dr. Spock and others in support of draft resisters). Lowell has credited this refusal with providing the initial impetus for his five-part poem *Near the Ocean*, which must therefore have been composed in a period of intense creative activity, since two parts of it were in print within three months after the festival.

In *Near the Ocean*, Lowell resumes, really for the first time since *Lord Weary's Castle*, the full authority of the poet-prophet. No longer an isolated observer cautiously and conscientiously locating himself in relation to intransigent realities, he seems, rather, to stand above history, grandly placing it at the disposal of his own thoughts and symbolic structures, and thus implicitly (as well as, more and more often, explicitly) judging it.

No doubt the temper of the times has something to do with Lowell's confidence here, as with his reticence in *Life Studies*. The climate of the middle 1960s tended to confer a bardic selfhood on politically engaged poets. The anti-war movement, though small, was fresher, more unified, more hopeful then than later; and it came, for many, as a philosophical, release from the myth of a benevolent technocracy beyond moral or ideological criticism which grew up in the Cold War years. The Left had the advantage, for morale and the symbolic imagination, of being able to concentrate the powers of evil in a single person—a person sufficiently complex and myth-conscious that, for a few moments in June, 1965, he conceivably saw himself as engaged in spiritual single combat by Robert Lowell. In the pages of the *New York Review*, coedited by Lowell's second wife, and in the work of Norman Mailer, a new kind of journalism put the author's personal commitments, even his free associations, squarely at the center of attention, arguing that this was more measurably objective than the impersonal style of Establishment writing, in which concealed prejudices could share the dignity of facts. When Eugene McCarthy's candidacy seemed to spring full-armed out of his own moral commitment, without the appurtenances of pragmatic power, the countermyth seemed to have become a reality. It was a good time for the idea of the Word against the world, the prophetic imagination against the reasoning spectre. Allen Ginsberg wrote, "I declare the end of the war"; and Lowell's authoritative tone (though accompanied by continued political pessimism) might be considered a distant echo of the same impulse.

On a more personal level, one might say that, as one cause of Lowell's earlier diffidence was self-distrust, one element in his new authority is an ability to make more radically imaginative connections between public and private experience. For the first time, the same poem can deal intimately with the poet's manias, depressions, artistic and sexual frustrations, and with poverty, assassinations, the war in Vietnam. And the "confessions" them-selves seem more inward—more experiential, less factual—than they were formerly. The advantages to both sides of Lowell's poetic endeavor are manifold. The artist's candor places the public beliefs in the context of a whole personality, but without thereby diminishing them, as the second stanza of "Memories of West Street and Lepke" seemed to do; while the "confession" ceases to be an end in itself and becomes an interpretive tool, illuminating by analogy the irrational motives of statesmen and masses.

Near the Ocean also becomes more bardic, perhaps, through an unusually wholehearted return to rhyme and meter. All but one of the five poems are written in tetrameter couplets, three in the four-couplet stanza of Marvell's "The Garden" and "Upon Appleton House." Marvell seems a significant ancestor; the tender irony with which he develops a double ambivalence toward the Edenic vision and the issues of ordinary experience very closely resembles Lowell's. But so, too, does Blake, in whose hands the short couplet could be a fierce instrument of political clarification and attack. Stimulated, perhaps, by these precursors, Lowell achieves a more suave and songlike tenderness, a calmer moral grandeur, than he allows himself elsewhere.

Yet *Near the Ocean* remains an extremely modern poem in which Lowell's taste for-variety and cacophony is given ample sway. In the personal poems of *For the Union Dead*, Lowell had learned—largely, I think, from Thomas Hardy—that a conspicuous, even an inept and thumping rhyme and meter, when set in counterpoint to a strong natural speech rhythm, can produce an extraordinary effect of mental energy, tension, or anguish. In *Near the Ocean*, this is achieved much more delicately; the meter itself is so emphatic, yet so limpid, that a mere inverted foot is a substantial disturbance. A jazzlike syncopation results, turning to wild improvisation when used—as it often is—in combination with heavy internal rhyming, off-rhymes, and conflicting alliterations. If the sound is jazzy, so, too, is the speech: Lowell's use of slang and hip terms is much more daring here than in *Life Studies*, and has little of its earlier derogatory overtone. Lowell seems to enjoy using vocabularies beyond his usual territory, and often makes them the starting point for brilliantly Empsonian verbal games. This new freedom, far from conflicting with Lowell's new high style, gives it the authority of a mind whose receptivity to contemporary experience is not merely intellectual but atmospheric and spiritual, whose speed is commensurate to the modern world's.

Another way one might distinguish *Near the Ocean* is to say that it is more symbolic than the preceding books—in the sense in which the last stanza of "Memories of West Street and Lepke" constitutes a return to symbolism. That is, the symbols seem to arise less from narrative particulars than from the unconscious, and to have an inborn capacity to organize the world of the poem rather than merely to participate passively in such an organization. This might be attributed simply to the exigencies of a tighter lyric, or to more daring methods of connecting the personal and the public. But I think it also suggests a turn toward a realm of archetypes—both in the sense of more inclusive and autonomous patterns of thought, and in the Freudian or Jungian sense. This is reflected, as we shall see later, in the reappearance of a mystical tendency—but expressed, now, as pure structure of experience, not a doctrinal belief.

The themes of *Near the Ocean* remain, it is true, pessimistic. They have to do with self-annihilating intensities, with processes of senescence and decay: in the Christian religion, in the American Dream, perhaps in the human species, certainly in the poet, as he ages and is forced to recognize cyclical patterns even in creative and sexual ecstasy. And yet, the sense of new possibilities found in the style is not missing from the content. Politically, there is an open expression of just anger which raises—if it never exactly defines—the possibility of radical action. Lowell's "confession" seems less clinical, more an utterance of his whole self, than it has before; and his metaphysical inquiry, too, seems at once to push toward more ultimate first principles and to rest in a richer context of inward experience. There is, as I have mentioned, the hint of a new kind of mystical consciousness. Finally, there is a quality I can only call tenderness toward humanity, which is quite new in Lowell's work; his previous poems are often tender, but always toward a single, indeed an isolated, object, the Christ Child, a friend, an animal. Lowell's attitude— at once more searching and more tender—toward his subjects, combined with the elements of strictly poetic freedom, gives the book a curious quality of lightness, vitality, and energy of vision which, in my experience, increases with rereading. Like the Puritans who continue to fascinate him, Lowell knows very well how to "*sing* of peace, and *preach* despair.". . .

The title of [*Near the Ocean*] expands in significance as the associations of the ocean do. On one level, the ocean is death, or devouring time, and the central consciousness of the poem feels close to that, certainly, in a number of senses. But the ocean is also the source of life and, symbolically, the life-impulse. We are near to it, in the poem, through the presence of intense creative and sexual energy, through the overriding image of the salmon's leap; but near also in the more dangerous, intellectual sense that modern science, and the poet's devastating intuitions, give us more knowledge and doubt about the nature of life than we are prepared to handle. Finally, the ocean may suggest a religious experience of liberation from, or dissolution of, the self in a total monistic unity, something like Freud's "oceanic feeling." Such experiences, in both their ecstatic and sinister aspects—both the "severed radiance" and the dark nirvana—come close at many points. The possibility of a total mystical experience vibrates through the opening and closing lines of the poem but is never completely realized; we remain "near," not in, the ocean.

We have seen how craftily water imagery is woven through the last poem, and the same is true elsewhere. The salmon's journey itself is a flight from water that ends in water, and still near the ocean; and the salmon cycle is neatly reversed in the last poem, where the protagonist feels the love impulse "inland" and then discovers its true limits in returning to the sea. Again, in "Waking Early Sunday Morning," the linking image gracefully juxtaposes such diverse elements as the "glass of water," the president's swimming pool, and the generals' "liquidations," and reinforces our sense of a "liquid" continuum of human energies.

Similar use is made of some less prominent symbols—for instance, the house as representative of a tradition or an attitude toward life. This is a dominant theme only in the formal house-poem "Fourth of July in Maine." But we note how, in the first poem, Lowell symbolizes his confessional material as "banished lumber," and compares it to the "Temple"; how he modulates into the New York scene through an "opposite house"; how houses (or their false analogues, apartments and theaters) appear in "*Near the Ocean.*"

The unifying power of the psychological themes derived from confession is similarly strong. We have already noted the use Lowell makes of the manic-depressive experience as a source for ideas of the patterned decay of energy and the final relativity of positive and negative attitudes toward life. An equally important theme is the psychoanalytic view of death, which we must consider briefly in the light of the theoretical background. The line of thought begins with Freud's *Beyond the Pleasure Principle.* Its argument, which I greatly oversimplify, is that man has a biological nirvana instinct which always seeks to move from tension or activity to rest, and which consequently, especially under conditions of life where tension is inescapable, ultimately desires death. Freud views this instinct as strong enough to play a dynamic role in masochism and to be converted outward into sadism, just as sexual sadistic feelings, converted inward, become masochism.

Freud's *Civilization and Its Discontents* and Marcuse's *Eros and Civilization* develop the implication that the tensions of advancing civilization must aggrandize the death instinct, a conclusion Lowell approached by a different route in "Beyond the Alps." Norman Brown's unique contribution, in *Life Against Death*, is his analysis of the fear of death (which, again, I greatly oversimplify). He contends that sexual repression prevents man from ever feeling fully alive in the moment, and makes him project fulfillment into the future or some form of immortality; hence, man must in turn repress his Freudian desire to die, which is thereby encouraged to take a concealed aggressive form. I have mentioned Brown's application of this doctrine to industrial societies in connection with "Central Park."

Lowell has possessed these themes, intuitively, from the beginning, and I bring in the theoretical background as a help to understanding rather than as an allegation of source. In "Memories of West Street and Lepke," Lowell shows us a professional murderer at first utterly terrorized by the prospect of his own death, and then unconsciously converting that very terror into a form of love. But in *Near the Ocean* these themes become more dominant, more complex, as we can see by reexamining the opening stanzas. There the poet, under conditions of sexual inhibition and guilt, becomes terrified of the idea that his energy is self-consuming and seeks to die; the result is the transmutation of the aroused energy into two forms, one outwardly aggressive (the dragon image), the other self-lacerating (the impulse expressed in the vermin stanza).

Throughout the poems, we see more or less dehumanized people, usually of the American ruling class or sharing in its ideology (the generals, the president, the policeman fingering his gun, the "Pharaohs") seeking some kind of self-expression or sexual satisfaction through the giving or receiving of death. The last poem deals with murderous feelings in sex and marriage, and the "abortion" theme relates them to civilized deflections of natural eroticism. Even the very last line of the poem can be read as stating the perverse equation of perfect sexual experience and death; though, as I have argued, at this point in the poem Lowell has substantially turned from this mystique toward what Brown conceives of as an opposite, life-serving mysticism, the liberation from time through total immersion in the present. Lowell states this attitude in traditional religious terms earlier: "Every time I take a breath, / my God you are the air I breathe."

Finally, we might consider *Near the Ocean*'s character as a long poem, in relation to the tradition, or traditions, of the personal epic. It has often seemed to me that critics too easily posit a single mainstream of the American long poem, where in fact there are at least two very distinct currents. One is the "open" tradition of Ezra Pound's *Cantos*, the longer works of the Black Mountain School poets, and (with some important reservations) William Carlos Williams's *Paterson* and John Berryman's *Dream Songs*. These poems tend to be very long, and to begin and end casually, almost arbitrarily; except in the case of Berryman, the subordinate units are also long, have no fixed meter, and could almost never be presented as separate lyrics. These poems can contain large sections of almost novelistic exposition and narrative; they tend to develop by loose but openly displayed links, and to make comparatively slight use of hidden symbolic networks. The author's presentation of himself is expansive and many-sided; his intelligence and observation, as well as his imagination, contribute to his authority.

This is the tradition of the personal epic that has received the most theoretical attention and, in general, the most praise in the past fifteen years—a fact that may help to explain the neglect of *Near the Ocean*. (Incredibly, many of the volume's hostile reviewers failed even to notice that it contained a long poem.) But there is another tradition: that of Eliot's longer poems, especially *The Waste Land*; of Hart Crane's *The Bridge*; Berryman's *Homage to Mistress Bradstreet*; and (with reservations) *Life Studies*. These poems tend to start from intense inward experience, to base their authority on the poet's imagination and symbol-making power rather than his secular self, and to incorporate the larger, public realm by epiphany rather than direct narrative. They center on a few subjectively crucial experiences and fall into short, but distinct and concentrated, lyrical units. Fixed forms and their variation or alternation, symbols and their cumulative associations, are very important to structure, which tends to be subtler and more interesting in and of itself than in the looser form. (None of these remarks, however, is intended to elevate one form over the other, but merely to point out that they have different virtues and powers, springing, ultimately, from a different sense of the important relations between the self and the world.)

Near the Ocean seems to me the one major poem of the last ten years to be written in the second tradition, the concentrated and lyrical sequence. Of all its predecessors, it seems closest to *The Bridge*. Like Crane, Lowell is concerned with the myth of America, the American Eden, and associates it, through his symbols, with an inward religious experience, pantheistic and perhaps (in the tradition of Whitman) pan-sexual, a vision of energy existing in intense harmony. Like Crane, too, Lowell is obsessed with the decline of America, and seeks an explanation for it in the history of consciousness more than in external history: both writers accuse their country of being a mental "convert to old age." Here, perhaps, the thematic similarities end; but the sheer rhetorical energy of *Near the Ocean*, its combination of the bardic and the contemporary, place Lowell among Crane's most direct heirs. (I have wondered, only half-fancifully, if Lowell's use of Crane's central symbols, Brooklyn Bridge and Atlantis, in his concluding stanzas does not constitute an oblique kind of tribute.)

The tendency to dismiss *Near the Ocean* as "an afterbeat of . . . *For the Union Dead*,"[1] or some similar phrase, generally comes from critics close to Lowell's own age, who are strongly attached to the realistic vein of *Life Studies*. Younger readers, I notice, often turn to the later book with equal, or greater, excitement. I myself am convinced that a

---

[1] M. L. Rosenthal, *The New Poets* (New York, 1967), 78.

work at once so haunting and so enormously ambitious, so profound and so inventive in structure, cannot ultimately fail to be recognized as a major American poem.

Pity the Monsters: The Political Vision of Robert Lowell (New Haven, 1974), 112-15, 150-55.

The Prophet Is a Fool:
On "Waking Early Sunday Morning"

Mary Kinzie

Sir Thomas Elyot in his *Castle of Health* (1534) wrote about the kinds of dreams the four Complexion types usually had. (The types are the Sanguine, the Melancholic, the Choleric, and the Phlegmatic.)[1] The Sanguine Man, who sleeps a great deal, dreams of red colors and pleasant things. The Sanguine mind has always seemed to me particularly suited to metaphysics or first philosophy because of the rapidity with which emotion is forgotten, and because of the merry abstractions into which this mind consistently retires. Among poets, the Sanguine type can be represented by Wallace Stevens.

The Choleric Man dreams of thunder and of bright, dangerous things. As far as his awful temper and deep, solitary violence are concerned, the Choleric Man might be Robert Frost. But I am not wholly pleased with this assignment. Frost, despite his excellent ear for song, is balked in his faculty of praise or celebration which the bright, dangerous things of which he dreams imply. I would assign the oneiric or poetic part of this Complexion to Richard Wilbur and James Merrill.

The Phlegmatic Man dreams of watery things or of fish. In the Phlegmatic Temperament are some aspects of Robert Lowell's themes and of his sensibility (his New England horror of the ocean and death by water, his intellectual battery of responses like repulsion and disgust). But nature and the watery and fishy are analogical in Lowell's work. The only American poet who is Phlegmatic by disposition and not by analogy must of course be Theodore Roethke.

---

[1] See C. S. Lewis, *The Discarded Image* (1964, rpt. Cambridge, 1972), 171-73

It is now obvious what Complexion one may divine for Robert Lowell—the Melancholic Man, who is such a bad sleeper and hence infrequent dreamer that the fearfulness of the dreams he does have are apt to be indistinguishable from the funks and fretting which dog him by day. The Melancholic is the man whom sleep seldom visits, and who has therefore no benefit from other realms. The self is the only realm he has.

This parable of the Humors may help to illustrate the special, massive irritability of Robert Lowell's poetic voice. While Lowell's religious conversion is the most documented of any poet since Eliot, there has, to judge from the poetry, been little relief or access of hope as a result. Yet he stands in a special relation to the Faith, similar in bitterness to that of the apostate, and complicated by the oddity of religious diction to our pursuits. As is evident in "Waking Early Sunday Morning," the political and cultural ambiance he confronts as a poet is conceived in terms of religious faithlessness. Lowell's verse is importantly that of a prophet on an a priori fruitless mission to a damned culture. It may be that he resents us for being unsalvageable as much as he despairs of himself for being displaced among us. Lowell's stance is thus much like the prophet Hosea's: "The prophet is a fool, the man of the spirit is mad, because of your great iniquity and great hatred (Hosea 9:7).

As the self who aspires but who falls into reckless moods, Robert Lowell is a particularly hard poet for most of us to write about. He has been our teacher; he has represented tradition to us; he has been grand, grave, parental, and deeply, purposively flamboyant. As one feels about a parent, then, who chronically becomes selfish or irretrievably emotional, Lowell's excesses in feeling and diction from *Lord Weary's Castle* to *History* elicit from us a sinister and difficult embarrassment. His accommodation to our fallen level hasn't helped. The looser, clever sounds of an after-generation make his voice oddly brittle, as does the shabbiness of current issues. Lowell perhaps is the most important of our poets to have made of being adrift in a world without cause or subject his chief poetic cause and subject.

The filial metaphor seems the more apt for our bond to Lowell in proportion as he too embodies the filial revolt against a somewhat stricter parentage. He revolted, perhaps as part of conversion, against his own intellectual gifts, so that we are always as dazzled by his poems as we are shocked by the unselective explosions of his prideful verbal skill. He consistently manifests a downhill kind of modesty, like that of the delinquent prodigy whose gifts it exhausts in shallowness. The jumble of the perceived world, as well as the cluttered solitude of the perceiving intelligence, are his subject as well as his way.

"Waking Early Sunday Morning" reveals the clutter, the anger, the intelligence, and the perverse carelessness which I take to be indicative of the aggressively delinquent posture from which Lowell writes his poems. It starts from that marvelous hypothesis which poets have often made use of: that they are sitting down to record their dreams, lying awake at night, meditating, making entries in journals, drowsing abed. The frame is loose, like the novel's, and whatever the mind's angle of vision discloses is meet and just. It's exciting to begin to read such an *essai*, and to test the play of another's daydreaming against one's own.

Like many another contest between harmony and invention "Waking Early Sunday Morning" begins with great freshness and promise, the poet conscious of his own enormous tensile strength and of the treasure of time tumbled out before him. It begins ("O to break loose") with a chinook salmon leaping up and bruising itself against the rocky falls, then clearing the top "alive enough to spawn and die." The poem ends with this planet a joyless cinder, a ghost orbiting "in our monotonous sublime." One could of course point out that the negative element was there from the beginning (as I suppose it always is for Lowell), in the frantic necrophilia of the salmon. But the first two stanzas, whatever else might creep in, are about his joy in the feeling of possibility:

> Stop, back off. The salmon breaks
> water, and now my body wakes
> to feel the unpolluted joy
> and criminal leisure of a boy—
> no rainbow smashing a dry fly
> in the white run is free as I,
> here squatting like a dragon on
> time's hoard before the day's begun! (st. 2)

Despite the pattern of definition-by-negation in the description of a joy which is "unpolluted" and leisure which is "criminal," there is still no way for us to second-guess Lowell about the course the poem will take; all we are prepared to do is await the *turn*.

There will be something, probably emanating from within, which will ruin the recitation, blot the gorgeous page. We may be dealing with a developmental pattern similar to that in "Tintern Abbey," where that young man's growth from blood to heart to purer mind finds echo here in the waking of the body in the second stanza, then in stanza four the "Fierce, fireless *mind,* running downhill," and then, in stanzas five and six, the introduction of the religious spirit. Our perceptual behaviorism differs so little from its eighteenth-century forbear that the gradual awakening of the self from the kinesthetic level (awareness of physical balance and interior borders) to mere affect and finally to intellectual or spiritual consciousness is as available to us as a metaphor for ontogenetic development as it was to Wordsworth. The chief difference in Lowell's application of the schema lies in the diminution of happiness and power as the mention of spirit and its exercise nears.[2]

The breaking loose of the first line is a strong kinesthetic theme echoed in various downhill runs, wanderings, "obsessive, casual" all-night motions, and in pointless impulses to energy (which are, as Lowell twice says, expended "anywhere, but somewhere else!"). The theme is finally capped by the perpetual motion of the lifeless star earth has become.

The ghost/spirit theme in the last stanza ("the earth, a ghost / orbiting forever lost / in our monotonous sublime") can also be traced back through the poem from, here at the end, the death of spirit in an off-hand or casual war, to the "ghost-written rhetoric" of that rough and doggy pol, President Lyndon Baines Johnson, in stanza twelve; the vague spiritual angst which manifests itself in random movement and the piling up of abstractions (restlessness, sanity, caution, deception) in stanza eleven; the vanishing of the emblems of God in stanza nine; and the emptiness of biblical histories and Hebraic credos, which promise "little redemption" (stanza ten). Borrowing Paul's image of a world without love in Corinthians, these biblical patterns are "old lumber banished from the Temple . . . the wordless sign, the tinkling cymbal."

The intermediate body-empty-of-soul metaphor is implicit in those tinkling cymbals and wordless signs of stanza eight, in the wordless hymns of stanza seven which are heard but not read and from which the soul is lucky to escape, and in the images of stanza six where the soul is "tinged" and "tarnished" by its "strain" (song, bent, tendency, or *ingenium*), just as the water glass in stanza five is silvery and neutral in its skyey reflections until a "shift, or change [in] mood" intrudes a dark wood-grained background. Here Lowell conflates the looking-glass/reflector idea with the idea of the holy vessel (man is what God puts it in him to become). The skewing comes because not God but man does all the putting, displacing, and mood changing.

"Waking Early Sunday Morning" thus arranges to cover important ground about Sunday, and Lowell's (or the speaker's—I don't think it matters which) recollections and present attitudes toward personal redemption and social religious forms. The transitions between ideas and

---

[2] Stephen Yenser elaborates his important corollary insight that "Waking Early Sunday Morning" develops diurnally as well, and that it parallels the progress of the morning church service: *Circle to Circle* (Berkeley, 1975), 249-60.

metaphors are fantastically abrupt, and one must suspect that Lowell is drawing on some mental formulas, some pre-arranged poetic signals in his thought which propel him across terrain which is indicated by map but, for us, at the moment, invisible.

Certain easy linkages we can make. The association of Sundays with something slightly criminal occurs in the poem "Law" (*For the Union Dead*). Practically asleep within four-line stanzas of irregular one- to five-measure lines, Lowell reaches for capsule images of frozen violence. On Sunday mornings as a boy the poet had gone "bass-plugging out of season on / the posted reservoirs": "Outside the law. / At every bend I saw / only the looping shore / of nature's monotonous backlash." It may be the same procedure whereby consciousness of wrongdoing heightens and more deeply impresses on the wrongdoer the majesty or exactitude of the adventure. Because Lowell's boyhood self had been poaching, his imagination was the more primed for the special fixation upon double rehearsals from which singular beauty comes. Because Wordsworth was either stealing a boat or rifling a nest for eggs or decimating the nut tree, the power of majestic otherness went more deeply into his mind. In Lowell's case, I think the special condition of breaking the Sabbath, by eliciting more associations and greater contrition, outweighed any other infraction.

One of the Sabbath associations for the boy in "Law" is with periods of historic conflict as represented in ritual form by the "battlefield" (the Civil War, or possibly where Puritans fought Indians) and by the Norman landscape. The ritual or quasi-religious aspect of wars, whether in Europe or America, was often the subject of Lowell's earlier verse. The old man in Lowell's "Falling Asleep Over the Aeneid" (*Mills of the Kavanaughs*) not only breaks the law by missing church, but finds himself involved in two funerals, one from the classical past, and one from his boyhood, both of which, along with his own death, are circumstantially connected to profaning the Holy Day. Like Lowell, the old man is at the end of a long line of glorious and strong-willed Puritans. He recollects meekly saying to his boyhood self, "It is I," while the bust of Augustus, Vergil's patron, is blankly reflected in his glasses. He is sedentary and impressionable while his cultural and religious forbears were active and convinced. This is a scenario which occurs frequently in all of Lowell's books, although in recent years his ancestors have tended to be more human and life-size.

The Protestant hymn "Faith of Our Fathers" which plays in stanza six of "Waking Early Sunday Morning" is thus doubly meaningful in terms of the Lowell canon, where not only do Devereuxs, Lowells, and Winslows abound, but where holy wars and satanic temptations have been

fiercely chronicled. In one of the two stanzas Lowell revised for the
poem's appearance in *Near the Ocean*, the particular anomie of his late-
born condition is evident:

> Empty, irresolute, ashamed,
> when the sacred texts are named,
> I lie here on my bed apart,
> and when I look into my heart,
> I discover none of the Feat
> subjects: death, friendship, love and hate
> only old china doorknobs, sad,
> slight, useless things to calm the mad.[3]

When he rewrote this stanza, Lowell wanted to make clear that his deep
personal anomie was not just a secular habit but part of a religious *crise*.

> When will we see Him face to face?
> Each day, He shines through darker glass.
> In this small town where everything
> is known, I see His vanishing
> emblems, His white spire and flag-
> pole sticking out above the fog,
> like old white china doorknobs, sad,
> slight, useless things to calm the mad. (st. 9)

The command to "put old clothes on" is in patent defiance of
Sunday habiliment. The search for "dregs and dreck" and "old lumber, on
the other hand, is so often enforced as a motif in "Waking Early Sunday
Morning" that the storeroom where discards are kept becomes a metaphor
for the poet's sentimentality. The junk of the "year's output, a dead wood
of dry verse" (from the rejected stanza three), like the "old china
doorknobs" found in his heart where love and hate should be (a ligature
removed from stanza nine), are the caked and random residues of a life
misspent in a particular way, and they lead to the frantic remorse we are
so flayed by in reading Lowell. The particular way in which the poet's
failings dog him becomes the more evident in the revisions, where the
"dead wood" of poems becomes the "dark nook" where mice roll marbles,
and the woodwork where termites sleep: "listen, the creatures of the night
/ obsessive, casual, sure of foot, / go on grinding, while the sun's / daily

---

[3] "Waking Early" was originally published in *New York Review of Books* (Aug.
5, 1965): 3

remorseful blackout dawns" (st. 3). As there are no great actions, he will sing of frogs and mice. Not the poet's detritus as in the original verses, but now a house undermined and inhabited by primitive smallfry who portion out the uneasy hours of the night. And the house, by implication, is hollow, decayed, and termite-ridden. The substitutions in stanza nine also emphasize the similarity between a hollow house and the equally hollow spirit within, since the ragtag junk and china doorknobs resemble the spire and pole-knob of a New England town's church. These emblems of worshipful belief then vanish in the general, dirty fog.

This double balance between his own spirit and its leavings on the one hand, and on the other between the world's "wake of refuse" (stanza four) and his own sympathetic harboring of dead and sundered objects, creates a Janus-posture from which the poem's peculiar invective is launched. Derision of self and derision of society go hand in hand where faith has been scrapped and shredded. Unlike the conduct of business under an edenic covenant in Psalm 107, going down to the sea in ships in 1965 does not enable men to see the works of the lord and his wonders in the deep, but only "refuse, dacron rope," and the messy trails of pleasure yachts. There are "No weekends for the gods now. Wars / flicker"—and President Johnson's compulsive, indecorous press conferences and the Vietnam "incidents" which cloaked destruction in euphemism are given an odd turn by Lowell. He compares our "action" in Southeast Asia with David's destruction of the Philistines. Both nations in each epoch, ours and David's, suffered. Both, by implication, were destroyed by the businesslike conduct of war. And, in a madly ugly phrase ("when that kingdom hit the crash: / a million foreskins stacked like trash"), the mutually binding death-to-the-spirit of Israelite and Philistine alike is rendered ambiguously (David was notorious, like Saul, for collecting foreskins from every tribe he defeated). Such verbal aggression is doubtless designed to plant the Great Society under the Philistine label, and in order that our period's dreck and its empty edifices, as well as the poet's own pottage of scraps, can be seen in the rubble. But the diction and the image are still nasty rather than tremendous, and something small lingers about the attempt of the whole.

The world of many Lowell poems, so full of dead foliage and scrubby, "frizzled" trees, gradually grows tattered and burned-out.[4] This

---

[4] Marjorie Perloff is especially sensitive to this class of images in *Poetic Art* (Ithaca, 1973). She also notes the peculiar prevalence of references to being off-balance, uncertain on one's feet, or stepping tentatively, as a version of giving up or yielding to the strong of the earth. It's the animals and the insurance brokers who stand their ground. See the quotation above from stanza three of "Waking Early," where the small-fry are "casual, sure of foot."

would be of secondary interest were it not for the infusion of emotion which makes the dreck and the cinders emblems of a deep and horrifying remorse. One example: "The Public Garden" in *For the Union Dead* is a place of dead leaves and the season's wreckage, as well as the wreckage of the passion David had for Bathsheba. Once, they drowned "in Eden, while Jehovah's grass-green lyre / was rustling all about us in the leaves / that gurgled by us, turning upside down," but this is very much a vision in *illo tempore* and has nothing but negative links to the present time, when the waters of the fountain "fail." In the last line Lowell avers that "Nothing catches fire" because the sin (the murder of Uriah, infidelity) broods and hectically burns like an ember which is almost spent. The last stanza of "Waking Early Sunday Morning" calls upon us to

> Pity the planet, all joy gone
> from this sweet volcanic cone;
> peace to our children when they fall
> in small war on the heels of small
> war—until the end of time
> to police the earth, a ghost
> orbiting forever lost
> in our monotonous sublime. (st. 14)[5]

Neither Shelley's "intense inane" nor Stevens's "perverse marine" (because the former was a borrowed and floundering expression of his theme, and because the latter was a phrase never intended to be important in its place) possesses the satisfactory and conclusive flourish of Lowell's resonant adjective nomination, "monotonous sublime." Embraced here are the final end both of hymns and belligerent racket, drawn down alike into a monotone; the "resolution" of faith into a ridiculous sublimity; and the reduction of trial and error into a final tablet, on which is written, "that which is done is irrevocable."

Perhaps there is nothing more frightening for a consciousness impelled by remorse than the closing of the book of the Recording Angel. By an interesting psychological reversal, the idea of death, like a veil, is taken down from the drafty corridor before which it hangs and wound about the figure of our living act, so that we can no longer move, nor work

---

[5] The rhymes of Lowell's last stanza do not keep to tetrameter couplets. Perhaps the *abba* quatrain envelope sounded more ironclad than another couplet pair, and acted for his purpose the way a couplet would at the end of a sonnet, or a tail line in terza rima. I suspect, however, that this was the only way he had to keep "monotonous sublime" for last.

our way out of an evil turbulence, nor redeem what we've done by
stepping into what we might do. We become a mummified vestige of
fallible intentions. Marlowe's Faustus may be the last and best exemplar
of the allegory of the eleventh hour (we do not find the same kind of terror
in Goethe). To posit other planes, afterlives, ways of going on, is another
sublimation of the fear and places the veil only further down amid dim
colonnades. Lowell wrote in "Jonathan Edwards in Western
Massachusetts," "We know how the world will end, / but where is
paradise. . . ."

In "Waking Early," the awareness of finality (punishment and
holocaust) looms on the horizon in the world's emblem as a "sweet
volcanic cone"—which refers to origins as well as ends, as Lowell's
etiologies tend to do. Even the Divinity was finished before He began:

> I suppose even God was born
> too late to trust the old religion
> all those settings out
> that never left the ground,
> beginning in wisdom, dying in doubt.

This is from the last stanza of "Tenth Muse" (*For the Union Dead*), a
poem about Sloth who comes to the speaker's bed and, strangely enough,
does not take him over, cushion him, or seduce him, but reminds him of
what she is *not*. And she is no fun at all; she is only that which he ought to
be doing, like opening his mail, or remembering Moses, who made the
effort and lugged down from Sinai the heavy stones of the old law. He
should make, receive, or at least abide by law. Due to Lowell's naturally
patristic[6] turn of mind, Acedia's pleasures, like God's trust in Himself, are
barely given time to breathe before doubt and vexations draw the cord.

Lowell's brave yet virulent fascination with late Rome possibly
has its meaning here. Caligula's depravity was not simple, easy, or merely
bad and promiscuous, but grotesquely anguished. Certainly, to ascribe to
Caligula even psychotic masochism would be a kindness, given how
repellent he was on every human level. But in Lowell's attention to him
there is an assumption of complicity between them which is not entirely
due to self-effacement or sheer, outrageous irony. Lowell claims for them
both "the lawlessness / of something simple that has lost its law"

---

6 Jerome Mazzaro's thorough examination of sources in Lowell's early verse,
and his assessment of the meditation-structure of his thought, are hardly
impugned by my addition of Augustine to the company of Sts. Ignatius and
Bernard of Clairvaux. See *Poetic Themes* (Ann Arbor, 1965).

("Caligula," *For the Union Dead*). Not only is this a splendid capsule of
what psychology has always claimed about our illnesses, but it's an
important position statement for Lowell as well: the world, and he as its
unemployed prophet, are simple at root, but it is a simplicity neither will
ever see face to face. In place of such simplicity, there is the exercise of a
conscience which is pained and even wrong-headed. There is thus no
probity except, by accident, among the meek and vaguely memorious—
those who "remember" how desire may once have been fitted to belief.
There is much anguish in conscience, the more for an intelligent and
learned poet who wrestles with the perversity of will and anarchic detours
on the part of lives and minds (including his own) which are probably, in
their best face, rather uninteresting, *simple*. Such intimations of the
character of a simple, conscienceless self are supremely withering: even
with all our meanness and self-consciousness aside, none of us would
exist very much.

  "Waking Early Sunday Morning" is a bleak, irritating, and
stunning poem. By its form it is a black parody of the elegance of
Marvell's "The Garden." Once the form draws us to the text, we find a
parody of substance as well. Within the rich and almost merry closure of
an engaged belief (I would call Marvell a Sanguine Temperament),
metaphoric and imaginative conceits blossom and dodge, retreating and
amplifying themselves. Marvell's aesthetic ebullience invents quite
broadly, but on themes which are hardly doubted. Because there is no
harmony among Lowell's beliefs, nor much clarity to his predications as a
whole except in attesting to ragged states of mind, there cannot be the
same contract for invention. He crosshatches his verse with allusions
because he must try to reinstate the recorded world each time he writes,
and cull from the ruins the pieces which seem intuitively important for the
building of some new, minor harmony. To this end, he culls from himself
as well, and much of the text of "Waking Early Sunday Morning" which I
have very sketchily presented has about it the air of critical apparatus.

  There is a sense in which most poets write one poem all the time,
however much they change. There is also a closet full of "tics" which
form a permanent wardrobe—speech tics, image tics, even moral ones.
Among those "tics" of Lowell's which I can see here, I am most interested
in two sorts. First, the ones I don't fully understand, but which Lowell
takes for granted because the associational links are private and familiar
to him. Second, the ones which seem to have leaped out of habitude into
full life. From among the former sort, I have already singled out a few of
the many images of things burned-out and used up: dead wood, the
volcanic cone, old lumber, the "Bible chopped and crucified," doorknobs,
candle-ends. A subclass presents itself, that of *wood* which can't be used

any more; the pattern will culminate in the tree of life which is being disposed of in stanza eleven. Still, I may not have fully understood the connections, and for this reason it's helpful to "Stop, back off," and see how a poem like "Where the Rainbow Ends" from the end of *Lord Weary's Castle* convenes similar images:

> The thorn tree waits
> Its victim and tonight
> The worms will eat the deadwood to the foot
> Of Ararat: the scythers, Time and Death,
> Helmed locusts, move upon the tree of breath;
> The wild ingrafted olive and the root
> Are withered . . .

The "tree of breath" (*spiritus* = breath, life), the thorn tree of the Passion and the deadwood on Ararat, as emblems of Adam, Christ, and Noah present the analogical discipline of finding types of Christ in a characteristic Lowell skewing: they are being eaten by worms defoliated by locusts, or made into cruel crowns. Nothing much flourishes in Lowell's Holy Land. There remains, however, something further or deeper about Lowell's fondness for the dead branch and the sickly stand of pines that I cannot locate, and which I must ascribe reductively, to an habitual swerve in the poet's memory.

An example of the second sort of "tic" which rises to metaphor is related to the indicated (but not fully visible) pattern of dying out, obsolescence, the tree of breath and the dead wood of dry verse, and to the diminishment of an irreligious present even (because pointedly disjoint from us) by a religious past. But naming and listing will never quite prepare one for the end of stanza eleven. As a further codicil, I should also say that I chose "Waking Early Sunday Morning" because of this stanza, and that I see in it the kind of personal nightmare which is absolutely embodied and absolutely unforgettable:

> No weekends for the gods now. Wars
> flicker, earth licks its open sores,
> fresh breakage, fresh promotions, chance
> assassinations, no advance.
> Only man thinning out his kind
> sounds through the Sabbath noon, the blind
> swipe of the pruner and his knife
> busy about the tree of life . . .

This is a suddenly quiet moment "sounding" in a poem otherwise full of conflicting song, ruckus, chimes, "stiff quatrains," tinkling cymbals. It is a dreadful, sinister hiatus which reminds me of the moment when Sir Gawain came to that turning in the dark ravine: suddenly an ear-splitting noise burst upon the air, and Gawain knew he was near to the heart of the mystery that the Green Knight was *there*, grinding his scissors and knives. I am also reminded of another great moment in literature, when Anna Karenina looked up to the platform from the wheels of the train that was crushing her, saw the old peasant doing something with metal and muttering, and realized what her recurrent nightmare about that peasant had finally meant. Tolstoy has given us here one of those terrible moments of truth when our triviality and our worst fate become indistinguishable: somewhere in their bond is the final modern horror.

The trivial is seldom far distant from the lethal in the verse we have been considering; but wretched death and the shallowness of our personal mystery are never so well bonded into true horror as when, having raised himself from a bad night into a quickly extinguishing joy, Robert Lowell picks his way through the babble and lost hope of centuries to see what the trouble could be. And after stumbling through four lines of substantives which mirror the rhetoric of the evil they denote, and skirting small war and open sore, he comes to the clearing where it's only man, working at something—"the pruner and his knife / busy about the tree of life." In language and symbols perfectly tuned to the poem's whole context, yet totally in the grip of an inspired private vision, Lowell meets the only kind of creature whose act and belief are in concord. And that is the Killer. The same eerie, tawdry figure who, with "the scythers, Time and Death," has managed to turn ploughshares back into spears. The tree of life, our dead wood, is his whetstone.

The prophet may be a fool, but the hatred and iniquity are commandingly perverse. This grim hypothesis, unlike the resounding imprecations in Hosea, Jeremiah, and Isaiah, creates in Lowell's work a psychic deadlock, for there is no counter-mood in the embrace of which it is possible to attain mildness, mercy, or peace of mind.

Salmagundi 37 (1977): 88-101; rev. and rpt. *The Cure of Poetry in an Age of Prose* (Chicago, 1993), 40-51.

Surviving the Marketplace:
Robert Lowell and the Sixties

Hilene Flanzbaum

In the 1960s, Robert Lowell took his career in an unexpected direction. Having won the Pulitzer Prize and inspired the devotion of literary critics and fellow practitioners in the previous two decades, he had established himself as the leading poet of his generation. But in the sixties, more than being warmly appreciated by a small elite audience, Lowell became a sensation: an American celebrity and a figure of political influence. In a few short years, he joined a select group of American poets who had bridged the great divide between academic and popular culture. This extraordinary stage in Lowell's career deserves wider critical attention than it has yet received, for it sheds significant light not only on his personal poetics but on the workings of America's literary and cultural history.

Scion of a dynastic American family, Lowell had always garnered more public attention than other modern poets, who, as we know, spent much of their time composing essays about the disappearance of their audiences. While the publication of *Life Studies* in 1959 guaranteed Lowell's critical reputation and reaffirmed his position as the preeminent poet of his generation, it also foreshadowed his dramatic rise to national prominence a mere five years later.

The story of Lowell's ascent begins in 1964, when President Lyndon Baines Johnson asked him to read at the White House Arts Festival. Citing his objections to LBJ's policies on Vietnam, Lowell declined. He also sent a copy of his letter of refusal to the *New York Times*, whose editors, knowing that a Lowell could always make news, decided to print it on the front page. Furious, Johnson responded, accusing Lowell of publicity seeking and grandstanding. When many of the nation's most important writers and artists lined up behind Lowell, the stage was set for a media battle between literati and the executive branch that took almost three months to play out and whose echoes could be heard now and again in the ideological war that raged for the better part of a decade.[1]

Lowell's opposition to the Vietnam War constituted the first and perhaps most essential ingredient in the hash of political and social

---

[1] The writers and artists who publicly supported Lowell's cause included, among others: Hannah Arendt, John Berryman, Jules Feiffer, Lillian Hellman, Alfred Kazin, Bernard Malamud, Philip Roth, and Robert Penn Warren.

changes in which he served himself up to the public sphere.[2] Politically he had always been a renegade—a conscientious objector to World War II and a persistent and harsh critic of American capitalism—yet the growing unpopularity of the Vietnam War, and the cultural revolution spawned in the wake of protests against it, found Lowell closer to mainstream American ideology and appetites than he would ever have thought possible. Abruptly, Lowell's iconoclasm was chic.

In 1965 Lowell wrote *The Old Glory*, an off-Broadway production that targeted the hypocrisy of American government and institutions; it ran for three years and won an Obie award for best play. In the years between 1964 and 1967, four of Lowell's dramas were staged and two books of his poetry published. His 1964 volume *For the Union Dead*, issued just months before the LBJ letter, had been applauded by the critics. By 1967, he drew thousands of anti-war protesters to the steps of the Pentagon and narrowly avoided being arrested with Norman Mailer. In 1968, Lowell frequently dined with Jacqueline Kennedy, and he joined presidential candidate Eugene McCarthy on the campaign trail.

Lowell found that when he walked his dog on the streets of Manhattan, paparazzi trailed him. While it has been argued that he abjured this particular aspect of celebrity, he had to be pleased, nonetheless, to see the entire texts of "The Quaker Graveyard in Nantucket" and "Memories of West Street and Lepke" reprinted in *Life* magazine, his portrait featured on the covers of *Time* and *Newsweek*, and articles touting his political views spreading to all comers of the world.

Despite Lowell's undeniable fame, curiously enough his career has never been appreciated, nor has his poetry been read, as a product of his lifelong ambition for popular, as well as critical, approbation. For it was not solely Lowell's political actions that brought him celebrity and influence; not every war resister, not even those who were poets, became stars. While certain external circumstances made Lowell popular—the turbulent political times, his maverick stance juxtaposed against his Brahmin background—Lowell's celebrity does not proceed simply from a

---

[2] From its inception, the anti-war movement attracted large crowds, which made protesting American involvement in Vietnam both respectable and profitable. Unlike many entrepreneurs who capitalized on the public's unhappiness with the war, Lowell's ambitions were not economic. As the heir to a diminished but still substantial family fortune, he had little financial need: he would never have to hold a job he did not want nor cater to readers' appetites to sell his poetry. Lowell becomes enmeshed in the vicissitudes of American commercialism, I argue, because for him success in the marketplace accorded him a level of popularity that assured him the platform and audience he had always sought.

serendipitous combination of biology and global events. Rather Lowell is exceptional because he had skillfully mastered the formula for media attention.[3]

A close friend of Lowell's, Blair Clark, explained the tremendous impact of the White House letter this way: "Lowell had a shrewdness in handling his public persona, and the 'LBJ letter' was an example of his brilliant timing. . . . He knew what he was doing. I'm sure there were people who were terribly envious of his ability to manipulate himself as a public figure. He did it without any pomposity—but he definitely believed he was a public figure."[4] Yet Lowell's prodigious talent for finding the spotlight should not be understood as a venal thirst for fame but rather as a result of his yearning to find common ground with the large American audience. Critics have mistakenly seen Lowell's gesturing to a popular audience as evidence of his poetic misprision instead of as a premeditated maneuver to widen his literary domain and to make contact with an audience that had become deeply alienated from most modern poetry. Lowell did manage his career shrewdly, but mere celebrity was not his aim: he wanted to be more than the poet literary critics acclaimed; he *also* wanted to be the poet the American people looked to for wisdom. While this conclusion has been occasionally and hurriedly noted in biographies of the poet, I believe that understanding Lowell means appreciating precisely how his conflicting ambitions directed his career decisions and affected the poetry he wrote.

For instance, many critics note that Lowell's career was a string of continual rebirths. A phoenix from the ashes, again and again Lowell reinvented his poetic persona with seeming ease: the student of obscure and inaccessible New Critical methods in *Lord Weary's Castle* transformed himself into the accessible, confessional poet of *Life Studies*, then turned himself into the political and public poet of *History*, then reinvented himself once more as the morose and withdrawn journalist of *Day by Day*. Critics have located the germs of these poetic evolutions in Lowell's tumultuous psychological profile, but they have failed to measure how his aspiration simultaneously to engage both an academic and a popular audience took its toll on him. Because the mass market and canonical poetry, especially in the post-Eliotic haze of high modernism,

---

[3] Dwight Macdonald maintained "that rarely has one person's statement of his moral unease about his government's behavior had such public resonance." He attributed the potency of Lowell's letter to LBJ to the fact it was "so unexpected, so private, and yet so expressive of a wide-spread mood of dismay and distrust." See Steven Axelrod, *Robert Lowell: Life and Art* (Princeton, 1978), 183.

[4] Quoted in Ian Hamilton, *Robert Lowell: A Biography* (New York, 1982), 323.

have always appeared implausible conspirators, literary scholars have
been slow to recognize the degree to which marketplace pressures have
driven American poetry. In Lowell's case, when the marketplace and the
academy briefly reconciled, that oversight has resulted in a missed
opportunity to examine the inner workings of literary history as well as
precluded a thorough understanding of many of Lowell's greatest poems.

    . . . Lowell's interaction with the marketplace of the sixties
culminated with the publication of *Near the Ocean*. The volume, hurried
to the stores by both a determined Lowell and an opportunistic publisher
eager to cash in on the heyday of the poet's prestige, stands as a telling
marker of Lowell's aspirations. Of the many clues in his career that he
sought to influence the larger culture and earn the plaudits of a wide
audience, none is more revealing than the collection of poems that
appeared in January 1967. Strongly critical of American ideology and
policy, the poems in *Near the Ocean* expose the corruption of America's
leaders and preach an end to imperialist violence.

    The message cannot be missed: the poems do not hide their
meanings in dense metaphors or obscure references; they mask neither
their political nor their commercial intentions. A conventionally popular
form, rhyming couplets, maximize the oral potential of the poems and thus
their public quality; we can be read before crowds, they announce, or
chanted and remembered. In "The Fourth of July," Lowell writes "dinner
waits / in the cold oven, icy plates— / repeating and repeating, one / Joan
Baez on the gramophone." The reference to Joan Baez reveals the
immediacy of Lowell's intentions and also identifies the poet with youth
culture, a youth culture that might adapt his verse to song.

    "Waking Early Sunday Morning," the first poem in the volume,
became "*the* political poem of the sixties," according to critic Richard
Howard.[5] When read aloud, it included a stanza that regularly received
howls of delight from Lowell's audiences and represented one of his most
Ginsberg-like moments:

> O to break loose. All life's grandeur
> is something with a girl in summer . . .
> elated as the President
> girdled by his establishment
> this Sunday morning, free to chaff
> his own thoughts with his bear-cuffed staff,
> swimming nude, unbuttoned, sick
> of his ghost-written rhetoric!

---

[5] "Fuel on the Fire," *Poetry* 110 (1967): 413.

The poem ends with a generalized plea against all war, but listeners could not help but hear the relevance to their own decade's aggression and imperialism:

> Pity the planet, all joy gone
> from this sweet volcanic cone;
> peace to our children when they fall
> in small war on the heels of small
> war—until the end of time
> to police the earth, a ghost
> orbiting forever lost
> in our monotonous sublime.

Other poems in the volume also take swipes at the American military. In Lowell's imitation of Juvenal's "The Vanity of Human Wishes," the poet rewrites the classic to make it more topical and pertinent to his own decade: . . .

Even more remarkable than the overt politics of the poems it contained was the physical appearance of the volume itself. *Near the Ocean* looked like, as a handful of reviewers dared mention, "a coffee table book." At 10 inches by 8 inches, it was larger than a standard-sized collection of poetry; Sidney Nolan had illustrated the poems with impressionistic pen-and-ink drawings; the lines were double spaced and the pages held at most sixteen lines—a markedly unserious and unliterary format. While the poems of *Near the Ocean* may or may not stand with his best work, in the context of Lowell's career, the appearance of a coffee table book is a significant piece of literary history. This volume evidences just how much Lowell labored to influence the wider culture; and more important, perhaps, the critical reception of the volume reveals the fate of the literary artist who struggles to satisfy a commercial market.

Lowell's biographer cautiously suggests that Lowell may have decided to issue a new collection of poetry at this stage of his career because "he felt himself to be at something of a dead end, or that the public or occasional aspects of poems like 'Waking Early Sunday Morning' made him see the book as his timely contribution to the intensifying antiwar campaign" (Hamilton 348). But in making his case so tentatively, Hamilton, like many Lowell scholars, underemphasizes the poet's commercial aspirations. Indeed, most critics have failed to recognize that *Near the Ocean* was Lowell's deliberate and premeditated attempt to ensconce his literary productions among the paraphernalia of the American household and to inscribe his message into American hearts and minds. Instead, the book has been viewed as an anomaly, virtually wished out of existence by supportive critics. To others, it has simply confirmed that Lowell's career was finished.

With the exception of Richard Howard, who, writing in *Poetry* called the book "devastating" and "Waking Early Sunday Morning" a masterpiece, reviewers for high culture publications panned *Near the Ocean*. Helen Vendler, writing in the *Massachusetts Review*, called it sensationalistic, shrill, and full of doggerel. Charles Philbrick, in the *Saturday Review*, dubbed it "the disappointment of the season." David Kalstone generously noted in the *Partisan Review* that "the slick coffee-table design of the volume entirely misrepresents the poems, which, at their best, challenge things that are shiny and bright." The reviewer for the *New Yorker*, Louise Bogan, condemned *Near the Ocean* for its "coldness and theatricality, its will towards pure shock and its horrifying illustrations that disqualify it as a coffee table object," although ultimately Bogan admits the book "is in that class." Explaining that a reviewer had "good reason to be annoyed with Robert Lowell's new book," Hayden Carruth commenting in the *Hudson Review*, elaborated on its many commercial aspects. . . .[6]

Despite the American literary establishment's dismay, *Near the Ocean* was widely and enthusiastically reviewed in both the British and American mass media. The *London Times* complained that "niggling critics were treating the book too harshly and that is was an important complement to [Lowell's] work"; Donald Davie, in the *Manchester Guardian Weekly*, said several poems were "elating and invigorating." In the American media, the book accumulated more plaudits: *Life* titled its review "The Poet as Folk Hero"; the *New York Times* and the *New York Herald Tribune Book Week* responded positively; and in the *Chicago Tribune of Books*, William Stafford claimed that Lowell's new book had immediate relevance to the national mood.[7]

Only *Life* magazine grasped the obvious: in *Near the Ocean*, Lowell's project had changed—he wanted to be a folk hero. No longer

---

[6] Howard, "Fuel on the Fire": 413; Vendler, "Recent American Poetry," *Massachusetts Review* 8 (1967): 55~60; Philbrick, "Debuts and Encores," *Saturday Review* (June 3, 1967): 32-34; Kalstone, "Two Poets," *Partisan Review* 34 (1967): 619-25; Bogan, "Verse," *New Yorker* (May 20, 1967): 179; Carruth, "A Meaning of Robert Lowell," *Hudson Review* (1967): 429-47.

[7] Bill Byrom, "Books Abroad," *London Times Weekly* (Dec. 30, 1967): 18; Davie, "Judgment in America," *Guardian Weekly* (July 20, 1967): 11; "Poet as Folk-Hero," *Life* (Feb. 17, 1967): 17; Thomas Lask, "Colors Run Dark," *NY Times* (Feb. 14, 1967): 41; Richard Gilman, "Securing the Beachhead," *NY Herald Tribune Book Week* (Jan. 29, 1967): 4; Stafford, "Critical Involvement of the Poet," *Chicago Tribune Magazine of Books* (Feb. 5, 1967): 5.

seeking to please the academician exclusively, Lowell tried his hand at poetry that advanced a political cause. Yet the critical reception of *Near the Ocean* proved that the large majority of reviewers for high culture publications could not tolerate Lowell's shift in intentions. Theatricality, doggerel; pretentious, sensationalistic: detractors used such descriptions to suggest that Lowell was no longer writing poetry worthy of serious attention. American critics, who had no criteria for the evaluation of, and no interest in, popular poetry, could only condemn a collection so blatantly commercial and aggressively political.

While the cultural revolution of the sixties opened a space for the critical recognition of certain popular art forms, it was not of the sort to accommodate *Near the Ocean*. Poetry designed exclusively for success in the political and commercial market not only suffered the slings and arrows of elite culture; it could not survive in a de-politicized mass culture. A modest fad in the sixties, Lowell's poetry soon succumbed to the fate of most timely products. By 1970, the anti-war movement had lost its steam with the election of Richard Nixon and the slow withdrawal of American troops. Lowell's politics and his poetry had outlived their usefulness. *Near the Ocean* was out of print by the early seventies, and in the 1990s critics dismiss the collection as containing his least important poetry.[8]

Yet the volume is central to an understanding both of Lowell's ambitions and conflicts and of the relationship between poetry and American culture. *Near the Ocean* marks the apex of a personal career perched on the brink of marketplace success, and, however fleetingly, it also represents a rare phenomenon in recent literary history: an academically credentialed, canonical poet exerting wide cultural influence and political leadership. On its own terms, *Near the Ocean* succeeded. It demonstrated that poetry could be relevant; it brought Lowell and his politics before the public; and it provided, with "Waking Early Sunday Morning," a poetic cry to ignite and rally war resisters.

Despite these notable accomplishments, Lowell would never think of himself as a success. He had gained cultural prominence and political stature, but he had sacrificed too much. In a sonnet for Robert F. Kennedy, composed in 1968, Lowell had written, "For them like a prince, you daily left your tower / to walk through dirt in your best clothes. Untouched" [*Notebook 1967-68*]. In 1964, Lowell had considered himself to be like Shaw, an aristocrat bending down to carry the people towards glory ["For the Union Dead"]. But by 1968, Lowell's clothes, supposedly

---

[8] Alan Williamson is the exception. Because *Pity the Monsters* (Yale, 1974) is exclusively about Lowell's political vision, Williamson praises *Near the Ocean*.

unlike those of Shaw and the equally heroic aristocrat RFK, *were* dirty;
Lowell had tumbled farther into the ditch than he had believed possible.
Literary critics had turned their backs on him; RFK had been
assassinated; the anti-war movement had spawned its own regrettable
violence; and he had been dragged into one distasteful partisan
controversy after the next in which his motives and his methods were
impugned. Indeed, "his commitment to see the whole thing through"
(Hamilton 323) waned as the anti-war movement wound down and as he
became a target for "New Left" bashers. Diana Trilling and Lowell had
argued in the politically conservative pages of *Commentary*.[9] Their
acrimonious volley extended for several months and encompassed more
than just their disagreement about the United States' involvement in the
Vietnam War. Trilling had attacked Lowell for his "grandstanding" and
"opportunism" during the student strikes at Columbia, and Lowell was
deeply troubled by her reproach, the violence that erupted at Columbia
during the demonstrations, and the critical indifference to his work.

But just as the critics forsook Lowell after *Near the Ocean*, he
forsook them, and the general reading audience as well. A poet who until
this point catered to critical trends and anticipated public appetites,
Lowell used his last three volumes to chasten himself for fashioning his
career to win public approval. Thus, after accomplishing what he always
thought he wanted—securing a podium to preach his convictions and a
popular audience to appreciate his poetry—Lowell retreated to a manor
house in England. Like a wounded warrior at the end of a ravaging and
futile battle, he repudiated the national crusade. And his bitterness
towards the critics he believed had misunderstood him and the American
public he thought had abandoned him haunt the final poems of his career.

New England Quarterly 68 (March 1995): 44-57.

---

[9] Trilling, "On the Steps of the Low Library," *Commentary* (Nov. 1968) 29-55;
Lowell, "Liberalism and Columbia," *Commentary* (Mar. 1969): 4-18;
"Controversy," *Commentary* (Apr. 1969): 19-20.

Still Bound: *Prometheus Bound*

Richard Gilman

Robert Lowell's "imitations" are actually new works which take the structures and themes of classic poems and convert them to Lowell's own, contemporary uses. The same is true of his "adaptations" of plays, his *Phaedra* and his newest work *Prometheus Bound*. In its world premiere last week at the Yale School of Drama, the play revealed itself to be not much more than the skeleton of the Greek original, filled out with Lowell's own imagination, which sometimes adheres closely to Aeschylus but more often veers sharply in very un-Greek-like directions.

The evening was puzzling, difficult, full of superb moments but also of stretches of barren event, enormously interesting in its ambitions and its central enterprise but not quite managing to bring it off. With its pure lyricism and nearly complete lack of physical action, *Prometheus Bound* is one of the hardest of all Greek tragedies to stage for modern audiences, and Lowell's free, colloquial, "existential" version doesn't make the problem much easier. It does however, suggest a line of approach, which director Jonathan Miller has energetically followed.

To get past the sterile faithfulness of most productions of Greek tragedy, he has replaced the original's wind-swept mountaintop and gloomy rock with a seventeenth-century castle keep—a brilliant, towering set by Michael Annals, with flaking dusty gray brick walls, enigmatic statuary in niches and two huge chains running from floor to flies like a cold symbolic armature of fate—and dressed his actors in dusty unkempt gray costumes of the period.

Lowell's construction follows the bare Greek outlines: as punishment for bringing fire (intelligence) to men, Prometheus is chained to a rock by Zeus, where he is visited by "seabirds" who function as a chorus; Ocean, the god who urges him to submit; Io, Zeus's former earthly lover; and Hermes, Zeus's messenger who brings a last appeal for submission. Lowell follows the structure of some of the original speeches, and there is a scattering of Aeschylus's lines, but everything else is pure Lowell.

Where Aeschylus shaped an elemental conflict—intelligence versus might, man's finiteness versus God's omnipresence—and looked forward to an eventual reconciliation, Lowell's *Prometheus* is a mostly dark, anguished poem (the writing is actually in a kind of loose, imagistic prose) about suffering, death and tyranny. Far more than in Aeschylus, Lowell's Zeus is a political tyrant, "blind with power," and at the same time he is a deity resembling the "helpless" God of certain contemporary theologies. And Prometheus is not so much Zeus's fierce adversary as he is a witty, mordant rebel, like a hero in Dostoevsky or Camus.

As Miller steers the play through its long arcs of lyricism and elegy and smaller ones of acrid commentary—"Cruelty is [Zeus's] form of courage"—and relaxed banter—"Why should I go on talking about monsters. When you have seen one, you have seen them all"—the work seems more and more to fall into a succession of shapely, intense but isolated dreams. This conception yields some splendors. In a beautiful long speech, Irene Worth as Io contrives to fashion a complete, miraculous little drama from what is essentially a narrative. And Kenneth Haigh as Prometheus also does some memorable work, including a soliloquy on death in which he tells Io how her own body, "that hound-pack of affliction," will close in "to kill you."

It is difficult to see how or why Miller might have "jazzed up" the play. Quietness, immobility, inwardness, make their own appeal to the mind. But perhaps the trouble is just there: *Prometheus Bound* in its ancient mythic incarnation remains available almost wholly to the mind—not the senses, except that of hearing. Whatever Lowell's poetry, distinguished as it is for the most part, has added or changed, his *Prometheus* remains uncomfortable on the stage, and at home in some much more private realm. Unlike his masterly adaptations of stories by Hawthorne and Melville, which were the basis of his brilliant trilogy, *The Old Glory*, the new work does not quite break out into its own hard, inescapable dramatic action.

Newsweek 69 (May 22, 1967): 109.

3

Late Period

Visions and Revisions: Three New Volumes

Calvin Bedient

History: dustjacket in rustic brown, midnight blue, muddied cream, ready for the deprivations of history. Over 360 poems, 80 new, the rest revised. Brief dramatic possessions of Roman tyrants, Dante, Goethe, Stalin, Capone . . . cannibalisms of difficult temperaments, of genius, of suffering; thumbnail summaries, the thumb pressed down. The poems are charged and claustrophobic. Here the minds of the great are flashlights in a mist; the poems steam with grandeur, deny perspective. At the beginning of many, Lowell potters about in his own life, waving across the distance to History—forlorn, inconsequent, gratuitous, wanting destiny. He offers himself, a figure with bent, stretched neck, to the weight of human overreaching, confusion, nobility, defeat, error. The student uprising being a mass conflagration, there is both fear and elation in the marching Lowell, a warming of hands.

Then frankly personal poems are hitched to the starry title, and the volume-comes to seem uncertain of its aim, like most of the poems. The end is affectingly open-eyed about aging—Lowell, midcentury America's grandest voice, now 56, taking us with him. Yet "the slush-ice on the east bank of the Hudson / is rose-heather in the New Year sunset": Lowell may prove one of the great poets of old age, having the necessary honesty, and showing signs of deepening fortitude and relenting love.

For Lizzie and Harriet: 67 poems, "for" and partly about, left over from *Notebook* after *History* was removed; all revised. A pale green tree under the title turning to chaff in the wind, like a hasty, unsatisfactory, choiceless goodbye. A dull cover, a wan volume, the-heart gone out: the end of 20 years of marriage. *"We never see him now, except at dinner, / then you quarrel, and he goes upstairs"*: Harriet, a lively sprig tolerating her "unwise" parents. Lizzie is admirably patient, admirably impatient. You like her but do not get close to her, screened as she is by the poetic "You." At moments she is stuck with the mask of universal Wife—a man's promised cure ("O when will I sleep out the storm, dear love, / and see at the end of the walk your dress glow / burnt-umber, as if you had absorbed the sun?") and his curse ("One doubts the wisdom of almighty God / casting weak husbands adrift in the hands of a wife") There is a battered hope almost to the end: "we smell as green as the weeds that bruise the flower." But the quarrels "seldom come from the first cause," and finally Fate lumbers in, with its convenient crush-all answers: "Our love will not come back on fortune's wheel"; "all men worsen"; "Home things can't stand up to the strain of the earth."

The Dolphin: 103 new poems, "For Caroline." She is British, "all muscle, youth, intention," a "Rough Slitherer" in her "grotto of haphazard," jolting, renewing: "When I was troubled in mind, you made for my body / caught in its hangman's-knot of sinking lines." As a mythic creature of loving energy, she is the dolphin sacred to Apollo, transport for the pale limbs of the poet-god. In another metamorphosis, however, she is the too-merry maid, the mermaid, the terrible menace of the female will:

> None swims with her and breathes the air.
> A mermaid flattens soles and picks a trout,
> knife and fork in chainsong at the spine,
> weeps white rum undetectable from tears.
> She kills more bottles than the ocean sinks,
> and serves her winded lovers' bones in brine,
> nibbled at recess in the marathon.

The cover: sea green and blue.

Adding that "further complication to / intense fragility," Lowell and Caroline have a child, and walk the glass of learning to live with each other. Meanwhile Lowell pays vacation visits to Lizzie and Harriet. Guilt. Doubt. "Even the licence of my mind rebels / and can find no lodging for my two lives." "One man, two women, the common novel plot": the formula is noted wearily. Nothing is really settled, and Lowell reaches into each day like a trailing plant, rooting as he goes.

In all three volumes feeling is like an enveloping sack; Lowell is largely confined to his passions. If his mind transcends them, it is in wondering grief, occasionally in surprised joy, coming upon them almost always after the fact. Or such is his poetic, a poetic of taking stock. When, years ago, Lowell turned to "life studies," evidently it was because, lacking will, perspective, philosophy, he had no choice—even in *History* the face of his poetry is held down to the echoing well surface of biography. What makes Lowell compelling is the groaning degree to which he suffers the general collapse not merely of faith but of its modern substitute, faith in reason. He has found himself enclosed by the accident of his birth and temperament, the wilderness of his needs, the squirrel-case of every 24 hours, without any hope of growth or construction. "I come on," he says, "walking off-stage backwards."

The result has been increasingly unfortunate for his poetry, now the poetry of a victim, not a master ("I'm sorry, I run with the hares now, not the hounds"). The great loss is the poem itself, the poem as distinct from lines of poetry. The idea of the poem as such is as dependent on the trappings of reason (coherence, logical economy, subordination, proportion) as on the submarine coupling, the dip and dive, of intuition. And Lowell, a nihilist who "has to live in the world as is, gazing the impassable summit to rubble," has let the idea of the poem fall to pieces.

His faithful 14-line poem (the sonnet razed, destructured) is a perfunctory repository for contingent facts and feelings. Inchoate and desultory, the poems never accumulate and break in the great way, like a waterfall seen from the lip, more felt than seen. In truth, they are under no pressure to go anywhere, expect to the 14th line. Prey to random associations, they are full of false starts, fractures, distractions. Lowell's lines are now like his "star-nosed moles. . . only in touch with what they touch." The scroll rolls as it unfolds, and the first lines are hidden from the last. "When I sit in my bath, I wonder why / I haven't melted like a cube of sugar— / fiction should serve us with a slice of life"; the dash has no meaning except to say, "My thought's slipping, I'm bored, changing the subject." Even when the poems cohere, they seem inconsequent and listless, Lowell not really believing in their necessity as poems—that is, as works intent on themselves, transcending contingency—but only as the record, the absorbing gauze, of the moment.

Perhaps 90 per cent of the revision in *History* and *For Lizzie and Harriet* are improvements, yet the effort seems wasted, being, after all the reworking of "rubble." Blocks are shifted or recut, but usually the poem is still random, not even a ruin. Repeated reversals of meaning create the sinking impression that all is arbitrary. "Often the player's outdistanced by the game," runs a line in *Notebook*; "Often the player outdistances the game," runs the revision. According to *Notebook*, "When we drank in the first blindness of courtship, / loving lost half its vice with all its virtue"; "When we joined in the sublime blindness of courtship," says the new version, "loving lost all its vice with half its virtue"—an improvement but, I should think, a little embarrassed.

Lowell may have turned to sequences to catch his life on the run, but the result was to encourage incompleteness in the poems. Each being

freed from the burden of comprehension and finality, they are abandoned
to the rapid piranhas of his lines. They are almost all situation and yet, as
if each counted on the others for exposition, the situations are obscure.
Verbal shadows, the poems undoubtedly mean more to Lowell than they
can to us, since he is hulking, perhaps deliberately, in the light. Lowell
may find himself in the predicament of wanting his privacy while needing
to write about his life. In these poems poetry approaches the
circumstantial interest of the novel or autobiography but without the
fullness of information, the clarifying consecutiveness, the architectural
intelligence, of those forms.

    Nor is what is lost in the parts regained by the sum. Isolated,
random, the poems in the sequences have neither ear nor memory for one
another; they follow Lowell's life with a groping and local apprehension,
as if learning Braille. Only once does a poem look back on the others as
from a summit, and that is at the end of "The Dolphin": yet even here the
best lines are independent of the volume: "My Dolphin, you only guide me
by surprise, / forgetful as Racine, the man of craft, / drawn through his
maze of iron composition / by the incomparable wandering voice of
Phèdre."

    Indeed, like the lines on the dining mermaid these are so very fine,
so nearly complete in themselves, that they make most of the poems seem
unlucky, if not apathetic. They display the true excitement of art, the
mind's joyful grasp, its almost playful mastery, of its own surprised
conceptions of experience. It is just a galling uncertainty of conception
that leaves most of the poetry uncreated.

    What survives in these volumes is an unimpaired vigor of
language, words "handled like the new grass rippling." Though Lowell
says of himself and John Berryman, "We used the language as if we made
it," in fact he differs from the latter in being not the inventor of an idiom
but—fluent, lustrous, acid, richly shadowed—a master of the common
tongue. If the poems are private, the style is public. It is never strained yet
never stale. The tact denied to the poems goes into the diction, the force
and beauty into the phrase. There are few poems here without remarkable
lines. "The minotaur steaming in a maze of eloquence"—such is the
eloquence, and such the situation, of the three new volumes.

New York Times Book Review (July 29, 1973): 15-16.

On *History, For Lizzie and Harriet,* and *The Dolphin*

Adrienne Rich

I have just been reading three (two revised) volumes by Robert Lowell, published by Farrar, Straus and Giroux. The first, called *History*, is a reworking of the (already reworked) poems in the second editions of *Notebook*, with 80 new poems added. From *Notebook*, Lowell has lifted a group of poems dealing with his second marriage and his daughter, and published them separately in a volume called *For Lizzie and Harriet,* These poems have also been revised since they appeared in the *Notebook* versions. The third volume, *The Dolphin*, consists of new poems which delineate Lowell's love-affair with his present wife, his divorce and remarriage. Of these seventy-odd poems, a number are placed in italics or quotation marks and are presumably based on letters written to Lowell by his wife, the writer Elizabeth Hardwick, during the period after he left her and through the time of their divorce.

I don't know why Lowell felt he wanted to go on revising and republishing old poems; why not let them stand and proceed on, since life itself goes on? Perhaps, as he says, "the composition was jumbled" in *Notebook*; but he chose, as a mature poet, to publish that jumbled composition, and it represents his poetic and human choices of that time. What does it mean to revise a poem? For every poet the process must be different; but it is surely closer to pruning a tree than retouching a photograph. However, the intention behind *History* is clearly to produce a major literary document encompassing the élite Western sensibility of which Lowell is a late representative; a work to stand in competition with the great long poems of the past.

The lesson of *Notebook/History* is that brilliant language, powerful images, are not enough, and that they can become unbelievably boring in the service of an encapsulated ego. I remember *Notebook* as a book whose language sometimes dazzled even though it often seemed intentionally to blur and evade meaning, even though Lowell's own rather pedantic notion of surrealism led to a kind of image-making out of the intellect rather than the unconscious. I remember saying to a friend that in poem after poem, at the moment when you thought Lowell was about to cut to the bone, he veered off, lost the thread, abandoned the poem he'd begun in a kind of verbal *coitus interruptus*. In *History* it strikes me that this is poetry constructed in phrases, each hacked-out, hewn, tooled, glazed or burnished with immense expertise; but one gets tired of these phrases, they hammer on after a while with a fearful and draining

monotony. It becomes a performance, a method, language divorced from
its breathing, vibrating sources to become, as Lowell himself says, a
marble figure.

History is a book filled with people: Robespierre, Timur, Allen
Tate, old classmates, old lovers, relatives, Che Guevara, Anne Boleyn,
King David, poets dead and alive, Kennedys and kings. Or perhaps I
should say that for his poetry Lowell *uses* real people, versifies and
fictionalizes them at will, and thus attempts to reduce or dominate them.
They are face-cards in a game of solitaire, but solitaire is what it remains.

There's a kind of aggrandized and merciless masculinity at work
in these books, particularly the third, symptomatic of the dead-end
destructiveness that masculine privilege has built for itself into all
institutions, including poetry. I sense that the mind behind these poems
knows—being omnivorously well-read—that "someone has suffered"—
the Jews, Achilles, Sylvia Plath, his own wife—but is incapable of a true
identification with the sufferers which might illuminate their condition for
us. The poet's need to dominate and objectify the characters in his poems
leaves him in an appalling way invulnerable. And the poetry, for all its
verbal talent and skill, remains emotionally shallow.

Finally, what does one say about a poet who, having left his wife
and daughter for another marriage, then titles a book with their names,
and goes on to appropriate his ex-wife's letters written under the stress
and pain of desertion, into a book of poems nominally addressed to the
new wife? If this kind of question has nothing to do with art, we have
come far from the best of the tradition Lowell would like to vindicate—or
perhaps it cannot be vindicated. At the end of *The Dolphin* Lowell writes:

> I have sat and listened to too many
> words of the collaborating muse,
> and plotted perhaps too freely with my life,
> not avoiding injury to others,
> not avoiding injury to myself—
> to ask compassion . . . this book, half fiction,
> an eelnet made by man for the eel fighting—
> my eyes have seen what my hand did.

I have to say that I think this bullshit eloquence, a poor excuse for a cruel
and shallow book, that it is presumptuous to balance injury done to others
with injury done to oneself—and that the question remains, after all—to
what purpose? The inclusion of the letter-poems stands as one of the most
vindictive and mean-spirited acts in the history of poetry, one for which I

can think of no precedent: and the same unproportioned ego that was capable of this act is damagingly at work in all three of Lowell's books.

American Poetry Review 2 (Sept.-Oct. 1973): 42-43.

Reply to Adrienne Rich

Diane Wakoski

. . . What could make Adrienne Rich read Robert Lowell's magnificent *The Dolphin* with a better critical eye when what she is angrily denouncing is the poet's own life, his own ill-treatment of women, and his morals? Her attack on Lowell in the last issue of APR seemed as irresponsible to me as that of a poetry student I had recently. He seemed to view the world as a prisoner who was locked in a room with only a pinhole to the outer world. Some bizarre jailer had obviously positioned a magnifying glass in front of this man's pinhole, and consequently he saw the world as a tiny dot magnified a thousand times in one spot. The fact that the spot was fixed and didn't necessarily take in any portion of the world relevant to what the rest of us saw daily did not curb his urgency to talk (effusively) about what he saw and try to make the rest of us believe it was a real view of the world.

Adrienne Rich's view of Lowell is certainly, for her, as urgent. And yet I think it is as mistaken. If I only read *The Dolphin* for one purpose, after her attack, and that purpose were to see how Lowell shamelessly exhibits his immorality and brags of his perfidy and "uses" his ex-wife, even then I would know that some maniacal view of literature was being pushed by Ms. Rich.

The poems present a world with a magnificent woman named Elizabeth in it. They present a man who is living as he feels he has to live, even when he knows he has no justification for it, but his own passions. He does not ask for pity. He asks one thing, I think, of the reader. Belief in the poems. They are a mythology with characters named Elizabeth and Harriet and Caroline in it. The myth of the prince, inheritor of a throne, father's favorite, who leaves bourgeois morality behind, adopts feudal values yet struggles with a puritan and (ironically) bourgeois conscience. The poems present this so well. It is, in fact, a beautiful book. And Lowell himself becomes the modern anti-hero. Who can love him? Or even pity him? Yet we admire him. Why? Because he has written the very document that chronicles all this. A beautiful book.

Surely what literary morality is about is not the justifying or condemning of an author as a good or bad person? Surely, it is about the presentation of a document in which we, the readers, can derive a morality, understand some lives, give credence to our humanity? If the real Elizabeth of those poems was wronged in real-life, then the poems surely have given her a fuller and more triumphant day in court (we all admire her eloquent and stately beauty now) than perhaps even she could have obtained for herself. If this represents tyranny in life, to Ms. Rich, perhaps she has forgotten for a moment that literature is once removed from life. That is both its limitations and precisely what makes it so valuable. It is not life. It gives life a second chance.

American Poetry Review 3 (Jan.-Feb. 1974): 46; rpt. *Toward a New Poetry* (Ann Arbor, 1979).

Voices in *History*

Robert Pinsky

. . . Attribution, quotation, borrowing of terms, allusion to what someone else hears, sees, said, or might have said—for Lowell these are ways to qualify or refine ironies and allegiances.

Without trying to treat ["For the Union Dead"] as a whole, one can observe that lines like those about the "bronze Negroes" suggest the general tone and subject of failed sympathy: spectatorhood. This modest, rather self-chastising subject also pervades the poems of *History*, sometimes under the guise of a seeming "topicality." Not denying the authentic topicality of those remarkable poems, or otherwise judging them, I would like to point out two aspects of the poems in *History*: the actual or implied quotation marks, sometimes surrounding whole poems, and the peculiar ambivalence of the volume, especially in its later poems.

A prominent instance is the poem which begins "It was at My Lai or Sonmy or something," and ends:

> "Lieutenant LaGuerre said, 'Shoot her.' I said,
> 'You shoot her, I don't want to shoot no lady.'
> She had one foot in the door. . . . When I turned her,
> There was this little one-month-year-old baby
> I thought was her gun. It kind of cracked me up."
>   ("Women, Children, Babies, Cows, Cats")

The poem is entirely enclosed between quotation marks. It may seem strange to suggest that such material is subjected to a systematic and pervasive ambivalence; "ambivalence" may not be precisely right, but whatever we call the attitude, Lowell seems to have undertaken the problem of atrocity precisely as a challenge to that sadly reflective attitude. It is hard to find words for what I perceive to be the poem's attitude toward most of the serious emotions raised—*potentially*—by the poem, the horror, fear, and need to condemn: these feelings are not exactly dismissed, but they are left to go without saying. We are not allowed to elaborate them, or even to concentrate upon them.

What we are allowed to feel in fairly elaborate detail and fluctuation are, first, the speaker's confusion, and then his peculiar, distinct dignity. But beyond the limits and somewhat unexpected contours of the speaker's character is the subject of remembering: how the dead possess our remembering, the small good it does them, and how accidental and sadly bewildering the contact is between historical actions and individual character.

These remarks may seem to neglect the poem's other, historical material: the American war-making in Indochina, and what it did to Indochinese and to Americans; but a similarly unhistorical and reflective emphasis is suggested by the poems before and after this one in *History*. "Remembrance Day, London 1970's" finds the poet looking for notices of his new book in the Sunday papers, where he finds instead tokens of mortality and remembrance and remembrance's limits. And perhaps the most penetrating of these tokens of vanity appears not in the newspaper, but as a slip of paper in the poet's coat: announcing a memorial evening— vain? futile?—for a poet whose work will not be found reviewed or remembered in the newspaper.

The third poem, "Identification in Belfast," also has to do with the traditional theme of vanity or futility—with what may be Lowell's special twist of gloomy comedy, the possibility that our futilities may be our most memorable or essential parts. A person's frailties may be more enduring than the frail bits of paper meant to memorialize larger claims on memory. "Identification" is spoken (except for three lines, about rubber bullets and children, in Lowell's own voice) by a father who identifies the dead body of his son by means of the son's trick matches which, as the father strikes them one by one, will not light. This is no less a token of absurdity, and no less convincing, than the things one says: "'When they first showed me the boy, I thought oh good, / it's not him because he is a blonde— / I imagine his hair was singed dark by the bomb.'" Or even more arbitrary, foolish, true at the same time: "'The police were unhurried and wonderful / they let me go on trying to strike a match. . . .'"

"Wonderful" and "oh good" have the same unexpected appeal, a sort of dignified humility or graceful silliness, as the word "lady" for the murdered My Lai victim. The same quality, humane and unhistorical as the clowns in a Shakespeare history play, pervades the solemnly marching veterans in the first poem of these three, "Remembrance Day, London 1970's": "The remembered live, bagpipers in tan kilts, / their old officers in black suit, bowler and poppy, / their daughters on the sidewalk keeping their step." The phrase "the remembered live," which seems to introduce a conventional profundity, turns into something funnier and more complexly touching.

So by a variety of means—context within the volume for example, and from that context reference to broad traditional themes like "all is vanity"—Lowell manages to convey a many-sided attitude, largely through quotation. The vanity of life and life's remembrances—one's book, daughters and fathers, powers (the doomed runner Lillian Board, the poet) and idiosyncrasies—are as movingly ineffective as trick matches, rubber bullets (which can be ineffectively "humane"), memorial poppies and pamphlets, our inherited soft or genteel diction ("I don't want to shoot no lady. . . . It kind of cracked me up").

This is not a poem that "contains history," then, in Pound's definition of the epic; rather, it is historical elegy, like the Anglo-Saxon poem "The Ruin": a meditation located in the places and voices and characters of history as though they constituted a landscape. We are familiar with this tradition. Unlike, say, Marvell's "Horatian Ode" or Gogol's "Dead Souls," Lowell's work does not present particular rulers, states, or peoples as of the first urgency: instead, they are there because they are ruined or ruinous, and so conduct the meditation of death and remembrance to deeper levels. It is extraordinary that Lowell can write such a poem about such "topical" material. In part, the reason he can write it and we can read it lies in "The Waste Land" and Canto LXXXI, and beyond them perhaps earlier salvaging of wisdom or repose from historical ruin, like Lionel Johnson's "By the Statue of King Charles at Charing Cross" and Browning's invented Italy. The mode goes back at least to Samuel Johnson's version of Juvenal, but the method and the feeling belong to the modernist tradition.

To speak less sweepingly, Lowell uses the dramatic technique as a means of caution and melancholy remove. Whether extended or rapid and indirect, reliance on views and voices other than the poet's own indicates hesitance, an often gloomy pre-occupation with failed sympathy. The ruin of history not only suggests mortality, it also forces the role of inert spectator upon one: spectator both of history itself and of its shady offspring News. At first, the following poem seems more straightforward, and perhaps even more straightforwardly topical:

> Had Pharaoh's servants slaved like Nasser's labor,
> Egyptian manhood under Russian foremen,
> the pyramid. . . . I saw the Russians and imagined
> they did more tangible work in a day than all Egypt. . . .
> Dr. Mohammed Abdullah Fattah al Kassas
> fears the Dam will slow the downstream current,
> dunes and sandbars no longer build up buffers
> along the Delta and repulse the sea—
> the Mediterranean will drown a million farms,
> wild water hyacinths evaporate Lake Nasser,
> snails with wormlike bloodflukes slide incurably
> to poison five hundred miles of new canals. . . .
> Rake-sailed boats have fished the fertile Nile;
> Pharaoh's death-ship come back against the shore.
>
> ("Aswan Dam")

But the eight-line attribution is essential, not incidental. For the man whose many, unmistakably traditional names Lowell relishes, the High Dam's ecological bad effects constitute, simply, a vivid disaster to come. The four lines preceding the attribution and the sonnet "couplet" following it suggest a much different attitude. The location-shifting modern technologists with their efficient empire appear to exceed the historical native empire in the area of "tangible work." The tone is too neutral and musing at this point to say that the phrase "tangible work" is ironic, but the fifth line, with its incantation of a name, suggests that possibility. And then the description of unforeseen derangement proceeds, increasingly less neutral and more charged in tone.

This incurable poisoning is reflected upon oddly by the final lines, the poet's response to the indirect quotation which has made up most of the poem. An historical observation linked by a semi-colon to a peculiarly seer-like last line: "Rake-sailed boats have fished the fertile Nile; / Pharaoh's death-ship come back against the shore." These lines present the predicted engineering and biological calamity—*if* it should come—as a reassertion or victory of the ancient past: a past not only feared for its persisting fatal power, but respected for its sinister dignity. But the disaster is only what Dr. Fattah al Kassas fears; could the lines be read in a second sense, dismissing those fears in the enormous context of time? or as a kind of perverse, self-destructive wishful thinking on the part of an ancient culture divided and invaded by a new one?

In the first sense, antiquity is allied with the natural world in a kind of revenge delivered upon the clever innovators and their projects. The optimism of multiplied tangible works is frustrated by the working of dark laws whose calamity seems nearly to satisfy the poet. But even in the second sense—that the prediction is wrong, and perhaps rooted in national feelings—a figurative longing remains, for some alliance between the ancient past and the physical setting of the terrain.

The effect of the reference to antiquity is to evoke an attitude toward such natural laws that is conservative, cautious, pessimistic. The poet's brooding sympathy is with the builders and with the man who criticizes them, as it was with the American soldier and the victim. But again that sympathy is limited or cut short, by a sense less of history than of time and ruin. Lowell is sure only that history and the physical world are allied, contingent, and ominous. The Russian engineers and their critic both seek to "contain" history by understanding the past and planning the future; but Lowell, remote and given to second thoughts, returns to the attitude of elegy, and qualification.

That qualification arises from a remarkably intricate play between the six lines in the poet's own voice—for instance, what he "imagined"— and the image of disaster attributed to another voice. We participate in a highly sophisticated technique and, with an illusion of relatively little effort, feel the poet's tentative, oblique relation to history and historical judgments.

History—or perhaps I should say "the past"—has a long-standing association with the post-Romantic ways of using a dramatic speaker. The nineteenth-century origins often involve a fascinated borrowing from the past of its belief, its fanaticism or wholehearted passion, vicarious emotional riches. Beginning perhaps with Landor, this stream includes Browning's fancy-dress Italian Renaissance and the English obsession with southern Catholicism echoed by such poems as Ernest Dowson's "Carthusians" or Lionel Johnson's "Our Lady of the Snows." The knights and troubadors of William Morris or of the early Ezra Pound seem to share in this reliance on the emotional life—more lucid or more approachable or of greater conviction?—of a largely invented past. The tradition is itself used as material in the rich folds of Richard Howard's *Untitled Subjects*. Different as Lowell's book is, he is linked to this line by the way he conducts the emotional battle between doubt and sympathy, with a rhetoric of attribution.

The Situation of Poetry (Princeton, 1976), 18-23.

The Dolphin

Steven Gould Axelrod

At the same time that Lowell chronicles his attainment of joy and his falling away from joy, he layers that chronicle with meditations on the relations between his life story and the artwork that expresses it. His meditations compose at once a running commentary on the story and a poetics. Thus *The Dolphin* is both a narrative of love's progress and a series of poetic statements about itself, an unfolding story and the story of its own unfolding. Lowell's point is that these two are so thoroughly interwoven, so reciprocally constructive, as to be inseparable. His love for Caroline has been an affair of the psyche just as is his writing of the poem. And conversely, his writing of the poem is an act of love, as were the events that precipitated the poem. Lowell sees that his life and art have permeable borders and a coextensive existence. The life gives birth to the art, and the art completes the life, for it reshapes and culminates his consciousness of that life.

Lowell explores the relationship between life and art by frequently commenting on his words as he writes them. He begins one fourteen-liner by calling attention to the blank page about to become "defiled / by my inspiration running black in type."[1] Throughout, he contemplates the nature and value of his poem. These self-reflexive comments serve a double function. First, they prevent any confusion that the poem is simply equivalent to the life by calling attention to the obvious fact that it *is* being written or invented. But second, they show how, in another way, art is intimately connected to life. Lowell makes us aware that the poem's composition is an act occurring within his life by bringing that composition into the life of the poem. By revealing its own writing

---

[1] *The Dolphin* (New York, 1973), 46.

process, the poem is able to suggest the place that writing occupies in the life of the poet who is at once subject, topic, and author.

Echoing D. H. Lawrence on the novel, Lowell calls his poetry "a book of life" (72), thus implying both that it affirms life and that it contains his own truest life. He muses on such propositions continuously, but tentatively, willing always to change his way of putting things. At one point, for example, he addresses to Caroline these words about the art-life relationship: "fiction should serve us with a slice of life; / but you and I actually lived what I have written"(52). This is first of all a corrective to his earlier complaint, made while mentally ill, that art is a knife that "slices," or a tapeworm that feed parasitically on his life (20). He now sees art as more life-sustaining that life-threatening. (He even states a few lines earlier, Stevens-fashion, that art "should support" [52]). Yet in the later line, Lowell suggests a simple identity between what was "actually lived" and what was "written." This suggestion cannot be entirely true. It ascribes to art a power of representational fidelity it does not in fact possess, and it denies art's very real power to heighten, clarify, shape, and change—to illuminate and to darken.

Later on, Lowell readdresses himself to this question and answers it more carefully: "Conscience incurable / convinces me I am not writing my life; / life never assures which part of ourself is life" (59). He now realizes that he can never be guilty of "writing his life," for he can never know what his life, shifting shape in every instant, truly is. Day-to-day existence is a continuing fiction of the mind; *The Dolphin* is a similar but inevitably different fiction. Although they are related since both are associated with himself, neither fiction is a pale reflection or mimesis of the other. Psychic text and literary text are overlapping but not identical spaces. Lowell continues: his "life" with Caroline "was never a book, though sparks of it / spotted the page with superficial burns; / the fiction I colored with first-hand evidence, / letters and talk I marketed as fiction" (59). *The Dolphin*, then, is not synonymous with what happened "first-hand," but is sparked and spotted, burned and colored, by the "first-hand." It is indeed a book of life, not precisely the life Lowell lived but that life as it bears on his writing desire. He frames his dialectic as paradox: the poem is fiction with only a "superficial" resemblance to truth or it is truth "marketed as fiction." Finally he turns the paradox back on itself in a concluding question, "but what is true or false?" (59). On the evidence of this text, "truth" is but a trope for the psyche that experiences objects and events and constructs something of itself and its world in the experiencing; a trope for the play of form and knowledge in art. It is this "truth"—of language, experience, and imagination together—that *The Dolphin* embodies.

To achieve *The Dolphin*'s particular kind of poetic truth, Lowell commingles art and life within the very texture of his language. He does this in two ways. First, he admits actual conversations and letters into his poem unaltered, except insofar as being selected, put in line form, and placed in the context of the poem inevitably alters them. By allowing into his poem voices other than his own—actual voices speaking unaware that their words would eventually appear in a poem—Lowell attempts to replace the "clangorous rhetoric" that he thinks mars Meredith's *Modern Love* with a language torn from life instead. His practice here most directly recalls *Paterson* (and indirectly "Song of Myself"). Like Williams' poem, *The Dolphin* is a collage, but it integrates its foreign materials into its poetic medium and narrative rather than having them stand apart as prose. Lizzie's letters, Caroline's conversations, are *objets trouvés* or "trouvailles" provided by actuality to the poem. In their suffering and humor and contingency they give *The Dolphin* human reality, a ground from which the lyric symbolism of mermaid-dolphin can grow. They also at times reveal an astonishing beauty of their own: Lizzie writing,

> I got the letter
> this morning, the letter you wrote me Saturday.
> I thought my heart would break a thousand times,
> but I would rather have read it a thousand times
> than the detached unreal ones you wrote before. (31)

Or Caroline saying, "Darling, / we have escaped our death-struggle with our lives" (61). Such passages suggest that everyday life and poetry cannot be divorced, for life becomes poetry all the time, however unexpectedly and unacknowledged.

Lowell's second way of commingling art and life is to regard his life consistently through the metaphor of art. This practice testifies again to his Jamesian notion that one's life, like art, is essentially a form of fiction, a structure of moral and esthetic perception. He introduces this motif at the very outset, when he and Caroline regard a storm through the window of his flat on Redcliffe Square. The stormy scene momentarily becomes a canvas, "the limited window of the easel painter"—a circumscribed but telling representation of their own emotional turbulence (16). Later in the poem he says of himself, "I cannot hang my heavy picture straight / I can't see myself" (28), and later still he compares himself both to Manet and Manet's model (52). For Lowell, his life has all the resonances of art, and he himself plays all the roles: artist, model, viewer, depicted character. If his life is not a painting, it is a movie, a "melodrama," a verse "tragedy," a "common novel," or even *War and Peace* (48-51). He interweaves his life with references to all artistic genres, from literature and the plastic arts to architecture, photography, music, film. Manet's bar-girls, Degas' dancers, Feininger's skyscrapers, a portrait of Dante, Ford's *Good Soldier*, Shakespeare's *Hamlet* and *Macbeth*, Raleigh, Racine, Hölderlin, Carpaccio, even popular culture (Muhammed Ali's "Float Like a Butterfly and Sting Like a Bee")—all these and more parade through Lowell's pages. They all image in some way the life story unfolding in *The Dolphin*, a story like Shakespeare's of doubt and guilt, like Ford's of passion.

Lowell has several points to make by this overlapping of art and life. First and most simply, we imagine and understand our lives in terms provided by art. Life does indeed, as Wilde contended, imitate art. Second, Lowell's depiction of himself as both the determined character and determining artist captures his (and our) inner sense of being both fated and free. As character, he has only a limited "choice of endings" and none at all as to the ultimate ending of death (72); as artist, though, he is free, able with the dolphin's help to cut his "net and chains" (54). Finally, the artistic references suggest the manner in which psychic life aspires to the condition of art, the superior structure of perception. In showing that his life is already a variety of artwork, a sequence of fiction-like moments, Lowell further problematizes the space between art and life. *The Dolphin* does not transform his life into art so much as it takes what was already art in fragments and in hiding and allows it to become the form of public artwork it always could be.

The Dolphin, then, begins with the dualism of life and art and tries in every possible way to complicate and undermine it. This desire is exemplified by the poem's proliferating verbal ambiguities, most of which involve the life-art dichotomy. *The Dolphin's* puns are "trouvailles"— lovely secret meanings waiting to reveal themselves to the observant eye, Thoreauvian invitations to see more deeply. What they invite us to see ultimately is not inner discord, as did the puns of *Lord Weary's Castle*, but harmonies. The puns in *The Dolphin* yoke similarities rather than dissimilarities. They surprise us with two meanings where we had expected only one, and then further surprise us by showing that the two are variants of each other after all. For instance, Lowell claims that he must "go on typing to go on living" (28). This may mean that art alone can give him the purpose necessary to sustain his life, and it may also mean that he truly lives only on his typed page. These two possible meanings reinforce rather than contradict each other. Both point to the interdependency of life and art. The most extended such conceit occurs in "Exorcism" and "Plotted," in which Lowell envisages his life in quick succession as movie, melodrama, novel, and revenge play. He describes his situation as "one man, two women, the common novel plot" (48). The double meanings of the last three words allow two different interpretations: his life centers around a plot (conspiracy) which is common (vulgar) and novel (new to him), and his life resembles the plot (story line) of a common (typical) novel (work of fiction). Neither reading excludes the other.

Most of the puns in *The Dolphin* are variations on the central pun of its title: the dolphin as double symbol of life-force (Eros) and artistic form (muse). The poem on every page seeks with miraculous inventiveness to bring its doubles together, to weld or to wed them. Its achievement lies not in any prolonged success, but in the imagination of the quest itself.

In "Dolphin," the final section of the poem, Lowell returns for one last time to his central trope and achieves its momentary apotheosis.

> My Dolphin, you only guide me by surprise,
> forgetful as Racine, the man of craft,
> drawn through his maze of iron composition
> by the incomparable wandering voice of Phèdre.
> When I was troubled in mind, you made for my body
> caught in its hangman's-knot of sinking lines,
> the glassy bowing and scraping of my will. . . .
> I have sat and listened to too many
> words of the collaborating muse,
> and plotted perhaps too freely with my life,
> not avoiding injury to others,
> not avoiding injury to myself—
> to ask compassion . . . this book, half fiction,
> an eelnet made by man for the eel fighting—
>
> my eyes have seen what my hand did. (78)

"Dolphin," the poem's epilogue, rhymes in its language and ideas with "Fishnet," the prologue. Its fifteen lines supply what the thirteen-line prologue lacks. The two "sonnet" structures, like their subjects life and art, are flawed in themselves but can correct the deficiency or the excess of the other. When fitted together, they suggest what *The Dolphin* has been all about, what Lowell's poetic career has been all about. They arc over the poem like a rainbow, a sign of peace.

In "Fishnet" Lowell could only praise the dolphin from afar, as a shimmering and transforming presence, baffling intimacy. Indeed

"Fishnet" contains hints of futility, even of terror. In "Dolphin," however, the poet has achieved a union with her. Where once she blinded him with surprise, now she only guides him by surprise. Where once her "wandering silences" drew him, now it is her "wandering voice." Where once she eluded his grasp, now she swims toward him unbidden. The "fishnet," catcher of life, has turned "eelnet," fighter of time. The "dolphin" has become holy "Dolphin." Lowell now sees more deeply than before into his being. Brilliantly resurrecting the pun in the word "plot," he apologizes for "collaborating" with the muse too often, at times without inspiration. He similarly apologizes for a life in which he has injured others as well as himself. In humility he accepts responsibility for all of his art and life, for all that his eye has seen and his hand has done. After a lifetime of kicking against the pricks, Lowell, in a moment of spiritual insight, unconditionally accepts his world and himself. The "dolphin" now, at the last, transcends both Eros and the muse, though she contains both. She is earthly grace.

Robert Lowell: Life and Art (Princeton, 1978), 225-32.

Ending: Lowell

Lawrence Lipking

Most ambitious poets harbor such suspicions, such fears. The life of the poet is achieved at the cost of many other possible lives; it fixes the poet in place like a worm in amber. Nor have poets in modern times always concluded that a sense of destiny is worth its price. The consciousness of a past and future time can easily impoverish the present, the immediate passing moment where a poem "*is* an event, not a record of an event."[1] Hence Robert Lowell agrees with Culler that "This living hand" is "Keats's most fascinating poem" precisely because it "eschews apostrophe for direct address" and produces an event.[2] No longer striving

---

[1] Lowell, quoted by Helen Vendler, *NYTBR* (Feb. 3, 1980): 28.
[2] The two quoted phrases are identical in Jonathan Culler's "Apostrophe" (*diacritics* 7, 1977, 68) and Lowell's remarks (28).... Professor Culler has informed me that "I delivered 'Apostrophe' as a Morris Gray lecture at Harvard in Feb. or March 1977, and I believe Lowell was there." Considering the rarity

to perfect his work (on this view), just before death the poet voices his raw will to survive. Life is stronger than destiny. "See here it is"—"Keats" surrenders to Keats. Or perhaps to Lowell. Focusing upon the impulsiveness and immediacy of "This living hand," we convert it to proto-Lowell. Certainly few poets have ever had a more ironic sense of destiny. Nor have many been more eloquent than Lowell on the doubts that accompany "Reading Myself."

> Like thousands, I took just pride and more than just,
> struck matches that brought my blood to a boil;
> memorized the tricks to set the river on fire—
> somehow never wrote something to go back to.
> Can I suppose I am finished with wax flowers
> and have earned my grass on the minor slopes of
>   Parnassus. . . .
> No honeycomb is built without a bee
> adding circle to circle, cell to cell,
> the wax and honey of a mausoleum—
> this round dome proves its maker is alive;
> the corpse of the insect lives embalmed in honey,
> prays that its perishable work live long
> enough for the sweet-tooth bear to desecrate—
> this open book . . . my open coffin.[3]

Lowell repudiates his life as a poet. Performing what this book has regarded as the essential action in bringing about a new stage of poetic life—rereading his work to find another meaning in it—he discovers not life but death. His technique has consisted of "tricks," his flowers are wax, his whole career congeals into a mausoleum. Nor is it his work alone that revolts him. The deliberate ambiguity of the title, which can apply either to reading poems (whether silently or in public) or to "reading" character, suggests that the petrifaction of the work is related to a psychological weakness. The poet has cared too much about building a great career. As a result he has wanted too much to please. Inflamed with pride, he thought to prove himself alive by erecting a dome of words, only to realize that death shows itself most proudly, as in a cathedral, when most denied. And in the meantime life has escaped him.

---

of the word "eschews," it seems likely that Lowell was consciously or unconsciously remembering Culler's phrase.
[3] *History* (New York, 1973), 194.

"Reading Myself" does not represent Lowell's final verdict on his career. The image of the book as mausoleum later tended to be replaced by more vital images, the fishnet or "eelnet made by man for the eel fighting."[4] Nor did he stop reading himself and others. The eel, for instance, with all its vitality, derives not only from Montale's great poem but from Lowell's own earlier imitation of it. And even "Reading Myself," notwithstanding its nausea in the face of classicism, might well be considered a classical type of modern poem—the failure of its "tricks" related to "The Circus Animals' Desertion," the bee and sarcophagus borrowed from Rilke,[5] the open book, its pages so in need of ruffling and its equation with death so manifest, beautifully adapted from "Le Cimetière marin." Yet readings like these should not be allowed to distract us from the genuine note of recantation in Lowell's own reading. He looks at his early work and does not find it good. He would not go back to it. Attempting to unlearn the brilliant formal structures and powerful rhythms with which he had once thought to storm Parnassus, he opened his book to the day-by-day, to events and history and family and politics and chance and America and the mistakes of a lifetime. His verse became a continuing journal, hesitant, vulnerable, and sometimes slack. The broken-backed unrhymed sonnet form of "Reading Myself," octave and sestet reversed to allow a long fall from the climax, is the staple of Lowell's later career. It is not a heroic form—"The line must terminate" (*Dolphin* 15). Refusing to let his lines deny death any longer, he sought to make his life as a poet identical with his life.

The project, as more than one critic has noted, derives from Whitman's. But Lowell puts far less confidence than Whitman in his readers—even when the reader is himself. The opening lines of "Reading Myself" exhibit an author who is very uneasy about resembling "thousands." Who are those thousands? The context implies them to be the whole herd of ambitious authors, carried away with their own eloquence and sense of future greatness. Yet clearly Lowell is not the poet to join a crowd. From another point of view the thousands seem associated with a political rally or protest, whose pride in solidarity the poet has helped to inflame. His lack of respect for this accomplishment is sufficiently defined by his view of how one stirs an audience: "I memorized the tricks." A similar uneasiness hovers round the "sweet-tooth bear," whose power to desecrate poetry can refer either to devouring time

---

[4] *The Dolphin* (New York, 1973), 78.
[5] The connection with Rilke is drawn by Phillip Cooper, *Autobiographical Myth of Robert Lowell* (Chapel Hill, 1970), 154, though the conclusion that "Lowell is actually doing what Rilke taught" seems extravagant to me.

or a hungry public. To be read at all, Lowell appears to hint, is to risk being inauthentic. Nor does his reading of himself allow any more comfort. For all his democratic mistrust of formalism, heroism, or an embalmed poetic, he does not seem to think of poetry as something to be shared with strangers. "The proof of a poet," Whitman had proudly concluded the preface to *Leaves of Grass*, "is that his country absorbs him as affectionately as he has absorbed it"—a declaration that would plague him later, when it became evident that his affections were not returned. But Lowell resists absorption. Taking just pride not only in his ability to move an audience but in his knowledge of what it costs, he withdraws from the race. Hence America, whose disorders at first seem monstrous counterparts to the poet's own psychological demons, ultimately turns into a foreign country. Even his early poems, reread, seem foreign.

In the image of the bee and the honeycomb Lowell's equivocal attitude toward his career receives its fullest expression. The organization of this particular hive is very peculiar. Surely no bee's labors have ever seemed more isolated or useless. Like a pharaoh aspiring to raise his pyramid by himself, this highly unsocial insect has no coworkers, no progeny, and no object but self-memorial. His own work keeps him prisoner. The dome of the honeycomb might stand for a human skull, whose outward calm conceals feverish, obsessive thoughts. But the figure that presides over the whole, above all, is death-in-life. Though three successive lines insist that the work and its maker "live," a heavy irony surrounds each use of the word; it is only a corpse that "lives." Lowell seems to regard his work and career as burying him alive.[6] Perhaps he also takes some secret pleasure in what he has accomplished; not every poet, after all, succeeds in building a mausoleum. "To die is life," an old man of Lowell's own creation had remembered while "Falling Asleep over the Aeneid." Yet the reading suffers woefully from its lack of issue. The old poems offer no nourishment and will not lead to new ones.

If the life of the poet depends on posterity, that is to say, Lowell considers it far from worth the cost. The sense of destiny withers when the future approaches like a tawdry motorway: "The Aquarium is gone. Everywhere, / giant finned cars nose forward like fish" ("For the Union Dead"). Why should one sacrifice one's life on an altar where no one worships? Lowell draws the logical conclusion. He writes for himself and tries to be true to himself, not greater than he is. He does not offer us his living hand. Yet another conclusion might be drawn from Lowell's reading

---

[6] The image of the honeycomb is regarded more benignly ("charming, witty," and sweet) by Irvin Ehrenpreis in *N Y Review of Books* (Oct. 28, 1976): 6.

of himself. Analysis of his career brings him no satisfaction, nevertheless it provides a new self-understanding. Perhaps a modern poet can hope for no more. In these terms the test of a true accomplishment may be less whether the poet has lived up to his dream of what he might be than whether he has perceived that nothing he has done is accidental. To perfect one's life as a poet, Lowell seems to say, would mean accepting full responsibility for it—the weakness as well as the strength. A poetic autobiography has the right to play with the truth, but it cannot afford to pretend that the past has not happened. Lowell's ruthlessness with his previous work (including his depredations of *Near the Ocean*) reflects his decision to judge himself again at every turn. His integrity, the shape of his career itself, consists of sparing nothing.

At the end of *The Dolphin*, the sequence that Lowell chose to conclude his *Selected Poems*, one line is separated from the rest. The fifteenth line of a sonnet, overflowing the space and standing alone, it may have been intended by Lowell as an epitaph for his life as a man and his life as a poet: "my eyes have seen what my hand did." I know what I have done, the poet says; and everything these poems record comes out of my own experience. Nor does he excuse himself. The terrible things a hand can do, the guilt of a Cain or the cunning stratagems of his creator, all burden the line. It holds a potential for horror. The disjunction between eyes and hand, between seeing and doing, is reminiscent of a stock Gothic effect: the murderer who observes himself in the act of murder, the criminal disconnected from his crime yet powerless to stop it. Exacerbated self-consciousness may be the ultimate horror. "See here it is." And it is possible that a poet who confesses to this disconnection in his own life, who may even regard the death-in-life of his poetry as both the cause and product of such disconnection, is asking not compassion but acceptance of what he has done.

Perhaps he is also accepting himself. To see what one has done is not to make amends; but responsibilities begin with clarity of vision. At least he has not averted his eyes. In the little world of the author and his page, moreover, where nothing matters more than coordinating the eye and hand, a proper vision of one's writing is all-important. It may even involve a transformation, as in Eliot: "to arrive where we started / And know the place for the first time" ("Little Gidding"). Lowell does not claim so much. He sees his handiwork without approving it.[7] Yet the line that he

---

[7] According to S. G. Axelrod, *Robert Lowell: Life and Art* (Princeton, 1978), the end of "Dolphin" shows that "Lowell, in a moment of spiritual insight, unconditionally accepts his world and himself" (232). But Lowell's own view of the relations between life and art is hardly so positive and unproblematical.

chooses to close his book and his career sounds almost religious—not the religion of Whitman and so many other great poets who believe in reincarnation, nor the religion of Dante and Eliot, who trust in the resurrection, but the religion of a poet who hopes only to be honest with himself. The past cannot be contravened and the future may never exist; there is only the present. If Lowell does not approve his life as a poet, nevertheless he puts his signature to it, his hand turned toward himself. Not "here it is," he says at last, but "here I am."

The Life of the Poet (Chicago, 1981), 184-88.

History

Vereen M. Bell

Notebook became *History* as an afterthought. Lowell's friend Frank Bidart, who participated in *History*'s revision, confirms what Stephen Yenser had guessed at: that *For Lizzie and Harriet* was the first book to be made from relevant materials excised from *Notebook* and that the plan of *History* came about as a device for reorganizing the materials that were left (along with the new poems to be added).[1] Without the personal poems that had formed the basis for *Notebook*'s seasonal structure, the remainder of *Notebook* was left with no structure at all. The solution that presented itself was to arrange the surviving and new poems in a rough chronological sequence, beginning with the very beginning of time. This was a resourceful but also somewhat arbitrary strategy, a virtue made of necessity; and since the results, in any case, are now fixed in place, *History* will eventually have to be dealt with on its own terms. Those terms, however, are markedly different from *Notebook*'s and not always to the later volume's advantage.

One damaging effect of the transformation of *Notebook* into *History* is that the eccentric style of the new volume is left without formal authorization. It is a notebook style, brilliantly effective at its best at registering what experience is like at the fluid border between subject and object, in the continuing present that is the consciousness-time of the

---

[1] Bidart in conversation; Yenser, *Circle to Circle* (Berkeley 1975).

original poem. *Notebook* is not a memoir or an autobiography or history but what it declares itself to be, which is its reason for being. The style of *Notebook*, in other words, is essentially appropriate for interior monologue in a moving present and justifiable only to the extent that it is harnessed securely and comprehensibly to that purpose. *History*, however, has no firmly identified protagonist whose consciousness we are attending; it is not invigorated by the quirky, palpable atmosphere of specific settings (Cambridge, New York, Castine, Mexico); and it presents no characterization of time whatever. Time in *History* is merely an idea, an abstraction, not a medium within which we live: the day-to-day, the seasonal, the real rhythm of experience, in other words, from which the written word of *Notebook* seems inseparable. The sense of intimacy that gave *Notebook* its mysterious life does not survive the transformation. *History* is not altogether successful, therefore, as a formal enterprise because it has merely adapted a style conceived for one design to a new design for which it is not suited. In this respect it is *History* rather than *Notebook* that is random, and careful readers of both volumes may perceive readily how the poems transposed from *Notebook* are stunned by *History*'s mechanical, symmetrical organization into the poetical equivalent of an inorganic state. This odd discontinuity—in effect, between style and point of view—is marginally less conspicuous after the chronology enters the time of Lowell's own life span, roughly at the point of "Wolverine, 1927"; but of course at that point the history paradigm itself has ceased to be relevant. The poet's consciousness in that subsequent time period is more personal and at least contemporaneous; but the first half of the book is then left seeming vaguely stranded.

Another important effect is that, epistemologically speaking, *History* turns *Notebook* inside out. It changes what was overtly subjective into an ostensibly objective structure, with the effect of hardening the attitudes. Whereas in *Notebook* the focus was first of all on the activity of consciousness and second on the contents of that consciousness, in *History* the content has achieved an autonomous status, and the mind's influence upon that material, though still evident, of course, in the idiosyncratic style, is downplayed. What was dominant in one volume is recessive in the other, and vice versa. In *Notebook* the cynicism shown toward historical figures could be taken at least partially as a projection of the poet's own identity, an aspect of an ongoing process of self-discovery; but in *History* Lowell takes the long aerial view, and the verdicts have edged toward the absolute authority of fact. *History* is therefore by a wide margin the more pessimistic of the two volumes. It is all the more so since the poignantly few domestic and extra-domestic romantic interludes that gave *Notebook* a faltering sense of human purpose, an affirmative orientation, in *History* have been cut away. The feeling man in the poems in *History* is claimed almost wholly by his won cynicism. Moreover, by linearizing for *History* the basic material of *Notebook*, Lowell has made the former volume's implicit anti-meliorism retroactive and therefore more emphatic. *History* fiercely spatializes time and human experience, and our moral nature in that stasis becomes inert. The obvious effect is that the familiar modernist recourse of nostalgic time-travel is disallowed. As there is no refuge before us (except death), there is now none behind us either, for whatever comfort the past may have been in any case. The powerful men and women of history in the new arrangement are more obviously simply replications of each other, domestic versions of Ozymandias; and their story, so exposed, becomes numbingly redundant, and poetically less interesting. It is not only no longer possible to be placated by illusions; it is also no longer possible to revere—or simply not be bored by—the truth.

When we move from *Notebook* to *History*, nothing ontologically has truly changed—human life is unfulfilling in either setting; but the emphasis is noticeably different. Yenser points out that *History* can also be read as his-story. The pun shows the margin of difference between the second version and the first, and the life of the one within the other. All of experience for Lowell tends to be "his story," no matter how it is laid out. It is all appropriated and internalized in radically personal ways. *History* as a concept seems grandiose, especially compared with the modesty of its predecessor, but it may in fact be quite the reverse—that is, a concession on Lowell's part of his failure to free himself from the confining patterns of his own thought.

The volume's first poem, itself called "History," foretells the themes of the volume by modifying the most familiar symbol of a more credulous romantic era.

> As in our Bibles, white-faced, predatory,
> The beautiful, mist-drunken hunter's moon ascends—
> A child could give it a face: two holes, two holes,
> My eyes, my mouth, between them a skull's no-nose—
> O there's a terrifying innocence in my face
> Drenched with the silver salvage of the mornfrost.[2]

It is important to recognize in passages such as this one the ambivalence that is indicated, almost unwillingly, in the diction—a conflict between a residual lyricism and the poem's grinding fatalism, which in the end prevails. In the preceding lines of the poem, it is made clear that the poet

---

[2] *History* (New York, 1973), 24.

is unable to envision our mythic beginnings in innocence without subordinating the Edenic aspect to the post-Edenic; what is stressed is the admonitory episode of Cain and Abel. The "terrifying innocence in my face" associates the poet with moon's skull face and with the innocence of Abel and its fateful consequence. If there is, as Yenser suggests, a bizarre pun on "no-nose," it might be understood to refer not only to a cosmic tyranny but also to a denial of possibility—a denial that the death's head in the moon's face only reinforces. But the moon's face is also Lowell's and therefore no portal but a mirror, another dead end. Perhaps that is an innocence—an inviolability of the ego—that is justly terrifying in its own right.

In "Flaw," later, that projecting solipsism is associated with the physically harmless but psychically pathogenic defect of his "old eye-flaw,"

> sprouting bits and strings
> Gliding like dragon-kites in the Midwestern sky—
> I am afraid to look closely, and count them;
> Today I am exhausted and afraid.
> I look through the window at unbroken white cloud,
> And see in it my many flaws are one,
> A flaw with a tail the color of shed skin,
> Inaudible rattle of the rattler's disks. (177)

Both curious and typical in this episode is the way in which this common spectacle of air travel, exhilarating to some observers (as is the moon), becomes for Lowell in a mood of anxiety and exhaustion simply one more sinister portent, a not merely hopeless but even threatening prospect. The shed skin becomes a rattler's disks—eerily inaudible—and the disks "the first scrape of the Thunderer's fingernail." The large meaning is hidden in the small, as the minute flaw is magnified in perspective upon the clouds. This is a gloss upon Lowell's many juxtapositions in both *Notebook* and *History* of the momentous and the trivial; but as both "History" and "Flaw" imply, he has somehow lost control over his own powers of signification. This theme stays in the foreground in *History*, especially in poems that have to do with the subject of his failing eyesight. Thus, in "Fears of Going Blind (For Wyndham Lewis)" two levels of meaning are quite clearly intended). . . .

Lowell is as ready to deglamorize the artist's vision as he is history, that vision's subject matter, and to concede that the vision is necessarily flawed and doomed. The "non sequitur" he speaks of is evidently the paranoid transition from simple stoplights to sinister leopard's eyes, and from the leopard to a four-legged predatory God. This nameless God is to the Christian vision what leaking eyeball jelly is to the artist's. His own vision is not something that he chooses, or by which he is redeemed or even gratified; it is something that he cannot escape. The "failed surgeon" who in this poem cannot save the eye and exits with "with a smile" suggests with irony "the wounded surgeon" of Eliot's "East Coker" whose "sharp compassion of the healer's art" resolves "the enigma of the fever chart" and saves the patient whose suffering in the world ensures his spiritual health.

Alan Williamson points out that the "concept 'God' has been making a surreptitious comeback in Lowell's [recent] poetry."[3] *History* contains as many as forty poems that make direct reference to God, but the God of this vision is no being with whom one would cheerfully consort. He is at his best as featureless as the God of Christian existentialism; at worst he is sinister and unpredictable, an adversary of humanity rather than an ally:

> But was there some shining, grasping hand to guide
> me when I breathed through gills, and walked on fins
> through Eden, plucking the law of retribution from the
>   tree?
> Was the snake in the garden, an agent provocateur?
> Is the Lord increased by desolation? (26)

Strictly speaking, this question is not necessarily facetious. Since in the Hebrew tradition, and in the Old Testament generally, there is no autonomous evil force such as the Christian Satan opposing God, there is logically no being for the serpent to represent in the unfallen garden but God himself. God and man in Lowell's revisions of history are therefore off to a considerably worse start than is generally supposed, each guilty of having betrayed the other. We are familiar with this contest from *Lord Weary's Castle*, where it is prosecuted less explicitly but with greater intensity. That it should now reassert itself at this later point in Lowell's career shows how deeply entrenched his religious nihilism has been all along. There is this difference now, though: the God of *Notebook* and *History* is so remote as to have become a kind of overbearing abstraction to whose existence may be attributed any number of recurring human tribulations. Cumulatively, the references to God in *History* insinuate that there must be some scheme at work in the universe that is vastly beyond our capacity for knowing—some principle that may as likely be irrational

---

[3] Williamson, *Pity the Monsters* (New Haven, 1974), 214n.

as rational or destructive as creative, having nothing remotely in common with the Gods of traditional religions, but somehow there. The idea of God in the poems of *History* signifies Lowell's unwillingness to envision a universe without a cause, or without an ultimate metaphysical boundary or limit. This may be the mystery that the nude and faceless figure in Frank Parker's frontispiece drawing broods upon as he sits amid ruins of war and glory glared down upon by evil faces in the sun and moon, with his own death waiting at his shoulder, half in shadow. So God in *History* at first is He "with whom nothing is design or intention" ("In Genesis," 26). Or later, "God is design, even our ugliness / is the goodness of his will" ("Flaw," 177). And at the last, "'God's ways are dark and very seldom pleasant'" ("Death and the Bridge," 205). History and God have this in common: each is, as Yeats said of Plato's nature, a "ghostly paradigm that plays upon the spume of things." The paradigms are indecipherable, but without them the things—the events and intuitions of human life—cannot be assigned certain value, except, seemingly, the negative value that owes to their contrast with the grand, failing paradigms themselves. With *History*, these grand paradigms themselves. With *History*, these grand paradigms have therefore been put away for good. From this point on, the poet's life will be conducted willingly— however unappeased—in the more intimate spaces of the world.

Robert Lowell: Nihilist as Hero (Cambridge, Mass., 1983), 188-94.

Robert Lowell's *History*

Robert von Hallberg

Of all the poets who have tried their hand at political poetry in the last thirty-five years, Lowell is the most accomplished and surely the most ambitious. One measure of the quality of his effort is the coherence of the poetry around several expressly political beliefs; another is the cogency of the beliefs themselves. *History* embodies nothing so systematic or impersonal as an ideology, but the judgments and sympathies in the poems reveal a set of political ideas that bear on each other—which is perhaps only to say that this is a more intelligent than opinionated book.

Lowell's politics were focused on the appeal of imperial and revolutionary cultures: opulence and excitement. Rome, even as late as the fourth century, offered enough of "The Good Life"—"trees flower and leaves pearl with mist, / fan out above them on the wineglass elms, / life's frills and the meat of life: wife, children, houses"—to make the officers left in Rome after Constantine withdrew (330 A. D.) "anxious to please," at the expense of "vomiting purple in the vapid baths."[1] Lowell made no bones about his own complicity in those experiences fostered by empires and revolutions—namely, quick changes.

> My live telephone swings crippled to solitude
> two feet from my ear; as so often and so often,
> I hold your dialogue away to breathe—
> still this is love, Old Cato forgoing his wife,
> then jumping her in thunderstorms like *Juppiter Tonans*:
> his forthrightness gave him long days of solitude,
> then deafness changed his gifts for rule to genius.
> Cato knew from the Greeks that empire is hurry,
> and dominion never goes to the phlegmatic—
> it was hard to be Demosthenes in his stone-deaf Senate:
> "Carthage must die," he roared . . . and Carthage died.
> He knew a blindman looking for gold
> in a heap of dust must take the dust with the gold,
> Rome, if built at all, must be built in a day.
>
> ("Marcus Cato 234-149 B. C.," 43)

The poem begins with self incrimination—for a common, domestic betrayal. His own willful deafness to his wife he compares to the deafness of demagoguery: Cato becomes a political genius when late in life he ceases listening to others, and of course the Roman senate was deaf as well. The imperialists hear not, and neither do they see, but they get the gold. What is all but stated is the painful truth that a poet trying to incorporate history from Eden to the Hudson must take a lot of dust for a little gold, and probably also betray the living ones he loves with insensitivity—a "petty decadence," he wrote in a draft of the opening line.[2]

As an alternative to imperial opulence and self-indulgence, history offers austerity, which Lowell regards as consistently loathsome. (In fact, as the case of Cato suggests, austerity too can be self-indulgent.) The

---

[1] *History* (New York, 1973), 50.
[2] Lowell collection (Harvard).

barbarians from the north were provincials with nothing more urging them on than "the wind / . . . and a gently swelling birthrate" (53). Lowell's criticism of America is not that it is imperialistic, like Rome, but that it is merely predatory where Rome was grand: "our bombers are clean-edged as Viking craft, / to pin the Third World to its burning house" (53). The grandeur of Rome was sensual, monumental, not ideological; Mediterranean, not Nordic. The austerity of the ideologue, Saint-Just and Cato the Elder are the type, is odiously inhumane (76). In an early draft of the poem he was then calling "Saint-Just, Saint of the Guillotine, 1767-1793," Lowell wrote: "It's deplorable that these men so young—still / unfinished, dead before the age 25 / should so violently force themselves on their / world. Lowell's complaint about austerity is not just that its severity is cruel but also that civilization, taste, is corrupted by it.

> A thundercloud hung on the mantel of our summer
> cottage by the owners, Miss Barnard and Mrs. Curtis
> a sad picture, 2/3's life-scale, removed now, and no
>   doubt
> scrapped as too raw and empire for our taste:
> *Waterloo, Waterloo!* You could choose sides then:
> the engraving made the blue French uniforms black,
> the British Redcoats gray; those running were French—
> an aide-de-camp, Napoleon's perhaps,
> wore a cascade of overstated braid,
> there sabered, dying, his standard wrenched from weak
>   hands;
> his killer, a helmeted, fog-gray dragoon—
> six centuries, this field of their encounter,
> kill-round of French sex against the English *no* . . .
> *La Gloire* fading to *sauve qui peut* and *merde*.
>   ("Waterloo," 78)

Cascade of braid, weakening hands, wicked dragoon—all of this was perfect, in its camp way, and sadly missed. Imperial grandeur is stagey, even crude, and indefensible in strictly moral terms (the landladies are right about that), but the last line claims that protestant moralism is ignoble and vulgar too in its effect on the French imagination. An empire is a conception of collective identity and of sublimity and gradation. Without it the picture is gray.

Lowell will take the power and the glory every time (how else should a poet choose?) even at the cost of championing Napoleon: "Dare we say, he had no moral center?" (77). Or, worse still, Stalin. . . .

Lowell was always inclined to go a long way in sympathy with the powerful, at least in his poems (in the polemical pages of *Commentary* he was more careful to align himself with the insistent anti-Stalinism of New York intellectual circles by saying that "No cause is pure enough to support these faces" of Stalin and Mao on posters upheld by students marching in Rome.[3]) The leaders he found most despicable were not the tyrants or the conquerors—a redeeming word or two could be found for Attila, Timur, or Hitler; but for the wholly predictable "Leader of the Left" he had only bitter contempt (150). Leaders ought, first, to be individuals; if they are humane as well, that is extra. Lowell, like most liberals, put a lot of stock in the ability of particular individuals to alter the course of history. In the winter of 1967, the editors of *Partisan Review* asked various intellectuals, "Does it matter who is in the White House? Or is there something in our system which would force any President to act as Johnson is acting?" To ideological leftists, the effects of American policy are determined by systematic priorities, not by individual executives. But to Lowell's mind, as to those of most liberals, "nothing could matter more than who is in the White House."

> It's not like the arts. Two very foolish novelists with opposed beliefs or temperaments would write equally foolish novels, but two equally foolish presidents would have widely differing effects on our lives, the difference between life and death. Yet a great president somehow honors his country, even if what he effects is debatable. I suppose Lincoln was our most noble and likable president. The country is somehow finer for having had him, yet much that he accomplished was terrifying and might have been avoided by the run-of-the-mill Douglas. I wish Stevenson had been elected. Maybe he would have done nothing (I don't believe this) but at least he would have registered what he was doing. I can't imagine him not losing a night's sleep over Hiroshima, even if he did drop the bomb. I think he might not have.[4]

A highly placed individual not only makes consequential decisions, determined partly by character, but he or she also serves as a measure (like *La Gloire*) of the state of the nation, its level of refinement. This is a poet's politics—Pound would have understood exactly. Lowell's forlorn glance back fifteen years to the defeat of Adlai Stevenson by Eisenhower

---

[3] "Liberalism and Activism," *Commentary* (Apr. 1969): 19.
[4] "What's Happening to America," *Partisan Review* 34 (1967): 14, 37-38.

shows how much this poet was of the intellectual, liberal, Democratic
Party. . . .

The leader to whom Lowell was most attached in the late 1960s
was Eugene McCarthy. He followed McCarthy along part of the
campaign trail and spoke publicly on his behalf. After the California
primary went to Robert Kennedy, and Kennedy was shot down, Lowell
realized that McCarthy's chances of receiving the Democratic nomination
were nil, and he wrote a sentimental poem about his candidate:

> I love you so. . . . Gone? Who will swear you wouldn't
> have done good to the country, that fulfillment wouldn't
> have done good to you—the father, as Freud says:
> you? We've so little faith that anyone
> ever makes anything better . . . the same and less—
> ambition only makes the ambitious great. (175)

Lowell's is a melioristic argument based on the liberal notion of progress,
and a belief that simple qualities of character, such as ambition, change
the world—this was a hard argument to render persuasive in 1968. Less
than a month before writing the poem "For Eugene McCarthy," he told a
group of Yale seniors that "we need a government of order and liberty, a
merciful and intelligent government."[5] Mercy and human kindness were
qualities Lowell thought worthy of political consideration, and about this,
as about the transience of life and the error of all efforts, he could write
well. . . .

About the time that the first version of *History*, then called
Notebook 1967-68, appeared, Lowell went on record as having "never
been New Left, Old Left, or liberal. I wish to turn the clock back with
every breath I draw, but I hope I have the courage to occasionally cry out
against those who wrongly rule us" ("Liberalism and Activism" 19). At
the time it seemed to some that he had committed his writing to the New
Left cause, though now the preoccupations of *History* seem far closer to
those of the liberal consensus of the 1950s. The poet who wishes to speak
only from time to time as the moral conscience of the body politic bears
no systematic opposition to the authority of his government; he rather
objects to some of the exercises of that authority. Lowell's interest in
individual leaders, his discounting of their particular ideologies and of
their class, his effort to psychologize the positions of those who were
plainly illiberal in their loyalties, his hope for some increment of progress
and a modicum of compassion—these are the concerns of the avowed

---

[5] Lowell collection (Harvard).

liberals of Lowell's generation. I make this point not to disparage Lowell's achievement, although the term "liberal" has indeed come to be used casually as a disparagement. Nor can this designation have an especially exact significance. On the contrary, from the end of World War II until the early 1960s, it was a usefully inclusive term for identifying the capacious center of American political opinion.

The years 1967-68, when Lowell was beginning work on *History*, were perhaps the height of the hunting season on liberals. After the Democrats chose that old liberal Hubert Humphrey in 1968, it was hard to hold the liberal ground with banners flying; for a while, the center of American politics was thoroughly debased in the eyes of many influential academic and literary intellectuals. That Lowell would then undertake his magnum opus in the liberal vein shows a kind of firm integrity that, to the literary historian who weighs the achievement of one poet against the mass of his or her contemporaries, looks especially impressive. How common it was in the late 1960s simply to assume that the center was uninhabitable.

Political positions have to be assessed in terms of their practicality, humaneness, consistency, inclusiveness, and justice, surely. American liberalism has been subjected to severe criticism on most of these grounds in the last fifteen years or so. This is not the place to defend liberalism from such attacks. But Lowell's work does demonstrate, to my judgment quite soundly, that postwar liberalism had sufficient range of vision and intelligence, and commanded enough emotional power, to enable a poet of unusual ability to write the sort of book that guarantees him the status of a major poet. It cannot be said that American liberalism has had no major imaginative embodiment in the last thirty-five years. It has indeed its *History*, which is one of the most successful book-length poems of this period. (Dorn's *Slinger* is the other, I believe). And the imaginative command of an ideology must also be measured when an ideology is assessed by historians, especially by literary historians.

American Poetry and Culture 1945-1980 (Cambridge, Mass., 1985), 158-65.

Robert Lowell: "Fearlessly Holding Back Nothing"

Marjorie Perloff

Let the trumpet of the Last Judgment sound when it will; I shall come, this book in my hand, to present myself before the sovereign judge. I shall declare here is what I have done, what I have thought, what I have been.

So writes Rousseau on the opening page of the *Confessions*. Robert Lowell, whose earlier poetry was haunted by visions of the Last Judgment, but who could not finally comfort himself with the belief in a sovereign judge, might have used Rousseau's words as his epigraph for *Day by Day*.[1] It is the triumph of this collection that it captures, with almost frightening accuracy, what Lowell has done, what he has thought, and especially what he has been. In his last years, he seems to have attained the self-knowledge he had always been seeking, a sense of self so sharp that in one poem he prefigures the very conditions of his own death:

> Under New York's cellular facades
> clothed with vitreous indifference,
> I dwindle . . . dynamite no more.
>
> I ask for a natural death,
> no teeth on the ground,
> no blood about the place . . .
> It's not death I fear,
> but unspecified, unlimited pain.

This passage appears on page 48 of *Day by Day*. Less than a week after the book was published, Robert Lowell died of a heart attack while traveling by taxi from Kennedy Airport to the home of Elizabeth Hardwick, his former wife, to whom he had been married for 25 years. There were "no teeth on the ground, / no blood about the place" in this "natural death." And surely this was justice, for the "unspecified, unlimited pain" Lowell longed to avoid in dying had been his portion while alive, especially during the years of terror and turmoil evoked with such candor in these new poems.

---

[1] *Day by Day* (New York, 1977).

Day by Day is Lowell's last testament, a book *self-centered* in the best sense of the word. For here, in successive "snapshot[s] . . . heightened from life, / yet paralyzed by fact," Lowell renounces, one by one, the roles he played in his earlier work: judge, preacher, surveyor of history, connoisseur of chaos. From the opening poem, in which Ulysses acknowledges his impotence to his young Circe, Lowell makes clear that there will be no more parades. The "I" of *Day by Day* offers no solutions to the political dilemmas of living in "the sunset of Capitalism." He has no hopes of being blessed by "the Queen of Heaven"; he passes judgment neither on Napoleon nor on Nixon, as he did in *History* (1973); he no longer berates his Puritan ancestors as he did in *Lord Weary's Castle* (1947). The fiery Lowell who once declared: "Our fathers wrung their bread from stocks and stones / And fenced their gardens with the Redman's bones" now speaks ruefully of "my dangerous ad hominem simplifications." Even Lowell's parents, immortalized in *Life Studies* (1959) as tragicomic representatives of Beacon Hill snobbery, decadence. and futility, now become merely Robert Lowell's parents, human beings whom he can actually love. The same process of demythologizing occurs in the case of Lowell's literary friends—John Berryman, Peter Taylor, W. H. Auden, Robert Penn Warren—as well as the women he has loved. Perhaps most remarkable, the machismo that made *The Dolphin* (1973) a rather problematic volume has wholly evaporated in this new book in which Lowell casts a cold eye on life and death, recognizing that "our bodies / are but as bodies are," that it is all "Gone / the sweet agitation of the breath of Pan."

In a poem called "The Withdrawal," Lowell notes: "and the years of discretion are spent on complaint— / until the wristwatch is taken from the wrist." "Complaint" in the broadest sense—political satire, moralizing about history, about the social condition, about sexuality—such topical poetry is now ruled out of order. Illness, both mental and physical, seems to have undermined the old desire to speak one's piece: "We feel the machine slipping from our hands, / as if someone else were steering; / if we see the light at the end of the tunnel, / it's the light of an oncoming train." Under these circumstances ("the wristwatch has been taken from the wrist"), Lowell opts for simplicity. "I thank God," he says in one poem, "for being alive— / a way of writing I once thought heartless." And in another poem he declares: "Alas, I can only tell my own story— / talking to myself, or reading, or writing, / or fearlessly holding back nothing from a friend."

But how does one tell one's "own story" without lapsing into solipsism? How to "say what happened" without resorting to cliché? This has always been a problem for the confessional poet, and Lowell has solved it variously. In *Life Studies*, his first autobiographical book, he creates beautiful circular structures; the typical lyric like "Man and Wife" begins in a moment of crisis in the present, moves backward into a closely related past, and then returns to the present with renewed insight. The model for these poems was the Greater Romantic Lyric—say Wordsworth's "Tintern Abbey"—but the texture was concrete and realistic—Flaubertian or Chekhovian as Lowell himself insisted whenever he discussed *Life Studies*.

The unrhymed blank verse sonnet sequences that began with *Notebook 1967-68* are closer to diary entries than to autobiography proper. In a recent commentary in *Salmagundi*, Lowell himself says of them: "I had a chance such as I had never had before . . . to snatch up and verse the marvelous varieties of the moment. I think perfection (I mean outward coherence not inspiration) was never so difficult. . . . Obscurity came when I tried to cram too much in the short space." Many readers including myself will concur with this self-judgment; one might add that, if obscurity was the Scylla of the sonnet cycles, their Charybdis was triviality. In recording the varieties of the moment, Lowell often resorted to sheer documentation. . . .

Such literal transcripts placed the reader in the position of voyeur, observing or overhearing things that were really none of anybody's business. But the "confessionalism" of *Day by Day* is of a very different order. In the *Paris Review* interview of 1961, Lowell spoke of the Chekhovian "detail that you can't explain. It's just there." And he added: "Almost the whole problem of writing poetry is to bring it back to what you really feel, and that takes an awful lot of maneuvering. You may feel the doorknob more strongly than some big personal event, and the doorknob will open into something you can use as your own. . . . Some little image, some detail you've noticed—you're writing about a little country shop, just describing it, and your poem ends up with an existentialist account of your experience."

The title sequence of *Day by Day* is precisely such an "existentialist account of experience," even though the individual poems lack the finish and complex network of images found in comparable poems in *Life Studies*, *For the Union Dead*, or *Near the Ocean*. *Day by Day* resembles a fragmented Chekhovian novella; it is a series of poignant and ironic variations on the title, which is that of a popular song, crooned over the airwaves of the early '50s by Frank Sinatra [entitled "Day by Day"].

Lowell takes these hyperboles and turns them inside out. His own "story" is one of day-by-day withdrawal; day by day, the love he shares with his new wife seems to decline, and there is an end to their mutual devotion. Significantly, husband and wife dwell in the "oceanless inland" of Milgate Park in Kent, and the poet thinks sadly that he hasn't heard "the Atlantic rattling paper" for "three years." In the idyllic "golden summer" world of cow pasture and "blond-faced wheat," each new day is threatening, the blinding sun reminding both poet and reader that "The reign of the kingfisher was short." Memories of his former life repeatedly crowd out the attempt to recapture "pastoral adolescence," and in the closing lines of "The Golden Summer," the speaker says laconically: "I will leave earth / with my shoes tied, / as if the walk / could cut bare feet."

In the poems that follow, Lowell gives us, not a realistic account of the breakdown of his marriage but a graph of his feelings in process. The ruling theme of the sequence is succinctly stated in "Milgate": "It's a crime / to get too little from too much." Or again in "Home": "*If he has gone mad with her, / the poor man can't have been very happy, / seeing too much and feeling it / with one skin-layer missing.*" Having everything a "man" could want, the protagonist is desperately unhappy; he is too old, too weather-beaten, too scarred by experience, too mentally disoriented to undergo the "*Arnolfini marriage*" he has set up for himself. And indeed it is not long before that marriage starts to dissolve: "This week the house went on the market— / suddenly I wake among strangers; / when I go into a room, it moves / with embarrassment and joins another room." These lines are as limpid as any Lowell has written: no moral comment, no judgment, no casting of blame; rather, the images do all the work. The room, no longer a space to be inhabited by the imperious poet, takes on a hallucinatory life of its own, avoiding his entrance by "join[ing] another room." It is as if everything he touches turns to dust.

In the remainder of the sequence, Lowell spells out, as few contemporary poets have done, what it means to be totally *alone*, spiritually adrift: "we learn the spirit is very willing to give up, / but the body is not weak and will not die." When his wife departs from Logan Airport, Boston, flying off into a "limitless prospect on the blue," the poet is left behind staring at a sketch that soon turns into a "blank sheet". . . . All attempts to communicate with old friends fail, and the poet loses himself in manic schemes: "Joy of standing up my dentist, / my X-ray; plates like a broken Acropolis. . . / Joy to idle through Boston, / my head full of young Henry Adams. . . ." Such "joy" quickly turns into anxiety: "No one has troubled to file away / the twisted black iron window-bar / their taunt of dead craft." And the poet's "Bright Day In Boston" ends on note of lassitude: "This house, that house— / I have lived in them all, / straight brick without figure."

His wife makes a brief return to Boston, but while she lies asleep in his "insomniac arms," Lowell's feverish thoughts turn to the "suburban surf" of nighttime cars, "Diamond-faceted like your eyes, / glassy, staring lights / lighting the way they cannot see." In daylight, *angst* gives way to "A false calm": "In noonday light, the cars are tin, stereotype and bright, / a, farce / of their. former selves at night—/ invisible as exhaust." But by this time, he too has become an invisible man, not seen by the woman in his bed. And a few poems later, the bed is empty: "The single sheet keeps shifting on the double bed, / the more I kick it smooth, the less it covers; / it is the bed I made.

These are the opening lines of "Ten Minutes," a remarkable example of the "grace of accuracy" Lowell longed to achieve in his last poems. In *Life Studies*, "Robert Lowell" was consistently presented as an exemplar of his time and place, a "Mayflower screwball" unable to "adjust" to the "savage servility" of modern Boston. But here, in "Ten Minutes," Robert Lowell is only himself:

> Mother under one of her five-minute spells
> had a flair for total recall,
> and told me, item by item, person by person,
> how my relentless, unpredictable selfishness
> had disappointed and removed
> anyone who tried to help—
> but I cannot correct the delicate compass-needle
> so easily set ajar.

One recalls the words of Jonathan Edwards. addressing his congregation, in a poem written 30 years earlier: "You play against a sickness past your cure." But in the new poems, "sickness" is not necessarily a universal condition; it is merely the condition of Robert Lowell, whose compass-needle points in the wrong direction:

> My frightened arms
> anxiously hang out before me like bent L's,
> as if I feared I was a laughingstock,
> and wished to catch and ward you off . . .
> This is becoming a formula:
> after the long, dark passage,
> I offer you my huddle of flesh and dismay.
> "This time it was all night," I say.
> Your answer, "Poseur,
> why, you haven't been awake ten minutes."

So much suffering, so little understanding! It is after this episode that Lowell, standing, like Lear, in his "nakedness," has a total breakdown and is taken to the hospital. Upon "recovery," he no longer wants to do anything but fish; he is content to record what he sees without comment or distortion:

> Ducks splash deceptively like fish;
> fish break water with the wings of a bird to escape.
>
> A hissing goose sways in stationary anger;
> purple bluebells rise ledges on the lake.
>
> A single cuckoo gifted with a pregnant word
> shifts like the sun from wood to wood.

Lowell himself calls these observations "description without significance, / transcribed, verbatim by my eye." But of course the poet's vision is still highly selective: ducks, fish, the "hissing goose," the "single cuckoo"—these are all creatures that can escape confinement, that are free. In contrast, the poet himself remains a prisoner, caught in the net of his past "crimes." And in the sobering "downlook" that accompanies his final "recovery," he realizes that he is responsible for everything that has happened: "It's impotence and impertinence to ask directions, / while staring right-and-left in two way traffic."

Day by Day internalizes the "unforgivable landscape" of Lowell's earlier poetry: the conflict is no longer between self and world but between the self and its false images. Such unrelenting self-criticism and self-examination might well be maudlin and embarrassing, not to say boring. But Lowell succeeds and succeeds brilliantly because he now recognizes that "We are poor passing facts / warned by that to give / each figure in the photograph / his living name."

"We are poor passing facts"—surely this statement (another oblique allusion to *Lear*) contains a bleak, despairing view of existence, and *Day by Day* is, to my mind, an almost unbearably painful book. Still, I find it comforting to think that, in artistic terms, Lowell's final poems constitute such a striking recovery. Rarely tendentious or sentimental—the respective vices of *History* and *The Dolphin*—*Day by Day* is the book that gives "each figure in the photograph / his living name."

Washington Post Book World (Sept. 25, 1977): H1.

Day by Day

Harold Bloom

The recent death of Robert Lowell now marks his final volume, *Day by Day*, with a particular poignance. *Day by Day* stakes everything on poignance in any case, and seems to have won the risk with most critics. Like nearly all of Lowell's verse in his last decade, the book is nevertheless a very problematic achievement. The most ambitious poem here, "Ulysses and Circe," seeks to elevate heroic wryness into a kind of sublimity, as when Ulysses-Lowell observes of himself: *He dislikes everything / in his impoverished life of myth*. But the poetic impoverishment becomes more the burden, in all the poems, than does the overt sorrow of personal mythology. A curious flatness or deadness of tone, indubitably achieved by considerable artistry, works against the expressive strength of the poet's struggle with tradition. The best poems in the book, to me, are the last four, where the pathos dares to become overwhelming, turning as it does upon the poet's reading of his life's losses as being the consequences of his mother's rejection. Yet I am left uncertain as to whether I am not being moved by a record of human suffering, rather than by a making of any kind. In his *Epilogue*, Lowell prays for "the grace of accuracy" and comes to rest upon the poetically self-defeating question: "Yet why not say what happened?"

John Berryman's *Henry's Fate* is very much a companion volume to *Day by Day*. This posthumous book collects unpublished work written during Berryman's last five years and adds little that is memorable to the substantial body of verse that already represents Berryman's final phase. Judgment of that phase cannot rest therefore upon this volume, yet reading it side-by-side with Lowell stimulates a sense of the almost opposed esthetic dangers that the two poets were driven to confront. Lowell's defense against poetic tradition was increasingly a fiction of nakedness or trope of vulnerability. Berryman resorted to a baroque mannerism, a heightened word-consciousness that compels a reader to struggle more directly with the poet's sense of belatedness. Both stratagems had the desperation of acute courage, and both seem to me noble and heroic failures, a judgment in which I seem to be as yet alone.

New Republic 177:22 (Nov. 26, 1977): 24.

Imitative Form in "Epilogue"

Norma Procopiow

. . . With the exception of a few translations in the Appendix, "Epilogue" is the last poem in *Day by Day*. Although it may not have been the last poem Lowell wrote, its order of appearance in this volume distinguishes it as a kind of farewell statement. Indeed, when critics review *Day by Day* they generally refer to "Epilogue" as Lowell's poetic apologia. . . .

The complaint, Lowell's customary approach to a theme, here becomes one about form. His efforts to achieve a painter's freedom and spontaneity have resulted in static constructions—snapshots rather than paintings. Or so the surface meaning suggests. But the phonetic and syntactic patterns suggest something different: a dialectic about the form of the poem itself. Frustration becomes determination, which becomes resignation; resignation becomes resolution. This is done through shift of mood in the order of its seven sentences: interrogative, declarative, declarative, declarative, interrogative, imperative, declarative. The imperative sentence beginning "Pray for the grace of accuracy / Vermeer . . ." emerges with a conviction not evident in earlier passages. But it is not sustained. The poem closes with a declarative statement of resolution: "We are poor passing facts. . . ." The attempt to imitate Vermeer seems to have failed; he can only draw on a technical resort: "to give / each figure in the photograph / his living name."

Syntactic order and parts of speech underscore this dialectic about technique. Verbs are used as past participles with adjectival rather than predicate force; this is especially significant in the modifiers for "snapshot" ("grouped, heightened," "paralyzed"). This reduces the quality of vibrance and action ordinarily associated with verbs. On the other hand, the most empathetic, sensuous verbals are used in reference to painting ("trembles," "caress"). A similar pattern occurs in the use of nouns. Lowell uses few concrete nouns and, when he does so, they refer to Vermeer's painting ("sun's," "map," "tide," "girl"). When speaking of his own creative ordeal, Lowell employs more remote abstract nouns ("structures," "plot," "facts," "figure"). The deadness of the abstract words functions as contrast to the vitality inherent in the concrete ones.

The syntax is as dialectically determined as the parts of speech. In sentences referring to Vermeer and, parenthetically, to the "painter's vision," syntax is simple, accretive, paratactic. The other lines contain more complex patterns, characterized by non-restrictive modifiers. The most pronounced examples of this are the modifiers for "snapshot":

"lurid, rapid, garish, grouped, / heightened from life, / yet paralyzed by fact." The grammatical structure has a formal duality, a dramatization of antithetical kinds of creativity. Lowell's last resort is to name. Caught in the clutch of time, he fixes the poem in the present tense and centres on the temporal adverb "now." Yet he knows that to make "something imagined, not recalled" is to be liberated from time. Thus, he produces no rooted sense of space or time in his lines on Vermeer.

The sound structure of "Epilogue" provides equally interesting evidence of the poet's dilemma. An inventory of its vowel patterns reveals that the tense, back vowel sound _ai_ appears most frequently, and figures predominantly in words which focus on the poet's self scrutiny ("why," "I," "my eye," "heightened," "paralyzed," "misalliance," "sometimes"). Tense back vowels, as opposed to lax front vowels, convey a more solemn mood to the text. This emotive power of vowels is a phenomenon requiring the analysis of a professional psycholinguist, which I cannot provide, but I believe that some elementary observations may be permitted regarding vocalic placement in the poem. The poem has few lax front vowels; the low frequency of lax front vowels is largely confined to unstressed syllables in parts of speech having relative insignificance (articles, prepositions). As for the tense back vowels, it has been argued by psycholinguists that the _ɔ_ sound conveys the most ominous emotional properties in comparison with other vowel articulations. This derives from the closeness in acoustical frequency of the vowel's formants. In "Epilogue," although _ɔ_ appears infrequently, it does so in strategic expressions: "_A_ll's misalliance," and "w_a_rned by that."

There are several phonetic climaxes in the poem which semantically pertain to the manner in which Lowell fears he is writing. The first climax comes with the word "snapshot" in line 10. Here it is positioned as a terminal word, abruptly concluding a barrage of images. Its terse quality is reinforced by the slow pacing of the line preceding it. Line 9 is not only longer, but it must be read slowly because of its stop consonants (d, b, t): "with the threa_d_bare ar_t_ of my eye / seems a snapshot." . . . The second climax is reached in line 14, which completes the references to "snapshot": "All's misalliance." Line 14 sounds like noise, or a bag of cacophony. This is due to the prevalence of short vowels ("m_i_s_a_ll_ia_nce") which carry little weight, leaving the consonantal aggregate to dominate sound.

A more subtle example of Lowell's technique with sound structure appears in the semantic device of echoing fricatives. The poet states that he would rather make something "imagined" than "recalled." He says: "I hear the noise of my own voice. . . . (line 5). Semantically, the line itself is suggestive of an echo; and phonetically, this is actualized in the movement from a voiced fricative (z), the echo sound, to a voiceless fricative (s). Then, in the next two lines (6, 7), Lowell states his aspirations regarding artistic perception: "The painter's vision is not a lens, / it trembles to cares*s* the light." Here he repeats the pattern of line 5: the movement from voiced fricative (z) and (3) to the voiceless fricative (s) . The duplication in these lines of the earlier line seems further proof of his inability to summon forth a "vision." This understated mode may be found in another passage—"seems a sna*p*shot, / luri*d*, rapi*d*, garish, group*ed*. . . ." (lines 10-11)—where the adjective string, both in its succession and symmetry, resembles the deadness and uniformity of snapshots. The released and unreleased dental stops simulate, in meaning, the click of a camera; in sound, they simulate Lowell's restrictive feeling about writing. Also, the word "fact," which appears twice in the poem (once in plural), is said to paralyze his imagination. The sound structure enforces this meaning, since the words appear after released diphthongs ("heightened," "paralyzed") only to be closed again on the word "fact."

The effect of "Epilogue" is a death-in-life dramatization of the poet's struggle. Even the vertical strategy of the poem underscores this. The last line, "his living name," is an iambic dimeter with the tense back vowel sound <u>ei</u>. It is in slant rhyme with the first line of the poem, "Those blessed structures, plot and rhyme." In effect, the poet has called on— imitated—his former tools and used them in ironic reversal. In this context, the pun embedded in "his living name" comes to signify the poet's wish for immortality. Interestingly, the liquids and nasals in this line provide an auditory pleasure that is absent in the earlier ominous line: "All's misalliance." Thus, the linguistic elements function to reveal that the poet's struggle is a success after all. As Vermeer fills out a bare pedestrian scene of the painter at work (in effect a snapshot of his studio), so Lowell in his contemplation of himself at his craft has created in the richness of sound and composition a work of art.

Ariel: A Review of English Literature 14 (1983), 4-14.

Memory and Imagination in *Day by Day*

Jeffrey Gray

> I want to make
> something imagined, not recalled . . .
> —Lowell, *Day by Day*[1]

> Imagination and memory are but one thing, which
> for divers considerations hath diverse names.
> —Thomas Hobbes, *Leviathan*

Robert Lowell's poetic career has frequently been seen as a journey along a distinct path, a path which by many accounts is that of American poetry itself in the twentieth century. The terms in which this story is told vary, and all are reductive, but setting them out may remind us of how we have accustomed ourselves to read American poetry in general and Lowell's work in particular. Lowell's poetry, then, from *Lord Weary's Castle* and *The Mills of the Kavanaughs* to the "breakthrough" of *Life Studies* and *For the Union Dead*, followed by the *Notebook* sequences and finally *Day by Day*, has been seen as tracing a course from the heavily clothed and indirect to the naked and direct; from "art" to "life"; from the masked to the unmasked; from poetry to prose; from the public to the private; from imagination to memory; from the painting to the photograph; from restraint to freedom; from exclusivity to inclusiveness; from mastery to surrender; from product to process; from a stable to an unstable ego; from a written to a visual trope.

While some of these versions of a poetic career demand elaboration, the parallelism of most will be obvious. It is right to find fault with them. One might argue, for example, that early Lowell poems as well as late are autobiographical, that some of the late poems are as dense and allusive as the early, or that the whole notion of a naked writing (think of the 1968 anthology *Naked Poetry*) lacks explanatory power, since writing is a medium and poetry is the genre that calls attention to its own mediatedness, its rhetoricity. But a more interesting project might be to see how these terms of a narrative toward authenticity serve as the *topoi* for the poems of *Day by Day*—that is, to see how the conversation *around* Lowell's poems is the conversation *within* the poems.

---

[1] *Day by Day* (New York, 1977), 127.

One set of the above terms, imagination and memory, belongs to Lowell and provides the framework for several of the most important poems of this book. "Day by Day," the title sequence, with its meditation on the poetic process and the relation of art to life, invites us, more than any other Lowell text, to consider the trajectory of his poetry, particularly the phase of it he had just passed through with the publication (in 1969-73) of *Notebook 1967-68, Notebook, History, For Lizzie and Harriet*, and *The Dolphin*. The structure of meaning, fought for in the transition from *Notebook* to the succeeding volumes, was relinquished in *Day by Day* (1977). The latter book's notational style, with its lack of syntactic rigor, corresponds instead to the concept of a drifting, non-teleological life. If this surrender, and the humility that comes with it, resulted in a certain slackness (one of several charges brought against the book when it appeared),[2] it also allowed a subjectivity capable of illuminating a crucial struggle within twentieth-century *poesis*.

Lowell's own remarks about his writing frequently supported the received view of a progressively more "naked" writing, and of a career trajectory toward an unmasking, a more complete identification of author and persona. In his account of the writing of "Skunk Hour," he worried that his earlier poems were "prehistoric monsters dragged down into the bog and death by their ponderous armor," and he spoke of turning for more immediacy to the prose models of Chekhov and Flaubert.[3] Elsewhere, he spoke of his qualm about the "glaze" in Browning "between what he writes and what really happened"; Frost's poems, by contrast, had the "virtue of a photograph but all the finish of art" (*Prose* 264). Lowell called *The Dolphin*, as Lawrence called the novel, "a book of life,"[4] saying in one of the poems, "fiction should serve us with a slice of life; / but you and I actually lived what I have written" (52).[5]

---

[2] Donald Hall called *Day by Day* "slack and meretricious" in "Robert Lowell and the Literature Industry," *Georgia Review* 32 (1978): 7-12 (see 8).

[3] *Collected Prose*, ed. Robert Giroux (New York, 1987), 227.

[4] *The Dolphin* (New York, 1973), 72.

[5] The extent to which Lowell's late books are "books of life" is the extent to which they allow not unaltered life into them, an obvious impossibility, but rather unaltered *writing*, actual letters and conversations, selected and put into line form as well as placed into the context of the poem(s)—and in this way of course altered. The *objets trouvés* that make up the collage of *The Dolphin* are Lizzie's letters and Caroline's conversations. A thorough discussion of this aspect is provided by Steven Gould Axelrod in *Robert Lowell: Life and Art* (Princeton, 1978), 214-32. The other reading of a "book of life" is that of life as a book, in Nietzsche's sense as well as Henry James's: life as an art form, a

Following the poet's lead, critics reinforced the idea of a narrative of authenticity. Harold Bloom, who never cared for Lowell's work, provides us with an instructive example. Although admitting the power of the final sequence in *Day by Day*, Bloom complained, "Yet I am left uncertain as to whether I am not being moved by a record of human suffering, rather than by a making of any kind. Lowell prays for 'the grace of accuracy' and comes to rest upon the poetically self-defeating question: 'Yet why not say what happened?'"[6] But does Lowell actually "come to rest" on this question? As one reads through *Day by Day*, the question of mediation or lack of it stands out in fact as the explicit theoretical problem of the book. Bloom's concern that he was being "moved by a record of human suffering, rather than by a making" shows a naiveté regarding *poesis*. Lowell's own probing of the question of a "record" versus a "making," in numerous poems of *Day by Day*, is richer and more nuanced.

Emerging out of a trope of poetic incapacity, the problem of mediation takes the form of a dialogue whose principal terms are the binaries of memory and imagination, for which Lowell substitutes, in several of the poems, the figures of the photographer and the painter, respectively. Memory implies, before we reflect on its constructedness, a kind of unmediated experience, which Lowell, like Bloom and others, rejects. Both poet and critic, then, fear losing Eliot's cherished separation between "the man who suffers and the mind which creates." The idea appears in "The Truth," from *The Dolphin*: "Nothing pushing the personal should be published, / Not even Proust's *Research* or Shakespeare's *Sonnets*" (67). This is a voice Lowell heard not only from within, but, as the quotation marks suggest, from all about him, first from Allen Tate and the New Critics, then from Elizabeth Bishop and other friends, and then from reviewers like Adrienne Rich, who took him severely to task for the injury he inflicted upon others, notably Elizabeth Hardwick. That the *Notebook*-style poems were composed, dialogically, of the speech of others—political figures, famous literary friends, loved ones—may reinforce the trope of poetic instability, but it also suggests

---

made thing. This trope is played out throughout *The Dolphin* but is more deeply problematized in *Day by Day*.

[6] Harold Bloom, "Introduction," *Robert Lowell* (New York, 1987), 1. In *The Western Canon* (New York, 1994), Bloom writes that, having been told by so many friends over so many years that he was wrong in his judgment of Lowell, he has decided to admit that possibility and to include Lowell in his canon after all (548).

inclusiveness, a less restrictive and centered ego, and a sense that any language he found was poetry, as indeed much of it was.[7]

In this framework of imagination versus memory, Lowell saw *Notebook* as *less* remembered and personal than *Life Studies* (out of the shadow of which he wanted to move): "It's terrible if you're bound to photograph your past, which I think I was doing in *Life Studies*. It's a decent book, but I don't want to write another *Life Studies*. Of course, you cheat and change things in giving what is supposedly the true story of your mother and father. But on the whole it seems as if it exactly happened in that kind of language."[8] In another interview, he said, "*Notebook* is more jagged and imagined than was desirable in *Life Studies*" (*Prose* 272). The roughness of the *Notebook* poems, according to this association of jaggedness and imaginedness, suggests its self-representation as a construction, while the relative clarity and, as most critics have agreed, the aesthetic emphasis (relative not to the preceding but to the succeeding books) that characterize *Life Studies* would make that work—again according to this view—more personal, more a portrayal of "life."

But in spite of the effort toward construction, against the narrative of authenticity and nakedness, in *Notebook* and the books that followed it, the speaker in *Day by Day* continues to worry that the poems are personal, mere snapshots from "life." The anxiety arises, I suggest, not out of the poems which take that anxiety as their theme, but out of the bulk of the previous period's work: the *Notebook* volumes. In this way *Day by Day* is a retrospect, surveying the work to date (but not, I think, making peace with it, as J. D. McClatchy has suggested).[9]

For *Day by Day* to have been written, Lowell had to have passed through the *Notebook* phase, with its sense of poems rising not out of narrative but out of unstoppable "writing." Alex Calder suggests, convincingly, that what Lowell learned from this phase was a suspicion of the sovereignty of the speaking subject, the norm of the modernist long

---

[7] Calvin Bedient's "Illegible Lowell (the Late Volumes)" discusses this facet of Lowell's work in the framework of Mikhail Bakhtin's "Discourse in the Novel" (*Robert Lowell*, ed. S. G. Axelrod and Helen Deese, New York, 1986, 139-55).

[8] Jeffrey Meyers, ed., *Robert Lowell* (Ann Arbor, 1988), 147.

[9] McClatchy, *White Paper* (New York, 1989), 124. Alan Holder, in a somewhat different sense, writes that "*Day by Day* repeatedly goes back to crucial elements of [Lowell's] past, as well as to earlier poems," pointing to a "retrospective or revisionary urge" ("Going Back, Going Down, Breaking," *Robert Lowell*, ed. Axelrod and Deese, 156).

poem.[10] The abandonment of the traditional ego, exploited in the hospital poems of several volumes, allows the late vulnerability of *Day by Day*. An open poetics and a referential language seem conventional after the relative murkiness of the *Notebook*-style poems, but the subject within the last poems is neither confessional nor solipsistic. Not only are the poems often highly crafted, without creating *Notebook* densities, but also the questions the poems pose preclude our viewing them as "confessional." The poems' explicit thematic concern is not a content of life but rather the representability of life in the poem.

The "drift of life," which Berryman saw Pound's *Cantos* as allowing, and which the other great high and late modernist long poems seem to aim at allowing (not, perhaps, containing) as well, is suggested as much in the phrase "day by day" as in the word "notebook." While the long poem tends to avoid consecutiveness, the feeling of mere diary, by inventing compositional strategies that will continually reactivate process (Calder 119), the "day-by-day" sequence has no such conviction or commitment. This may be a Poe-like argument for the shorter poem, or for a series of poems linked loosely in a temporal and thematic chain. Pound's *Cantos* and Lowell's *Notebook* have in common a culture-mulcher quality, a compulsive assimilation of historical detritus. Is this the enabling "drift of life" which Berryman admired?

What Lowell looks back on in *Day by Day* is the cutting up of letters and other found writing, the daily work of making poetry out of whatever came to hand, poems of notes and observations, mediated but "personal." *Day by Day* too consists of notes from life, but the "notes" in the *Notebook*-style books serve a different end: they are taken and worked up in order to keep poems coming; the inner directive is to produce, to accumulate, to form an opus. Lowell consciously tried for an effect of speed, and yet the impression of the fourteen-liners of the *Notebook*s is not one of spontaneity or lightness, but rather of thickness. Fitted into a rough mold, their bringing together of notes and selected found language is a technique producing opaque, often structurally-fractured poems. In the *Notebook*-style poems of 1969-73, Lowell seems to bracket aesthetic judgments, a move which could be argued to place those works (always keeping in mind distinctions Lowell himself made between these volumes) in a different class—that of the long poem, or the postmodern process poem.[11] The "notes" of *Day by Day*, by contrast, serve—or are made to

---

[10] Calder, "*Notebook 1967-68*: Writing the Process Poem," *Robert Lowell*, ed. Axelrod and Deese, 117-38.

[11] Calvin Bedient has pointed out the many "illegible" passages in *Notebook* (though he argues this also for *Day by Day*). Vereen M. Bell points to a line

seem to serve—the more contemplative end of a heightened awareness of a fleeting subject in a fleeting world. The poems retain the casual quality of notes, especially in the sense of eschewing grand unities in favor of a "day by day" craft and record, as transient as their themes and referents. But they are notes with a nimbler, clearer, airier touch than those of the *Notebook* period.

Notes, the poems of *Day by Day* say, help one to notice. In "Notice," appearing toward the end of the title sequence, notes are seen as a way into life, renewal, innocence, freedom. Some of this is explicit ("I am free"); the rest branches out metonymically from the images of spring and the speaker's astonished tone. Poems, on the other hand, have brought the poet only sorrow and the inability to connect. The poet asks his doctor: "'These days of only poems and depression— / what can I do with them? / Will they help me to notice / what I cannot bear to look at?'" (118). The doctor's failure to reply has already been suggested by his saying, "'We are not deep in ideas, imagination or enthusiasm— / how can we help you?'" (118). With this remark, he reveals himself as also anchored in "mere" experience, as—in terms of the "Epilogue" to come—"paralyzed by fact." But, absent any response to the question of what to do with poems and depression, or to the problem of noticing, the poet-patient moves to a scene years later, where he sits on the rush-hour train making notes about trees in spring, suggesting that the note-making process *does* help the poet notice. The poems-depression metonym of the first section gives way, toward the poem's end, to one of notes-elation.

But the nature of "notes" also educes the problematic of imagination versus memory. Notes are not, the poet worries, real imagination; they are a way of noticing what is "out there," a way of recording, taking photographs. The one note quoted refutes that worry, however, showing the inextricability of imagination and memory, painting and photography: "'When the trees close branches and redden, / their winter skeletons are hard to find'" (118). Far from being photographic, merely recording the change of season, the note bespeaks an intelligence in search of imagined forms (forms of *memory*, as it happens: the barely visible but remembered "skeletons" of the trees in spring). The speaker is

---

like "four windows, five feet tall, soar up like windows," which Lowell allowed to remain intact through two revisions, thus, according to Bell, "permit[ting] objects to retain their indifferent, unmodified presence" (*Robert Lowell: Nihilist as Hero*, Cambridge, 1983, 145).

"free," he emphasizes, to make such a note, or any note; that is the important thing.[12] He is free to notice:

> . . . after long rest
> and twenty miles of outlying city
> that the much-heralded spring is here,
> and say,
> "Is this what you would call a blossom?" (118)

The poem's closing lines, "But we must notice— / We are designed for the moment" (118), are in fact a protest. The struggle, the desire, is still to say something from the imagination, not from memory. We see the course of the poem as an effort do so, with mixed results. The doctor's words have indicated the poverty of not living in an imagined world. But, by the testimony and tone of the final long verse-paragraph, we see that taking notes, *with* imagination, produces in the poet that missing enthusiasm.

The most celebrated of these last poems that frame Lowell's Platonic dialogue between memory and imagination is surely the one that closes the sequence, "Epilogue," a poem of anxiety not so much about a new stage of writing as about a stage already passed through. It is a poem of emergence in a book of emergence—into a new light, into texts of often indeterminate transcendence. These improvisatory texts concern both "noticing" and noting, and they explicitly ponder the problem of writing.

The question on which Harold Bloom claimed that Lowell "settles" in "Epilogue" actually represents one voice in a dialogue that is never carried to conclusion. Yeats's "Ego Dominus Tuus" consists of a similar dialogue between two selves, the self ("Hic") as a reporter who believes an essential content is accessible, if difficult to locate, and the self ("Ille") as a maker who believes that a mediating image is all we have. The latter accuses the former of sacrificing beauty and craft in pursuit of an illusion. When the first self declares, "I would find myself and not an image," the other responds, "That is our modern hope, and by its light / we have lit upon the gentle, sensitive mind / And lost the old nonchalance of the hand. . . ."[13] This loss, the loss of "art," is what Bloom mourns, but

---

[12] The fact that Lowell works these lines into a poem titled "Suicide" (16), much earlier in the book than "Notice," supports Bell's argument that *Day by Day*, by reversing chronology, moves from dark to light, having gotten the worst of Lowell's history of this time out of he way in order to move to other questions and themes.

[13] One might do more with Yeats's mind/hand dialogue in Lowell's work. In "Dolphin," for example, Lowell would seem to agree with Yeats that the craft sustains, supports (though ultimately also entraps) the life. The poet's body is

of course Lowell mourns it too, even while the poem constitutes a valediction against that mourning. Lowell's dialogue is between rememberer and imaginer, the former wishing to tap a prior content, the latter an explicit artificer, inventing his Other in *poesis*. "Why not say what happened?" is a question asked by the first self. It is not a rhetorical question, but it is never conclusively answered.

"Why not say what happened?" *could* be read as a plea for engagement, for a public, even political reportage or advocacy, for a facing of the "facts" as they are reflected in the headlines. But Lowell's sense of "what happened," given the context of "Epilogue" and the context of the poet's life work, refers more broadly to whatever passes through his consciousness—whether a photograph, a balsa head from Brazil, a book, a rosary, or a protest march. And his question is not a plea, as some have read it, but a response to his own desire *not* merely to report or remember but to imagine, invent: "I want to make / something imagined, not recalled (127). Indeed, as the poet's "own voice" reminds him: *"The painter's vision is not a lens, / it trembles to caress the light"* (127).[14]

The loss feared in "Epilogue" is the loss of the ability to imagine, the loss of *poesis* if not of poetry. It is the fear that the very historical narrative under discussion—the narrative of twentieth-century "artlessness"—might be an accurate description. This was Yeats's fear also when he spoke of modern poems as "the sort now growing up / All out of shape from toe to top" ("Under Ben Bulben"). In spite of the poet's "own voice" telling him that his is not a mere camera lens, he nevertheless fears that he has stopped imagining, that he is artistically impotent. Looking at the snapshots that he takes his poems to be, bereft of vision or

---

"caught in its hangman's-knot of sinking lines," just as "Racine, the man of craft, / [is] drawn through his maze of iron comprehension / by the incomparable wandering voice of Phèdre" (*Dolphin* 78). (Alternatively, in "Reading Myself" in *Notebook* and *History* the bee's poetic work, its honeycomb, is also its coffin.) "Dolphin" worries—as Yeats did and as "Epilogue" will do—over the poet's having "plotted perhaps too freely with my life, / not avoiding injury to others, / not avoiding injury to myself." This anxiety is more pertinent in *The Dolphin* than in any other book Lowell wrote. The book, the poet claims, "is half fiction, / an eelnet made by man for the eel fighting." Yeats suggests that what the hand makes is craft, what the mind thinks and remembers is life. But "Dolphin," like the poems of *Day by Day*, suggests that this opposition cannot be sustained. In "Dolphin," what the hand did was life and craft, to both of which the mind has been witness: "my eyes have seen what my hand did."

[14] See also "July-August" in *The Dolphin*: "I love you, / a shattered lens to burn the clinging smoke" (26), where love is not a passive lens but one that focuses light with a will to create intensities.

craft, Lowell, anticipating his critics, sees them as "lurid, rapid, garish, grouped, / heightened from life, / yet paralyzed by fact" (127). It is in response to the anxiety caused by this "misalliance," this dreaded paralysis of art by fact, that the other voice of the internal dialogue asks, well, "Why *not* say what happened?"—as if to say, What could be wrong with that? The art of recall is not so much defended as its accuser is challenged to find anything wrong with it. After all, "Memory is genius," as Lowell said at one of his last readings.[15] The poet (the "voice" in italics that identifies with the painterly view) ultimately suggests a paradoxical combination of both sides when he prays for Vermeer's "grace of accuracy." With the touchstone of the Old Master, the photographic is again subordinated to the painterly, and, thus, too, memory to the imagination. Poet and reader realize that memory never did exist apart from imagination, and that paralysis of art by fact was a fear, never a reality. But it is not a fear fully exorcised by this poem.

In "Shifting Colors," which follows "Notice" in the third section of the "Day by Day" sequence, we see the conflict again between imagination and memory, between creation and description, between the painting and the photograph, all of these framed by the anxiety of representation. The categories, inexact in their correspondences, shift in "Shifting Colors," and the ambivalence at the poem's end is even more pronounced than that in "Epilogue"—but it is the same consciousness poring over the same question. The poem opens with the aged pastoral poet (Lowell's self-image) fishing "until the clouds turn blue, / weary of self-torture, ready to paint / lilacs or confuse a thousand leaves, / as landscapists must" (119). On the surface, this is a retiree's poem—fishing, taking up watercolors; even the poem's title suggests a fuzzy impressionist painting, not energized by sharp definition.

But to read these lines in the context of Lowell's work is to read them both rhetorically and biographically, since the books preceding *Day by Day* do indeed contain a great deal of sensitive and self-wounding material. "Shifting Colors," then, announces a shift: being "weary of self-torture," the poet is ready to turn from the personal (from uttering "what happened") to painting, to the non-personal, whether imagined or real. But the shift is so problematic that its own contradictions become the poem's *topos*. The quoted lines introduce a survey not of an imagined landscape

---

[15] Introducing "Epilogue," Lowell recalled Randall Jarrell's poem "The Lost World," of which Jarrell's brother had said that it wasn't a poem at all, because "it was something remembered, not imagined." Lowell commented, "I'm not sure of that distinction. . . . Memory is genius, really, but you have to do something with it" (*Reading*, Dec. 8, 1976, Cadmon recording TC1569, 1978).

but of the "natural" world around the poet, beginning with "my double, / an ageless big white horse," and spreading over the pond to include ducks, geese, bluebells, and "a single cuckoo gifted with a pregnant word" (119). Before this world, the poet finds himself inadequate, too weak to imagine or even to recall in any way that would prove helpful:

> I am too weak to strain to remember, or give
> recollection the eye of a microscope. I see
> horse and meadow, duck and pond,
> universal consolatory
> description without significance,
> transcribed verbatim by my eye. (119-20)

What can it mean to "transcribe verbatim"? It is, of course, the question that worries the speaker in "Epilogue"—the idea that the writing is mere reproduction and yet the consciousness that it is not possible to transcribe verbatim. *Can* we say "what happened"? By way of an answer, "Shifting Colors" offers the conundrum that closes the poem:

> This is not the directness that catches
> everything on the run and then expires—
> I would write only in response to the gods,
> like Mallarmé who had the good fortune
> to find a style that made writing impossible. (120)

"This" we must take to mean this *writing*, "without significance," the writing a poet must do who has neither the strength to remember nor the capacity to represent what is before him, but who insists on mediation, indirectness, on not merely recording.

But the conundrum lies in the last two lines. One suspects the final word, "impossible," of being an instance of the kind of revision noted by Jonathan Raban: "For almost every sentence that Cal ever wrote if he thought it made a better line he'd have put in a 'never' or a 'not' at the essential point. His favorite method of revision was simply to introduce a negative into a line, which absolutely reversed its meaning but very often would improve it."[16]

Unable to settle on an explanation of the best way of writing, but certain in his rejection of what has been tried and found wanting, the poet opts for writing "in response to the gods / like Mallarmé. . . ." Given the

---

[16] Quoted in Ian Hamilton, *Robert Lowell: A Biography* (New York, 1982), 431.

choice of painter or photographer as poetic functions, we would have to place Mallarmé, with his dense texts and poems written on fans, in the painterly category. But Mallarmé, who continued to write until the end of his life, even under great duress, did not find writing *impossible*. Instead, his poetry became more unorthodox, elliptical, and opaque (and, after the death of his son, more personal!)—aspiring to the blank page, so "pure" it rejected all language as tainted. His writing, that is, became "impossible" in the other sense, that is, *non-lisible*. The poet's prayer, then, may be double: to find a style to make writing *possible* (as Lowell's last line may first have been written); and also (with what measure of perversity on the part of the supplicant?) to diverge still more sharply from the burden of representing that unrepresentable world of nature, where the poet finds himself fishing, and to find a style that would finally make writing *unreadable*. An additional reading may even be added, without contradiction: "impossible" in the sense of incredible or amazing, as in "the day breaks, impossible, in our bed" ("The Day"51).

To a certain degree, the prayer to be unreadable is answered. The poems, however much written in a language of presence, full of both light and melancholy, are also poems of a dispersed subject. They are kin, in fact, to those of the American poet who could now be said to occupy the position that Lowell occupied at mid-century: John Ashbery. Here, one could list examples of hermetic, incoherent, or ludic passages, as Calvin Bedient has done with Lowell's late work. And indeed, the dispersed subject and the poem of non-sequiturs are carry-overs from the *Notebook*-style poems. But what is different in *Day by Day* is, again, the glowing sense of lyric presence. It is this quality, along with the irreferentiality, that likens Lowell's last volume to the work of Ashbery.[17]

In "Marriage," as a final example of the internalizing of the *topoi* of authenticity and representation, the photograph / painting opposition is spelled out with an explicit comparison. The poet, on the occasion of being photographed with wife and children, reflects on another family portrait, equally "middle-class and verismo" (69), that of Jan Van Eyck's *Arnolfini Marriage*. The wife in the painting is with child, like the poet's

---

[17] W. S. Di Piero misses an opportunity in "Lowell and Ashbery" of dealing with the striking similarities between Ashbery and the Lowell of *Day by Day* (*Southern Review* 14, 1978: 359-67). *Day by Day*, far from surrendering to mere description and notation, as Di Piero claims, repeatedly creates ironic and yet sunlit spaces through a diction and prosody of which Lowell had only given subtle indications previously. Lowell's strong likeness to Ashbery here lies not only in his use of the language of amazement but in his sense of the poem as found language and his use of a syntax that promises meaning but a logic that inhibits or defies (though it does not preclude) it.

"wife." (Lowell and Blackwood were not yet legally married.) Indeed, everything about the Renaissance couple (and, by inference, about the present portrait's subjects) is too real, too veristic, too closely wedded to mere fact: "The picture is too much like their life— / a crisscross, too many petty facts. . . . (70).

Some of those "petty facts" the poet then sets out as the material of his poem: a description of the bedroom, its furnishings and colors, and a windowsill where peaches ripen. We must take the sentence, "the picture is too much like their life," at least in part as a reference to the poem being written, mediated though it is through Van Eyck. Both of the poem's topics—the family photo and the Van Eyck painting—are seen as suffering from the condition of the poem. But, as in "Notice" and "Epilogue," that worry over imaginative decline is negated by the descriptions, the poetic portraits themselves, whether through imagery, simile, diction, or the turning from the visible to the unseen, historical, or metonymic. As in the "note" of "Notice," where the unseen "skeletons" of the trees are the focus, here, in the family photo, the unborn son Sheridan is the "center of symmetry" (69). And here too, in the Arnolfini portrait, we are constantly led out of the frame, into history ("In an age of Faith, / he is not abashed to stand weaponless") as well as into simile and imagination, as in the powerful penultimate verse-paragraph:

> They are rivals in homeliness and love;
> her hand rests like china in his,
> her other hand
> is in touch with her unborn child.
> They wait and pray,
> as if the airs of heaven
> that blew on them when they married
> were now a common visitation,
> not a miracle of lighting
> for the photographer's sacramental instant. (70-71)

Of this commentary on the couple's mutual devotion and on the devotional atmosphere, the strand to separate out, in order to highlight the late Lowellian dialogue between imagination and memory, is again the contrast between the historical and more or less hallowed painting and the contemporary, belated, and relatively trivial photograph. The juxtaposition of the two portraits in "Marriage" highlights an anxiety of artistic belatedness, an inadequacy in relation to the achievements of Old Masters (in a poetic sense as well). One might say that this is a revival of early Lowell and the New Critical poem of allusion; indeed, much of the power of "Marriage" does depend on the transcendental quality of the above passage, which, by imbuing the Van Eyck painting with an iconic religious awe, soars above the supposed "facts" of the earlier sections. The juxtaposition of the two portraits is also, however, a juxtaposition of lives and of marriages—one solidly embedded in monocultural, bourgeois Italian wealth and commitment as well as in sanctification by the Church, the other destabilized by the British-American "ambivalence of the revolution" as well as by the narrator himself, whose decenteredness is a given in the poems of *Day by Day* as it is through much of late Lowell. If photography cannot live in the shadow of Van Eyck's painting, can this third marriage live in the shadow of the Arnolfinis' example?

Thus, by the end of the poem, "the airs of heaven," which have visited the Arnolfinis since their marriage, seem to be invoked for the present marriage in the hope that they will be a "common visitation" here too. But the fear behind the hope is that a marriage in our time is analogous to its mode of representation. In place of a marriage already established and a painting executed over weeks, we have, contemporarily, the incomplete marriage and only the photographic instant to serve as sacrament.

A last parallel between the two couples is suggested in the final anticlimactic two-line verse-paragraph: "Giovanni and Giovanna, / who will outlive him by 20 years. . ." (71). With Caroline Blackwood's death in 1997, that prediction turns out to have been almost exact. But, while the issue of age difference provides another reason to ponder the Arnolfini marriage, the ellipsis suggests there is no commentary possible on this given of the two marriages. It remains the question of representation (via painting or photograph, imagination or memory), the question of a viable *poesis*, that predominates, in "Marriage," over the question(s) of life.

We might re-think the teleology of authenticity in Lowell to suggest that *Day by Day* enacts a movement not so much toward the personal, the remembered, or the unmasked as toward a language of patience, humility, and light. Alan Holder, while acknowledging that there are "nuggets that gleam" in *Day by Day*, speaks of the "prevailing gloom" of the book (Holder 177). But perhaps the figure and ground of light and darkness need to be reversed, since the tone and diction of most of the poems suggest a different prevailing mood. A volume about age, helplessness, and obsolescence, focused obsessively on death and regret, *Day by Day* yet brings to these concerns an almost constant wonder, innocence, and even cheer. We may leave to the compilers of concordances the task of listing the number of times "sun" (or variations such as "sunslant," "sunfall," "sundrunk") occurs in *Day by Day*, but it is often enough to make even the poems of death seem far from wintry. The poems are, in fact, largely vernal, though some have the colors of a sunny autumn. "Logan Airport, Boston" provides a representative example of this palette. At the airport, the blouse worn by the speaker's beloved "shone blindingly" in the light, and though the apartment is dim as the speaker moves from window to window "to catch the sun," he is "blind with seeing" (74). The light, both at the airport and across time ("blindingly" and "blind with seeing"), is so strong as to be almost unendurable to the subject. In the poem's last two verse-paragraphs, "the undrinkable blaze / of the sun" and the partly figurative "bright sun of my bright day" make what is certainly a poem about deliquescence anything but gloomy (75). What colors it, for a moment, as autumnal is the description of a year-old bruise on the shin: "firm brown and yellow, / the all-weather color for death" (75). Other colors, notably the color of oxidation, contribute to the palette of decay, but even that decay is dynamic, never at rest: "We are things thrown in the air / alive in flight . . . / our rust the color of the chameleon" ("Our Afterlife I" 22).

The forces behind these shifting colors in *Day by Day*—the shift in affective tone, toward a kind of earned lightness of being, along with the shift toward an explicit theorizing of *poesis*—are indicated by the book's title. The received meaning of the title-phrase should not be overlooked. That we should live "day by day" is the therapeutic advice we receive when we are ill, troubled, or dying. In seeming to count his remaining days, Lowell composes poems of days, moments, and perceptions on the wing, almost in the spirit (though not in the form or the economy) of haiku. Even the persona of the poems has something in common with that of the poems of Basho or Li Po—the old, nostalgic, wine-drinking sage struck dumb by a falling leaf. "Day by day" may also suggest a certain despair, what Vereen Bell calls the "demoralized experience of living on redundantly from one day to the next, without willing or meaning to" (205). Warner Berthoff suggests Lowell might have got his title from Henry Miller's *Tropic of Cancer*.[18] Miller wrote: "The present is enough for me. Day by day . . . Day by day. No yesterdays and no tomorrows," suggesting a Nietzschean commitment to being rather than becoming. (See Lowell's "Obit" in *Notebook* on this point.) Or we may turn to *The Tempest*, where Prospero says of his years in exile, "tis a chronicle of day by day," too much to be told at a single meeting. All of these meanings, even Bell's, suggest at once the keenness, ephemerality, and vulnerability of dwelling, and writing, in the present.

---

[18] Werner Berthoff, *A Literature Without Qualities* (Berkeley, 1979), 173.

Day by Day picks up the thread of *Life Studies* in searching for a way of writing that preserves life, an experience-centered mode of writing. In a sense the cultural and historical tours conducted in the *Notebooks* and *History* were a regression to a depth model, requiring a reader steeped in symbols as well as historical points of reference. *Day by Day* emerges from that model (albeit with Ulysses, Vermeer, and Freud in tow), and, to recur to the narrative of a "breakthrough," it is as clear an emergence from Lowell's preceding books as that of *Life Studies* was from the densities of *Lord Weary's Castle* and *The Mills of the Kavanaughs*.

Day by Day stands as a crowning achievement not only because, at the end of his life, Robert Lowell moved back toward a style that had marked a breakthrough for him in *Life Studies*, but also because the poet, expanding on a strand running through *The Dolphin*, wrote a book in which the principal *topoi* are the writing of poetry and, elegiacally and self-reflectively, the mourning of the loss of the power to write poetry. These *topoi* are declared as such, not submerged as in the *Notebooks*. In continuing Lowell's life-long questioning of the bewilderingly porous boundaries between memory and imagination, *Day by Day* becomes principally a meditation on the paradox of getting "life" into art. To argue that the book is or isn't "life" or "art"—as critics often have done—is to ignore the work the poems are doing in thinking over Lowell's, and perhaps any poet's, profoundest problem.

Essay written for this volume, 1999.

Robert Lowell's *Agamemnon*: The Price of Dominion

Helen Deese

> Glory to Zeus, whatever he is:
> he cut off the testicles of his own father,
> and taught us dominion comes from pain![1]

The direct, brutal language shocks. These lines are more savagely oedipal than anything Freud inferred from Oedipus. They are Robert Lowell's compressed version of a passage in the original Greek of Aeschylus's *Agamemnon* that is known familiarly as the "Hymn to Zeus." The passage—twenty-four lines in the original Greek—occurs early in the play.[2] Lowell's three-line compression exemplifies the plainness, irony, and bitter clarity that characterize his verse throughout his rendition not only of *Agamemnon* but also of the other two plays of the *Oresteia*: a clarity about dominion as it relates to the chief god, the family, and the polis. The wish to kill is seeded in both the human heart and that heart's projection of itself to heaven. Aeschylus's trilogy concerns killing in the family, killing one's seed, spouse, and progenitor, and killing as a political act. Lowell's verse strips away any ameliorating metaphor, any ennobling of the human will to dominion when custom allows it. His play adapts Aeschylus's fifth-century BCE play to the cruelties of our own century.

In Lowell's prefatory note to his rendition of the *Oresteia*, published in 1978 after his death, he briefly explains his method and intention: "I have written from other translations, and not from the Greek. One in particular, Richmond Lattimore's, has had my admiration for years, it is so elaborately exact. I have aimed at something else: to trim, cut, and be direct enough to satisfy my own mind and at a first hearing the simple ears of a theater audience." Writing for the theater, Lowell wanted the performance to be directly understood, visually and aurally, by its twentieth-century audience. He had been asked by Elia Kazan, sometime in 1964, to translate Aeschylus's *Oresteia* as the first production of the Vivian Beaumont Theater at New York City's Lincoln Center.[3] We can see just how much he trimmed text, stripped it of metaphor, and shaped it to his own ends by comparing his three-line version of the Hymn to Zeus to two other translations he clearly knew well, first that of Richmond

---

[1] Lowell, *The Oresteia of Aeschylus* (New York, 1978), 6.
[2] A. W. Verrall, tr., *"Agamemnon" of Aeschylus* (London, 1889, 1904), 21-24.
[3] Paul Mariani, *Lost Puritan: A Life of Robert Lowell* (New York, 1994), 326.

Lattimore and then that of Edith Hamilton. Both have twenty-two lines,
two less than Aeschylus's twenty-four.

Lattimore begins with a seven-line strophe that addresses the god
with an evident desire to please:

> Zeus: whatever he may be, if this name
> please him in invocation,
> thus I call upon him.
> I have pondered everything
> yet I cannot find a way,
> only Zeus, to cast this dead weight of ignorance
> finally from out my brain.[4]

Lowell, in contrast, radically cuts the first seven lines of Aeschylus's
Hymn to a curt six words: "Glory to Zeus, whatever he is." Just the
change of Lattimore's first line "whatever he may be" to Lowell's
"whatever he is" harshens the tone from semi-reverence to a flip
challenge. Lattimore's choral speaker recognizes a transcendent being of
an undefined nature who has, at least, not indicated any displeasure at
being invoked by the name of Zeus. The implication is that there could be
other names or no name. The speaker's address seems a civilized one, and
he is speaking to a civilized deity. He wants relief from the "the dead
weight of ignorance" that burdens his brain; perhaps Zeus might cast out
that ignorance.

In the next lines, the antistrophe, Lattimore follows Aeschylus in
alluding most delicately to the oedipal struggles through which Zeus came
to power. Like Aeschylus, Lattimore—as well as Hamilton, Robert
Fagles, and other translators—omits the primitive, archetypal details that
Hesiod presents of the three-generational, masculine struggle for deific
dominance.[5] Here are Lattimore's lines:

> He [Uranos] who in time long ago was great,
> throbbing with gigantic strength,
> shall be as if he never were, unspoken.
> He [Cronos] who followed him has found
> his master, and is gone.

---

[4] Lattimore, tr., *Aeschylus I: Oresteia*, (Chicago, 1953), 39-40.
[5] In his translation Fagles updates archetype with a sporting metaphor:
wrestling. Of Zeus's victory over his father, he writes: "And then his son
[Cronos] who came to power / met his match in the third fall" (*Aeschylus: The
Oresteia*, New York, 1975, 109).

> Cry aloud without fear the victory of Zeus,
> you will not have failed the truth: . . . (40)

The myth that those lines adumbrate is told by Hesiod in his *Theogony*.[6] Ouranos, the first Greek sky-god, born from Gaia, the earth, the ultimate mother of all immortals and mortals, married his mother and ruled orgiastically. Despite his primal, masculine strength, he feared the children he and Gaia engendered, and he would not let them be born. Gaia was finally able to bear the youngest son, Cronos, in secret. She gave him a sickle she had made of adamant and hid him in a bush. When Ouranos came that night to lie with her and was "fully extended," Cronos reached out from hiding and with his sickle "quickly severed / his own father's genitals" (17). He threw them into the Mediterranean, and from their semen Aphrodite was created. Now Cronos ruled over the immortals. He made his sister Rhea his consort, but, like his father, he was nervous about children. Thinking it likely that a son would try to replace him, he swallowed his children as soon as they were born. Rhea, when she was about to give birth to her youngest son, descended to the island of Crete where she hid the baby she named Zeus. Instead of the baby, she gave Cronos a large stone to swallow. Sometime later Cronos vomited up the stone and all his other children. Zeus rescued his siblings, who became known as the Cyclops, and, in gratitude, they allowed him mastery over thunder and lightning. With these weapons, he defeated Cronos in battle, became Cronos's master, and ruled as king of immortals and mortals.

For compression and power, Lowell changes Zeus's weapon from thunder and lightning to a knife and attributes Cronos's castrating action to Zeus. Lowell reduces the myth to its oedipal, one-line core: "He cut off the testicles of his own father." That line, in stripping Zeus of his grandeur, intensifies the sardonic irony of the preceding line: "Glory to Zeus, whatever he is."

In Lattimore's translation, the choral singers of the Hymn to Zeus urge their listeners to "cry aloud without fear" in praise of Zeus's victory. If they do so, they "will not have failed the truth." But what is the victory? The victory may be that of Zeus over Cronos, but more likely it is the Greeks' hoped-for victory over the Trojans. We're not sure what "the truth" is, either. Lattimore puts a colon after the word, so we can assume that the strophe that follows explains it:

> Zeus, who guided men to think,
> who has laid it down that wisdom

---

[6] Richard S. Caldwell, tr., *Hesiod's Theogony* (Cambridge, 1987), 17.

> comes alone from suffering.
> Still there drips in sleep against the heart
> grief of memory; against
> our pleasure we are temperate.
> From the gods who sit in grandeur
> grace comes somehow violent. (40)

In Lattimore's translation, the truth is what Zeus has decreed: that wisdom can be attained *only* from suffering, that grace, the loving favor of the deity, rather than being freely given, has somehow a violent genesis.

Again Lowell cuts the truth of Zeus to one line: Zeus "taught us dominion comes from pain." Zeus achieved his dominion, if not his glory, by castrating his father. Thus, the price of Zeus's power is his father's pain. The notion is at once barbarous and psychoanalytical. The anguish is that of the castrated father, or of whoever is disciplined. Pain is the price of dominion in any relationship—interpersonal, familial, political, or theological. All contemporary English-language translations of this passage echo Lattimore in reproducing Aeschylus's tropes that idealize the will to power.[7] Only Lowell foregrounds the agony that is the price paid by the dominated.

Edith Hamilton, in her translation, depaganizes Zeus.[8] He becomes God. Whereas Lowell states, "whatever he is," she asks, "God—who is he? If that name he choose, / by it I will cry to him" (169). Like Lattimore and Aeschylus himself, Hamilton emphasizes the faith that from suffering will come knowledge and wisdom. Essentially she Christianizes the Hymn to Zeus:

> Guide of mortal man to wisdom,
> he who has ordained the law,
> knowledge won through suffering.
> Drop, drop—in our sleep, upon the heart
> sorrow falls, memory's pain,
> and to us, though against our very will,
> even in our own despite,
> comes wisdom
> by the awful grace of God. (169-70)

---

[7] Fagles again finds a sporting metaphor: "From the gods enthroned on the awesome rowing-bench / there comes a violent love" (109).

[8] Hamilton, tr., *Three Greek Plays: Prometheus Bound, Agamemnon, The Trojan Women* (New York, 1937).

God, or Zeus, decrees that wisdom is won from suffering that is "against our very will." The theological concept of evil under the rule of an omnipotent God presents a quandary for those who believe that the omnipotent force has purpose, the purpose being moral discipline. Suffering is not the synonym of evil, if "evil" be defined as the demeaning of life, but it is the corollary, the natural consequence of evil. The Hymn that Aeschylus's chorus sings in the original Greek roughly translates as "Zeus has decreed that wisdom shall come from experience" (Verrall 21-22n). In the Hymn as translated by Hamilton and Lattimore, "experience" becomes "suffering." Both versions address the moral dilemma that suffering imposes upon us, comforting us with the assurance that out of suffering we gain "wisdom," through the "awful grace of God" or through the "somehow violent" gift of grace.[9]

---

[9] In a dark time in American history, this strophe from the Hymn to Zeus, as translated by Hamilton, assuaged the pain of hearts terribly wounded by civil struggle and assassination. Late on the infamous date of April 4, 1968, Robert Kennedy invoked these lines from his memory. On his campaign tour for the Democratic presidential nomination, he had just made the short flight from Muncie to Indianapolis. The night was windy and chill. Under the bright glare of small search lights, he stood on the back of a flat bed truck, hunching in his black overcoat, against the cold. Five or six hundred people, all African Americans except for the press, had come to this street corner in the ghetto of a racially divided city to listen to the candidate. They had been waiting for nearly an hour and a half in a festive mood, for they did not know that Martin Luther King had been attacked. Kennedy had to tell them what he had just learned on his short flight: that King had been shot and killed by a white man. In his brief, extemporaneous speech, he alluded for the first time in public to his brother's assassination: "I had a member of my own family killed. He was killed by a white man. But we have to make an effort in the United States, an effort to understand." Then he said: "My favorite poet was Aeschylus. He wrote: 'In our sleep, pain which cannot forget falls drop by drop upon the heart until, in our own despair, against our will, comes wisdom through the awful grace of God.'"

These lines from *Agamemnon*, remembered by Kennedy and changed by his remembering, are carved as he recalled them on the wall facing his grave site in Arlington National Cemetery. Two months after that night in Indianapolis, Robert Kennedy was himself assassinated in Los Angeles. (See R. W. Apple, "Kennedy Appeals for Nonviolence," *N Y Times*, Apr. 5, 1968, 133; Leroy Aarons, "RFK, His Voice Quivering, Tells Rally Very Sad News," *Washington Post*, Apr. 5, 1968, A2; Arthur M. Schlesinger, Jr., *Robert Kennedy and His Times*, New York, 1979, 938-40).

Robert S. McNamara also alludes to Aeschylus's lines in his recent book admitting erroneous judgment of the Vietnam War. He says in his preface that he wants Americans to understand the mistakes that "we" made so that we learn from them: "That is the only way our nation can ever hope to leave the

Lowell's brevity, however, perceives no wisdom gained either by the sufferers or the perpetrators of pain. His version of the Hymn helps explicate, and is explicated by, the play that surrounds it. At the center of *Agamemnon* is an assassination: Clytemnestra kills her husband, Agamemnon. The murder is her carefully considered act of vengeance, a blood-for-blood answer to Agamemnon's sacrifice of their daughter, Iphigenia. Because the Chorus sings the Hymn to Zeus directly before telling of the sacrifice, their recitation includes an unspoken knowledge of that human sacrifice. Thus, the various iterations of murder—Zeus of Cronos, Agamemnon of Iphigenia, Clytemnestra of Agamemnon, and the Greeks and Trojans of each other—become imbricated narratives, each repeating the others.

Agamemnon begins on a bare area before the doors to Agamemnon's palace in Argos, with one actor on stage, the sentinel who has been watching every night for the last beacon in a relay of fiery beacons set out by Clytemnestra to signal, from Troy to Argos, that Troy has fallen to the Greek army. In this early morning, in the darkness before dawn, the sentinel finally sees the signal and, shocked by the possibilities of what will now happen, hastens to tell Clytemnestra. A chorus of old men, representing the populace of Argos, enters, pacing in step as the day begins to dawn. They chant an expository song, one that includes the Hymn to Zeus. In Aeschylus, as in the translations by Lattimore and Hamilton, the song is one long poem spoken in one voice by the Chorus—217 lines in Lattimore and a similar length in Hamilton. Lowell trims this chant to 104 succinct and powerful lines of contemporary English.

In the Greek dramatic tradition, the chorus always sings in one voice. Aeschylus usually limited the voices on stage to three: two actors plus either the Chorus as a whole or the Leader of the Chorus. Translators primarily concerned with fidelity to the original text rightly follow that dramatic structure. Lowell, writing not a translation but a "version" or "imitation," breaks with the tradition. To enhance the ability of a contemporary audience to hear the meaning, he breaks the Chorus into multiple Voices with which he creates short bursts of contrapuntal dialogue that hold the listener's attention more effectively than would a single exposition.

---

past behind. The ancient Greek dramatist Aeschylus wrote, 'The reward of suffering is experience.' Let this be the lasting legacy of Vietnam" (*In Retrospect*, New York, 1995, xvii). In contrast to Kennedy's, McNamara's memory and application of Hamilton's lines from *Agamemnon* seem sadly shallow.

In Lowell's version, the Leader takes the first Voice. He begins the play's exposition ten years back when Menelaus and Agamemnon "gathered the fighting men of Greece, / and marched them on a thousand ships" (4). What follows is a brutal, primitive story, and Lowell's Chorus tells it bluntly. The two kings, brothers and sons of the House of Atreus, were "like eagles screaming with bloodlust," circling "over the nest of their choked young" (4-5). The wasting of the young by the Greek kings and their uncaring, masculine gods becomes a dominant theme in Lowell's version. The Chorus is composed of old men, whose infirmities make them unsuitable for war service. In contrast, the young fighting men shipped off to Troy were slaughtered *en masse*: "Thousands have died there for one loose woman. / Legs break, knees grind / in the dust, the wounded are killed without mercy"(5).[10] Apollo or Zeus heard the cries of the eagles and gave them "his fury," but the resulting burnt flesh, oil, tears, and blood failed to satisfy "the thirst of the gods" (5).

A Second choral Voice breaks in, addressing Clytemnestra who has silently come onto and across the stage: "Lady Clytemnestra, Queen of Argos, tell us what to do" (5). This Voice prays that "hope" after Troy's fall may "shine in the bright flames" of the beacons (6). The Leader, however, returns the song to the war's beginning and to the brutal metaphor of the eagles. Before the palace in Aulis, where the ships awaited the winds to take them to Troy, two eagles appeared and, diving into the square, killed and feasted upon a hare, "her unborn young . . . bursting from her side." The Leader concludes this awful visual metaphor with a refrain of desperate hope: "Cry death, cry death, but may the good prevail" (6). Hamilton's translation of that line is much more assertive: "Sorrow, sing sorrow, but good shall prevail with power" (167). Lattimore's translation suggests a tenuous sentiment nearer to Lowell's: "Sing sorrow, sorrow: but good win out in the end" (38). Unlike both Hamilton and Lattimore, however, Lowell directly states the cause of the sorrowful crying, the destruction of what is female—the hare and her birthing.

In Lowell's version, the Leader reports that Calchas, "the prophet of the Army," interpreted the eagles' feast that everyone, mortal and immortal, had seen. The two eagles feasting on the hare, said Calchas, are Agamemnon and Menelaus. The scene prefigures their success. "In time," their armies will "fall on Troy, and butcher its rich / herds of people." Unfortunately, Calchas continues, a goddess who is watching (Lattimore

[10] These words echo Ezra Pound's in "Hugh Selwyn Mauberly": "And of the best, among them, / There died a myriad, / For an old bitch gone in the teeth, / For a botched civilization."

and Hamilton both identify her as Artemis) "is sick off the eagle's banquet. She pities / the unborn young and the shivering mother." The Leader ends this strophe with the refrain "Cry death, cry death, but may the good prevail" (6).

Now the Second Voice candidly answers that refrain's desperate hope with the "Hymn to Zeus":

> Glory to Zeus, whatever he is:
> he cut off the testicles of his own father,
> and taught us dominion comes from pain! (6)

In Lowell's version, then, what will prevail is not "good" but "dominion" and its associated "pain." Perhaps that dominion will be for the good and perhaps not, but anguish is inevitable. We understand now half the context of the Hymn. Lattimore and Hamilton follow Aeschylus in expressing hope that wisdom will follow our experiential knowledge of violent death. And perhaps wisdom does follow, if that wisdom acknowledges the horror of dying in pain. But does that wisdom derive from the grace of a god or from the god's need for control, a need mirroring in magnification the human need? Lowell's version amplifies the irony of Aeschylus's structure: the Hymn to Zeus in all translations is preceded and followed by the most awful images of young suffering, occurring so that gods and men and eagles may achieve dominion.

After the last line of the Hymn, the Leader returns to the narrative of the war's inception. The winds died, the ships could not sail, men starved. The Leader now reminds Clytemnestra, and the audience, how Calchas turned the situation into a crucial dilemma for Agamemnon: Calchas prophesied that "the death of a girl will free the winds. / Iphigenia, the King's daughter, must die." (7) In both the Lattimore and Hamilton translations, Calchas suggests but does not state that Artemis is the goddess that must be appeased. In Lowell's version, Calchas himself is clearly the instigator of Agamemnon's dilemma. The predicament derives from a human will, not a divine one.

The Third choral Voice then takes up the story of Agamemnon's response. An angry Agamemnon smashed his staff on the ground, saying "the gods / will curse me if I disobey this order" but "I shall be cursed if I murder my child, / the love of my house": "whatever I do will destroy me" (7). In Lattimore, Agamemnon understands that "My fate is angry if I disobey these, / but angry if I slaughter / this child , the beauty of my house" (41). Hamilton's Agamemnon similarly says in sorrow: "Heavy my load / if I refuse and obey not. / But heavy too if I must slay / the joy of my house, my daughter" (171). The "angry fate" and the "heavy load" are not commensurate with the concept of the "curse" in Lowell's version, for the "curse" implies a Puritan foreknowledge of eternal damnation, destruction without redemption.

Still, the choice that Agamemnon makes is a man's choice, not a divine reflection, and his reasoning is pragmatic: "How can / I betray my ships and lose faith in the war?" (7). The military loyalties necessary to battle and to the patriarchal state that must punish the abductor of a wife are political arrangements of power. To doubt their necessity, and therefore their moral rightness, would be to subvert the whole masculinist social structure. It is a dilemma not unlike the one facing President Johnson in 1965, when Lowell was writing these lines. Agamemnon resolves his dilemma quickly. Loyalty to the war is primary: "My soldiers are mutinous. They cry for winds, / and care nothing for the blood of a child. / The winds must blow. May all be well" (7).

The Chorus proceeds to probe Agamemnon's motives. In Lowell's version, the Fourth Voice chants directly and bluntly: "When the King accepted this necessity, / he grew evil" (7). Lattimore renders the response in more muted words: "But when necessity's yoke was put upon him / he changed" (41). Hamilton's translation uses metaphoric indirection to express a spiritual perspective on Agamemnon's decision:

> But when he bowed beneath the yoke of fortune,
> shifting his sails to meet a wind of evil,
> unholy, impious, bringing him to dare to think
> what should not be thought of—
> For men grow bold
> when delusion leads them. (171-72)

Lattimore employs a different metaphor, that of the body, to make a similar point: "he changed, and from the heart the breath came bitter / and sacrilegious, utterly infidel, / to warp a will now to be stopped at nothing" (41). Lowell's Fourth Voice picks up the trope of "wind" or "breath" and the warping of mind and will from both translations:

> he grew evil. Crosswinds darkened
> his mind, his will stopped at nothing.
> It pleased him to imagine the infatuation
> of his hard heart was daring and decision. (7)

Lowell's lines, revealing Agamemnon's delusory sense of "daring and decision," seem not merely more condemnatory than those of Lattimore and Hamilton but more accurate: Agamemnon likes his self-image of boldness. The Fourth Voice provides stern judgment. Agamemnon, he sings, "was willing to kill his own daughter / to avenge the adultery of his brother's wife" (7). The key words in the sentence are "willing," "kill," "avenge," and "adultery." In contrast, Lattimore's Agamemnon "endured then / to sacrifice his daughter / to stay the strength of war waged for a woman" (41); and Hamilton's Agamemnon "dared the deed, / slaying his child to help a war / waged for the sake of a woman" (172). Although each passage presents the sacrifice with distaste, that distaste is mitigated in Lattimore and Hamilton, whereas Lowell harshly reveals both the triviality of the war's purpose (to recover a straying wife) and its brutal execution ("avenge," "kill").

Now Lowell adds to the choral recital a Fifth Voice. In its narrative, Iphigenia at the altar pleads, "Father, help me," but Agamemnon orders the priests to lift his child "like a goat above the altar" and to "gag her lovely mouth" (8). A Sixth choral Voice enters the colloquy, producing one of the few extended tropes in Lowell's text: Iphigenia "looked with pity at her familiar killers" as if she were seated at her father's banquet, dutifully ready to address the guests and to sing in her father's honor (8). The Sixth Voice abruptly ends its recital: "I will not talk of what happened next. / I didn't see it. The ships sailed." The short, bare, kernel sentences—separated by the sharp pauses of the period—enforce a tone of overwhelming emotion, stoically suppressed.

The Second Voice, the voice that spoke the Hymn to Zeus, concludes the choral exposition with two more terse lines, starkly predictive of Clytemnestra's vengeful act: "The future will be plain when it comes. / The killer will be killed" (8). In Lattimore's translation, the Chorus concludes its exposition by returning to its consolatory mode: "Justice so moves that those only learn / who suffer; and the future / you shall know when it has come" (42). Hamilton's lines are similar: "The scales of God / weigh to all / justice: those that suffer learn. What shall be / slow time will show" (173). Both Lattimore and Hamilton reflect the verse of Aeschylus far more accurately than does Lowell. The latter has chosen to use *Agamemnon* as a dramatic structure from which to create his own text, one that is informed by Aeschylus's dramatization of human cruelty and also by Lowell's perception of the tortured social and political conditions of his time.

We have seen how the Hymn to Zeus is preceded by the image of two eagles consuming a pregnant hare and followed by that of a father sacrificing his daughter upon an altar (6-8). In each image the pain of dominion is suffered solely by the victim. In the larger context of the play, however, the killer (as Lowell's line predicted) will be killed. Clytemnestra assassinates Agamemnon. It is an act she has planned for the ten years of the war's duration. During the ten years she has also, in an aptly ironic action, been cuckolding Agamemnon with his cousin Aegisthus. Aegisthus, we recall, is the son of Thyestes, who seduced the wife of his brother, Atreus, the father of Agamemnon. In retaliation for the seduction, Atreus murdered three sons of Thyestes and served them to him at a feast of mock reconciliation. Aegisthus, the one son who escaped, later killed Atreus in revenge, and then achieves further vengeance in the death of Agamemnon. The whole legend of the House of Atreus is one of crime and vengeance. In the second play of the *Oresteia*, Orestes must, at Apollo's urging, continue the pattern. He kills both Aegisthus and his own mother, Clytemnestra. He then is pursued by the avenging Furies. In the final play of the trilogy, however, the motif of personal vengeance through murder is broken. Orestes undergoes a trial by the Athenian citizens, presided over by Athena, the goddess of wisdom. When the jury splits six to six, Athena breaks the tie with a thirteenth vote for acquittal. The third play thus transforms the tragic action of the first two plays, replacing the tribal compulsion for revenge with the rule of law.[11]

In 1964, when Lowell was asked to write a play for the Lincoln Center, he began to write his version of Aeschylus's *Oresteia*. By September, 1965, he had completed the first two plays of the trilogy and was at work on the third. The production, however, was first postponed to the 1966-67 season and then canceled.[12] The cancellation may have been political. Lowell's trilogy, *The Old Glory*, which opened at the American Place Theater in November, 1964 and won a Tony award as the best

---

[11] In *Notebook: 1967-68* and *Notebook*, Lowell included three sonnets on the House of Atreus: "Agamemnon: A Dream," "The House in Argos," and "Clytemnestra." In *History*, he revised these sonnets into a seven-poem group: "Helen," "Cassandra" 1-2, "Orestes' Dream," and Clytemnestra" 1-3.

[12] Sam Zolotow, "Blau-Irving Team Weigh 'Oresteia,'" *N Y Times* (Mar. 14, 1966): L36. A decade later, in early 1977, Joseph Papp proposed to produce the trilogy—again at Lincoln Center—and, in response, Lowell completed his version of "The Furies." But the Romanian director Andrei Serban vetoed Lowell's version. (Thomas Lask, "Book Ends," *NYTBR*, July 13, 1978, 35). He chose, instead, to use Edith Hamilton's translation, supplemented with chanted lines from the original Greek and music by Elizabeth Swados. In this production, the chants of the Chorus and the Hymn to Zeus were accompanied by actors miming the reported actions. Music and visual action replaced the poetry. Bernard Knox, writing for *New York Review of Books*, commented: "Now that the work once done by the words alone is given to the actors, the words themselves become superfluous; indeed, if recited at full length and so as to be intelligible to the audience they might constitute a dangerous distraction" (July 14, 1977: 17). Lowell's powerful language would have resisted that kind of reduction.

drama of the year, critiques the abuse of individual and national power. Then in June, 1965, after Lowell had been invited to write a play for the Lincoln Center but before he had completed it, he wrote a letter to President Lyndon Johnson refusing to participate in the White House Festival of the Arts. In February, 1965, three months after Johnson's re-election, he had begun the systematic bombing of North Vietnam and a massive troop build-up. Lowell's letter was courteous, but sharply worded: "Every serious artist knows that he cannot enjoy public celebration without making subtle public commitments. . . . I can . . . only follow our present foreign policy with the greatest dismay and distrust."[13] The refusal infuriated President Johnson and caused a great stir in the public press and among artists. Each invited artist had to decide whether to attend or not, and to justify that decision publicly.

    Although we cannot be certain that Lowell's political action contributed to the decision to cancel production of his play, we can be sure that Lowell's political thinking had an effect on the play itself. In his letter he had written: "I know it is hard for the responsible man to act; it is also painful for the private and irresolute man to dare criticism." Lowell's *Oresteia* is centrally concerned with difficult and painful political acts— acts that can perpetuate or terminate destructive cycles of war, vengeance, and dominion.

> Glory to Zeus, whatever he is:
> he cut off the testicles of his own father,
> *and taught us dominion comes from pain!*

Informing the Hymn to Zeus and the entire choral exposition is Agamemnon's decision to sacrifice his daughter, an image of the price of dominion. There is now a black wall on the green sward in Washington, D. C. that names the price thousands of American men and women paid for a lost dominion in Southeast Asia. Tens of thousands of Vietnamese paid the price as well. Lowell's *Agamemnon*, like the wall, does not permit us to create heroes of those who make the decision to sacrifice others on the altars of war. In his bare lines we hear the dark pulse of the human heart as we are led to meditate the complexities of our desire and history.

Essay written for this volume, 1999.

---

[13] *Collected Prose* (New York, 1987), 370-71. Lowell's anti-war activities are described in Steven Gould Axelrod's *Robert Lowell: Life and Art* (Princeton, 1978) and Mariani's *Lost Puritan*.

4

Overviews

Robert Lowell

Randall Jarrell

More than any other poet Robert Lowell is the poet of shock: his effects vary from crudity to magnificence, but they are always surprising and always his own—his style manages to make even quotations and historic facts a personal possession. His variant of Tolstoy's motto, "Make it strange," is "Make it grotesque"—largely grotesque, grandly incongruous. The vivid incongruity he gives the things or acts he uses is so decided that it amounts to a kind of wit; in his poetry fact is a live stumbling block that we fall over and feel to the bone. But it is life that he makes into poems instead of, as in Wilbur, the things of life. In Wilbur the man who produces the poems is somehow impersonal and anonymous, the composed conventional figure of The Poet; we know well, almost too well, the man who produces Lowell's poems. The awful depths, the plain absurdities of his own actual existence in the prosperous, developed, disastrous world he and we inhabit are there in the poems. Most poets, most good poets even, no longer have the heart to write about what is most terrible in the world of the present: the bombs waiting beside the rockets, the hundreds of millions staring into the temporary shelter of their television sets, the decline of the West that seems less a decline than the fall preceding an explosion. Perhaps because his own existence seems to him in some sense as terrible as the public world—his private world hangs over him as the public world hangs over others—he does not forsake the headlined world for the refuge of one's private joys and decencies, the shaky garden of the heart; instead, as in his wonderful poem about Boston Common, he sees all these as the lost paradise of the childish past, the past that knew so much but still didn't *know*. In *Life Studies* the pathos of the local color of the past—of the lives and deaths of his father and mother and grandfather and uncle, crammed full of their own varied and placid absurdity—is the background that sets off the desperate knife-edged absurdity of the jailed conscientious objector among gangsters and Jehovah's Witnesses, the private citizen returning to his baby, older now, from the mental hospital. He sees things as being part of history; if you say about his poor detailedly eccentric, trust-fund Lowells, "But they *weren't*," he can answer, "They are now."

Lowell has always had an astonishing ambition, a willingness to learn what past poetry was and to compete with it on its own terms. In many of his early poems his subjects have been rather monotonously wrenched into shape, organized under a terrific unvarying pressure; in the later poems they have been allowed, in comparison, to go on leading their own lives. (He bullied his early work, but his own vulnerable humanity has been forced in on him.) The particulars of all the poems keep to an extraordinary degree their stubborn toughness, their senseless originality and contingency; but the subject matter and peculiar circumstances of Lowell's best work—for instance, "Falling Asleep over the Aeneid," "For the Union Dead," "Mother Marie Therese," "Ford Madox Ford," "Skunk Hour"—justify the harshness and violence, the barbarous immediacy, that seem arbitrary in many of the others. He is a poet of great originality and power who has, extraordinarily, developed instead of repeating himself. His poems have a wonderful largeness and grandeur, exist on a scale that is unique today. You feel before reading any new poem of his the uneasy expectation of perhaps encountering a masterpiece.

The Third Book of Criticism (New York, 1969), 332-34.

On Robert Lowell

Frank Bidart

One day in Robert Lowell's class, someone brought in a poem about a particularly painful and ugly subject. A student, who was shocked, said that some subjects simply couldn't be dealt with in poems. I've never forgotten Lowell's reply. He said, "You can say anything in a poem—if you *place* it properly."

I think that this is one of the reasons one can't think about literature in the twentieth century without thinking about the body of Lowell's work. He has stayed alive as a poet by never drawing a line around what a poem can or should be. Again and again, his style has changed in an attempt to deal with intractable, unfashionable, or intolerable subject matter. He has kept his poetry close to the intuitions, concerns, obsessions that dominate his mind. Many of us would be terrified to face or write the record of our lives. He says at the end of *The Dolphin*: "my eyes have seen what my hand did."

One of the great subjects of poetry is whether poetry itself is possible. Lowell's work seems to me the most significant taking up of this subject since Eliot's *Four Quartets*. He writes in *History*: "Even if I should indiscreetly write / the perfect sentence, it isn't English . . . ." His whole career has been an embodiment of the traditional formal possibilities of English—in terms of meter, rhyme, stanzaic form, even genre—as well as an unending argument with the expressive limits and assumptions of the language. Perhaps this is why critics are often at first bewildered by his new work, and compare it unfavorably to his next-to-last.

In December 1974, the United States First Circuit Court of Appeals, upholding Judge Garrity's Boston school desegregation decision, wrote:

> . . .while Boston is unique in some of its traditions, demographic profile, and style, its uniqueness cannot exempt it from complying with a national policy forged long ago and laboriously implemented throughout the land. The poet, Robert Lowell, wrote of the Beacon Hill statue commemorating the young white Colonel Shaw and our first black regiment, commissioned in 1863, "Their monument sticks like a fishbone in the city's throat."

I think I am not alone in feeling that—personally, and as a nation—one way we have come to understand and judge ourselves is by reading Robert Lowell.

Salmagundi 37 (Spring 1977): 54-55.

The Child Who Writes / The Child Who Died

Maria Damon

. . . Empathetic as my reading of Lowell may be on a personal level, I hope to emphasize his poetry and personal conduct *as social practice*—privileged white male poet(ry) in crisis, as it were. Supremely privileged, preeminently public, and insistent on self-disclosure, Lowell serves as a powerful case study of the pathos of failed liberalism.

The titles of the collections from the period on which this essay focuses—*Life Studies, For the Union Dead, Imitations*[1]—echo Lowell's identification with official textbook history and the personalizing of institutional discourse. *Life Studies* plays on the delicate sense of life in death and death of life: biography as still life, or even as "death studies" of both the child "always inside" longing to die and of the decaying Boston aristocracy to which Lowell was heir; the "union dead" are not only the Northern soldiers who died in the Civil War, but the death of national unity as well as of union/marriage/intimacy/wholeness, and also the shattering of a dignified and controllable "unified self" into mental illness; the translated *Imitations* reverberate with alienation and struggle for authenticity under the shadow of oppressive family history; the insistence on and simultaneous despair of autonomy ("selfhood") and difference. But Lowell seems to have experienced this flickering between various understandings of his poetic project and of his "self" in the light of psychiatrically and poetically inspired self-exploration and confession (influenced particularly by Snodgrass's *Heart's Needle*), rather than as a challenge to the idea of selfhood. Lowell's poetry is a long and painful meditation on the awareness that "Robert Lowell" embodies a set of historically determined relationships—and the desire that "he" be more beyond that. The poetry enacts a desperate faith in Ego—if one could only get to it—in the face of experience that countermands that faith. It is as if Lowell, suffering a mental illness whose diagnosis tears his experience into dichotomous halves, tries to get it right by willing a unified self into being through a belief in history and intimate human relationships, rather than questioning the very idea of a unified self. He enacts the violent disjunction between Robert Lowell, historical personage with all the obligations of American aristocracy to engage publicly the national politics, and Robert Lowell, fragmented and free-floating subjectivity set

---

[1] *Life Studies, Imitations*, and *For the Union Dead* (New York, 1959, 1961, and 1964 respectively). Henceforward cited in the text as *LS*, *I*, and *FUD*.

awash in various mental institutions ranging from the patrician McLean's ("Waking in the Blue") to Boston Psychopathic, where he was once interned after refusing commitment unless it were to a public facility.[2] My essay examines one or two works from each of the three volumes of this period, which I formulate as Lowell's poetic "adolescence"—that is, the period in which his work attempts to constitute an identity both other than and continuous with his former familial and poetic histories. This era reflects a .sharp change in his style, represented especially in the prose piece "91 Revere Street"; indeed, Marjorie Perloff has referred to the publication of *Life Studies* not only as "Lowell's central achievement" but as a "turning point in the history of twentieth-century poetry," with specific reference to the fusion, in "91 Revere Street," of the "romantic 'poetry of experience'" with the innovations of nineteenth-century realist prose.[3] I discuss the transition indicated by that particular prose piece in its environment of original poems and translations—in particular, the Rimbaud translations in *Imitations* and "The Neo-Classical Urn" from *For the Union Dead*.

For Lowell, individual poems became salutary mirrors in which he could experience and represent himself as unified; even his writings about his manic-depressive episodes and periods of extreme psychic fragmentation became unified aesthetic objects. . . . Although "91 Revere Street" can't be taken as unmediated diaristic recollection or unselfconscious prose, the choice to write this material in prose rather than verse indicates an association of personal disclosure with relaxing boundaries formally as well as thematically. In that the poems' formal unity allows Lowell to say "I," the prose represents a step toward allowing fluidity into the concept of "I," even as the subject of his prose is autobiographical pain and psychic suffocation. After "91 Revere Street," the prose continues to be highly stylized and the verse relaxes, as Lowell finds a way to write about his psychic disorders in which any sense of unity cracks apart. The subject *becomes* division, the object absence: the dead parents, the dying child inside him, whose efforts at emergence are manifest and reified in writing.

Lowell translated Rimbaud the adolescent, who tried to shatter the lyric and whose subject matter often involved orphaned children. Lowell initiates the Rimbaud translations in *Imitations*, with "Mémoire," which Lowell translates as "Nostalgia" and to which he appends a note telling the reader that the poem is autobiographical. . . . In it, a young boy escapes his family, comprising his arch-rigid mother (Rimbaud's epithet

[2] Ian Hamilton, *Robert Lowell: A Biography* (New York, 1983), 239.
[3] Perloff, *Poetic Art of Robert Lowell* (Ithaca, 1973), xi, 99.

for his mother was "la bouche d'ombre") and sisters (their alcoholic father
has deserted them), and daydreams in a moored boat on the river. In a
later, more famous poem, the one with which Rimbaud made his entry into
Paris and the favors of the homosocial and homosexual Parnassian
patriarchy, the boy himself becomes "le bateau ivre," tearing loose from
his moorings, bursting through the strictures of traditional lyric as he
bathes himself in the tempestuous "Poème de la mer."

Lowell identifies—perhaps overidentifies—with the more
oppressive aspects of Rimbaud's childhood, although he takes liberties
and wide leeway in translation, appropriating the adolescent symbolist's
memories of childhood as his own. Significantly, however, his translation
of "Le Bateau Ivre" loudly omits the poetically self-reflexive phrase "je
me suis baigné dans le Poème / De la Mer. . . ." (Lowell's poetry does not
engage, for the most part, the question of writing itself apart from the
agency of a writing personality.) In his own words, the point of the
Imitations was to "do what my authors might have done if they were
writing their poems now and in America" (xi)—that is, what they might
have done had they been Robert Lowell. "Les Poètes de sept ans," which
Lowell renders in the singular, becomes his own self-portrait—the child-
poet matches Lowell's autobiographical sketches in *Life Studies* and *For
the Union Dead*. Compare the following portraits:

> his lumpy forehead knotted
> with turmoil, his soul returned to its vomit.
> All day he would sweat obedience.
> He was very intelligent, but wrung,
> and every now and then a sudden jerk
> showed dark hypocrisies at work.
> . . . As for compassion,
> the only children he could speak to
> were creepy abstracted boys . . .
> . . . His Mother was terrified,
> she thought they were losing caste. This was good—
> she had the true blue look that lied.
>   ("Poet at Seven," *I* 77)

> I rub my head and find a turtle shell
> stuck on a pole,
> each hair electrical
> with charges, and the juice alive
> with ferment. Bubbles drive
> the motor, always purposeful . . .

> Poor head! ("Neo-Classical Urn," *FUD* 47)

My mind always blanked and seemed to fill with a clammy hollowness when Mother asked prying questions. Like other tongue-tied, difficult children, I dreamed I was a master of cool, stoical repartée. ("91 Revere Street," *LS* 20)

and the final lines of "Child's Song":

> Help, saw me in two,
> put me on the shelf!
> Sometimes the little muddler
> can't stand itself. (*FUD* 22)

These unflattering self-portraits dwell on physical discomfort and awkwardness. In direct contrast to Wordsworthian harmony, Lowell's child "muddler" is disproportioned—head overlarge, a gooey, seething ooze encased in hard bulkiness. The turtle in its shell imagistically governs "The Neo-Classical Urn"; the subject "I" of the poem tortured turtles as a child, and is a turtle, captured and claustrophobic in his own self-protection. After the opening just cited, this poem savagely twists the Wordsworthian code of blissful boyhood. It shows a boy, ostensibly blissful, or at the very least, boyishly energetic.

> I sprinted down the colonnade
> of bleaching pines . . .
> . . . Rest!
> could not rest. At full run on the curve,
> I left the caste stone statue of a nymph . . .

It then undermines our assumptions about that poetic code: far from expressing a natural joie de vivre, the boy is frantically torturing animals, cramming an ornamental garden urn with painted turtles, who inevitably die.

> the turtles rose,
> and popped up dead on the stale scummed
> surface—limp wrinkled heads and legs withdrawn
> in pain. What pain? A turtle's nothing. No
> grace, no cerebration, less free will
> than the mosquito I must kill—
> nothings! Turtles! I rub my skull,

that turtle shell, and breathe their dying smell,
still watch their crippled last survivors pass,
and hobble humpbacked through the grizzled grass.

The boyish energy turns out to be self-hate compulsively turned on other small creatures. As the poem's title indicates, Wordsworth is not the only Romantic whom Lowell takes on here. He likewise savages the Keatsian strain of his Romantic heritage, and through oblique reference to the New Critical manifesto *The Well Wrought Urn*, he defies the idea of aesthetic self-containment represented by the well-wrought urn. Rather than on a lover trapped in mid-passion on the outside of an urn, rather than on an autonomous work of art transcending personality and history, Lowell focuses on the all-too-historically specific "I" trapped inside the urn of his own body and consciousness, and trapped as well in the constraints of conventional lyric production. The masturbatory opening images, in which the head/mind is the only sex organ, indicate that he can relate to no one but himself. The subjectivity of lyric becomes obsessive self-hatred. The stasis of solipsism reproduces a split, cerebral self that mocks Keats's vision of beauty and art by showing us one of its possible endpoints: the history of Romantic lyric as a family history terminating in degenerative, inbred deformity of consciousness.

     The poet's psyche breaks the rigidity of neat dichotomies—hard/soft, inside/outside—and then blurs in the confusion of subject/object, self/other: the boy tormenting the turtles is himself a tormented turtle. Like them, he is sluggish and vulnerable, hard and ungainly and inaccessible, loath to acknowledge the depths of his pain. The grown poet's pain in the opening and closing passages is not, as Marjorie Perloff suggests (13), remorse at acts impulsively and unconsciously committed in a carefree youth, and sudden and mature recognition of creaturely kinship. Rather, it reflects pain continued from childhood and now brought to articulate consciousness. The opening lines suggest that science and psychiatry have mutilated the speaker/poet through electroshock treatment, as the wanton child mutilated the turtles. But beyond that, he acknowledges that even in childhood, this sense of victimization underwrote all activity. Although there are no adults in the poem and no explicit mention of oppressive authorities, the ordered, suffocating claustrophobia of the parental garden with its ominous "caste stone statue of a nymph, / her soaring armpit and her one bare breast / gray from the rain and graying in the shade" and the "two seins of moss" the boy "swerves" between, suggest that the boy is trapped inside his parents', especially his mother's, body, just as later the man feels trapped inside his own head/mind and the poet inside generic constrictions. The landscape, the projected world of his parents' passions in which the boy feels "drenched" (*LS* 19), is both wet and sterile, oppressively sensuous and infertile, like an incestuous or otherwise inappropriately undifferentiated affective relationship; and the boy imprisons the turtles as he feels imprisoned—only violence can break him out of himself ("Help, saw me in two"). He cannot understand relationship except in terms of domination and possession.

Here the monolithic and static female figure parallels neatly "la bouche d'ombre" as she is described in "Nostalgia," though Lowell does not grant the softness of grief and abandonment to *his* female overseer. Lowell outdoes even Rimbaud in his refusal, of a golden childhood. Rimbaud, whose popularity was growing in the United States in the wake of several lurid, pathos-drenched biographies and the popularity (especially among the Beats of the fifties and sixties) of vagabonding pretensions and the *maudit* tradition in literary production, wrote some stunning poems in the golden vein—"Ma Bohème," for example, or many of the pieces in *Illuminations*. The substitution, in "The Poet at Seven," of "naked, red / Hawaiian girls dancing" for "des Espagnoles . . . et des Italiennes" further Americanizes, updates, and Lowellizes Rimbaud's lines. The other Rimbaud poems Lowell includes are also typically Lowellian, or rendered thus, in subject matter: childhood, in "Les Poètes de sept ans" and "Les Chercheuses de poux"; and the historical interest of his series "Eighteen Seventy," which includes "L'Eclatante victoire," "Rages de Césars"—which Lowell entitles "Napoleon After Sedan"—and so on.

In identifying with Rimbaud, in creating through translation a family of poets, as he did through early apprenticeship to the distinctly anti-Bostonian but equally patrician (in aspiration if not in literal genealogy) and even more conservative Agrarians and New Critics, who often explicitly functioned "in loco parentis" (Hamilton 65, 57), Lowell is both replicating and repudiating the (for him) unbearable sociohistorical visibility of his biological family and its decline. When Lowell first committed himself to being a poet, and demonstrated that commitment by leaving Harvard for Kenyon College to study under John Crowe Ransom, a patriarchy of high art, of poesy, replaced the oppressive matriarchy of the Winslow-Lowell heritage embodied by his overbearingly caste-conscious ("stone caste") mother. However, the new family had much in common with his nuclear family, especially through the linking character of Merrill Moore, Agrarian sonneteer and both Charlotte Lowell's and her son Robert's psychiatrist—and possibly Mrs. Lowell's lover. The work produced during Lowell's early Tate/Ransom-influenced years, while it constituted a breakaway from his family in that writing poetry was itself a heretical activity for the son of a naval lineage, did not especially embody values in conflict with the conservative and genteel tenets of American aristocracy—especially in a family that ambivalently boasted James Russell Lowell and Amy Lowell as members. Lowell simply exchanged Northern for Southern aristocratic values, and his poetry followed the ethics and aesthetics of the latter.

If *Imitations* represented Lowell's attempt to place himself in a transnational and transhistorical poetic family extending beyond both biological and New Critical families, *Life Studies* and *For the Union Dead* represent a stylistic and thematic breakthrough. By common consensus, *Life Studies* constitutes the turning point in Lowell's career, in which the "cooked" aspect of his style—its highly wrought, "difficult," self-conscious poeticity—and the grandeur and public historical interest of his subject matter, gives way to the influence of the "raw": the spontaneity and unmetrical influence of the Beats; the relaxation, following his mother's death in 1954, of strictures against close scrutiny and public utterance of his own family secrets—most notably his suffering as a child; the aftermath of devastating manic attacks, the most recent of which had led to a three-month internment in McLean's, Boston's famous private and exclusive psychiatric hospital. *Life Studies* is Lowell's descent, after bouts of "enthusiasm" for Catholicism and manic madness, for various "girls" (his manic episodes were usually signaled by obsessive attachments to clearly inappropriate women: young women he barely knew, the lesbian Elizabeth Bishop, Delmore Schwartz's wife, the widowed Jackie Kennedy, et al.), into simple family history, both public and private. Lowell studies his own life through that of his family, which he takes, through its social prominence and decline, as a kind of representative family. But he is not, like Whitman, the Poet as Emerson's Representative Man, though the poetic establishment worked hard to accord him premier status. He does not contain multitudes; unlike Whitman's self-proclaimed heir, his contemporary Beat complement Allen Ginsberg, his reach is not gargantuanly democratic. His focus is him-Self, which atomic unit becomes as mythically large as he felt dominated by it; and his democracy consists not in claiming everyman's voice as his own, but in giving a voice to his own most oppressed self, his stifled and stifling patrician childhood. As representatives, Whitman is diffusion; Lowell, distillation and then violent, rending explosion. . . .

The poles of assimilation and defiance, Heaven and Hell, innocence and experience, that characterize adolescence, and on which we can look back with the pleasure/pain of nostalgia, work themselves permanently and horrifyingly into Lowell's life in the manic-depression of mental illness, and less dramatically into his work as an attempt to negotiate the controlled decorum of the old-world, patriarchal New Critics and his new Confessional mode. *Life Studies* and to a lesser extent *For the Union Dead* mark Lowell's poetic adolescence, in that he emerges semiautonomous and self-conscious from under the influence of both biological family and poetic family: he views his parents and ancestors with detached pathos that cuts them down to size, even as he finally acknowledges their crushing power over his psyche, and he declares independence from the New Critics and Agrarians with his new relaxed style and personal subject matter.

Revealing family secrets allows Lowell to break the formal rigidity that fueled hyperdramatic, manically religious earlier poems whose praise from New Critical quarters had brought him instant fame. "Colloquy in Black Rock," the Jonathan Edwards poems, and "The Quaker Graveyard in Nantucket" especially exemplify Lowell's early cryptic and overwrought style. "91 Revere Street" opens with Lowell's public announcement of a Jewish ancestor, Major Mordecai Myers, a jibe at the sanitized reference to him as "M. Myers" in a cousin's "Biographical Sketches" (*LS* 11). Lowell goes beyond simply broadcasting this family secret—he identifies with and romanticizes his forefather, who, after a distinguished career in the military, "sponsored an enlightened law exempting Quakers from military service"; thus, the poet could imagine, this heroic man might have sanctioned Lowell's own defiant conscientious objector position in World War II. Mocking his own romantic illusions in the text, Lowell confesses that he was also yearningly certain that "Major Mordecai had lived in a more ritualistic, gaudy and animal world than twentieth century Boston." This reference to the Major's Jewishness demonstrates the extent to which Lowell starved for the mystique he projects onto Jews, the Mediterranean mystical ambience so lacking in his own family experience; his own earlier movement toward Catholicism had attempted to fill the sterile void of Boston Protestantism. At the same time, he hopes to discover family antecedents, still trying to construct a "legitimate" biological subfamily, an alternative undercurrent that would be the "hidden truth" to the overt coldness of his lived experience. Especially important is Myers's place in his father's family line, as Lowell attempts to counterbalance his mother's power with a dynamic and interesting forefather, and the stultifying Lowell/ Winslow scenario with subcultural ethnic warmth. (Lowell did not explore the actual Jewish communities of Boston or New York; rather, he sought to undermine the family structure from within, reenacting his ambivalence about moving out of the family into a world of others.)

Lowell's description of Myers's portrait, and the feelings and fantasies it elicited from him, constitute a modified instance of a technical convention of the modern lyric: that of Eliot's objective correlative, the projection outward of private emotions onto a presumably corresponding object, and the corollary introjection of these external objects. "Modified" here in that Mordecai's quality of Jewishness, rather than a bounded object, serves to externally anchor Lowell's desire for warmth and liveliness. The constant projection of inner experience onto what Marjorie Perloff has termed, in Lowell's words, the "unforgiveable landscape" of modern decay and detritus is mitigated in these confessional poems, especially, again, in "91 Revere Street"; here, finally, Lowell implicitly acknowledges that his perception of the "earth choking its tears" (Perloff 3-4) has its analogue in his own childhood asthma, dismissed by female relatives as "growing pains" (*LS* 41). This disease is increasingly understood in contemporary medical circles as internal crying. The mitigation is never complete; Lowell's externals are never freed from emotional coloring, and they continue to play an integral part in setting the psychological atmosphere of each poem. But the poet loosens the strict and repressive (imperialistic, even, and born of self-abnegation) insistence on objective correlative, not requiring natural objects, or anything outside the poet's psyche, to bear the entire burden of conveying emotional content. The attempt to "own" Mordecai's imagined "Jewish" qualities by placing these qualities within Lowell's own genealogy brings the correlative closer to its emotional referent. Furthermore, Lowell himself figures prominently in the passage as the child full of fantasies—Lowell shows the process of splitting off and projecting particular qualities onto an absent person/object, rather than presenting the correlative as a *fait accompli*. In this sense, the slightly pejorative term "confessional" can be understood as the poet's taking responsibility for his presence in the poem, for his agency in appropriating objects for self-representative purposes.

Again, the hoary Self raises its problematic unwieldy head. Confessional poetry has, like any other poetic genre, its conventions. Especially in the context of modern debates about voice and presence, the confession can be accorded no special status as truth-telling. But with the heavy emphasis in the 1950s on psychotherapy as a way of "getting to" a "true self," rather than constructing one through narrative, the re-membering or invention of the past was seen as a liberating move, one designed to promote rather contradictory ideas: both an autonomous "healthy" ego and a successful social unit—that is, someone who is able to conform to social norms with a minimal degree of discomfort. The psychotherapeutic practices of the 1950s and early 1960s (including, for instance, prescription of addictive pharmaceuticals in combination with a talking cure, or, in a different vein, Merrill Moore's intimate relations with the Lowell family and his plan to collaborate with Mrs. Lowell on a biography of Lowell's early years [Hamilton 200]) seem fraught with fallacies, unprofessional conduct, and double binds impossible for the client to negotiate with any sense of empowerment. Contemporary psychoanalytic revisionists have refined and clarified the process: while one does not engage the process of verbal self-invention/exploration to posit a "true self," the trying out of various possibilities, the telling of family secrets, the acknowledgment of pain and the retrieval of memories does, inevitably, allow one to see oneself differently. . . . Narrative's truth is contingent and provisional—"true" for as long as its undomesticated, defamiliarizing insights enable change. One does not, at best, "confess to" a fixed and monolithic set of experiences of which there is only one real interpretation. But this is not clear to the person confessing until those taboos have been broken and those memories retrieved and articulated. In other words, the "self" does not acquire transparency until one acknowledges and releases one's illusions, attachments and beliefs about that "self." Herein lies the value of Lowell's confessional poetry; this is why *Life Studies* indicates such a shift in his style and content. The style, especially, becomes more fluid and inclusive because he understands himself differently. I want to acknowledge the provisional nature of the subject "Robert Lowell" as the poet understands it in *Life Studies* and passing into *For the Union Dead*, and address the later ramifications of those revelations of oppressed childhood.

In a sweeping and flattering statement, [Alice] Miller proclaims that "it is not the psychologists but the literary writers who are ahead of their time." Lowell's writings accurately reflect the psycho-therapeutic practices of his time, which tended toward the pharmaceutical and the Freudian, although he claimed to mistrust the "talking cure," submitting to it only because he had to, regarding visits to his therapist as "necessary chores" (Hamilton 287). Read against the grain of his intentions, however, self-disclosures anticipate by several decades the findings of primarily feminist philosophers and therapists, who see the subtle cruelty of childrearing in the modern family as inevitably perpetrating both socially and personally destructive and self-destructive behavior—resulting in the obvious and endless family merry-go-round of physical and emotional violence and neglect. What then of the possible fertile alliance [Ricky] Sherover-Marcuse speaks of between the socially privileged and the world of others? What of, the confirmation and corroboration of collective experience—the empathy—that indicates "authentic" (in Sartrean terms) experience? Did Lowell find or does his poetry enact, through acknowledging the pain of childhood, an empathetic participation in emancipatory activities? Lowell's politics and those of his poetry have been much discussed. An explicitly political poet, a self-appointed "witness to his age," he took well-publicized stands on a number of political issues throughout his life; in his "day" he was the leading national poet of the United States. Having served time in prison as a conscientious objector during World War II (his grounds for objection being the Allied bombing of Germany, and of Dresden in particular), he later opposed the Vietnam War in the March on the Pentagon, declined President Johnson's invitation to read at the White House, campaigned for Senator Eugene McCarthy on the latter's antiwar platform, and supported the student movement of the sixties. In each of these instances, he used his standing as an American aristocrat and premier national poet to draw attention to the position he took.

However, his poems show no sympathy for a structural critique of social injustice; as with his preoccupation with writers rather than writing, his interest in history lay in personalities—military or political leaders' integrity or lack thereof (and his "efforts to psychologize" the latter),[4] and the poignancy of the down-and-out in prisons and mental institutions. As Alan Williamson argues in *Pity the Monsters: The Political Vision of Robert Lowell*, Lowell's personal and "public" political poetry became increasingly interdependent.[5] Some of his best poems play with an identification with or alienation from his socially outcast "monsters": "Memories of West Street and Lepke," "Waking in the Blue," and the prose piece "Near the Unbalanced Aquarium" show the poet as one among the world's outcasts, one among the criminal and the insane. (During manic episodes, even such "monsters" as Hitler and Stalin took on a sympathetic glamor for Lowell.) But there is a bemusement in these pieces, as if Lowell were wondering, "What am I, a Boston Lowell, doing here? I feel kinship with these people because we are all alien from the respectable world; I feel alien from them because of my investment in the respectable world". . . .

Lowell's bemused irony and the gentle, self-conscious sense of noblesse oblige behind these desperate empathies differs from the self-consciousness of . . . writers from across the tracks—Walt Whitman, for example, or Etheridge Knight (compare "West Street," for instance, with Knight's "Hard Rock Returns to Prison from the Hospital for the Criminally Insane"). Divided against itself, Lowell's sense of inside/outside, participant/alien symmetrically complements these other writers' feelings of community/exclusion—but it has a different internal logic; their concerns were not his. One senses that in order to preserve the integrity of his psychic struggle, Lowell has to preserve "Otherness," like

---

[4] Robert von Hallberg, *American Poetry and Culture* (Cambridge 1985), 173.
[5] Williamson, *Pity the Monsters* (New Haven 1974).

a sensitive and vulnerable version of the hypothetical newscasters covering the lives of Southie's poor. The creative and emotional catharsis Lowell gets from his acts of empathy *depend* upon structural inequity.

Lowell conducted his act of "consciousness-raising"—writing—in a community of writers presumably more interested in the craft and integrity of their art than the benefits of psychotherapy or social change. The prose piece "Near the Unbalanced Aquarium" offers a poignant, almost scathing instance of ineffectual "art therapy," in which Lowell competes with a fellow inmate of the Payne-Whitney Clinic in making imitations of Klee and Pollock—the use of ekphrasis barely wards off painful questions about the psychic utility of his preferred craft. Lowell's writing did not take place in conditions designed to help loosen the tight grasp he tried to maintain on self-hood, on authorship and authority. His compulsive "desire to confess"[6] was not necessarily matched with a desire to let go of the secrets he was confessing—at least not to the extent of relinquishing to a collectivity the control and identity that self and secrets appear to offer. While Lowell could take pacifist, antiviolent positions in the public arena; and while his obsessive stranglehold on form, language, and personal information relaxed with the relatively colloquial syntax and open forms of *Life Studies*, he continued to suffer psychic and emotional inner violence which never entirely abated, and he continued to inflict psychic and physical violence on those close to him.

Without wishing to detract from Lowell's achievement, Robert von Hallberg has called him a quintessential liberal, unusual for postwar America in his insistence on the personal and his distaste for systematic social change; for von Hallberg, the weight of Lowell's political/historical opus demonstrates that "American liberalism has had . . . major imaginative embodiment in the last thirty-five years" (174). Given its consistency with notions of individuality and personal experience, Lowell's preferred but embattled genre, the lyric, could be called the exemplary liberal literary form. But further, the term "liberal," with its roots in *liber*, freedom, and its emphasis on tolerance rather than change, points toward Lowell's own need, once again projected onto the landscape of history and the political arena, to be free and tolerated rather than changed—his task, perhaps, was not to change himself or to effect change in others but simply to learn to find the world and himself tolerable. If a radical nostalgia impelled him outward, he was also, perforce, tremendously preoccupied with simply maintaining a clear sense of who "he" was—which maintenance, according to the desperate faith in self he had learned from the world of privilege and from self-defense against the

---

[6] C. David Heymann, *American Aristocracy* (New York, 1980), 363.

chaos of mental illness, meant pushing others away. making sure he, and they, recognized their otherness. Lowell ripped away the sham nostalgia of the golden childhood, thus permitting himself the possibility of identification with others. But it remained an empathy based on shared pain and deprivation, an empathy tinged with a constant sense of superiority-run-aground, rather than an active building toward a new way of conceiving relations from which a new meaning of "Robert Lowell" could emerge.

The Dark End of the Street (Minneapolis, 1993), 123-41.

The Postmodern Sublime:
Lowell, Wilson, and Jameson

Henry Hart

Although for many critics Lowell is the central poet of the postwar era, consolidating advances made by modernists and pushing beyond them, whether he is postmodernist is open to debate. Arguing against the very terms of this debate, a critic like James Breslin unwittingly places Lowell at its center by fastening on a topic repeatedly scrutinized by theorists of postmodernism—the sublime. Quoting the 1965 interview with Alvarez in which Lowell differentiates American culture from English culture, Breslin concludes: "Lowell's theory [of the American sublime] is most valuable when understood as a projection onto the American past of his own struggles as a beginning poet."[1] If Lowell's early poetry courted the apocalyptic violence the sublime entails, making him one "of Ahab's party without knowing it" (113), his later poetry (from *Life Studies* on), according to Breslin, renounces the sublime and embraces the prosaic: "It discards rhetorical sublimity and religious myth in a quest to enter a demystified present. Lowell touches what had hurt him most, the prosaic and everyday, and he finds that his fiery creative self can survive within the quotidian" (124).

　　Does this tell the whole story? Can Lowell's career be divided so neatly between sublime ascent and prosaic descent, religious myth and

---

[1] Breslin, *From Modern to Contemporary* (Chicago, 1984), 113.

demystified fact, or did his ambivalence toward the sublime simply decrease in intensity without ever really disappearing? If *Lord Weary's Castle* and *The Mills of the Kavanaughs* represent an apotheosis of modernist and New Critical methods of deploying myth, ritual, symbol, poetic form, wit, paradox, and other tropes, and *Life Studies* as well as later books express a postmodern fascination with a "demystified present," would it not be more accurate to say that Lowell's early compulsions, repressed as they were in his middle and late periods, had an uncanny way of returning in the form of a postmodern sublime? . . .

Although critics are certainly right to point out the change in the intensity of Lowell's attachment to the sublime in his middle and later periods, they are wrong to claim that he shut the door entirely on its beguiling power. Certainly in his personal conduct, which was so intimately tied to his poetry, he never quelled the seductions of sublimity. Dudley Young recounts Lowell's visit to Essex University in 1970, when he was "burning manic energy and whiskey at about twice the rate of us who were half his age. He was the large and lethal Carnival King, the Candlemas Bear come to release us from common prose; sublime, sexy, and frequently mad."[2] Like a ghost from the past, the sublime insinuated itself through cracks in Lowell's best defenses. One of the implications of his interviews with Alvarez is that the awesomeness and awfulness of the postwar era haunted even those, like Lowell, determined to repudiate it. But what is the postmodern sublime that beleaguered Lowell with such persistence? How does it figure in his poetry, and how do his shifting attitudes to it affect his stylistic shifts?

Wilson's provocative, wide-ranging study, *American Sublime: The Genealogy of a Poetic Genre*, provides clues to many of these questions.[3] To elucidate Lowell's inconsistent appraisal of the sublime, he quotes the last stanza of "Waking Early Sunday Morning," in which those standard sites of sublimity—volcanoes and wars—and the sublime rhetoric they occasion appear hollow. Wilson explains: "Such a fall into 'the monotony of the sublime'—which Lowell early feared as a stylistic peril—is decried as one consequence of our American will-to-sublimity, now displaced from natural ('sweet volcanic cone') or human centers ('our children') to soul-dead icons such as satellites and nuclear warheads—hence comprising, in all dread and terror, *'our monotonous sublime'*" (59). Natural grandeur, military power, financial hegemony, literary prestige, romantic potency—these are only some of the sublime

---

[2] Young, "Life with Lord Lowell at Essex U.," *Robert Lowell: Interviews and Memoirs*, ed. Jeffrey Meyers (Ann Arbor, 1988), 312-17; see 312.
[3] Rob Wilson, *American Sublime* (Madison, 1991).

fruits that tantalized Lowell and that, at least after descending from his manic highs, he branded monotonous, ignominious, or both.

Wilson's disquisition on the sublime repeatedly returns to Wallace Stevens's claim in "The American Sublime" [that the sublime equates to the "spirit" itself in "vacant space" (131)]. Lowell's "Waking Early Sunday Morning" echoes Stevens's "Sunday Morning," and it echoes "The American Sublime" as well. As Lowell contemplates the globe as a gutted spaceship or ghostly satellite orbiting through space, his spirit empties itself of apocalyptic yearnings, at least for the moment, and confronts that other aspect of the sublime—the mesmerizing horror of the void, of infinite space. Eternal vacancy is a type of "mathematical sublime," as Kant explained. For Wilson it has emerged in recent art as a Hydra-headed monster inspiring dread and wonder: "This vastness for the nineteenth century primarily meant the counterforce of Nature-writ-large, whereas for poets of postmodernism, this newer sublime entails an experience of technological space and commodity-infinitude which ungrounds and decenters the human agent to a condition of mute subjugation and fresh wonders of accommodation" (204). In the space abandoned by the natural sublime, which was so popular for Romantics, technological and capitalist sublimes have established their ambiguous allure.

Before the immense destructiveness of nuclear warheads and the prodigious waste of capitalist overproduction Lowell articulates his postmodern protest. Wilson quotes Lowell's "Fall 1961" as an example of the sort of diminishment and despair instilled by the postmodern sublime:

> All autumn, the chafe and jar
> of nuclear war;
> We have talked our extinction to death.
> I swim like a minnow
> behind my studio window. (*FUD* 11)

Similarly, in "Waking Early Sunday Morning" the salmon leaping for the sublime will suffer tragic diminishment and death. The mushroom cloud is a postmodern analogue of the "bone-crushing waterfall" that for Romantics would have been a symbol of nature's awesome power.

Wilson contends that the invidious aspects of the postmodern sublime emanate inevitably from the origins of American culture. Lowell would certainly agree that seeds sown by America's founding fathers and cultivated by their political heirs have burgeoned into a poisonous yet seductive garden. According to Wilson: "Nuclear power. . . seems to emanate from the innermost depths of American poetics articulating self-rapture and national empowerment like a first fate, a fact of nature. Poets, too, stand implicated in this fascination with icons of national superiority, self-sublation into nature and God, the death of European history back into the primal scene of the desert—poets and scientists conjuring the technology of the Over-Soul in the sublime solitude of Los Alamos" (226). Oedipal son that he was, Lowell craved self-rapture and self-empowerment; he wanted to dethrone the American patriarchs and prove his strength was greater than theirs. If he protested against Kennedy's nuclear buildup, he also embraced Kennedy, and in his dreams even became Kennedy. If he rebuked Roosevelt for criminal war policies, he also drew attention to their similar patrician "family traditions" (*CP* 368). He liked to assume common ground with his formidable adversaries and then assume moral superiority.

Like other theorists of the postmodern sublime, Lowell interprets his aesthetic concept in ideological terms. Whether the conflict is between son and father, citizen and president, worker and executive, power is always the crucial issue. For Marx and Freud, class strife and family strife were part of a Romantic narrative whose happy conclusion depicted an empowerment of the oppressed and a reconciliation of antitheses—a classless utopia or an oedipal resolution. Lowell's response to the postmodern sublime of military and industrial power is not so simple or auspicious. It embraces antitheses while discountenancing syntheses. In his early formalist phase, Lowell attacked the excesses of American might in a style that was as imperious and impassioned as what he condemned. Devoted New Critic that he was, if he gestured toward reconciliations, he undercut them with ambiguities. In the end opposites were suspended in tension rather than happily wedded. Like Romantics before him, having given up his apocalyptic hopes for political renovation, he later retreated inward to concentrate on psychological and religious renovation, which turned out to be just as elusive. Although his forays into history and politics continued, they consistently reconnoitered figures who, for better or worse, mirrored his personal obsessions. If the postmodern sublime in its political manifestations meant Cold War power struggles, threats of nuclear Armageddon, and capitalist plunder on a massive scale, Lowell would search for a style that, like Perseus's shield, reflected and simultaneously resisted the terror, chaos, and splendor of postmodern existence.

Lowell's vision of the postmodern scene as an agon without an end recalls Jean Baudrillard's view of history's vertiginous dialectic. In the postmodern world antitheses have burned up their theses like so much fuel, according to Baudrillard, but have failed to reach a synthesis. Baudrillard's interpretation of current events recalls Yeats's grim appraisal of totalitarian movements at the beginning of the twentieth century. In "The Second Coming" everything is spiraling out of control, "the centre cannot hold," "the best lack all conviction, while the worst / Are full of passionate intensity." Multitudes clamber heroically but suicidally for terrible beauties. Baudrillard proposes that the high-tech revolutions in the latter part of the twentieth century offer similar grim seductions. They have instigated a horrendous apocalypse in which the natural world has been eclipsed. Having virtually died, nature has made way for a vast array of spectacular simulations designed for transient entertainment. The sublime now emanates from commodities and ads engineered by corporate executives and advertising agencies to stimulate perpetual cycles of artificial appetite, conspicuous consumption, and stupendous waste. Baudrillard comments: "The passion of intensification, of escalation, of mounting power, of ecstasy, of whatever quality so long as, having ceased to be relative to its opposite (the true to the false, the beautiful to the ugly, the real to the imaginary), it becomes superlative, positively sublime as if it had absorbed the energy of its opposite."[4] The simulation of the real has created a "hyper-reality," a capitalist's dream like Disneyland, a space glutted with garish fictions so captivating that they seem facts.

This postmodern sublime in which transcendence of natural exigencies is read in capitalist rather than Kantian terms is one facet of the sublime that Lowell repeatedly addresses. In a way it is at the heart of his multi-perspective narrative of postmodern times. His divided attitudes toward the postmodern sublime predict those expressed by Marxist and post-Marxist critics like Jean-Francois Lyotard, Christopher Norris, [Fredric] Jameson, and [Terry] Eagleton. What Jameson says about the Marxist ambivalence toward capitalism and how the sublime best captures that ambivalence rings true for Lowell. In "Postmodernism, or The Cultural Logic of Late Capitalism," Jameson notes: "Marx powerfully urges us to do the impossible, namely . . . to achieve . . . a type of thinking that would be capable of grasping the demonstrably baleful features of capitalism along with its extraordinary and liberating dynamism."[5] According to Jameson, the postmodern sublime derives from a similar contradictory sense of elation and despair over culture's glut of simulations, of depthless images and tawdry signs.

As nature dissolves into a "glossy skin, a stereoscopic illusion, a rush of filmic images without density," is the capitalist apocalypse "a terrifying or an exhilarating experience" (76-77)? Borrowing concepts

---

[4] Baudrillard, *Selected Writings*, ed. Mark Poster (Stanford, 1988), 186-87.
[5] Jameson, "Postmodernism," *New Left Review* 146 (1984): 53-92; see 86.

from Burke and Kant to formulate what he calls "the hysterical sublime," Jameson analyzes texts that embrace the unreality of this state of affairs much as Lowell does—in psychological and political contexts. Behind the depthless images and fragmentary narratives, behind the words that seem to come from nowhere and go nowhere, he finds cultural hysteria and schizophrenia. Because the artist's imagination is structured politically, Jameson concludes morosely: "This whole global, yet American, postmodern culture is the internal and super-structural expression of a whole new wave of American military and economic domination throughout the world: in this sense, as throughout class history, the underside of culture is blood, torture, death and horror" (57).

Kant believed that sublimity arose from the imagination's confrontations with scenes so awesome or horrible that the mind at first shuddered without being able to find concepts or words to describe them; Jameson finds that same language-baffling power in high-tech culture. He suggests that "our faulty representations of some immense communicational and computer network are themselves but a distorted figuration of something even deeper, namely the whole world system of present-day multinational capitalism" (79). In contradistinction to Jameson, Kant would stipulate that the true sublime comes only when reason makes sense of overwhelming phenomena like the "immense communicational and computer network . . . of present-day multinational capitalism" and when it thereby recognizes its superior conceptual power. For Jameson the postmodern sublime inheres in a mind that merely encounters the faulty representations, schizophrenic writings, and other nonrepresentational artifacts of postmodernism, and is bemused, baffled, or horrified by them.

According to Jameson, the postmodernist's unwillingness to subdue the meteor shower of images in "mass culture" to the rational mind's intelligible order, and to locate sublimity in the mind's power to construct such an order, is due to cultural amnesia, collective irresponsibility toward the past, and breakdowns between history and its referent. "The new spatial logic of the simulacrum," he writes in his critique of avant-garde art, "can now be expected to have a momentous effect on what used to be historical time" (66). An ordinary sense of narrative time in many postmodern texts has been thrown to the winds, and what readers confront instead is a scattering of broken images—the fractured space of a collage rather than the temporal fluidity of a history. Hence we have "the randomly heterogeneous and fragmentary and the aleatory . . . or schizophrenic writing" (71) of postmodern artists who blissfully ignore temporal continuity and indulge in chaotic linguistic play. In his view, texts in which signifiers float free from signifieds and from coherent narrative structures are comparable to texts written or uttered by schizophrenics and hysterics. Their expressive, chaotic bliss resembles the "pathological enthusiasms" that Lowell, too, associated with sublimity.

In the poetry written between *Land of Unlikeness* and *Near the Ocean*, Lowell generally deplores the situation in which "the retrospective dimension . . .has . . . become a vast collection of images, a multitudinous photographic simulacrum" (Jameson 66). He is hesitant to embrace the postmodernist's (and modernist's) narrative of spatial discontinuity and to abandon the temporal coherence of a history that points toward a definite past and future. In his late volumes of sonnets, however, Lowell edges closer to a postmodernist style of sublime disorder even while intimating his dissatisfaction with its reduction of the past to a melange of fragmentary simulacra. Discussing Lowell's late "photographic" aesthetic, Calvin Bedient convincingly asserts: "That he was not happy with the aesthetic is plain from the poems, which sweat out their confinement to snapshot rapidity and rectilinear form."[6] History in his seemingly endless sequence of free-form, aleatory, idiosyncratic sonnets is a collage of personal obsessions from Alexander and Napoleon to Hitler and Mussolini bizarrely juxtaposed with vignettes about parents, literary mentors, lovers, and friends. *Notebook, The Dolphin, For Lizzie and Harriet*, and *History* can be read as an extended elegy for an orderly history, both ancient and recent. While these volumes reflect time's bewildering flux, they also self-reflexively diagnose, as Jameson does, the postmodern sublime as if it were symptomatic of contemporary America's pursuit of political, military, and economic hegemony. As America pursues its morally dubious goals with the cunning of a high-tech Lucifer or Ahab schooled in nuclear physics, Lowell fabricates a postmodern style that tries to mime more faithfully the frenzy and fragmentation of his and his nation's psyche. Somewhat like Eliot, who responded to his own modernist moment by offering in *The Waste Land* a diagnostic X ray of "the immense panorama of futility and anarchy which is contemporary history,"[7] Lowell pursues a helter-skelter style to delineate personal and cultural history on the verge or in the midst of collapse.

Robert Lowell and the Sublime (Syracuse, 1995), 136-42.

---

[6] Bedient, "Illegible Lowell (The Late Volumes)," *Robert Lowell*, ed. Steven Gould Axelrod and Helen Deese (New York, 1986), 139-55; see 141.
[7] Eliot, *Selected Prose*, ed. Frank Kermode (London, 1975), 177.

Damaged Grandeur: The Life of Robert Lowell

Richard Tillinghast

When *Life Studies* appeared in 1959, John Thompson wrote in the *Kenyon Review* that "the great past, Revolutionary America, the Renaissance, Rome, is all contemporary to [Lowell]. He moves among its great figures at ease with his peers. . . . This is why, perhaps alone of living poets, he can bear for us the role of the great poet, the man who on a very large scale sees more, feels more, and speaks more bravely about it than we ourselves can do." Earlier in Lowell's career Peter Viereck had judged him "best qualified to restore to our literature its sense of the tragic and the lofty."

Largeness of scale was part of Lowell's makeup. He came into the world with a sense of grandeur: "I too was born under the shadow of the Dome of the Boston State House and under Pisces, the Fish, on the first of March 1917. America was entering the First World War and was about to play her part in the downfall of four empires." Thus begins an unfinished autobiographical piece, unpublished during his lifetime, which appeared in his posthumously published *Collected Prose* under the title "Antebellum Boston." The two sentences I have quoted wonderfully capture Lowell's essence. If the dramatic self-proclamation seems presumptuous—well, the phenomenon of Robert Lowell really was awe-inspiring. The juxtaposition of the personal with a crucial historical moment became a trademark of his poetry.

Lowell has, as a historical poet, few rivals among modern writers. Few poets have the erudition (not to speak of the brazenness) to link their birth with a world war and the decline of the British, German, Hapsburg, and Czarist Russian empires. But Lowell's preoccupation with historical turning points was characteristic. His manic-depressive mental illness (bipolar disorder) expressed itself in flights of enthusiasm, which took the form of highly excited identifications with powerful figures from history such as Napoleon, Alexander the Great, Churchill, Stalin, Hitler. This tendency began in childhood:

> And I, bristling and manic,
> skulked in the attic,
> and got two hundred French generals by name,
> From A to V—from Augereau to Vandamme.
> I used to dope myself asleep,
> naming those unpronounceables like sheep. (*LS* 70)

An obsession with Napoleon runs through Lowell's madness, an enthusiasm he shared, or so he claims in "Antebellum Boston," with his mother when she was a girl: "She began to bolt her food, and for a time slept on an Army cot and took cold dips in the morning. In all this she could be Napoleon made over in my grandfather's Prussian image. It was always my grandfather she admired, even if she called him Napoleon." Napoleon as a pint-sized image of domination. "Mother, her strong chin unprotected and chilled in the helpless autumn, seemed to me the young Alexander, all gleam and panache. . . . Mother, also, was a sort of commander in chief of her virgin battlefield." Alexander was another of Lowell's favorite tyrants; Robert Silvers, quoted by Ian Hamilton, recalls that "at Mt. Sinai [hospital] he talked in a wandering way about Alexander the Great how Philip of Macedon had been a canny politician but Alexander had been able to cut through Asia." His manic attacks were sometimes heralded by his wearing a medallion of Alexander the Great around his neck, or reading *Mein Kampf* (Jonathan Miller writes that Lowell kept a copy of it inside the dust jacket of Baudelaire's *Les Fleurs du mal*), or buying a bust of Napoleon and displaying it on his dining room table in his apartment on West 67th Street in New York.

If we are to come to a better understanding of Robert Lowell's life and art, we need first of all to examine some of the misconceptions engendered by what has until recently been the only biography of him available: Ian Hamilton's massive, handsomely turned out, but often misleading 1982 work. . . . It is unfortunate that the "definitive" biographer of Robert Lowell, the subtleties of whose poems are extremely hard to grasp outside the American context, should not be an American. As an Englishman, Hamilton simply lacks the ear to interpret, or misses the tone of, much of the material he is confronted with. A sensitivity to social nuance is essential to an understanding of much of Lowell's work, *Life Studies* above all. As one small instance of how lost Hamilton is in this most important area, he presents Lowell's grandfather Arthur Winslow as "a Boston boy who had made his middle-sized pile as a mining engineer in Colorado . . . almost ridiculously proud of his descent from the New England Winslows who had supported George III," as though Winslow were some sort of jumped-up, socially insecure *nouveau riche*, and not what he was: a typical son of a good Boston family. I've never heard the expression "a Boston boy" in my life.

If Sylvia Plath's *Ariel* was, as Lowell wrote in his introduction to the book, "the autobiography of a fever," Hamilton's biography of Lowell is the biography of a psychosis. But Lowell was, like Hamlet, "but mad north-north-west"; when the wind was southerly he too knew "a hawk from a handsaw." His attacks, and the subsequent recovery periods, typically lasted one to two months. My calculations indicate that Hamilton devotes, by a rough page-count, one-fourth of his account of Lowell's adult life to the poet's madness, thereby giving readers of the biography the impression that Lowell was off his rocker more than twice as much of the time as he actually was. Caroline Blackwood comments in a 1993 interview in *Town and Country*, "There was the mad Cal, but that was less than half the person—only a few months every year" (and even here, she is speaking of Lowell's last years, when the bouts of insanity came more frequently).

What astounded Lowell's friends was how quickly and substantially he was able to recover from his manic episodes: "In between," Blair Clark wrote in a letter quoted by Hamilton, "Cal functions brilliantly, and I mean this to apply not only to his writing but to his personal and family life." Writing in the 1986 collection, *Robert Lowell: Essays on the Poetry*, which he also edited, Steven Gould Axelrod endeavors to explain why Hamilton's book has left readers with the sense that having read it, they know what there is to know about Robert Lowell:

> First, of course, Hamilton's ability to persuade Lowell's intimates and executors to help him has seemed to give his book an official imprimatur. Second, Hamilton does indeed reveal more information about Lowell's private life, especially its scandalous side. . . . But I believe another factor has played a crucial role in the book's success. Hamilton's genius is in relating the most sordid personal details in a tone of effortless, agreeable superiority. Reading *Robert Lowell: A Biography* is like reading the *National Enquirer* firm in the conviction that one is actually perusing the *Times Literary Supplement*.

Lowell's second wife, Elizabeth Hardwick, who was in the best, or worst, position to speak of his attacks and recoveries is quoted by Hamilton as saying that

> It seemed so miraculous that the old gifts of person and art were still there, as if they had been stored in some serene, safe box somewhere. Then it did not seem possible that the dread assault could return to hammer him into bits once more.
>
> He "came to" sad, worried, always ashamed and fearful; and yet there he was, this unique soul for whom one felt great pity. . . . Out of the hospital, he returned to his days, which were regular, getting up early in the morning, going to his room or separate

place for work. All day long he lay on the bed, propped up on an elbow. And this was his life, reading, studying and writing. The papers piled up on the floor, the books on the bed, the bottles of milk on the window sill, and the ashtray filled. . . . The discipline, the dedication, the endless adding to his *store*, by reading and studying—all this had, in my view, much that was heroic about it.

To reverse the terms of the old Aristotelian chestnut, Lowell had the qualities of his defects. He had not only that sense of self-assurance without which it is hard to see how anyone writes poetry at all, but also the luck to have been born with a name and family tradition that lent authority to his utterances. Elizabeth Bishop was keenly aware of the many advantages life had dropped in Lowell's lap—advantages that had been denied her. When she remarks [in a letter to Lowell], "In some ways you are the luckiest poet I know!," the first three words of her sentence are weighty ones. This luckiest of all our poets turned out to be one of the unluckiest. Both as poet and man, Lowell presents an awesome spectacle of great gifts, great luck, and great misfortune. This tragic imbalance is what gives his story overtones of classical heroism.

The young Lowell was notorious for his single-mindedness, ambition, lack of humor, and belief in aristocratic ideals. "I am not flattered by the remark that you do not know where I am heading or that my ways are not your ways," he wrote at age twenty-three to his tyrannical mother: "I am heading exactly where I have been heading for six years. One can hardly be ostracized for taking the intellect and aristocracy and family tradition seriously." As a teenager, he had prescribed for his friends not only a reading and self-improvement program, but even, during a summer on Nantucket with two schoolmates, the daily menu: "We had dreadful health food all the time. The diet was eels cooked by me, badly—and a dreadful cereal with raw honey. All decided by Cal."

Lord Weary's Castle, Lowell's first major collection, can be seen as a proud, forbidding citadel that the poet erected around himself. The title was already a good indication that here was a poet who would concern himself with the exercise of power, both on the personal and political levels. Robert Hass, in the essay "Lowell's Graveyard" from *Twentieth Century Pleasures*, writes:

"The Quaker Graveyard" is not a political poem. I had assumed that it was, that its rage against the war and Puritan will and the Quakers of Nantucket who financed the butchery of whales was an attack on American capitalism. But a political criticism of any social order implies both that a saner one can be imagined and the hope or conviction that it can be achieved. . . . I went back to the poem looking for the vision of an alternative world. There is none.

If optimism about alternative political solutions is a *sine qua non* of political poetry, then it must be concluded that Lowell was never a political poet at all. But I would have to disagree with Hass's strictures on political poetry. While remaining pessimistic about change, Lowell constantly engaged himself with the world of politics and power. His view of the radical alternatives to capitalism was just as dark as his critique of capitalism itself.

Received opinion has it Lowell started writing "personal" poetry only with *Life Studies*, a view that Robert Hass counters brilliantly in his essay:

I still find myself blinking incredulously when I read—in almost anything written about the poetry—that those early poems "clearly reflect the dictates of the new criticism," while the later ones are "less consciously wrought and extremely intimate." This is the view in which it is "more intimate" and "less conscious" to say "my mind's not right" than to imagine the moment when "The death-lance churns into the sanctuary, tears / The gun-blue swingle, heaving like a flail, / And hacks the coiling life out . . ."

which is to get things appallingly wrong.

Lowell's manner in "The Quaker Graveyard at Nantucket" is to manhandle the iambic pentameter with strong spondees and enjambments learned from Milton, and to express an extreme mental derangement through violent imagery and logical absurdities. Speaking of the lines "Where the heelheaded dogfish barks its nose / On Ahab's void and forehead," Hass comments, "The lines depend on our willingness to let barking dogs marry scavenging sharks in the deep places where men void and are voided. To complain about this is not to launch an attack on 'consciously wrought' but the reverse." So much for the fiction that in *Life Studies*, Lowell conformed to a culture-wide shift from the cooked to the raw, from paleface to redskin, though he himself publicly made the case for such a view. For poets like Galway Kinnell, Robert Bly, and Adrienne Rich, free verse really did mean what the name implies. For Lowell, what are misleadingly called fixed forms meant freedom and madness, while free verse meant prose, sanity, and control.

In the deepest part of his psyche, Lowell was, I suspect, that tyrant, that pure id that always longed to "break loose," to dominate, to be the entire world. Writing "imitations" of poets from Homer to Pasternak, for example, he "Lowellized" (Hamilton's term) his originals, making their poems sound like his own. There was not a drop of Wordsworthian "wise passivity" in his veins. In a poem written later in life, he addressed a bit of light but telling raillery to his wife and daughter: "I hope, of course, you both will outlive me, / but you and Harriet are perhaps like countries / not yet ripe for self-determination." (Alan Williamson, in a letter to me dated 5 December 1993, reports Lowell's claim that the words here were Elizabeth Hardwick's, not his, which puts the matter in quite a different light.)

In person he could shamelessly bully the weak and even the strong, often charmingly. But the tyrant shared a bed with the rebel, as Lowell himself understood. His sense of humor—and Hamilton gives little sense of it—was mischievously subversive. In "Grandparents," written when he inherited his grandfather's summer place, he grieves for his grandfather, who is "Never again to walk there, chalk our cues, / insist on shooting for us both," but concludes with: "I hold an *Illustrated London News*—; / disloyal still, / I doodle handle-bar / mustaches on the last Russian Czar." Being both dictator and revolutionary allowed him a unique view of politics. Given the contradictions inherent in this position, naturally he was a pessimist. Prometheus, in Lowell's *Prometheus Bound*, sums up the position: "It is impossible to think too much about power."

Lowell as a political poet remains, for all his brilliance and insight, something of a creature of the 1960s, along with the Kennedys, Eugene McCarthy, Che Guevara, and Lyndon Johnson, all of whom appear in his poems. Pronouncements on America from those years have a way of sounding, in retrospect, excitedly and unjustifiably apocalyptic. Hamilton's evaluation is sound: "His difficulty was that his image of America was not too sharply different from his image of himself." On the other hand, it was Lowell's own violent nature, perhaps, that made him healthily skeptical of the glibness with which many of us promoted a potentially violent revolution during that giddy decade. If James Atlas's "Robert Lowell in Cambridge: Lord Weary" is accurate, Lowell's comments on former students who, like me—fictionalized as "Leonard Wiggins"—had been swept up in left-wing politics, were rather caustic but not unfair:

"What about Leonard Wiggins?" I said. He had gone out to California for the semester and "been through a lot of heavy changes," he reported in a letter I now quoted to Lowell.

"Yes, I gather he's brimming with revolutionary zeal," Lowell said, leaning forward to concentrate on my words. (What a keen pleasure that was!) He loved news of anyone he knew. "I like his early poems, but I can't follow what he's writing now. You wonder if there isn't too much California in it." (He always switched from "I" to "you," as if attributing his opinions to someone else.)

The side of Lowell's personality that needed to dominate was balanced by a side that liked to be led. Writing about his acrimonious home life with his parents, John Crowe Ransom (quoted in Steven Gould Axelrod's *Robert Lowell: Life and Art*) calls it "a bad hurt for a boy who would have revered all his elders if they were not unworthy." In the 1940s both Ransom and Allen Tate were to some degree surrogate fathers to Lowell, though Tate winced at being called "Father Tate." And Randall Jarrell, Lowell's elder by only three years—Lowell's pet name for him was "the Old Man"—always, though a lifelong close friend, remained a distant and austere critic of Lowell's poetry.

His relationship with Jarrell, who had the surest taste in poetry of anyone in his generation, is another example of Lowell's wonderful luck. An even more important bit of luck was his marriage to Elizabeth Hardwick. Hardwick's acerbic wit, in conversation and in print, is famous if not notorious. The tintype saint from Hamilton's book is an image that few of her friends would recognize. She married, took care of, and tolerated all manner of outrageous behavior from a man who could be impossible. Part of what made Hardwick stick with him must have been love and family loyalty; part must have been a dedication to literature. Jarrell expressed what many people thought: "You feel before reading any new poem of his the uneasy expectation of perhaps encountering a masterpiece." It's clear that Lowell needed something like Hardwick's astringency to keep his native wildness under control: "your old-fashioned tirade / loving, rapid, merciless / breaks like the Atlantic Ocean on my head." He had also loved the gift his first wife, Jean Stafford, had for malicious gossip and slander. "Calumny!" he would shout delightedly. "Here comes the black tongue!" Readers with a Freudian inclination will not be surprised to learn that Lowell's mother also had a wickedly sharp tongue.

It was inevitable that Lowell would bite the hand that fed him. "O to break loose!" the opening of "Waking Early Sunday Morning," could have been his motto. After he left Hardwick, he wrote her: "What shall I say? That I miss your old guiding and even chiding hand. Not having you is like learning to walk. I suppose though one thing worse than stumbling and vacillating is to depend on someone who does these things." Yet the sense of "breaking loose" that accompanied Lowell's estrangement from

Elizabeth Hardwick and his move to England eventually brought personal
unhappiness and confusion rather than clarity. His third marriage, to
Caroline Blackwood, turned into a disaster—though not all of Lowell's
friends would agree with my assessment. A friend writes:

> True, Caroline didn't have the stamina to deal with Cal's
> breakdowns, whereas Lizzie did. But, according to [mutual
> friends], the marriage with Lizzie had gotten so combative by
> 1970 as to be really unpleasant to be around. And there was
> something touching in Cal's sexual and protective affection for
> Caroline, and the way their slapdash, improvisatory approach to
> life made them good companions for each other, for a while.

On the fourteen-line poems (it is not accurate to refer to them as
sonnets) he began writing in 1967 for *Notebook* and continued writing
through 1973, which constitute *History*, *For Lizzie and Harriet*, and *The
Dolphin*, I am inclined to agree with Ian Hamilton:

> The death of Randall Jarrell had removed the one critical voice
> that Lowell was in fear of—What will Randall think of *this?* had
> always been one of his first worries. It is possible that Jarrell
> might have found most of these new fourteen-liners slack, near-
> journalistic, or too much like casual diary jottings; they might
> have seemed to him too mumblingly unrhetorical, too self-
> indulgent. This is guessing; but there *is* a sense in which Lowell's
> new surge of eloquence is also a surge of truancy from the idea of
> some absolute critical authority, a "breaking loose" from the
> requirement *never* to write badly.

Part of what is wrong with the fourteen-liners is a formal
problem. Lowell's willfulness led him to think that if he could convince
himself of the truth of something, then that was all that needed to be done.
The fourteen-liners were little molds into which he could pour whatever he
wished. The mere fact that they *resembled* sonnets was enough to make
them do what sonnets have traditionally done in English poetry. In an
Afterthought to *Notebook 1967-68*, he avers, "My meter, fourteen line
unrhymed blank verse sections, is fairly strict at first and elsewhere, but
often corrupts in single lines to the freedom of prose. Even with this
license, I fear I have failed to avoid the themes and gigantism of the
sonnet." He was guarding the wrong flank: the poems need more, not less,
of the traditional virtues (which he derides as "gigantism") of the sonnet

sequence. The gigantism came not from his approximation of the sonnet form, but from his own megalomania.

"Those blessed structures, plot and rhyme— / why are they no help to me now / I want to make / something imagined, not recalled?" Lowell asks in his last book, *Day by Day*. Perhaps they *would* have been a help to him, if he had had the discipline and deliberation to return to them. Hamilton identifies another problem of the "sonnets," one of tone: "there is something glazed and foreign in their manner of address, as if they sense an audience too far-off, too blurred to be worth striving for." Lowell at his best is a very grounded, personal writer, and his prefatory remark to *Notebook 1967-68*, "Accident threw up subjects, and the plot swallowed them—famished for human chances," suggests an impersonality far from his genius. *Notebook* and its later incarnations have been seen by some critics as attempts to rival John Berryman's *Dream Songs*. If this was the case, Lowell might have done well to emulate the *Dream Songs'* formal division into stanzas.

Furious debate surrounded the ethics of Lowell's having included the letters, telephone conversations, and so on of Elizabeth Hardwick in his late books, *The Dolphin* and *For Lizzie and Harriet*. His friend William Alfred was strongly against it. W. H. Auden said he would never speak to Lowell again if he published the Hardwick material. Elizabeth Bishop wrote him an impassioned letter trying to dissuade him from publishing an earlier version of *The Dolphin*:

> That is "infinite mischief," I think. The first one, page 10, is so shocking—well, I don't know what to say. . . . One can use one's life as material—one does, anyway—but these letters—aren't you violating a trust? IF you were given permission—IF you hadn't changed them . . . etc. *But art just isn't worth that much*. . . . It is not being "gentle" to use personal, tragic, anguished letters that way—it's cruel.

To Lowell, though, life and art were one. His loyalties were, finally, to his work.

But in his last book, *Day by Day*, Lowell seems to say that he has botched not only his life, but his poetry as well. Perhaps he was writing his own epitaph when he addressed these words to his namesake: "yours the lawlessness / of something simple that has lost its law, / my namesake, not the last Caligula." He could perhaps have endured the pain of inflicting pain on his family. In fact, in the last poem of *The Dolphin* he shoulders that responsibility:

> I have sat and listened to too many
> words of the collaborating muse,
> and plotted perhaps too freely with my life,
> not avoiding injury to others,
> not avoiding injury to myself—
> to ask compassion . . . this book, half fiction,
> an eelnet made by man for the eel fighting—
>
> my eyes have seen what my hand did.

Writing in the *American Poetry Review* in 1973, Adrienne Rich delivered the strongest condemnation of the three books of "sonnets." Harsh as her words are, it is hard to disagree with Rich's assessment of the lines from *The Dolphin*, except that what she sees as vindictiveness is more truly a colossal thoughtlessness. . . .

Lowell was not completely written out when he died at sixty. The poems in *Day by Day* demonstrate that he had abandoned the crutch the fourteen-line form had become for him during the period of *History*; the anguished candor of the new poems suggests that, had he lived, he might have achieved another poetic breakthrough as important as the one he brought off in *Life Studies*. Sixty might, in some people, seem a ripe enough age to die. Not for Lowell, of whom one can say that he "should have died hereafter." In the meantime Paul Mariani's new biography of Lowell gives readers a more rounded picture of the "Cal" his friends put up with, laughed about, became exasperated with, but always admired and deeply loved.

To say that his friends laughed about him may sound cruel; but sad as his life in some ways was, why not grant the man credit for being one in a long line of aristocratic Boston eccentrics? Ian Hamilton quotes Keith Botsford, who accompanied Lowell on a Congress for Cultural Freedom junket to South America. Botsford would visit Lowell in the hospital in Buenos Aires during one of his attacks and recalls:

> I was brought up as a composer, and all he wanted me to do was whistle. Sometimes it was "Yankee Doodle Dandy" or "The Battle Hymn of the Republic." Or it was Brandenberg concertos, Mozart piano concertos, anything. It was the one thing he craved, the one thing that would calm him. I'd be there two or three hours, just whistling until I was dry in the mouth. I'd whistle all the parts in the Ninth Symphony, or whatever, and he'd say, "Yeah, but do the tympani bit."

I leave the last word to Peter Taylor, one of Lowell's oldest friends, in his funeral oration:

> As poet, as man, he approaches the great mystery playfully and seriously at the same time. From the very beginning or from the time when I first knew him in his later teens, he seemed determined that there should be no split in his approach to understanding profound matters. He was searching for a oneness in himself and a oneness in the world. He would not allow that any single kind of experience denied him the right and access to some opposite kind. . . . He would boast at times that he had never lost a friend. He never even wanted to give up a marriage entirely. He wanted his wife and children around him in an old fashioned household, and yet he wanted to be free and on the town. Who *doesn't* wish for all that, of course? But he *would* have both. He wanted it all so intensely that he became very sick at times. . . . When one heard that he was dead and how he died in the back seat of a New York taxi cab, one could not help feeling that he had everything, even the kind of death he had always said he wanted.

Sewanee Review 102:1 (Winter 1994), 121-31; rpt. *Robert Lowell's Life and Work: Damaged Grandeur* (Ann Arbor, 1995), 43-56.

~~The Age of~~ Lowell

Jed Rasula

The poet who personified the postwar American bard was Robert Lowell. He was the poet whose actions set the pace and dramatized the Puritan backdrop into the bargain. But was he indicative? Was it really, after the Age of Auden, the Age of Lowell? Thomas Parkinson admits "It makes me uneasy to hear the period from c.1945 to the present referred to as 'The Age of Lowell'—the phrase has a tinny fabricated sound. Lowell was something we reacted to and against, but there was never a sense of coziness about the whole thing."[1] Parkinson's phrasing reveals more than he's willing to concede: his Lowell, it turns out, is not a person but a force, "something we reacted to," or as he subsequently puts it, "an other and representative reality." Lowell was attractive because he personified self-determination and force of will, at a time when these were the qualities that appeared to have left America intact and endowed with leadership in a broken world. But this was, in the classic Madison Avenue and Hollywood sense, personification as production. Shapiro offers this insight: "Robert Lowell took to poetry instinctively as one of the deepest forms of abuse: he was pliable in the hands of the New Critics, the most powerful literary caucus of the mid-century, and he was not discovered but created by them."[2] This would be sufficient incentive for a quality that many besides Shapiro noted: "one feels that Lowell writes poetry to *get even*," he said, adding that "competition is the sole inspiration of such a poet."

It's not difficult to see Lowell as the "self-made" poet that Robert Duncan disapproves of, pridefully asserting the marketability of his verse as the public struggle of a *persona*. It was a role Yeats had pioneered, and Lowell made his difference explicit by putting the mask on upside down or backwards from time to time. It's not an accusation Duncan himself leveled, possibly because he saw, as I am inclined to, that Lowell was compelled in part to destroy the terms of valuation that had canonized him in the first place. His career charts a set of hurdles, each of which is a calculated affront to a coterie of admirers. What is alarming about Lowell, in the end, is the amount of *calculation* involved. The will to power is nowhere more brazenly apparent in poetry than in Lowell's trajectory. "Lowell is primarily a figurehead which he himself personally carved out of solid rock," Shapiro observed, contradicting his version of Lowell as New Critical putty (136). His success is a classic American perplexity: that of the self-made man who is, for all that, enabled to triumph by powerful backers with their team of handlers and public relations experts. He was *the* poet prepared, golem-like, by the founders of New Criticism, programmed as it were to produce the poems that would confirm for a contemporary audience that their *tastes* (as honed by the curriculum of *Understanding Poetry*) could handle the new poetry as readily as the old.

"'You didn't write, you rewrote,'" Jarrell's voice says reproachfully in a poem from *History* (135). Lowell's way of explaining his own work was to direct attention to the past, then offer a solution for

---

[1] Parkinson, *Poets, Poems, Movements* (Ann Arbor, 1987), 215.
[2] Karl Shapiro, *To Abolish Children, and Other Essays* (Chicago, 1968), 137.

its liabilities: "Shelley can just rattle off *terza rima* by the page," he explained. "And I think both Tate and I felt that we wanted our formal patterns to seem a hardship and something that we couldn't rattle off easily" (*CP* 241). In his final years, when Lowell rattled off volume after volume of blank verse sonnets, it seems that history itself has been grasped as a technical problem, disgorging epiphanies by squeezing equal portions of data and sensibility into a stunted receptacle. . . .

Lowell certainly called up powers of some kind. His manic-depressive episodes are well documented, and he exemplifies more than anyone the sustaining power of poetry in the face of personal crisis. So, while Parkinson is unwilling to recognize an Age of Lowell, he does validate Lowell as a barometer of public record. "Lowell was a reminder of pain. He dramatized, not knowing it himself any more than the rest of us, that pain was normal for our generation because of the irreconcilabilities we had chosen as our substance, and then the ultimate numbness that great pain imposes" (215-16). His private pain could signify a public grief, that is, at a time when public space was being remorselessly privatized. In the wake of the McCarthy hearings, which made it clear just how much punishment could be brought to bear on the private lives and beliefs of individuals, a poetry that glamorized laceration offered irresistible attractions. "Pain was what we expected society to impose," Parkinson continues, "and all our cultural conditioning has led us to associate purgation and genuine suffering with that pain." "In the Cage," from *Lord Weary's Castle*, reappears in *History* like a refrain Lowell couldn't stop feverishly handling. "It is night, / and it is vanity, and age / Blackens the heart of Adam" becomes, thirty years later, "I am night, I am vanity." Both versions end "Fear, the yellow chirper, beaks its cage" (*H* 129). But pain with Lowell was a private matter preceding public life (a distinction not so clear in the case of one whose genealogy was notably public): reminiscing about his boyhood pugilism, he admitted in the fifties "I wanted to handle and draw strength from my scar."[3] . . .

What the "age demanded" in Pound's phrase, after the Second World War, was its "accelerated grimace" in the figure of the poet as virile youth, a role which fit Lowell to a tee. The poet did not compel the age (as, in some measure, Yeats, Eliot and Auden had). What had changed from Pound's time was the way in which literary expectations were gratified. Lowell was the all but official laureate for an age that cared little for poetry. Quite apart from his personal traumas, he suffered the indignity of being canonized while alive and installed into what I hope has been conveyed as the *kitsch* proportions of exhibit in the Wax Museum.

---

[3] Ian Hamilton, *Robert Lowell: A Biography* (New York, 1982), 17.

Trapped in a display space nicely prefigured as the jail cell of "In the Cage," Lowell kept one eye on the idolators, sycophants and tourists of literature, and another on the ward bosses, all on behalf of Poetry with a capital P. "If you look at the poetry of Robert Lowell," Michael Palmer points out, "a certain amount of it is stultified by having to exist under the sign of Literature. Am I making Great literature? Is Delmore Schwartz going to be angry with this poem? Is Allen Tate going to scold me?"[4] Lowell may have been The Man, but he was also the front for a committee.

Even his closest admirers could be disconcerted by the way he seemed pliable to the will of others. In his commemorative tribute to Lowell in *The New York Times Book Review*, Kunitz describes how "he made his friends, willy-nilly, partners in his act, by showering them with early drafts of his poems, often so fragmentary and shapeless that it was no great trick to suggest improvements."[5] Kunitz was both fascinated and disconcerted by the legibility of so many contributing hands in Lowell's finished work. Frank Bidart, Lowell's student amanuensis at Harvard, testifies that "He wanted you to like his poems, obviously, but he didn't want you to be a yes man." Bidart nicely captures the plight of canonization as a kind of premature burial as he describes the process of revision: "I said I didn't think this line was quite right, or something, and he changed it right in front of me, and it was unnerving, it was scary. It was a little like going into a museum and you say, 'I'm not crazy about that arm,' and the statue moves" (Hamilton 392). In his last years Lowell was performing the biopsy of his career, which had been one of perpetual overexposure. Nothing may be quite so haunting as the last lines of "Endings": "The wandering virus never surmounts the cluster / it never joined. // My eyes flicker, the immortal / is scraped unconsenting from the mortal" (*Day by Day* 50). The viral poet, never fully dissociated from the pack because he been adopted too young to have sensed any personal agency in the matter: helplessly contagious, impassively dominant, a colossus of contradictions. David Perkins writes, "He understood that in poetry 'life' must be an illusion produced by art."[6] The opposite, I think, was the case: Lowell gullibly credited poetry with producing the facticity of a life, the public reputation of which might be illusory but, for all that, needed to be *lived*.

Lowell's evident dismay at his own eminence, in the end, can best be analogized to a prizewinning boxer who knows he had the moxie but

---

[4] Palmer, Interview, *Talking Poetry*, ed. Lee Bartlett (Albuquerque, 1987), 131.
[5] Stanley Kunitz, "Sense of a Life," *NYTBR* (Oct. 16, 1977): 34.
[6] Perkins, *History of Modern Poetry* (Cambridge, 1987), 415.

whose career was an orchestrated series of fixed fights. Convinced of his own superiority, he's nevertheless haunted by his awareness that the public show was rigged. As indeed it was for Lowell, mascot of the New Criticism during the decades of its imperium. Lowell—along with Jarrell and Schwartz to lesser degrees—represents the establishment's quest for poetry's Right Stuff (to evoke Tom Wolfe's phrase), lofted into canonical orbit; and we see, in the late work especially, the g-force *introjected* into the poetry, the masking function of the personae becoming an apotropaic grimace: the poet, suited up and deposited in the claustrophic body-contour of the space capsule, cultivated like so much raw material for the purpose of Making History. And under it all the suspicion that "The Age of Lowell" is really another movie: *The Set-Up.*

Lowell's epitaph could very well be Mailer's wager, in *Armies of the Night* (subtitled "History as Novel, the Novel as History"): "Once History inhabits a crazy house, egotism may be the last tool left to History" (68). It's not coincidental, I think, that in the wake of global war—under the sign of History as Apocalypse—the poets most notable for energetically engaging history have been figures of complex polymathic egotism, foremost of which are Pound, Lowell, and Olson. Donald Hall, reviewing Olson for *The Nation* in 1961, found his historicizing impulse practically without precedent in recent years. . . . This might seem a surprising slight of Lowell, but Hall may have discovered by way of Olson that Lowell's variety of history was attenuated. As David Antin complains, Lowell "manages to get as much grade-school history into a poem as he can."[7] For a friendlier view which I think amounts to the same thing: Elizabeth Bishop enviously exclaimed in a letter to Lowell "In some ways you are the luckiest poet I know!" Most poets could write about their ancestors, "but what would be the significance? Nothing at all. . . . Whereas all you have to do is put down the names!" (Hamilton 233).

Bishop's remark suggests a distinction that cleaves American poetry in two in the anthology wars, and into a myriad of splinters thereafter. Where Lowell could write of "The farm, entitled *Char-de-sa* / in the Social Register, / . . . named for my Grandfather's children: / Charlotte, Devereux, and Sarah" (*LS* 60), a comparable passage in Olson might be "Althan says / Winslow / was at Cape Ann in April, / 1624"—a specification which immediately follows Olson's declaration "I would be an historian as Herodotus was, looking / for oneself for the evidence of / what is said" (*Maximus* 104-5). Lowell tends to monument, Olson to document. The Boston Common statue of Colonel Shaw's troops in "For

---

[7] Antin, "Modernism and Postmodernism," *Boundary 2* 1(1972): 112.

the Union Dead" ("William James could almost hear the bronze Negroes breathe") is a hieratic view; whereas Olson registers the stark traces of the transatlantic economy that fetched so many millions as raw material in the first place. . . .

The density of Olson's documentation in *The Maximus Poems* is for most readers distressingly far from anything resembling "gradeschool history." But scholars have been more successful annotating *Maximus* than they have *History*, for all the convenience of Lowell's specimen label titles. The reason is not hard to find: Lowell's work is accessibly subordinated to the thematic register of the heroic ego. In his final year, reflecting on his life's work, he concluded that "the thread that strings it together is my autobiography, it is a small-scale *Prelude*, written in many different styles and with digressions, yet a continuing story" (Hamilton 233). Lowell's work is compulsively fascinating precisely because it takes on the waxwork character of the freak show, the exhibit of a human life assuming monstrous proportions. What is "monstrous," I should clarify, comes from the root *monstrum* and *monere*, portent and warning: Lowell warns us, by self-exhibition, of the pitfalls of life lived on a pedestal, in the showcase; life as continual self-dramatization; poetry as public monument. His celebrated jawbreaker lines have an integrity that detaches them from the very poems they inhabit, bringing to mind Albert Speer's penchant for designing Third Reich buildings for the elegance of the rubble that would eventually be left of them. . . .

The American Poetry Wax Museum (Urbana, 1996), 247-56.

After Enjoying Six or Seven Essays On Me

Robert Lowell

I am not an authoritative critic of my own poems, except in the most pressing and urgent way. I have spent hundreds and hundreds of hours shaping, extending and changing hopeless or defective work. I lie on a bed staring, crossing out, writing in, crossing out what was written in, again and again, through days and weeks. Heavenly hours of absorption and idleness . . . intuition, intelligence, pursuing my ear that knows not what it says. In time, the fragmentary and scattered limbs become by a wild extended figure of speech, something living . . . a person.

I know roughly what I think are my better poems, and more roughly and imperfectly why I think they are; and roughly too, which are my worst and where they fail. I have an idea how my best fall short. To have to state all this systematically, and perhaps with controversial argument, would be a prison sentence to me. It would be an exposure. But which is one's good poem? Is it a translation? Can one write something that will sing on for years like the sirens, and not know it?

Reading other critics on me, as I have the pleasure of doing here [in *Salmagundi*], gives me the surprise of seeing my poems through eyes that are not mine. Younger, older . . . refreshingly different and perhaps keener eyes . . . mercifully through the eyes of another, for a poem changes with each inspection. Variability is its public existence. Yet variety has limits; no one could call *Macbeth* or my *Quaker Graveyard* hilarious minuets. That would take an insensately amusing theorist.

Politics? We live in the sunset of Capitalism. We have thundered nobly against its bad record all our years, yet we cling to its vestiges, not just out of greed and nostalgia, but for our intelligible survival. Is this what makes our art so contradictory, muddled and troubled? We are being proven in a sort of secular purgatory; there is no earthly paradise on the horizon. War, nuclear bombs, civil gangsterism, race, woman—the last has always been the writer's most unavoidable, though not only, subject, one we are too seriously engaged in to be fair, or . . . salvationists.

It seems our insoluble lives sometimes come clearer in writing. This happens rarely because most often skill and passion are lacking, and when these are not lacking it happens rarely because the goddess Fortuna grudgingly consents. It is easier to write good poems than inspired lines.

Influences: I assume this is a live subject. When I began to publish, I wrote literally under the rooftree of Allen Tate. When I imitated him, I believed I was imitating the muse of poetry. When I erred, I failed, or accidentally forced myself to be original. Later, I was drawn to William Carlos Williams and Elizabeth Bishop. I can't say how much I hope I learned. Yet I differed so in temperament and technical training (particularly with Williams) that nothing I wrote could easily be confused with their poems. How many poets I wish I could have copied, the Shakespeare of *The Winter's Tale*, the Wordsworth of the *Ruined Cottage*, the Blake of "Truly my Satan . . .", the Pound of the best *Pisan Cantos*. Baudelaire? Hardy? Maybe I have. The large poet of the nineteenth century who attracts and repels us is Robert Browning. Who couldn't he use, Napolean III, St. John, Cardinal Manning, Caliban? He set them in a thousand meters. Nor was his ear deficient—take the opening of *Andrea del Sarto*, hundreds of lines of *Christmas Eve*, all of the *Householder*, most of *Mr. Sludge the Medium*. And yet Browning's idiosyncratic robustness scratches us, and often his metrical acrobatics are too good. One wishes one could more often see him plain, or as he might have been rewritten by some master novelist, Samuel Butler or George Eliot, though not in her Italian phase. Yet perhaps Browning's poems will out last much major fiction. Meanwhile he shames poets with the varied human beings he could scan, the generosity of his ventriloquism.

Looking over my *Selected Poems*, about thirty years of writing, my impression is that the thread that strings it together is my autobiography, it is a small-scale *Prelude*, written in many different styles and with digressions, yet a continuing story—still wayfaring. A story of what? Not the "growth of a poet's mind." Not a lesson and example to be handed to the student. Yet the mind must eventually age and grow, or the story would be a still-life, the pilgrimage of a zombi. My journey is always stumbling on the unforeseen and even unforeseeable. From year to year, things remembered from the past change almost more than the present.

Those mutilating years are often lenient to art . . . If only one's selected poems could keep their figure like Madame Bovary!

I haven't said what I wished to write in poems, the discordant things I've tried. It isn't possible, is it? When I was working on *Life Studies*, I found I had no language or meter that would allow me to approximate what I saw or remembered. Yet in prose I had already found what I wanted, the conventional style of autobiography and reminiscence. So I wrote my autobiographical poetry in a style I thought I had discovered in Flaubert, one that used images and ironic or amusing particulars. I did all kinds of tricks with meter and the avoidance of meter. When I didn't have to bang words into rhyme and count, I was more nakedly dependent on rhythm. After this in the *Union Dead*, I used the same style but with less amusement, and with more composition and stanza-structure. Each poem was meant to stand by itself. This stronger structure would probably have ruined *Life Studies*. Which would have lost its novelistic flow. Later on in *For the Union Dead*, free verse subjects seemed to melt away, and I found myself back in strict meter, yet tried to avoid the symbols and heroics of my first books. After that I wrote a long sequence in Marvell's eight-line four-foot couplet stanza. God know why, except that it seemed fit to handle national events. Indeed the stanza was a Godsent task that held me almost breathing couplet all one summer and deep into the next autumn. Shine compensated for the overcompression. For six years I wrote unrhymed blank verse sonnets. They had the eloquence at best of iambic pentameter, and often the structure and climaxes of sonnets, with one fraction of the fourteen lines balanced against the remaining fraction. Obscurity and confusion came when I tried to cram too much in the short space. Quite often I wasn't obscure or discontinuous. I had a chance such as I had never had before, or probably will again, to snatch up and verse the marvelous varieties of the moment. I think perfection (I mean outward coherence not inspiration) was never so difficult. Since then, I have been writing for the last three years in unrhymed free verse. At first I was so unused to this meter, it seemed like tree-climbing. It came back—gone now the sonnet's cramping and military beat. What I write almost always comes out of the pressure of some inner concern, temptation or obsessive puzzle. Surprisingly, quite important things may get said. But sometimes what is closest to the heart has no words but stereotypes. Stereotypes are usually true, but never art. Inspired lines from nowhere roam through my ears . . . to make or injure a poem. All my poems are written for catharsis; none can heal melancholia or arthritis.

    I pray that my progress has been more than recoiling with satiation and disgust from one style to another, a series of rebuffs. I hope there has been increase of beauty, wisdom, tragedy and all the blessings of this consuming chance.

Salmagundi 37 (Spring 1977): 112-15.

Chronology

1917   Robert Traill Spence Lowell IV born March 1 in Boston, the only child of Robert Traill Spence Lowell III, USN, and Charlotte Winslow Lowell. Maternal ancestors include Pilgrim leader Edward Winslow (1595-1655), Plymouth colony governor Josiah Winslow (1629-1680), and Revolutionary War general John Stark (1728-1822); paternal ancestors include author Robert Traill Spence Lowell (1816-1891), poet James Russell Lowell (1819-1891), astronomer Percival Lowell (1855-1916), Harvard president A. Lawrence Lowell (1856-1943), and poet Amy Lowell (1874-1925).

1924   Lowell family settles permanently in Boston after periods in Philadelphia and Washington, D. C.

1924-30   Brimmer School in Boston.

1930-35   St. Mark's School in Southborough, Mass. Studies with Richard Eberhart, befriends Frank Parker.

1935-37   Harvard University. Fight with father.

1937   Spring and summer with Allen Tate at Clarksville, Tenn.

1937-40   Kenyon College. Studies with John Crowe Ransom, befriends Randall Jarrell and Peter Taylor. Graduates summa cum laude in Classics.

1940   Marries writer Jean Stafford on April 2.

1940-41   Converts to Roman Catholicism. Graduate study in English at Louisiana State University with Cleanth Brooks and Robert Penn Warren.

1941-42   Move to New York. Editorial assistant at Sheed & Ward.

1942-43   Writes poetry during year's stay with Allen Tate and Caroline Gordon at Monteagle, Tenn.

1943   Refuses military induction, sentenced in October to a year and a day for violating Selective Service Act. Serves five months in West Street detention center in New York and federal prison at Danbury, Conn. Parole in Black Rock, Conn.

1944   *Land of Unlikeness.* Jean Stafford's novel *Boston Adventure.* Move to Damariscotta Mills, Maine.

1946   *Lord Weary's Castle* (Pulitzer Prize). Befriends Delmore Schwartz and John Berryman. Separates from Stafford, moves to New York.

1947   Guggenheim Fellowship and American Academy grant. Befriends William Carlos Williams and Elizabeth Bishop.

1947-48   Poetry Consultant to the Library of Congress.

1948   Divorce from Jean Stafford. Leaves Roman Catholic Church.

1948-49   Yaddo Writers' Colony.

1949   Returns to New York. Member of committee awarding the Bollingen Prize to Ezra Pound for *Pisan Cantos.* Hospitalized for mental disturbance in March. Marries writer Elizabeth Hardwick, July 28.

1950   Teaches creative writing at the University of Iowa in spring and at Kenyon College in summer. Father dies in August.

1950-53   Lowell and Hardwick live in Europe.

1951   *The Mills of the Kavanaughs* (Harriet Monroe Prize).

1952   Supports Stevenson for president. Teaches at the Seminar in American Studies at Salzburg.

1953   Teaches at the University of Iowa. Students include W. D. Snodgrass and Philip Levine. Teaches summer session at the University of Indiana.

1954   Lectures at the University of Cincinnati. Mother dies in Italy in February. Lowell and Hardwick relocate to Boston. Manic-depressive breakdown. Begins drafting autobiography.

1954-60 Lowell and Hardwick live on Marlborough St. in Boston.

1955-60 Teaches at Boston University Students include Sylvia Plath, Anne Sexton, and George Starbuck.

1957   Daughter Harriet Winslow Lowell born. January 4. West Coast speaking tour in March-April. Drafts "Skunk Hour" at summer home in Castine, Maine. Bi-polar illness.

1958   Hospitalized in January. Continues work on *Life Studies*.

1959   *Life Studies* (National Book Award, Guinness Poetry Award).

1960   Reads "For the Union Dead" at Boston Arts Festival, June 5. Move to New York. Supports Kennedy for president.

1960-70 Residence on upper west side in Manhattan.

1961   *Imitations* (Harriet Monroe Prize, Bollingen Prize). *Phaedra*.

1962   Summer in South America.

1963-77 Teaches at Harvard (on leave 1970-72, commutes from England for one semester yearly 1973-76). Students include Frank Bidart, who becomes a close friend.

1964   *For the Union Dead*. "My Kinsman, Major Molineux" and "Benito Cereno" premiere in New York. November 1 (Obie Award). Ford grant for drama.

1965   *The Old Glory*. Protests Vietnam War by publicly declining President Johnson's invitation to the White House Festival of the Arts. *Phaedra* premieres at Wesleyan University.

1966   Defeated for Oxford Chair of Poetry by English poet Edmund Blunden. Wins Sarah Josepha Hale Award.

1967   *Near the Ocean*. Joins Allen Ginsberg, Denise Levertov, Norman
          Mailer, and others in March on Pentagon. *Prometheus Bound*
          premieres at Yale University.

1968   *The Old Glory*, revised edition. "Endecott and the Red Cross"
          premieres in New York, April 18. Campaigns for Eugene
          McCarthy in primaries, refuses to vote for president in November.

1969   *Notebook 1967-68*. *Prometheus Bound*. Visits Israel.

1970   *Notebook*. Visiting Fellow, All Souls' College, Oxford.

1970-76   Residence in England with writer Caroline Blackwood.

1970-72   Teaches at Essex University. Befriends Seamus Heaney.

1971   Son Robert Sheridan Lowell born to Blackwood and Lowell.

1972   Divorce from Elizabeth Hardwick, marriage to Caroline
          Blackwood in October.

1973   *The Dolphin* (Pulitzer Prize). *For Lizzie and Harriet. History.*

1974   Copernicus Award for lifetime achievement in poetry.

1976   *Selected Poems*.

1977   *Day by Day* (National Book Critics Circle Award). *Selected
          Poems*, revised edition. American Academy Medal for Literature.
          Returns to Elizabeth Hardwick in the United States. Dies of heart
          failure in New York, September 12. Episcopalian funeral service in
          Boston, September 16. Burial in family plot at Dunbarton, N. H.

1978   *The Oresteia of Aeschylus* published posthumously.

1987   *Collected Prose* published posthumously.

Selected Bibliography

BOOKS BY LOWELL

Land of Unlikeness. Cummington, Mass.: Cummington Press, 1944.

Lord Weary's Castle. New York: Harcourt, Brace, 1946.

The Mills of the Kavanaughs. New York: Harcourt, Brace, 1951.

Life Studies. New York: Farrar, Straus & Cudahy, 1959; London: Faber & Faber, 1959, 1968.

Imitations. New York: Farrar, Straus & Cudahy, 1961; London: Faber & Faber, 1962.

Phaedra and Figaro. By Jean Racine and Pierre Baumarchais; translated by Robert Lowell and Jacques Barzun. New York: Farrar, Straus & Cudahy, 1961; London: Faber & Faber, 1963.

For the Union Dead. New York: Farrar, Straus & Giroux, 1964; London: Faber & Faber, 1965.

The Old Glory. New York: Farrar, Straus & Giroux, 1965; London: Faber & Faber, 1966; revised edition, New York: Farrar, Straus & Giroux, 1968.

Near the Ocean. New York: Farrar, Straus & Giroux, 1967; London: Faber & Faber, 1967.

Notebook 1967-68. New York: Farrar, Straus & Giroux, 1969.

Prometheus Bound. Derived from Aeschylus. New York: Farrar, Straus & Giroux, 1969; London: Faber & Faber, 1970.

Notebook. New York: Farrar, Straus & Giroux, 1970; London: Faber & Faber, 1970.

The Dolphin. New York: Farrar, Straus & Giroux, 1973; London: Faber & Faber, 1973.

For Lizzie and Harriet. New York: Farrar, Straus & Giroux, 1973; London: Faber & Faber, 1973.

History. New York: Farrar, Straus & Giroux, 1973; London: Faber & Faber, 1973.

Selected Poems. New York: Farrar, Straus & Giroux, 1976; revised.
    edition, New York: Noonday, 1977.
Day by Day. New York: Farrar, Straus & Giroux, 1977; London: Faber
    & Faber, 1978.
The Oresteia of Aeschylus. New York: Farrar Straus Giroux, 1978.
Collected Prose. Edited by Robert Giroux. New York: Farrar Straus
    Giroux, 1987; London: Faber, 1987.
Collected Poems. Edited by Frank Bidart. Forthcoming.

WORKS ABOUT LOWELL

BIBLIOGRAPHIES

Axelrod, Steven Gould and Helen Deese. *Robert Lowell: A Reference
    Guide*. Boston: G. K. Hall, 1982.
Mazzaro, Jerome. *The Achievement of Robert Lowell: 1939-1959*.
    Detroit: University of Detroit Press, 1960.
Miehe, Patrick. *The Robert Lowell Papers at the Houghton Library*. New
    York: Greenwood Press, 1990.
Procopiow, Norma. *Robert Lowell: The Poet and the Critics*. Chicago:
    American Library Association, 1984.

BIOGRAPHIES

Bawer, Bruce. *The Middle Generation: The Lives and Poetry of Delmore
    Schwartz, Randall Jarrell, John Berryman, and Robert Lowell*.
    Hamden, Conn.: Archon Books, 1986.
Doreski, William. *The Years of Our Friendship: Robert Lowell and Allen
    Tate*. Jackson: University Press of Mississippi, 1990.
Hamilton, Ian. *Robert Lowell: A Biography*. New York: Random House,
    1982.
Heymann, C. David. *American Aristocracy: The Lives and Times of
    James Russell, Amy, and Robert Lowell*. New York: Dodd, Mead,
    1980.
Kalstone, David. *Becoming a Poet: Elizabeth Bishop with Marianne
    Moore and Robert Lowell*. New York: Farrar Straus Giroux, 1989.
Mariani, Paul. *Lost Puritan: A Life of Robert Lowell*. New York: W. W.
    Norton, 1994.
Meyers, Jeffrey. *Manic Power: Robert Lowell and his Circle*. London:
    Macmillan, 1987.

Stuart, Sarah Payne. *My First Cousin Once Removed: Money, Madness, and the Family of Robert Lowell.* New York: HarperCollins, 1998.

Tillinghast, Richard. *Robert Lowell's Life and Work: Damaged Grandeur.* Ann Arbor: University of Michigan Press, 1995.

CRITICAL BOOKS

Axelrod, Steven Gould. *Robert Lowell: Life and Art.* Princeton: Princeton University Press, 1978.

Bell, Vereen M. *Robert Lowell: Nihilist as Hero.* Cambridge, Mass.: Harvard University Press, 1983.

Cooper, Phillip. *The Autobiographical Myth of Robert Lowell.* Chapel Hill: University of North Carolina Press, 1970.

Cosgrave, Patrick. *The Public Poetry of Robert Lowell.* London: Gollancz, 1970; New York: Taplinger, 1972.

Crick, John. *Robert Lowell.* Edinburgh: Oliver & Boyd, 1974.

Fein, Richard J. *Robert Lowell.* New York: Twayne, 1970; revised edition, Boston: Twayne, 1979.

Hart, Henry. *Robert Lowell and the Sublime.* Syracuse, N.Y.: Syracuse University Press, 1995.

Hobsbaum, Philip. *A Reader's Guide to Robert Lowell.* London: Thames & Hudson, 1988.

Mackinnon, Lachlan. *Eliot, Auden, Lowell: Aspects of the Baudelairean Inheritance.* Atlantic Highlands, N.J.: Humanities Press 1983.

Martin, Jay. *Robert Lowell.* Minneapolis: University of Minnesota Press, 1970.

Matterson, Stephen. *Berryman and Lowell: The Art of Losing.* Totowa, N.J.: Barnes & Noble, 1988.

Mazzaro, Jerome. *The Poetic Themes of Robert Lowell.* Ann Arbor: University of Michigan Press, 1965.

Meiners, R. K. *Everything to Be Endured: An Essay on Robert Lowell and Modern Poetry.* Columbia: University of Missouri Press, 1970.

Perloff, Marjorie. *The Poetic Art of Robert Lowell.* Ithaca, N.Y.: Cornell University Press, 1973.

Raffel, Burton. *Robert Lowell.* New York: Ungar, 1981.

Ramakrishnan, E. V. *Crisis and Confession: Studies in the Poetry of Theodore Roethke, Robert Lowell, and Sylvia Plath.* Delhi: Chanakya Publishers, 1988.

Rudman, Mark. *Robert Lowell: An Introduction to The Poetry.* New York: Columbia University Press, 1983.

Smith, Vivian. *The Poetry of Robert Lowell.* Sydney: Sydney University Press, 1974.

Staples, Hugh. *Robert Lowell: The First Twenty Years.* New York: Farrar, Straus & Cudahy, 1962; London: Faber & Faber, 1962.

Tokunaga, Shozo [Yozo]. *Robert Lowell: Horo to Hangyaku no Bostonian.* Tokyo: Kenyusha, 1981.

Travisano, Thomas. *Midcentury Quartet: Bishop, Lowell, Jarrell, Berryman.* Charlottesville: University of Virginia Press, 1999.

Williamson, Alan. *Pity the Monsters: The Political Vision of Robert Lowell.* New Haven, Conn.: Yale University Press, 1974.

Witek, Terri. *Robert Lowell and "Life Studies": Revising the Self.* Columbia: University of Missouri Press, 1993.

Yenser, Stephen. *Circle to Circle: The Poetry of Robert Lowell.* Berkeley: University of California Press, 1975.

ESSAY COLLECTIONS

Anzilotti, Rolando, editor. *Robert Lowell: A Tribute.* Pisa: Nistri-Lischi, 1979.

Axelrod, Steven Gould, and Helen Deese, editors. *Robert Lowell: Essays on the Poetry.* New York: Cambridge University Press, 1986.

Bloom, Harold, editor. *Robert Lowell.* New York: Chelsea House, 1987.

London, Michael, and Robert Boyers, editors. *Robert Lowell: A Portrait of the Artist in His Time.* New York: David Lewis, 1970.

Mazzaro, Jerome, editor. *Profile of Robert Lowell.* Columbus, Ohio: Merrill, 1971.

Meyers, Jeffrey, editor. *Robert Lowell: Interviews and Memoirs.* Ann Arbor: University of Michigan Press, 1988.

Parkinson, Thomas, editor. *Robert Lowell: A Collection of Critical Essays.* Englewood Cliffs, N.J.: Prentice-Hall, 1968.

Price, Jonathan, editor. *Critics on Robert Lowell.* Coral Gables, Fla.: University of Miami Press, 1972; London: Allen & Unwin, 1974.

ARTICLES AND BOOK SECTIONS

Altieri, Charles. "Robert Lowell and the Difficulties of Escaping Modernism." *Enlarging the Temple: New Directions in American Poetry.* Lewisburg, Penn.: Bucknell University Press, 1979. 53-77.

——. "Poetry in a Prose World: Robert Lowell's 'Life Studies.'" *Modern Poetry Studies* 1.4 (1970): 182-99.

Alvarez, A. "Robert Lowell." *Beyond All This Fiddle.* London: Allen Lane, 1968. 3-21.

Anonymous. "Robert Lowell Dies at 60." *Boston Globe* (Sept. 13, 1977): 1, 36.

——. "Robert Lowell, Leading American Poet." *London Times* (Sept. 14, 1977): 18.

——. "The Second Chance." *Time* 89 (June 2, 1967): 67-74.

Antin, David. "Modernism and Postmodernism: Approaching the Present in American Poetry," *Boundary 2* 1 (1972): 98-133.

Atlas, James. "Robert Lowell in Cambridge: Lord Weary." *Atlantic Monthly* 250 (July 1982): 56-64.

Axelrod, Steven Gould. "Baudelaire and the Poetry of Robert Lowell." *Twentieth Century Literature* 17 (1971), 257-74.

——. "Colonel Shaw in American Poetry: 'For the Union Dead' and Its Precursors." *American Quarterly* 24 (1972): 523-37.

——. "Introduction: Lowell's Living Name." Axelrod and Deese collection. 1-26.

——. "Revolt." *Sylvia Plath: The Wound and the Cure of Words.* Baltimore: Johns Hopkins University Press, 1990. 51-79.

——. "Robert Lowell and Hopkins." *Twentieth Century Literature* 31 (1985), 55-72.

Barry, Jackson G. "Robert Lowell's 'Confessional' Image of an Age: Theme and Language in Poetic Form," *Ariel*, 12 (1981): 51-58.

——. "Robert Lowell: The Poet as Sign." *Semiotics 1995*: 179-87.

Baumel, Judith. "Robert Lowell: The Teacher." *Harvard Advocate* 113 (Nov. 1979): 32-33.

Bayley, John. "Robert Lowell: The Poetry of Cancellation." *London Magazine* new series 6 (June 1966): 76-85.

Beach, Christopher. "Who Else Has Lived Through Purgatory?: Ezra Pound and Robert Lowell." *Papers on Literature and Language* 27 (1991): 51-83.

Bedient, Calvin. "Illegible Lowell (The Late Volumes)." Axelrod and Deese collection. 139-55.

Belitt, Ben. "*Imitations*: Translation as Personal Mode." *Salmagundi* 4 (1966-1967): 44-56.

Berryman, John. "On Robert Lowell's 'Skunk Hour': Despondency and Madness." *The Contemporary Poet as Artist and Critic.* Edited by Anthony Ostroff. Boston: Little, Brown, 1964. 99-106.

Bidart, Frank. "On Robert Lowell." *Salmagundi* 37 (Spring 1977): 54-55.

Bloom, Harold. "Introduction." Bloom collection. 1-4.

Bly, Robert. "The Dead World and the Live World." *The Sixties* 8 (Spring 1966): 2-7.

Bobbitt, Joan. "Lowell and Plath: Objectivity and the Confessional Mode." *Arizona Quarterly* 33 (1977): 311-18.

Borroff, Marie. "Words, Language, and Form." *Literary Theory and Structure*. Edited by Frank Brady, John Palmer, and Martin Price. New Haven, Conn.: Yale University Press, 1973. 63-79.

Bowen, Roger. "Confession and Equilibrium: Robert Lowell's Poetic Development." *Criticism* 11 (1969): 78-93.

Boyers, Robert. "On Robert Lowell." *Salmagundi* 13 (Summer 1970): 36-44.

Breslin, James E. B. "Robert Lowell." *From Modern to Contemporary*. Chicago: University of Chicago Press, 1984. 110-142.

Breslin, Paul. "Robert Lowell: The Historical Self and the Limits of 'Conflation.'" *The Psycho-Political Muse*. Chicago: University of Chicago Press, 1987. 59-94.

Brooks, Esther. "Remembering Cal." Anzilotti collection. 37-44.

Calder, Alex. "*Notebook 1967-68*: Writing the Process Poem." Axelrod and Deese collection. 117-38.

Calhoun, Richard J. "The Poetic Metamorphosis of Robert Lowell." *Furman Studies* 13 (Nov. 1965): 7-17.

Cambon, Glauco. " Robert Lowell: History as Eschatology." *The Inclusive Flame*. Bloomington: Indiana University Press, 1963, 219-28.

Carne-Ross, Donald S. "The Two Voices of Translation." Parkinson collection. 152-70.

Cazé, Antoine. "Polyphony in Robert Lowell's Poetry." *Journal of American Studies* 28 (1994): 385-401.

Cooper, Phillip. "Lowell's Motion: *Notebook* and After." *South Carolina Review* 12 (Spring 1980), 18-30.

Corcoran, Neil. "Lowell's Retiarius: Towards *The Dolphin*." *Agenda* 18 (Autumn 1980): 75-85.

Crowley, Sue Mitchell. "Mr. Blackmur's Lowell: How Does Morality Get into Literature?" *Religion and Literature* 19 (Fall 1987): 27-47.

Damon, Maria. "The Child Who Writes / The Child Who Died." *The Dark End of the Street: Margins in American Vanguard Poetry*. Minneapolis: University of Minnesota Press, 1993. 77-141.

Deese, Helen. "Lowell and the Visual Arts." Axelrod and Deese collection. 180-216.

Dolan, Paul J. "Lowell's 'Quaker Graveyard': Poem and Tradition." *Renascence* 21 (Summer 1969): 171-180, 194.

Donoghue, Denis. *Connoisseurs of Chaos—Ideas of Order in Modern American Poetry*. New York: Macmillan, 1965. 150-157.

Doreski, Carole. "Robert Lowell and Elizabeth Bishop: A Matter of Life Studies." *Prose Studies* 10 (1987): 85-101.

Doreski, William. "Cut Off from Words: Robert Lowell's 'Tranquilized Fifties.'" *Prospects* 21 (1996): 149-68.

———. "The Sudden Bridegroom: The Dialectic of *Lord Weary's Castle*." *Modern Philology* 93 (1996): 352-70.

———. "Vision, Landscape, and the Ineffable in Robert Lowell's *History*." *Essays in Literature* 14 (1987): 251-68.

Dover, K. J. "Translation: The Speakable and the Unspeakable." *Essays in Criticism* 30 (Jan. 1979), 1-7.

Dubrow, Heather. "The Marine in the Garden: Pastoral Elements in Lowell's 'Quaker Graveyard.'" *Philological Quarterly* 62 (1983): 127-45.

Eddins, Dwight. "Poet and State in the Verse of Robert Lowell." *Texas Studies in Literature and Language* 15 (1973): 371-86.

Edwards, Thomas R. *Imagination and Power—A Study of Poetry on Public Themes*. London: Chatto & Windus, 1971. 3-6, 210-25.

Ehrenpreis, Irvin. "The Age of Lowell." *American Poetry* Stratford-upon-Avon Series 7 (1965), 68-95.

Epstein, Joseph. "Mistah Lowell—He Dead." *Hudson Review* (Summer 1996): 185-202.

Estrin, Barbara. "Lowelling and Laureling: Revising Gender and Genre in Robert Lowell's *Day by Day*." *Modern Language Quarterly* 57 (1996): 77-105.

Fein, Richard J. "The Life of *Life Studies*." *Literary Review* 23 (Spring 1980): 326-38.

Fender, Stephen. "What Really Happened to Warren Winslow?" *Journal of American Studies* 7 (1973): 187-190.

Fitzgerald, Robert. "Aiaia and Ithaca: Notes on a New Lowell Poem." *Salmagundi* 37 (Spring 1977): 25-31.

Flanzbaum, Hilene. "Surviving the Marketplace: Robert Lowell and the Sixties." *New England Quarterly* 68 (1995): 44-57.

Fraser, G. S. "'Near the Ocean.'" *Salmagundi* 37 (Spring 1977): 73-87.

Furia, Philip. "'IS, the whited monster': Lowell's Quaker Graveyard Revisited." *Texas Studies in Literature and Language* 17 (1976): 837-54.

Gelpi, Albert. "The Reign of the Kingfisher: Robert Lowell's Prophetic Poetry." Axelrod and Deese collection. 51-69.

Gewanter, David S. "Child of Collaboration: Robert Lowell's *Dolphin*." *Modern Philology* 93 (1995): 178-203.

Gilbert, Sandra M. "Mephistophilis in Maine: Rereading 'Skunk Hour.'" Axelrod and Deese collection. 70-79.

Hass, Robert. "Lowell's Graveyard." *Salmagundi* 37 (Spring 1977): 56-72.

Heaney, Seamus. "Lowell's Command." *Salmagundi* 80 (Fall 1988): 82-101.

Hochman, Baruch. "Robert Lowell' s *The Old Glory.*" *Tulane Drama Review* 11 (Summer 1967): 127-38.

Hoffman, Steven K. "Impersonal Personalism: The Making of a Confessional Poetic." *English Literary History* 45 (1978): 687-709.

Holder, Alan. "The Flintlocks of the Fathers: Robert Lowell's Treatment of the American Past." *New England Quarterly* 44 (1971): 40-65.

——. "Going Back, Going Down, Breaking: *Day by Day.*" Axelrod and Deese collection. 156-79.

Holloway, John. "Robert Lowell and the Public Dimension." *Encounter* 30 (Apr. 1968): 73-79.

Ilson, Robert. "*Benito Cereno* from Melville to Lowell." *Salmagundi* 4 (1967): 78-86.

James, Stephen. "Revision as Redress?: Robert Lowell's Manuscripts." *Essays in Criticism* 46 (1996): 26-51.

Johnson, Barbara. "Ode on a Public Thing ['For the Union Dead']." *Field Work.* Edited by Marjorie Garber, Paul Franklin, and Rebecca Walkowitz. New York: Routledge, 1996. 137-41.

Johnston, Allan. "Modes of Return: Memory and Remembering in the Poetry of Robert Lowell." *Twentieth Century Literature* 36 (1990): 73-94.

Kalstone, David. "Robert Lowell: The Uses of History." *Five Temperaments.* New York: Oxford University Press, 1977. 41-76.

Kinzie, Mary. "The Prophet Is a Fool: On 'Waking Early Sunday Morning.'" *Salmagundi* 37 (Spring 1977): 88-101.

Kramer, Lawrence. "Freud and the Skunks: Genre and Language in *Life Studies.*" Axelrod and Deese collection. 80-98.

Labbé, Evelyne. "Mort et crise: Le Travail du négatif dans deux poèmes de Robert Lowell: 'The Flaw' et 'Ice.'" *Eclats de voix.* Edited by Christine Raguet-Bouvart. La Rochelle: Rumeur des Ages, 1995. 125-35.

Labrie, Ross. "Reassessing Robert Lowell's Catholic Poetry." *Renascence* 47 (1995): 117-33.

Leibowitz, Herbert. "Robert Lowell: Ancestral Voices." *Salmagundi* 4 (1967): 25-43.

Lensing, George. "Robert Lowell and Jonathan Edwards: Poetry in the Hands of an Angry God." *South Carolina Review* 6 (Apr. 1974): 7-17.

Libby, Anthony. "The Ocean Gods of Robert Lowell." *Mythologies of Nothing.* Urbana: University of Illinois Press, 1984. 73-100.

Lindsay, Geoffrey. "Robert Lowell's 'Common Novel Plot': Names, Naming, and Polyphony in *The Dolphin.*" *Dalhousie Review* 75 (1996): 351-68.

Lipking, Lawrence. "Ending: Keats, Lowell, Rilke." *The Life of the Poet*. Chicago: University of Chicago Press, 1981. 180-91.

Logan, William. "Lowell in the Shadows." *New Criterion* 13 (Dec. 1994): 61-67.

Longenbach, James. "What Was Postmodern Poetry?" *Modern Poetry After Modernism*. New York: Oxford University Press, 1997. 3-21.

Lunz, Elizabeth. "Robert Lowell and Wallace Stevens on Sunday Morning." *University Review* 37 (1971): 268-72.

McClatchy, J. D. "Robert Lowell: Learning to Live with History." *American Poetry Review* 6 (Jan.-Feb. 1977): 34-38.

McFadden, George. "'Life Studies'—Robert Lowell's Comic Breakthrough." *PMLA* 90 (1975): 96-106.

——. "'Prose or This': What Lowell Made of a Diminished Thing." Axelrod and Deese collection. 231-55.

McGill, Meredith L. "Enlistment and Refusal: The Task of Public Poetry ['For the Union Dead']." *Field Work*. Edited by Marjorie Garber, Paul Franklin, and Rebecca Walkowitz. New York: Routledge, 1996. 144-49.

McNeil, Lynda Donnelly. "Robert Lowell's *Imitations*: Tone and Meaning in the Rimbaud Sonnet Sequence." *Comparative Literature Studies* 21 (1984): 323-44.

McWilliams, John P. "Fictions of Merrymount." *American Quarterly* 29 (1977): 3-30.

Malkoff, Karl. "Testing the Boundaries of the Self." *Escape from the Self*. New York: Columbia University Press, 1977. 92-139.

Manousos, A. "'Falling Asleep over the Aeneid': Lowell, Freud, and the Classics," *Comparative Literature Studies* 21 (1984): 16-29.

Martin, Jay. "Grief and Nothingness: Loss and Mourning in Lowell's Poetry." Axelrod and Deese collection. 26-50.

Mazzaro, Jerome. "The Classicism of Robert Lowell's *Phaedra*." *Comparative Drama* 7 (1973): 87-106.

——. "*Prometheus Bound*: Robert Lowell and Aeschylus." *Comparative Drama* 7 (1973): 278-90.

——. "Robert Lowell and the Kavanaugh Collapse." *University of Windsor Review* 5 (Fall 1969): 1-24.

——. "Robert Lowell's '*Benito Cereno*.'" *Modern Poetry Studies* 4 (1973): 129-58.

——. "Robert Lowell's Early Politics of Apocalypse." *Modern American Poetry*. Edited by Mazzaro. New York: David McKay, 1970. 321-50.

Meyers, Jeffrey. "Robert Lowell: The Paintings in the Poems." *Papers on Literature and Language* 23 (1987): 218-39.

——. "Robert Lowell: Wild-Genteel." *Contemporary Literature* 29 (1988): 294-99.

Middlebrook, Diane Wood. "What Was Confessional Poetry?" *The Columbia History of American Poetry*. Edited by Jay Parini and Brett Millier. New York: Columbia University Press, 1993. 632-49.

Miller, James E., Jr. "Poetic Metamorphoses: Lowell and Berryman." *The American Quest for a Supreme Fiction*. Chicago: University of Chicago Press, 1979. 3-11.

Molesworth, Charles. "Republican Objects and Utopian Moments: The Poetry of Robert Lowell and Allen Ginsberg." *The Fierce Embrace*. Columbia: University of Missouri Press, 1979. 37-60.

Newmyer, Stephen. "Robert Lowell and the Weeping Philosopher." *Classical and Modern Literature* 1 (1981): 121-131.

Nielsen, Aldon. "The Poetry of Race and Liberalism." *Reading Race*. Athens: University of Georgia Press, 1988. 123-43.

North, Michael. "Boston Common." *The Final Sculpture: Public Monuments and Modern Poets*. Ithaca: Cornell University Press, 1985. 228-43.

Oberg, Arthur. "Lowell Had Been Misspelled Lovel." *Modern American Lyric*. New Brunswick: Rutgers University Press, 1978. 5-47.

Parkinson, Thomas. "Robert Lowell: The Final Phase." *Poets, Poems,. Movements*. Ann Arbor: UMI Press, 1987. 225-34.

—— "For the Union Dead," *Salmagundi* 4 (1967), 87-95.

Pearson, Gabriel. "Robert Lowell." *Review* 20 (Mar. 1969): 3-36.

Perloff, Marjorie. " *Poètes Maudits* of the Genteel Tradition: Lowell and Berryman." Axelrod and Deese collection. 99-116.

Petry, Alice Hall. "That 'Tudor Ford' Reconsidered: Robert Lowell's 'Skunk Hour.'" *Papers on Literature and Language* 22 (1986): 70-75.

Pfister, Manfred. "Gedicht und Denkmal Robert Lowells *For the Union Dead*." *Poetik und Geschichte*. Edited by Dieter Borchmeyer. Tubingen: Niemeyer, 1989. 163-86.

Pinsky, Robert. "The Conquered Kings of Robert Lowell." *Salmagundi* 37 (Spring 1977): 102-105.

——. "Lowell." *The Situation of Poetry*. Princeton: Princeton University Press, 1976: 16-23.

Price, Jonathan. "Fire Against Fire." *Works* 1 (1967): 120-26.

Procopiow, Norma. "*Day by Day*: Lowell's Poetics of Imitation." *Ariel* 14 (Jan. 1983): 4-14.

——. "William Carlos Williams and the Origins of the Confessional Poem." *Ariel* 7 (Apr. 1976): 63-75.

Prunty, Wyatt. "Allegory to Causality: Robert Lowell's Poetic Shift." *Agenda* 18 (1980): 94-103.

Raizis, M. Byron. "Robert Lowell's *Prometheus Bound.*" *Papers on Language and Literature* 5 (1969): 154-68.

Ramazani, Jahan. "Robert Lowell." *The Poetry of Mourning.* Chicago: University of Chicago Press, 1994. 226-40.

Rasula, Jed. "~~The Age of~~ Lowell." *The American Poetry Wax Museum.* Urbana, Ill.: National Council of Teachers of English, 1996. 247-67.

Reed, John R. "Going Back: The Ironic Progress of Lowell's Poetry." *Modern Poetry Studies* 1 (1970): 162-181.

Remaley, Peter P. "Epic Machinery in Robert Lowell's *Lord Weary's Castle.*" *Ball State University Forum* 18 (1977): 59-64.

Ricks, Christopher. "Racine's *Phèdre*: Lowell's *Phaedra.*" *Arion* 1 (Spring 1991): 44-59.

Rollins, J. Barton. "Young Robert Lowell's Poetics of Revision." *Journal of Modern Literature* 7 (1979): 488-504.

Rosenthal, M. L. "Our Neurotic Angel: Robert Lowell (1917-77)." Anzilotti collection. 143-55.

——. "Robert Lowell and 'Confessional' Poetry." *The New Poets.* New York: Oxford University Press, 1967. 25-78.

Ruddick, Nicholas. "A New Historiography of the Self: Robert Lowell's *History* as History." *Wascana Review* 20 (1985): 3-15.

Russo, J. P. "'I Fish Until the Clouds Turn Blue': Robert Lowell's Late Poetry." *Papers on Literature and Languages* 20 (1984), 312-25.

Saffioti, Carol Lee. "Between History and Self: The Function of the Alexander Poems in Robert Lowell's *History.*" *Modern Poetry Studies* 10 (1981): 159-72.

Shaw, Robert B. "Lowell in the Seventies." *Contemporary Literature* 23 (1982): 515-27.

Simon, John. "Abuse of Privilege: Lowell as Translator." *Hudson Review* 20 (1967): 543-62.

Souza, Maria Helena de. "Robert Lowell's 'Dropping South: Brazil': An Analysis." *Estudos Anglo-Americanos* 5-6 (1981-82): 145-51.

Spacks, Patricia Meyer. "From Satire to Description." *Yale Review* 58 (1968): 232-48.

Spears, Monroe K. "Poetry Since the Mid-Century." *Dionysus and the City.* New York: Oxford University Press, 1970: 229-60.

Spivack, Kathleen. "Robert Lowell: A Memoir." *Antioch Review* 43 (1985): 189-93.

Staples, Hugh. "A Graph of Revelations." *Northwestern University Triquarterly* 1 (1959): 7-12.

Sterne, Richard Clark. "Puritans at Merry Mount: Variations on a Theme." *American Quarterly* 22 (1970): 846-58.

Stone, Albert E. "A New Version of American Innocence: Robert Lowell's *Benito Cereno*." *New England Quarterly* 45 (1972), 467-83.

Strand, Mark. "Landscape and the Poetry of Self." *Prose* 6 (1973): 169-83.

Strout, Cushing. "Refractions of History: Lowell's Revision of Hawthorne and Melville." *Southern Review* 25 (1989): 549-62.

Sullivan, James. "Investing the Cultural Capital of Robert Lowell." *Twentieth Century Literature* 38 (1992): 194-213.

Sullivan, Rosemary. "*Notebook*: Robert Lowell as a Political Poet." *Etudes Anglaises*, 27 (1974): 291-301.

Taylor, Peter. "Robert Traill Spence Lowell: 1917-1977." *Ploughshares* 5 (1979): 74-81.

Thurley, Geoffrey. "The Poetry of Breakdown: Robert Lowell and Anne Sexton." *The American Moment*. London: Edward Arnold, 1977. 70-90.

Tokunaga, Shozo. "Private Voice, Public Voice: John Berryman and Robert Lowell." *John Berryman Studies* 1 (1975): 18-23.

Veitch, Jonathan. "'Moondust in the Prowling Eye': The *History* Poems of Robert Lowell." *Contemporary Literature* 33 (1992): 458-79.

Vendler, Helen. "Reading a Poem ['For the Union Dead']." *Field Work*. Edited by Marjorie Garber, Paul Franklin, and Rebecca Walkowitz. New York: Routledge, 1996. 129-36.

——. "Robert Lowell." *Part of Nature, Part of Us*. Cambridge: Harvard University Press, 1980. 125-73.

——. "Robert Lowell and History." *The Given and the Made*. Cambridge: Harvard University Press, 1995. 1-28.

von Hallberg, Robert. "Lowell's *History*." *American Poetry and Culture 1945-1980*. Cambridge: Harvard University Press, 1985: 148-74.

Waggoner, Hyatt H. "Centering In: Robert Lowell." *American Poems From the Puritans to the Present*. Boston: Houghton Mifflin, 1968. 577-85.

Walcott, Derek. "On Robert Lowell." *New York Review of Books* 31 (Mar. 31, 1984): 25-31.

Weatherhead, A. Kingsley. "*Day by Day*: His Endgame." Axelrod and Deese collection. 217-30.

Wiebe, Dallas E. "Mr. Lowell and Mr. Edwards." *Contemporary Literature* 3 (1962): 21-31.

Wilbur, Richard. "On Robert Lowell's 'Skunk Hour.'" *The Contemporary Poet as Artist and Critic.* Edited by Anthony Ostroff. Boston: Little, Brown, 1964. 84-87.

Williamson, Alan. "'I Am That I Am': The Ethics and Aesthetics of Personal Poetry." *Introspection and Contemporary Poetry.* Cambridge: Harvard University Press, 1984. 7-25.

———. "Robert Lowell: A Reminiscence" and "The Reshaping of 'Waking Early Sunday Morning.'" *Eloquence and Mere Life.* Ann Arbor: University of Michigan Press, 1994. 3-28.

Willis, Gary. "The Masculine and the Feminine as Seen in the Poetry of Robert Lowell." *English Studies in Canada* 6 (1980): 444-59.

Willis, G. D. "Afloat on Lowell's Dolphin." *Critical Quarterly* 17 (1975): 363-76.

Woodson, Thomas. "Robert Lowell's 'Hawthorne,' Yvor Winters and the American Literary Tradition." *American Quarterly* 19 (1967): 575-82.

Xiang, Fei. "Holy Bitterness and Brilliant Despair." *Foreign Literature Studies* 40 (June 1988): 203-11. [In Chinese]

Yankowitz, Susan. "Lowell's *Benito Cereno*: An Investigation of American Innocence." *Yale Theatre* 1 (Summer 1968), 81-90.

BOOK REVIEWS

Land of Unlikeness (1944)

Blackmur, R. P. "Notes on Eleven Poets." *Kenyon Review* 7 (1945): 339-52.

Drew, Elizabeth. "Challenging Vitality." *New York Herald Tribune Weekly Book Review* (Dec. 17, 1944): 18.

Dupee, F. W. "Some Young Poets and a New Genre." *Nation* 160 (Feb. 10, 1945): 159-61.

Jarrell, Randall. "Poetry in War and Peace." *Partisan Review* 12 (1945): 120-26.

Nims, John Frederick. "Two Catholic Poets." *Poetry* 65 (1945): 264-68.

Tate, Allen. "Introduction." *Land of Unlikeness.* By Robert Lowell. i-ii.

Lord Weary's Castle (1946)

Berryman, John. "Lowell, Thomas &tc." *Partisan Review* 14 (1947): 73-85.

Bogan, Louise. "Verse." *New Yorker* 22 (Nov. 30, 1946): 137-40.

Deutsch, Babette. "In These Home Waters." *New York Herald Tribune Weekly Book Review* (Nov. 24, 1946): 16.

Eberhart, Richard. "Four Poets." *Sewanee Review* 55 (1947): 324-36.

Fiedler, Leslie. "The Believing Poet and the Infidel Reader." *New Leader* 30 (May 10, 1947): 12.

Jarrell, Randall. "From the Kingdom of Necessity." *Nation* 164 (Jan. 18, 1947): 74-77.

Rodman, Selden. "Boston Jeremiad." *New York Times Book Review* (Nov. 3, 1946): 7, 32.

Warren, Austin. "A Double Discipline." *Poetry* 70 (1947): 262-65.

The Mills of the Kavanaughs (1951)

Arrowsmith, William. "Five Poets." *Hudson Review* 4 (1952): 619-27.

Bogan, Louise. "Verse." *New Yorker* 27 (June 9, 1951): 94-97.

Engle, Paul. "Poems in Which You Hear Human Voices." *Chicago Tribune Magazine of Books* (June 10, 1951): 4.

Jarrell, Randall. "A View of Three Poets." *Partisan Review* 18 (1951): 691-700.

West, Ray B. "The Tiger in the Wood: Five Contemporary Poets." *Western Review* 16 (Fall 1951): 76-84.

Williams, William Carlos. "In a Mood of Tragedy." *New York Times Book Review* (Apr. 22, 1951): 6.

Life Studies (1959)

Alvarez, A. "Something New in Verse." *London Observer* (Apr. 12, 1959): 22.

Baraka, Amiri [Le Roi Jones]. "Putdown of the Whore of Babylon." *Yugen* 7 (1961): 4-5.

Bennett, Joseph. "Two Americans, a Brahmin and the Bourgeoisie." *Hudson Review* 12 (1959): 431-39.

Bogan, Louise. "Verse." *New Yorker* 35 (Oct. 24, 1959): 194-96.

Davie, Donald. *"Life Studies."* *Twentieth Century* 166 (1959): 116-18.

Dupee, F. W. "The Battle of Robert Lowell." *Partisan Review* 26 (1959): 473-75.

Eberhart, Richard. "A Poet's People." *New York Times Book Review* (May 23, 1959): 4, 27.

Engle, Paul. "A Great Year for Poetry and Light." *Chicago Tribune Magazine of Books* (Nov. 29, 1959): 24.

Fraser, G. S. "I, They, We." *New Statesman* new series 57 (May 2, 1959): 614-15.

Hollander, John. "Robert Lowell's New Book." *Poetry* 95 (1959): 41-46.

Kazin, Alfred. "In Praise of Robert Lowell." *Reporter* 20 (June 25, 1959): 41-42.

Kermode, Frank. "Talented and More." *Spectator* 202 (May 1, 1959): 628.

Kunitz, Stanley. "American Poetry's Silver Age." *Harper's* 219 (Oct. 1959): 173-79.

Rosenthal, M. L. "Poetry as Confession." *Nation* 189 (Sept. 19, 1959): 17.

Spender, Stephen. "Robert Lowell's Family Album." *New Republic* 140 (June 8, 1959): 17.

Standerwick, DeSales. "Pieces Too Personal." *Renascence* 13 (Fall 1960): 53-56.

Thompson, John. "Two Poets." *Kenyon Review* 21 (1959): 482-90.

Imitations (1961)

Alvarez, A. "A Poet's Re-Creations." *London Observer* (May 27, 1997): 29.

Carruth, Hayden. "Toward, Not Away From." *Poetry* 100 (1962): 43-47.

Cluysenaar, Anne. "*Imitations.*" *Dubliner* 1 (July-Aug. 1962): 65-66.

Enright, D. J. "Common Market." *New Statesman* 63 (June 22, 1962): 901-902.

Hill, Geoffrey. "Robert Lowell: 'Contrasts and Repetitions.'" *Essays in Criticism* 13 (1963): 188-97.

Phaedra (1961)

Kenner, Hugh. "The Art of Translation: Memory Refreshed." *National Review* 11 (Dec. 2, 1961): 385-86.

Kunitz, Stanley. "Some Poets of the Year and Their Language of Transformation. *Harper's* 223 (Aug. 1961): 86-91.

Mercier, Vivian. "Great Racine." *Commonweal* 74 (May 12, 1961): 184-85.

Steiner, George. "Two Translations." *Kenyon Review* 23 (1961): 714-21.

For the Union Dead (1964)

Alvarez, A. "Poetry in Extremis." *London Observer* (Mar. 14, 1965): 26.

Anonymous. "Eastern Personal Time." *Times Literary Supplement* (July 1, 1965): 558.

Bogan, Louise. "Verse." *New Yorker* 41 (Apr. 10, 1965): 193-96.

Carruth, Hayden. "Freedom and Style." *Poetry* 106 (1965): 358-60.

Fraser, G. S. "Amid the Horror, A Song of Praise." *New York Times Book Review* (Oct. 4, 1964): 1, 38.

Hartman, Geoffrey. "The Eye of the Storm." *Partisan Review* 32 (1965): 277-80.

Howard, Richard. "Voice of a Survivor." *Nation* 199 (Oct. 26, 1964): 278-80.

Jacobsen, Josephine. "Poet of the Particular." *Commonweal* 81 (Dec. 4, 1964): 349-52.

Martz, Louis. "Recent Poetry: The Elegiac Mode." *Yale Review* 54 (1965): 285-98.

Poirier, Richard. "Our Truest Historian." *New York Herald Tribune Book Week* (Oct. 11, 1964): 1, 16.

Ricks, Christopher. "The Three Lives of Robert Lowell." *New Statesman* 69 (Mar. 26, 1965): 496-97.

Rosenthal, M. L. "Poets of the Dangerous Way." *Spectator* 214 (Mar. 19, 1965): 367.

Stafford, William. "Poems that Deal a Jolt." *Chicago Tribune Books Today* (Nov. 15, 1964): 11.

Wain, John. "The New Robert Lowell." *New Republic* 151 (Oct. 17, 1964): 21-23.

The Old Glory (1965)

Brustein, Robert. "Introduction." *The Old Glory*. By Robert Lowell. xi-xiv.

Gelpi, Albert. "He Holds America to Its Ideals." *Christian Science Monitor* (Dec. 16, 1965): 11.

Jarrell, Randall. "A Masterpiece." *New York Times* (Nov. 29, 1964): II.3.

Kroll, Jack. "New Glory." *Newsweek* 87 (May 3, 1976): 83-84.

McDonnell, Thomas. "Poet as Playwright." *Critic* 24 (Apr. 1966): 72-74.

Oliver, Edith. "Off Broadway." *New Yorker* 40 (Nov. 14, 1964): 143-44.

Simon, John. "Strange Devices on the Banner." *New York Herald Tribune Book Week* (Feb. 20, 1966): 4, 12.

Snodgrass, W. D. "In Praise of Robert Lowell." *New York Review of Books* 3 (Dec. 3, 1964): 8-10.

Near the Ocean (1967)

Anonymous. "Open Sores." *Times Literary Supplement* (Aug. 3, 1967): 705.

Fraser, G. S. "Unmonotonous Sublime." *New York Times Book Review* (Jan. 15, 1967): 4-5, 17.

Garrigue, Jean. "A Study of Continuity and Change." *New Leader* 50 (Mar. 27, 1967): 23-25.

Hoffman, Daniel. "Robert Lowell's *Near the Ocean*: The Greatness and Horror of Empire." *Hollins Critic* 4 (Feb. 1967): 1-16.

Howard, Richard. "Fuel on the Fire." *Poetry* 110 (1967): 413-15.

Kalstone, David. "Two Poets." *Partisan Review* 34 (1967): 619-25.

Martz, Louis. "Recent Poetry." *Yale Review* 56 (1967): 593-97.

Raz, Hilda [Hilda Link]. "A Tempered Triumph." *Prairie Schooner* 41 (1967): 439-42.

Stafford, William. "Critical Involvement of the Poet." *Chicago Tribune Magazine of Books* (Feb. 5, 1967): 5.

Symons, Julian. "Cooked and Raw." *New Statesman* 74 (July 21, 1967): 87.

Prometheus Bound (1969)

Bermel, Albert. "Closet Openings." *Nation* 209 (Aug. 25, 1969): 156.

Fergusson, Francis. "Prometheus at Yale." *New York Review of Books* 9 (Aug. 3, 1967): 30-32.

Gilman, Richard. "Still Bound." *Newsweek* 69 (May 22, 1967): 109.

Notebook 1967-68 (1969) / *Notebook* (1970)

Anonymous. "The Chameleon Poet." *Time* 93 (June 6, 1969): 112-13.

Bayley, John. "The King as Commoner." *Review* 24 (Dec. 1970): 3-7.

Boyers, Robert. "On Robert Lowell." *Salmagundi* 13 (1970): 36-44.

Cooley, Peter. "Reaching Out, Keeping Position." *North American Review* new series 6 (Fall 1969): 67-70.

Feldman, Burton. "Robert Lowell: Poetry and Politics." *Dissent* 16 (1969): 550-55.

Ignatow, David. "Puritan Paradox." *New Leader* 52 (Sept. 1, 1969): 16-18.

Mazzaro, Jerome. "Sojourner of Self." *Nation* 209 (July 7, 1969): 22-24.

Spivack, Kathleen. "In the Midst of Life." *Poetry* 116 (1970): 190-93.

The Dolphin (1973) / *For Lizzie and Harriet* (1973) / *History* (1973)

Bedient, Calvin. "Visions and Revisions:Three New Volumes." *New York Times Book Review* (July 29, 1973): 15-16.

Bertholf, Robert. "An Elegant Inconclusion." *Caterpillar* 5 (1973): 121-34.

Cotter, James Finn. Review. *America* 129 (Sept. 8, 1973): 150-51.

Dale, Peter. "Fortuitous Form." *Agenda* 11 (1973): 73-87.

Davie, Donald. "Lowell." *Parnassus* 2 (1973): 49-57.

Hall, Donald. "Knock, Knock: A Column." *American Poetry Review* 2 (Nov.-Dec. 1973): 46.

Perloff, Marjorie G. "The Blank Now." *New Republic* 169 (July 7, 1973): 24-26.

Rich, Adrienne. "Carydid: A Column." *American Poetry Review* 2 (Sept.-Oct. 1973): 42-43.

Ricks, Christopher. "The Poet Robert Lowell." *Listener* 89 (June 21, 1973): 830-32.

Wakoski, Diane. "The Craft of Carpenters, Plumbers, & Mechanics: Column." *American Poetry Review* 3 (Jan.-Feb. 1974): 46.

Yenser, Stephen. "Half Legible Bronze?" *Poetry* 123 (1974): 304-9.

Day by Day (1978)

Adcock, Fleur. "Versions of Death." *Encounter* 51 (Aug. 1978): 84-86.

Alvarez, A. "Intimations of Mortality." *London Observer* (Mar. 5, 1978): 32.

Bayley, John. "If Life Could Write." *New Statesman* 95 (Mar. 10, 1978): 323.

Bedient, Calvin. "Desultorily Yours." *Sewanee Review* 86 (1978): 286-93.

Bloom, Harold. "Harold Bloom on Poetry." *New Republic* 177 (Nov. 26, 1977): 24-26.

Chasin, Helen. "Escape from Safety." *Village Voice* 22 (Sept. 5, 1977): 24-26.

Di Piero, W. S. "Lowell and Ashbery." *Southern Review* 14 (1978): 359-67.

Donoghue, Denis. "Lowell at the End." *Hudson Review* 31 (1978): 196-201.

Hall, Donald. "Robert Lowell and the Literature Industry." *Georgia Review* 32 (1978): 7-12.

Kazin, Alfred. "Robert Lowell and John Ashbery: The Difference between Poets." *Esquire* 89 (Jan. 1978): 20-22.

Luria-Sukenick, Lynn. "*Day by Day*." *American Book Review* 1 (Dec. 1978): 6.

Perloff, Marjorie. "Robert Lowell: 'Fearlessly Holding Back Nothing.'" *Washington Post Book World* (Sept. 25, 1977): H7-9.

Index

About the Editor

STEVEN GOULD AXELROD is Professor of English at the University of California, Riverside. He is the author of several books, including *Robert Lowell: Life and Art* (1978), *Robert Lowell: A Reference Guide* (1982), *Robert Lowell: Essays on the Poetry* (1986), *Critical Essays on Wallace Stevens* (1988), and *Sylvia Plath: The Wound and the Cure of Words* (1990).

ISBN 0-313-29037-7

90000>

9 780313 290374

EAN

HARDCOVER BAR CODE